WAKEFIELD PRESS

EVER YOURS,
C.H. SPENCE

Catherine Helen Spence, c.1900,
photograph courtesy of the State Library of South Australia, SLSA: 36575

Ever yours,
C.H. Spence

CATHERINE HELEN SPENCE'S
AN AUTOBIOGRAPHY (1825–1910),
DIARY (1894) AND
SOME CORRESPONDENCE (1894–1910)

EDITED BY SUSAN MAGAREY
WITH BARBARA WALL
MARY LYONS AND MARYAN BEAMS

Wakefield Press

Wakefield Press
1 The Parade West
Kent Town
South Australia 5067
www.wakefieldpress.com.au

First published 2005

Copyright © Susan Magarey, 2005

All rights reserved. This book is copyright. Apart from any fair dealing for the purposes of private study, research, criticism or review, as permitted under the Copyright Act, no part may be reproduced without written permission. Enquiries should be addressed to the publisher.

Designed and typeset by Clinton Ellicott, Wakefield Press
Printed in China at Everbest Printing Co Ltd

National Library of Australia
Cataloguing-in-publication entry

Spence, Catherine Helen, 1825–1910.
Ever yours, CH Spence: Catherine Helen Spence's an autobiography (1825–1910), diary (1894) and some correspondence (1894–1910).

Bibliography.
Includes index.
ISBN 1 86254 656 8.

1. Women – Suffrage. 2. South Australia – Social conditions.
I. Magarey, Susan. II. Title.

303.484

Contents

Introduction   1
A Note on the Text   15

Catherine Helen Spence: *An Autobiography*

1   Early Life in Scotland   19
2   Towards Australia   30
3   A Beginning at Seventeen   38
4   Lovers and Friends   45
5   Novels and a Political Inspiration   51
6   A Trip to London   61
7   Melrose Revisited   69
8   I Visit Edinburgh and London   77
9   Meeting with J.S. Mill and George Elilot   88
10   Return from the Old Country   94
11   Wards of the State   99
12   Preaching, Friends, and Writing   109
13   My Work for Education   119
14   Speculation, Charity, and a Book   126
15   Journalism and Politics   132

16 Sorrow and Change   139
17 Impressions of America   146
18 Britain, The Continent, and Home Again   157
19 Progress of Effective voting   166
20 Widening Interests   173
21 Proportional Representation and Federation 181
22 A Visit to New South Wales   187
23 More Public Work   195
24 The Eightieth Milestone and the End   204

Catherine Helen Spence's Diary: 1894

A Preface   213
A Note on the Text   216
An Introduction   218
The Diary   228

Catherine Helen Spence's Letters

An Introduction   327
To Alice Henry   331
To Rose Scott   351

Appendices

A: Family Tree   359
B: Sources of Notes and additional information   375

Index
378

Introduction

It is Saturday, 2 April 1910 in Adelaide, South Australia. Catherine Helen Spence, now 84 years old, is in bed. 'I cannot depend on my health as I used to do', she wrote to Rose Scott, leader of the campaign for votes for women in Sydney, on Easter Monday,

> The last eight months I have had little recurrent attacks proceeding from the internal growth which was discussed in 1903 – which force me to lie in bed for two three four or five days.

There is nothing malignant, but she must 'keep recumbent'. And that is a nuisance because she is hard at work, writing the history of her life.

For some months Miss Spence has been 'drawing in' her engagements and saving herself as much as she can for the completion of this work. She wants it published in the *South Australian Register*, the daily newspaper with which she has been most closely associated throughout her career as a journalist, and as the 'prophet' of the 'effective vote', her extended campaign for the introduction of proportional representation into South Australian elections. She has been delighted to learn that the paper's editor has, he said, already had the same idea; the first three chapters are already typeset and the proofs are waiting for her to correct them. She is excited about the work. In March she complained:

> My chief trouble is that I cannot sleep; the 'life' is helping the hot weather to keep me awake.

On 2 April she has the proofs and a further 13 chapters in manuscript, and has had a discussion with the people that she lives with – the householders, Kate and John Quilty, and Catherine Spence's companion, Ellen Gregory – about how she can write in bed with indelible pencil, for, as she says herself, 'A nice state I and the sheets would be in if I used ink'.

The doctor has been to see her in the morning, and has been so reassuring that her niece, Lucy Spence Morice, very nearly decides not to go and see her that evening. Lucy Morice, herself, is in low spirits because her mother has died recently and she has spent the day 'looking through the old house' and choosing keepsakes. But there is no telephone in the house where her 'dearly beloved "Good Aunt"' is living, and therefore no other way of finding out how she is. So Lucy comes after all, and is immediately alarmed at Auntie Kate's condition. She spends more than an hour on the telephone in a neighbour's house, trying to summon the doctor and find a nurse. Neither can arrive until close on midnight. At first Catherine Spence is unaware of any reason for her niece's anxiety –

'Why don't you go home Lucy, you'll make me think I am very ill.'

But later she realises 'this is the beginning of the end', and prepares herself, reciting poems, parts of the gospels and psalms. Her one anguished protest still echoes today:

Oh my book, my book.[1]

Catherine Helen Spence died on 3 April 1910.

And her book lay only two-thirds complete, the last chapter that she had begun writing, titled 'Sorrow and Change' recounting the death in 1887 of her mother. 'It was', noted her friend and colleague Jeanne Young, 'as if the task of recording one of the deepest sorrows of her own life – the death of her mother – had been too much for the brave heart, for it was at that point of her life's narrative that the facile pen of the well-known writer had been abruptly stopped'.[2]

1   All of this account is drawn from Lucy Morice to Rose Scott, 12 April 1910, and Eleanor Wren to Rose Scott, 13 April 1910, printed as Appendices A and B in Helen Jones, 'A Postscript to the Life of Catherine Helen Spence', *Journal of the Historical Society of South Australia*, no.15, 1987, pp. 82–92. A version of the same account appeared in Susan Magarey, *Passions of the First Wave Feminists* (UNSW Press), Sydney, 2001, pp. 173–4.
2   Jeanne F. Young, 'Introductory' in Catherine Helen Spence, *An Autobiography* (reprinted from the *Register*), Adelaide, 1910. The chapter titled 'Sorrow and Change' in the manuscript copy of the autobiography includes a good deal of material in another hand, not Catherine Spence's.

Lucy Spence Morice, c.1886,
photograph courtesy of the State Library of South Australia,
SLSA: B58523

Catherine Spence had certainly loved her mother very dearly. Even before her father died in 1846, she and her mother were especially close. She remained at home when her mother was widowed, and when her siblings went off to form households and families of their own. She and her mother formed a household that came to the rescue when Catherine's younger sister, Mary, was widowed, and again, when Mary herself died, leaving two children, Charles and Eleanor Wren, in their care. When her mother fulfilled an old dream, having a gracious house built in Trinity Street, College Town (now College Park), it included a little study for Catherine Spence's books where she would write her articles for the newspapers with her 'dear old mother sitting with her knitting on her rocking chair at the low window'. 'I generally read the MS to her before it went to the office', she recalled. 'I had the knowledge that she was interested in all I did'. When Helen Brodie Spence took to her bed for the last thirteen months of her ninety-six years, it was her daughter Catherine who nursed her, remaining with her always, anguished at 'a gradual decay of the faculties which had previously been so keen'. This was the central relationship of Catherine Spence's life. Her mother's death was, she said, 'an exceedingly great loss to me': 'I missed her untiring sympathy'.[3]

Even so, this loss also meant a major change in the possibilities of life for Catherine Spence. 'Henceforth I was free to devote my efforts to the fuller public work for which I had so often longed, but which my mother's devotion to and dependence on me rendered impossible', reads a sentence in this chapter. 'Crowded and interesting as my life had been hitherto, the best was yet to be.'

> My realization of Browning's beautiful line from "Rabbi Ben Ezra" – 'The last of life, for which the first was made,' came when I saw opening before me the possibilities of public service undreamed of in my earlier years.

By the end of the chapter of the autobiography in which her mother's death is related, she had discovered 'some of the gifts of a public speaker'; undertaken a campaign – speaking on public platforms all over South Australia, then in Melbourne and Sydney – for proportional representation, which she had renamed 'effective voting'; sailed for the United States as a 'Government Commissioner and delegate to the Great World's Fair Congresses' to take place in Chicago in 1893; and arrived in San Francisco. She travelled without escort, indeed without much money – hoping to earn enough to support herself from public lectures and letters sent back to the Australian press: all this at the age of 67. And that was but a beginning to the last seventeen years of her life which were packed with 'the fuller public work' for which she had longed. Clearly, some account of these event-laden years was necessary for the life-story that was to be published in the *Register*.

But there were strains and difficulties between Catherine Spence's heirs over her tiny property, her literary remains, and the completion of the autobiography.[4] Lucy Morice, who shared some of her aunt's interests in politics, feminism and kindergartens, believed that her aunt wanted her to be her literary executor. Indeed, by the time she was writing a set of reminiscences about Auntie Kate, probably in the 1930s, Lucy Morice went so far as to suggest that her aunt's wishes were sabotaged.

---

3   All of these details are in Catherine Spence's autobiography.
4   Helen Jones sets out a version of these stresses and strains which differs from the one provided here, in her 'Postscript to the Life of Catherine Helen Spence'. The information given here about Ellen Gregory's age – born in 1852 – has been unearthed by Barbara Wall.

> She told me that I was to be her literary executor and that to me she was leaving her books and papers. She thought that she had not left a will and gave me verbal instructions. These I could not carry out as there was a will. This, I believe, she thought she had destroyed, but there it was in her own handwriting dated many years before and entirely forgotten. How it came to be in one of her drawers on the top of underclothes was difficult to understand. I think it must have been secreted for long and when the moment came it was produced.

The will, signed and dated 4 March 1895, appointed Catherine Spence's brother, John Brodie Spence, and her nephew, Charles William Wren, to be her executors. It instructed JB Spence to select keepsakes for himself and her personal friends from her 'books, manuscripts, pictures, photographs, letters and other relics', and then bequeathed the remainder of her library to another nephew, son of her older sister Jessie, John David Murray. At the time of Catherine Spence's death, fifteen years later, her brother had already died in 1902, and her nephew Charles Wren, his wife, and his sister, Eleanor, were living in Melbourne. A telegram summoned Eleanor Wren to Adelaide, though 'too late', she told Rose Scott, 'to see the darling alive'. But once there, she could assume her brother's responsibilities and wind up Catherine Spence's affairs.

For the Wrens, the fifteen year-old will was probably no surprise. They had grown up in the household formed around them by Catherine Spence and her mother, when their mother, Catherine Spence's youngest sister, Mary, had died. They were close. Catherine Spence called Charles 'Charlie' and Eleanor 'Nell'. At one time, Eleanor had copied out the whole text of Catherine Spence's novel, *Handfasted*, when her aunt decided that Eleanor's handwriting might give the work a better chance of winning a prize. At another, Catherine Spence shared Charles's Latin tutor with him. In later years, Catherine Spence decided that Charlie was a 'cold devil', but her letters to Alice Henry and Rose Scott during the final decade of her life show her still close to Nell, and eager to spend time with her. The Wrens clearly regarded Catherine Spence as a substitute mother. She reciprocated by naming Charles as one of her executors.

They had another bond, too, and this may have been the source of Lucy Morice's sourness. In 1866, while on her visit to England, Catherine Spence met a cousin of the young Wrens, Ellen Louisa Gregory. Born in 1852, the girl was only 14 years old, the same age that Catherine Spence had been when she arrived in South Australia. Thinking that she might be a help to an aunt living in the country in South Australia, Catherine Spence persuaded young Ellen Gregory to migrate to Adelaide. Once there, though, the Wrens' country aunt did not find Ellen Gregory to her liking. So she joined the Spence-Wren household instead, living with her cousins; Catherine Spence called her 'Cousin'

Eleanor Wren,
photograph in the private collection of Mrs Marjorie Caw (1970)

when referring to her in letters to the Wrens, 'coz' in her diary. She would go out sewing in other people's households to earn something towards her living, but it was never an independent living. Catherine Spence considered her to be one of her own financial responsibilities. Ellen Gregory remained with Catherine Spence through the succession of households that she formed, to be, Spence wrote, 'the prop and mainstay of my old age'. She, too, and the Quiltys, were with Catherine Spence when she died. Since Ellen Gregory eventually died in Victoria, it seems likely that Eleanor Wren took her back to Melbourne with her when she had finished sorting out her aunt's affairs.

Can this explain why Lucy Morice came so close to slandering Ellen Gregory with her insinuations over finding Catherine Spence's will? Yes, if it is regarded in a context of long-standing resentment among members of her own family, that of Catherine Spence's brother John Brodie Spence. Lucy Spence's father became a wealthy and prominent figure in Adelaide; Lucy, the eldest of his three children, was growing up to great expectations in the 1880s. At the same time, she learned from her mother a scepticism and impatience over her Auntie Kate's reliance upon her father's interest and generosity, and this could extend to interest and generosity expressed beyond what they saw as 'the family' by Auntie Kate herself. Ellen Gregory's failure to get on with the country aunt meant, wrote Lucy Morice, that 'Auntie Kate was saddled for life with a protégée who, less than kin, was much resented by my part of the family'.

Once arrived in Adelaide, one of Eleanor Wren's first actions was to write to Lucy Morice asking her to complete their aunt's autobiography. Lucy Morice did not reply immediately: 'I was too ill to think the day I got her letter'. She did write an answer accepting the task, she related later, but before she posted it, she heard from Eleanor Wren again. Eleanor had decided that the best person for the job was Jeanne F. Young.

Jeanne Young, born Sarah Jane Forster, who would become a well-known welfare worker, journalist, social worker and political activist,[5] sought an introduction to Catherine Spence in 1896, when she was a young mother of almost thirty years with four children under the age of seven, and Miss Spence was a household name. 'Had my tastes been merely literary or social', Jeanne Young was to reflect,

---

5   Jeanne F. Young also served as a magistrate, was the first woman on the Board of Governors of the Public Library, Museum and Art Gallery, stood for election to the Senate, unsuccessfully, in 1937, and formed the Democratic Women's Association of South Australia. See the Archival Database in the State Library of South Australia. This information differs from that given in Dirk Van Dissell, 'Sarah Jane (Jeanna) Young (née Foster)', in Wilfrid Prest, Kerrie Round and Carol Fort (eds), *The Wakefield Companion to South Australian History* (Wakefield Press), Kent Town, South Australia, 2001, p. 603.

>Miss Spence would assuredly have found nothing to bind us together. It was the combination of these, with my deep interest in public affairs, that welded the links in our chain of friendship.[6]

In Mrs Young, Catherine Spence discovered a young, energetic and enthusiastic supporter for her campaign for effective voting. It was Jeanne Young who prompted the small party to celebrate Miss Spence's 71st birthday and raise her spirits, when she professed herself weary of campaigning for electoral reform. This move was so successful that Miss Spence followed it up promptly, inviting a group of women to her house for a supper which her companion Ellen Gregory prepared, and spending the evening teaching them how to count the votes in an election carried out by proportional representation. In one account, it was Jeanne Young who proposed to Catherine Spence that she stand for election to the Federal Convention when it was held in Adelaide in 1897, an action that made Miss Spence the first female political candidate in the world.[7] In response, Catherine Spence effectively made Jeanne Young into her deputy in the struggle. It was Jeanne Young who accompanied Catherine Spence interstate to promote effective voting.

>'Please see that Aunt keeps her bonnet on straight',

said Eleanor Wren, seeing them off on the train from Melbourne to Sydney in 1900. Jeanne Young also notes, in her 'study and … appreciation' of Catherine Helen Spence, published in 1937, that Miss Spence used to take particular pleasure, too, in her visits to the Youngs' household where she talked literature with Jeanne Young's husband Alfred Howard Young, who admired Miss Spence's 'very terse, and excellent literary style, of which' Jeanne Young commented, 'she rather naively claimed to be unconscious'.[8] Some of Catherine Spence's letters included later in this collection suggest that her pleasure gave way to a very different view of Mr Young.

There were gulfs between Jeanne Young and Catherine Spence, to be sure. 'How far apart we were fundamentally', wrote Jeanne Young in 1937,

---

6   Jeanne F. Young, *Catherine Helen Spence: A Study and An Appreciation* (Lothian Publishing Co. Pty. Ltd.), Melbourne, 1937, p. 11.

7   In Catherine Spence's own account, it was her brother John who made this suggestion, see *An Autobiography*, p. 80.

8   Young, *Catherine Helen Spence*, pp. 24–5; Susan Magarey, *Unbridling the tongues of women* (Hale & Iremonger), Sydney, 1985, pp. 161–2; Young, *Catherine Helen Spence*, pp. 28, 13. See also, below, pp. 216.

Jeanne Forster Young, c.1921,
photograph courtesy of the State Library of South Australia, SLSA: B 26285/211

may be understood, when I say that Miss Spence's great sympathy with, and love for, humanity in general particularly for those who suffered from oppression, tended to give her at that time a leaning to State Socialism, then floating into the atmosphere of political thought on the wings of Bellamy's "Looking Backward," while I, trained in the school of freedom, became more and more an Individualist.[9]

Indeed, since Jeanne Young would become an ardent supporter of Australia's engagement in the Great War of 1914–18, they would undoubtedly have parted company, for Catherine Spence was strongly opposed to war, as any reader of her future-vision novella, *A Week in the Future*, would know. However, world war was still in the future when Catherine Spence died, and their close collaboration in the campaigns for the principal cause of Catherine Spence's last decades made Jeanne Young a logical choice for the writer to complete Catherine Spence's autobiography.

Between them, Eleanor Wren, Jeanne Young and the editor of the *Register*, William Sowden, decided that the remaining chapters should be written in the first person, 'to avoid a break in the story'. Eleanor Wren handed over to Jeanne Young the diaries that Catherine Spence kept every year of her life after she had turned twenty-four, and a 'mass of notes' which Catherine Spence had prepared for the remainder of her life-story,[10] and Jeanne Young valiantly set about the final eight chapters. The whole book was published in December 1910. The Libraries Board of South Australia republished it in 1975, to mark the year that the United Nations designated International Women's Year, and portions of it were reproduced in Helen Thomson's selection of Spence's writings.[11] It is re-published again here, in its entirety. After almost a century, the work – however hybrid a product it might be – has its own history, and that gives it an integrity of a kind. It speaks for itself, especially with the addition of Barbara Wall's helpful and informative annotations.

Yet readers of the whole work will have no difficulty in distinguishing the hand of Catherine Spence from that of Jeanne Young. Years after its first appearance, novelist Miles Franklin was to write, rudely, of 'that Young person': 'She doesn't know how to make paragraphs even'.[12] Later still, Helen Jones, pre-eminent historian of South Australian women, remarked:

---

9 Young, *Catherine Helen Spence*, p. 12.
10 Jones, 'A Postscript to the Life of Catherine Helen Spence', p. 86.
11 Helen Thomson (ed.), *Catherine Helen Spence* (University of Queensland Press), St. Lucia, 1987, a volume in the Portable Australian Authors series.
12 Stella Miles Franklin to Alice Henry, 8 September 1937, Miles Franklin Papers, Mitchell Library MSS 364/114.

> The sections on proportional representation, which dominate this part of the book, are strong and studded with anecdotes. The remainder varies: some parts are thin, lacking background ... [She] ignores other causes, episodes and people of importance.[13]

Any comparison between Jeanne Young's chapters and the richly-textured record that Spence kept of her work and travels in 1894 prompts the thought that even Jeanne Young may have found Catherine Spence's atrocious handwriting difficult to read.

So we are supplementing *An Autobiography* with two further essays as well. They set out for the reader a selection of the material to be found in Catherine Spence's correspondence, and in the single diary that has survived, the diary for 1894.

In October 1905, in a church schoolroom in Adelaide, a public gathering celebrated Catherine Spence's eightieth birthday. Miss Spence received her guests, with Jeanne Young on one side and Ellen Gregory on the other – her political deputy and her household companion. South Australia's chief justice, Sir Samuel Way, proclaimed her

> The most distinguished woman they had had in Australia ... There was no one in the whole Commonwealth, whose career covered so wide a ground. She was a novelist, a critic, an accomplished journalist, a preacher, a lecturer, a philanthropist, and a social and moral reformer.

Miss Spence responded:

> I am a new woman, and I know it.[14]

This was, at first blush, an extraordinary statement. The New Woman – in the novels and periodicals of the 1880s and 1890s in Victorian England – had come to symbolise transgression against all the traditional distinctions of sex, gender and class. In public intellectual debate in Australia in the 1890s, the New Woman stood for feminist challenge to the double standard of sexual morality, and assertion of women's own sexual desires and their right to determine how they might be satisfied.[15] By juxtaposing a shocking image

---

13 Jones, 'A Postscript to the Life of Catherine Helen Spence', pp. 86–7.
14 *Catherine Helen Spence 1825–1905*, pamphlet reprinted from the *Register*, Adelaide, 1905.
15 See Magarey, *Passions of the First Wave Feminists*, pp. 41–4.

associated with sexual radicalism with her own person – a short, square, white-haired spinster of eighty – Catherine Spence prompted attention to the larger dimensions of the image: a concern with women's participation in public politics.

> I mean an awakened woman ... awakened to a sense of capacity and responsibility, not merely to the family and the household, but to the State; to be wise, not for her own selfish interests, but that the world may be glad that she had been born.[16]

It was an astute gesture.

It might not have been as outrageous as it first appeared. The rights of women had been firmly on the public political agenda in South Australia for about two decades by the time of Miss Spence's birthday party. For South Australian women had gained the right to vote – and, accidentally, to sit in the parliament – in 1894. Since then, female suffrage had been won everywhere else in the new Commonwealth of Australia, except in Victoria. In Catherine Spence's view, if women were to vote, then their votes needed to be well-informed, just as, though she didn't say it on that occasion, men's votes should be as well. Women must be responsible to their communities and their societies, not merely to the hearthstones and husbands to which they had formerly been confined. Nevertheless, Catherine Spence's statement – as does her earlier support for the campaigns for votes for women – sets her firmly in the forefront of the ranks of Australia's pioneering feminists, even if, as *An Autobiography* shows, she considered the introduction of proportional representation a more important electoral reform than female suffrage.[17]

She was a major pioneer in other ways as well. Her first published novel, the witty story of South Australia during the gold rushes, *Clara Morison*, was the first work of fiction about Australia to have been written by a woman.[18] Her last

---

16 *Catherine Helen Spence 1825–1905*.
17 Magarey, *Unbridling the tongues of women*, pp. 181–2, 185.
18 Grahame Johnston, *Annals of Australian Literature* (Oxford University Press), Melbourne, 1970; C.H. Spence, *Clara Morison a tale of South Australia during the gold fever*, 2 vols., (John W. Parker and Son), London, 1854; reprinted (Rigby Limited), with an Introduction and Notes on the Text by Susan Eade [Magarey], Adelaide, 1971; reprinted facsimile edition (Wakefield Press), Netley, South Australia, 1986. See also Susan Magarey, 'Catherine Helen Spence: Novelist' in Philip Butterss (ed.), *Southwords: Essays on South Australian Writing* (Wakefield Press), Kent Town, 1995.

full-length novel, *Handfasted*, was a visionary depiction of an arcadian society, presented as a utopia. So radical was it that it was dismissed by the judges of the competition for which it was entered – one of whom 'had a wife who kept a ladies school' – as 'calculated to loosen the marriage tie – it was too socialistic, and consequently dangerous'. Catherine Spence, herself, did not think this novel as good as her others: '[I]t is rather overweighted with social and economic speculations', she wrote in a passage left out of *An Autobiography*, probably by the *Register*'s editor. Yet this novel contains the entrancing story of Marguerite de Launay, possibly the best of Catherine Spence's fictional writing, compelling reading at any time.[19] Even so, this work was so radically progressive that it had to wait almost a century to achieve publication.

Catherine Spence broke new ground in other places, too. Her work for education, and – with Caroline Emily Clark – for destitute children[20] is recognised in the image of the South Australian State Children's Department next to her portrait on the $5 bills in use in the early twenty-first century. Following the example of Martha Turner, visiting Adelaide from Melbourne where she was the pastor of the Unitarian Church, Catherine Spence took to the pulpit of the Unitarian Christian Church in Adelaide, and subsequently in Sydney, Melbourne and across the United States of America.

But the cause that took her to the United States was not the gospel of the Unitarian church, nor was it the practice of boarding out destitute children with families, rather than keeping them in large institutions, the subject on which she was to address the Congress of Charities in Chicago. Rather, it was the promotion of Hare-Spence proportional representation, a quota preferential voting system, as the 'fairest' electoral system that a democracy could devise. 'Effective voting' was Catherine Spence's own contribution to electoral reform, and the cause about which she cared most. In the twenty-first century, it is in operation throughout Australia in elections to the Senate, and in every state where there are two houses of parliament. Surely, it is time to recognise this contribution and give her credit for it?

Catherine Helen Spence is commemorated in several ways. In South Australia there is a scholarship named after her; a primary school in Aberfoyle Park and a building at Brighton Secondary School; a portrait by Margaret Preston in the

---

19 Catherine Helen Spence, *Handfasted*, edited with a preface and afterword by Helen Thomson (Penguin Books), Ringwood, 1984, *passim*, and pp. viii, 156–211.
20 There is an account of this work in the autobiography, here. But see also C.H. Spence, *State Children in Adelaide: a History of Boarding Out in its Development*, Adelaide, 1907, and Magarey, *Unbridling the tongues of women*, chapter 4.

Art Gallery of South Australia and a statue by Ieva Pocius in Light Square; a plaque in the pavement of Norwood Parade, a street in the City of Adelaide and a new wing of the State Library of South Australia – all acknowledge and applaud her outstanding achievements. Nationally, her portrait appeared on our currency in 2001, to mark the centenary of Federation and to issue an invitation to all Australians to know her better.

The portrait on the five dollar bill is not an especially accurate representation, even though it appears to have been drawn from Margaret Preston's splendid and deeply moving portrait. 'Short in stature, and symmetrically broad', wrote Jeanne Young, 'with delicate hands, generally half-veiled with black silk mittens – soft, pliable, capable hands – of which she was rather proud'. Young's description goes on to detail 'a face marked by strong features which matched her tone of confidence and power', her 'silvery grey hair … with a parting that was kept meticulously straight', her 'alert, eager and almost searching grey eyes', and her 'broad, Scotch accent'.[21] Alice Henry would have queried the description of her accent as 'broad': 'it was a refined accent' she told Miles Franklin, 'she was a lady'. Henry noted as well her keen sense of humour and her shining intelligence: 'you felt the soul within her, clever, competent, intellectual, through and through'.[22]

'The Grand Old Woman of Australia', people had been calling her since 1894. It was a title that Alice Henry took into the international arena, when Catherine Spence died.[23] Another friend, Sydney suffrage leader Rose Scott, could have been sending an envoy for *An Autobiography*, even though it was still to be completed, when she wrote:

> To live in hearts we leave behind is not to die! The shadows of time will no doubt eventually dim the vision we now hold of that vivid personality, but her works will live after her, and be the most fitting monument to her memory.[24]

---

21 Young, *Catherine Helen Spence*, p. 13.
22 Alice Henry to Miles Franklin, 3 October 1937, Mitchell Library MSS 364/11.
23 References to Catherine Spence as 'the Grand Old Woman of Australia' appeared in the Adelaide *Advertiser*, 18 December 1894; in *Quiz and the Lantern*, 9 May 1895; in the Melbourne *Leader*, 4 June 1904; in the *Australian Woman's Sphere*, 14 February 1905; in the *Express*, 30 October 1905; and then in Alice Henry, 'Catherine Helen Spence: the grand old woman of Australia', *Survey* (1910), pp. 117–18; see also Diane Kirkby, *Alice Henry: The Power of Pen and Voice: The Life of an Australian-American Labor Reformer* (Cambridge University Press), Cambridge, 1991.
24 Quoted by Jeanne Young, writing as Catherine Spence, *An Autobiography*, p. 4.

A Note on the Text

Corrections have been made to words mis-read by the *Register*'s compositors, and to last names spelled wrongly.

Catherine Helen Spence

An Autobiography

CHAPTER 1

EARLY LIFE IN SCOTLAND

Sitting down at the age of 84 to give an account of my life, I feel that it connects itself naturally with the growth and development of the province of South Australia, to which I came with my family in the year 1839, before it was quite three years old. But there is much truth in Wordsworth's line, 'the child is father of the man',[1] and no less is the mother of the woman; and I must go back to Scotland for the roots of my character and ideals. I account myself well-born, for my father and my mother loved each other. I consider myself well descended, going back for many generations on both sides of intelligent and respectable people. I think I was well brought up, for my father and mother were of one mind regarding the care of the family. I count myself well educated, for the admirable woman at the head of the school which I attended from the age of four and a half, till I was thirteen and a half, was a born teacher in advance of her own times. In fact, like my own dear mother, Sarah Phin was a New Woman without knowing it. The phrase was not known in the thirties.

I was born on 31 October 1825, the fifth of a family of eight[2] born to David Spence and Helen Brodie, in the romantic village of Melrose,[3] on the silvery Tweed, close to the three picturesque peaks of the Eildon Hills, which

1 William Wordsworth (1770–1850), 'My heart leaps up', 1807.
2 Agnes Spence, 1818–1835; Jessie Spence, 1821–1888 (married Andrew Murray 1841); William Richard Spence, 1822–1903 (did not marry); John Brodie Spence, 1824–1902 (married Jessie Cumming 1858); Catherine Helen Spence, 1825–1910 (did not marry); David Wauchope Spence, 1827–1890 (did not marry); Mary Brodie Spence, 1830–1870 (married William John Wren 1855); Eliza Brodie Spence, 1833–1836, see Appendix A, Family Tree.
3 Roxburghshire, Scotland. In October 1999 a plaque was placed on the wall of the house in which Spence was born, now the Bon Accord Hotel.

Michael Scott's[4] familiar spirit split up from one mountain mass in a single night, according to the legend. It was indeed poetic ground. It was Sir Walter Scott's ground.[5] Abbotsford was within two miles of Melrose, and one of my earliest recollections was seeing the long procession which followed his body to the family vault at Dryburgh Abbey. There was not a local note in *The Lay of the Last Minstrel* or in the novels, *The Monastery* and *The Abbot*, with which I was not familiar before I entered my teens. There was not a hill or a burn or a glen that had not a song or a proverb, or a legend about it. Yarrow braes[6] were not far off. The broom of the Cowdenknowes[7] was still nearer, and my mother knew the words as well as the tunes of the minstrelsy of the Scottish Border.[8] But as all readers of the life of Scott know, he was a Tory, loving the past with loyal affection, and shrinking from any change. My father, who was a lawyer (a writer as it was called), and his father who was a country practitioner, were reformers, and so it happened that they never came into personal relations with the man they admired above all men in Scotland. It was the Tory doctor who attended to his health, and the Tory writer who was consulted about his affairs.

I look back to a happy childhood. The many anxieties which reached both my parents were quite unknown to the children till the crisis in 1839. I do not know that I appreciated the beauty of the village I lived in so much with my own bodily eyes as through the songs and the literature, which were current talk. The old Abbey,[9] with its 'prentice window',[10] and its wonders in stonecarving, that Scott had written about and Washington Irving[11] marvelled at – 'Here lies the race of the House of Yair'[12] as a tombstone – had a

---

4 Scottish scholar (c.1160–1235), who gained a reputation as a wizard. The legend told that he set demons to split Eildon Hill into 'the three picturesque peaks'.
5 Sir Walter Scott (1771–1832), poet and novelist, who lived at Abbotsford, had a great influence on Spence. *The Lay of the Last Minstrel* (1805), *The Monastery* (1820) and *The Abbot* (1820) are all set in the Melrose district.
6 The steep banks of the river Yarrow.
7 The low hills of the Cowden area.
8 The *Minstrelsy of the Scottish Border* (1802–3). Scott's collection of border ballads.
9 Melrose Abbey, one of the best preserved ruins in Scotland.
10 The legend of the beautiful eastern window in Melrose Abbey, known as the Prentice Window, is that the master builder lacked the skill to construct it. He went to Rome to consult the masters of his craft. During his absence his apprentice completed the window, and cut on the wall 'The best mason of masonry, except the man that learned me'. On his return the master killed his apprentice after reading only the first few words.
11 Washington Irving (1783–1859), American writer and traveller, published *Abbotsford*, an account of his visit to Scott and the Melrose area, in 1815.
12 These words are among the memorials carved on the walls of the ruined Melrose Abbey.

grand roll in it. In the churchyard of the old Abbey my people on the Spence side lay buried. In the square or market place there no longer stood the great tree described in *The Monastery* as standing just after Flodden Field,[13] where the flowers of the forest[14] had been cut down by the English; but in the centre stood the cross with steps up to it, and close to the cross was the well, to which twice a day the maids went to draw water for the house until I was nine years old, when we had pipes and taps laid on. The cross was the place for any public speaking, and I recalled, when I was recovering from the measles, the maid in whose charge I was, wrapped me in a shawl and took me with her to hear a gentleman from Edinburgh speak in favour of reform to a crowd gathered round. He said that the Tories had found a new name – they called themselves Conservatives – because it sounded better. For his part he thought conserves were pickles, and he hoped all the Tories would soon find themselves in a pretty pickle. There were such shouts of laughter that I saw this was a great joke.

We had gasworks in Melrose when I was ten or eleven, and a great joy to us children the wonderful light was. I recollect the first lucifer[15] matches, and the wonder of them. My brother John had got sixpence from a visiting uncle as a reward for buying him snuff to fill his cousin's silver snuffbox, and he spent the money in buying a box of lucifers, with the piece of sandpaper doubled, through which each match was to be smartly drawn, and he took all of us and some of his friends to the orchard, we called the wilderness, at the back of my grandfather Spence's house, and lighted each of the 50 matches, and we considered it a great exhibition. My grandfather (old Dr Spence) died before the era of lucifer matches. He used to get up early and strike a fire with flint and steel to boil the kettle and make a cup of tea to give to his wife in bed. He did it for his first wife (Janet Park), who was delicate, and he did the same for his second wife until her last fatal illness. It was a wonderful thing for a man to do in those days. He would not call the maid; he said young things wanted plenty of sleep. He had been a navy doctor, and was very intelligent. He trusted much to Nature and not too much to drugs. On the Sunday of the great annular eclipse of the sun in 1835, which was my brother John's eleventh birthday, he had a large double tooth extracted – not by a dentist, and gas was then unknown or any other anaesthetic, so he did not enjoy the eclipse as other people did. It took place in the afternoon and there was no afternoon

---

13　The battle of Flodden Field in Northumberland in 1513, when the English defeated the Scotch and killed James IV of Scotland.

14　'Flowers of the Forest', a popular lament for those who fell at Flodden, by the Scottish poet Jane Elliot (1727–1805).

15　The early name given to a friction match made with a splint of wood tipped with an inflammable substance.

church. In summer we had two services – one in the forenoon and one in the afternoon. In winter we had two services at one sitting, which was a thing astonishing to English visitors. The first was generally called a lecture – a reading with comments, of a passage of Scripture – a dozen verses or more – and the second a regularly built sermon, with three or four heads, and some particulars, and a practical summing up.

Prices[16] and cost of living had fallen since my mother had married in 1815, three months after the battle of Waterloo. At that time tea cost 8s a pound, loaf sugar, 1s.4d, and brown sugar 11½d. Bread and meat were then still at war prices, and calico was no cheaper than linen, and that was dear. She paid 3s.6d a yard for fine calico to make petticoats. Other garments were of what was called home made linen. White cotton stockings at 4s.9d, and thinner at 3s.9d each; silk stockings at 11s.6d. I know she paid 36s for a yard of Brussels net to make caps of. It was a new thing to have net made in the loom. When a woman married she must wear caps at least in the morning. In 1838 my mother bought a chest of tea (84 pounds) for £20, a trifle under 5s a pound; the retail price was 6s – it was a great saving; and up to the time of our departure brown sugar cost 7½d, and loaf sugar 10d. It is no wonder that these things were accounted luxuries. When a decent Scotch couple in South Australia went out to a station in the country in the forties and received their stores, the wife sat down at her quarter-chest of tea and gazed at her bag of sugar, and fairly wept to think of her old mother across the ocean, who had such difficulty in buying an ounce of tea and a pound of sugar. My mother even saw an old woman buy a quarter ounce of tea and pay 1½d for it, and another woman buy a quarter pound of meat.

We kept three maids. The cook got £8 a year, the housemaid £7, and the nursemaid £6, paid half-yearly, but the summer half-year was much better paid than the winter, because there was the outwork in the fields, weeding and hoeing turnips and potatoes, and haymaking. The winter work in the house was heavier on account of the fires and the grate cleaning, but the wages were less. My mother gave the top wages in the district, and was considerate to her maids, but I blush yet to think how poorly those good women who made the comfort of my early home were paid for their labours. You could get a washer-woman for 1s or 1s.6d a day, but you must give her a glass of whisky as well as

---

16 It is impossible to give equivalents for money then and now. Some idea may be gained by comparing the prices of different commodities with their modern counterparts. In Spence's time there were twelve pence (d.) in a shilling (1s.) and twenty shillings in a pound (£). £1/16 or 36s equals one pound sixteen shillings. 1s.4d equals one shilling and four pence. 11½d equals eleven pence and a half penny. One pound weight (lb.) is roughly equivalent to half a kilogram.

her food. You could get a sewing girl for a shilling or less, without the whisky. And yet cheap as sewing was it was the pride of the middle-class women of those days that they did it themselves at home. Half of the time of girls' schools was given to sewing when mother was taught. Nearly two hours a day was devoted to it in my time.

A glass of whisky in Scotland in the thirties cost less than a cup of tea. I recollect my father getting a large cask of whisky direct from the distillery which cost 6s.6d a gallon, duty paid. A bottle of inferior whisky could be bought at the grocer's for a shilling. It is surprising how much alcoholic beverages entered into the daily life, the business, and the pleasures of the people in those days. No bargain could be made without them. Christenings, weddings, funerals – all called for the pouring out of strong drink. If a lady called, the port and sherry decanters were produced, and the cake basket. If a gentleman, probably it was the spirit decanter. After the 3 o'clock dinner there was whisky and hot water and sugar, and generally the same after the 10 o'clock supper. Drinking habits were very prevalent among men, and were not in any way disgraceful, unless excessive. But there was less drinking among women than there is now, because public opinion was strongly against it. Without being abstainers, they were temperate. With the same heredity and the same environment, you would see all the brothers pretty hard drinkers and all the sisters quite straight. Such is the effect of public opinion. Nothing else has been so powerful in changing these customs as the cheapening of tea and coffee and cocoa, but especially tea.

My brothers went to the parish school, one of the best in the county. The endowment from the tiends or tithes, extorted by John Knox[17] from the Lords of the congregations,[18] who had seized on the church lands, was more meagre for the schoolmasters than for the clergy. I think Mr Thomas Murray had only £33 in money, a schoolhouse, and a residence and garden, and he had to make up a livelihood from school fees, which began at 2s a quarter for reading, 3s.6d when writing was taught, and 5s for arithmetic. Latin, I think, cost 10s.6d a quarter, but it included English. Mr. Murray adopted a phonic system of teaching reading, not so complete as the late Mr Hartley[19] formulated for our South Australian schools, and was most successful with it. He not only

17 John Knox (1505–1572), Scottish minister and reformer.
18 Lords of the Congregation were a group of powerful Scottish nobles who cooperated after 1557 to oppose French influence in Scotland and who were in favour of a reformed faith.
19 John Anderson Hartley (1844–1896), educationist, Inspector-General of Schools in South Australia from 1878 to 1895 and permanent head of the South Australian Education Department. Hartley was a personal friend of Spence, who lived near him and championed him when his authority was challenged.

used maps, but he had blank maps – a great innovation. My mother was only taught geography during the years in which she was 'finished' in Edinburgh, and never saw a map then. She felt interested in geography when her children were learning it. No boy in Mr Murray's school was allowed to be idle; every spare minute was given to arithmetic. In the parish school boys of all classes were taught. Sir David Brewster's[20] sons went to it; but there were fewer girls, partly because no needlework was taught there, and needlework was of supreme importance. Mr Murray was session clerk, for which he received £5 a year. On Saturday afternoons he might do land measuring, like Goldsmith's schoolmaster in *The Deserted Village*[21] –

> Lands he could measure, terms and tides presage,
> And even the rumour ran that he could gauge.

My mother felt that her children were receiving a much better education than she had had. The education seemed to begin after she left school. Her father united with six other tenant farmers in buying the third edition of the *Encyclopedia Britannica*, seven for the price of six. Probably it was only in East Lothian[22] that seven such purchasers could be found, and my mother studied it well, as also the unabridged Johnson's Dictionary[23] in two volumes. She learned the Greek letters, so that she could read the derivations, but went no further. She saw the fallacy of Mr Pitt's sinking fund[24] when her father believed in it. To borrow more than was needed so as to put aside part on compound interest, would make the price of money rise. And why should not private people adopt the same way of getting rid of debts? The father said it would not do for them at all – it was only practicable for a nation. The things I recollect of the life in the village of Melrose, of 700 inhabitants, have been talked over with my mother, and many embodied in a little MS. volume of reminiscences of her life.[25] I hold more from her than from my father; but, as

---

20 Sir David Brewster (1781–1868), natural philosopher, born at Jedburgh, editor of the *Edinburgh Journal* and a founder of the Royal Scottish Society of Arts.
21 Oliver Goldsmith (1730–1774), Irish poet, novelist and playwright, author of *The Deserted Village*, (1770).
22 South East maritime county of Scotland, two counties north of Roxburghshire.
23 Samuel Johnson (1709–1784), scholar and lexicographer. Johnson's *A Dictionary, with a Grammar and History of the English Language* was published in two volumes in 1755.
24 William Pitt the Younger (1759–1806) was Prime Minister of Great Britain in 1783–1801 and 1804–1806. He introduced a 'sinking fund' which enabled loans to be used for the reduction of the national debt.
25 This MS was published in 1994, Judy King and Graham Tulloch (eds), *Tenacious of the Past*,

he was an unlucky speculator, I inherit from him Hope, which is invaluable to a social or political reformer. School holidays were only a rarity in harvest time for the parish school. At Miss Phin's we had besides, a week at Christmas. The boys had only New Year's Day. Saturday was only a half-holiday. We all had a holiday for Queen Victoria's coronation, and I went with a number of school fellows to see Abbotsford, not for the first time in my life.

Two mail coaches – the Blucher and the Chevy Chase – ran through Melrose every day. People went to the post office for their letters, and paid for them on delivery. My two elder sisters – Agnes, who died of consumption at the age of 16, and Jessie, afterwards Mrs Andrew Murray, of Adelaide and Melbourne, went to boarding school with their aunt, Mary Spence, at Upper Wooden, halfway between Jedburgh and Kelso.[26] Roxburghshire is rich in old monasteries. The border lands were more safe in the hands of the church than under feudal lords engaged in perpetual fighting, and the vassals of the abbeys had generally speaking, a more secure existence. Kelso, Jedburgh, and Dryburgh Abbeys lay in fertile districts, and I fancy that when these came into the hands of the Lords of the congregation, the vassals looked back with regret on the old times. I was not sent to Wooden, but kept at home, and I went to a day school called by the very popish name of St Mary's Convent, though it was quite sufficiently Protestant. My mother had the greatest confidence in the lady who was at the head of it. She had been a governess in good situations, and had taught herself Latin, so that she might fit the boys of the family to take a good place in the Edinburgh High School. She discovered that she had an incurable disease, a form of dropsy, which compelled her to lie down for some time every day, and this she considered she could not do as a governess. So she determined to risk her savings, and start a boarding and day school in Melrose, a beautiful and healthy neighbourhood, and with the aid of a governess, impart what was then considered the education of a gentlewoman to the girls in the neighbourhood. She took with her her old mother, and a sister who managed the housekeeping, and taught the pupils all kinds of plain and fancy needlework. She succeeded, and she lived till the year 1866, although most of her teaching was done from her sofa. When my mother was asked what it was that made Miss Phin so successful, and so esteemed, she said it was her commonsense. The governesses were well enough, but the invalid old lady was the life and soul of the school. There were about fourteen boarders,

(Centre for Research in the New Literatures in English and the Libraries Board of South Australia) Adelaide, South Australia.

26 Jedburgh is south east of Melrose and Kelso almost due east. There are abbey ruins at Kelso, Jedburgh and Dryburgh which is six kilometres east of Melrose. Sir Walter Scott was buried at Dryburgh Abbey.

and nearly as many day scholars there, so long as there was no competition. When that came there was a falling off, but my young sister Mary and I were faithful till the day when after nine years at the same school, I went with Jessie to Wooden, to Aunt Mary's, to hear there that my father was ruined, and had to leave Melrose and Scotland for ever, and that we must all go to Australia. That was in April, 1839.

As I said, I had a very happy childhood. The death of my eldest sister at 16, and of my youngest sister at 2 years old, did not sink into the mind of a child as it did into that of my parents, and although they were seriously alarmed about my health when I was 12 years old, when I developed symptoms similar to those of Agnes at the same age, I was not ill enough to get at all alarmed. I was annoyed at having to stay away from school for three months. When the collapse came Jessie had a dear friend of some years' standing, and I had one whom I had known only for some months, but I had spent a month with her in Edinburgh at Christmas, 1838, and we exchanged letters weekly through the box which came from Edinburgh with my brother John's washing. It was too expensive for us to write by the post. Well, neither of our friends wrote a word to us. With regard to mine it was not to be wondered at much – she was only 13 – but the other was more surprising. It was not until 1865[27] that an old woman told me that when Miss F.B. came to return some books and music to her to give to my aunt in Melrose, 'she just sat in the chair and cried as if her heart would break'. She was not quite a free agent. Very few single women were free agents in 1839. We were hopelessly ruined, our place would know us no more.

The only long holidays I had in the year I spent at Thornton Loch, in East Lothian, 40 miles away. I did not know that my father was a heavy speculator in foreign wheat, and I thought his keen interest in the market in Mark Lane[28] was on account of the Thornton Loch crops, in which first my grandfather and afterwards the three maiden aunts were deeply concerned. My mother's father, John Brodie, was one of the most enterprising agriculturalists in the most advanced district of Great Britain. He won a prize of two silver salvers from the Highland Society for having the largest area of drilled wheat sown. He was called up twice to London to give evidence before Parliamentary committees on the corn laws,[29] and he naturally approved of them, because, with three large farms he'd on 19 years' leases at war prices, the influx of cheap wheat from abroad would mean ruin. He proved that he paid £6,000 a

---

27 Spence visited Great Britain in 1865.
28 The London Corn Exchange was situated in Mark Lane, formerly Market Lane, London.
29 The British Corn Laws regulated the import and export of corn to protect the income of farmers.

year for these three farms – two he worked himself, the third was for his eldest son; but he was liable for the rent. On his first London trip, my aunt Margaret accompanied him, and on his second visit he took my mother. That was in the year 1814, and both of them noted from the postchaise that farming was not up to what was done in East Lothian.

My grandfather Brodie was a speculating man, and he lost nearly all his savings through starting, along with others, an East Lothian Bank, because the local banker had been ill used by the British Linen Company. He put in only £1,000; but was liable for all, and, as many of his fellow shareholders were defaulters, it cost £15,000 before all was over, and if it had not been that he left the farm in the capable hands of Aunt Margaret, there would have been little or nothing left for the family. When he had a stroke of paralysis he wanted to turn over Thornton Loch, the only farm then had, to his eldest son; but there were three daughters, and one of them said she would like to carry it on, and she did. She was the most successful farmer in the country for 30 years, and then she transferred it to a nephew. The capacity for business of my Aunt Margaret, the wit and charm of my brilliant Aunt Mary, and the sound judgment and accurate memory of my own dear mother, showed me early that women were fit to share in the work of this world, and that to make the world pleasant for men was not their only mission. My father's sister Mary was also a remarkable and saintly woman, though I do not think she was such a born teacher as Miss Phin. When my father was a little boy, not 12 years old, an uncle from Jamaica came home for a visit. He saw his sister Janet a dying woman, with a number of delicate-looking children, and he offered to take David with him and treat him like his own son. No objections were made. The uncle was supposed to be well-to-do, and he was unmarried, but he took fever and died, and was found to be not rich, but insolvent. The boy could read and write, and he got something to do on a plantation till his father sent money to pay his passage home. He must have been supposed to be worth something, for he got a cask of rum for his wages, which was shipped home, and when the duty had been paid was drunk in the doctor's household. But the boy had been away only 21 months, and he returned to find his mother dead and two or three little brothers and sisters dead and buried, and his father married again to his mother's cousin, Katherine Swanston, an old maid of 45, who, however, two years afterwards was the mother of a fine big daughter, so that Aunt Helen Park's scheme for getting the money for her sister's children failed. In spite of my father's strong wish to be a farmer, and not a writer or attorney, there was no capital to start a farm upon, so he was indentured to Mr Erskine, and after some years began business in Melrose for himself, and married Helen Brodie. His elder brother John went as a surgeon in the Royal Navy before he was 21. The demand for surgeons was great during the war time. He was made a Freemason before the set age, because in case of capture friends from the fraternity might be of great use. He did not like his original profession, especially when after the peace he must be a country practitioner like his father, at every one's beck and call, so he was articled to his brother, and lived in the house till he married and settled at Earlston, five miles off. Uncle John Spence was a scholarly man, shy but kindly, who gave to us children most of the books we possessed. They were not in such abundance as children read nowadays, but they were read and re-read.

In these early readings the Calvinistic teaching of the church and the shorter catechism[30] was supported and exemplified. The only secular books to counteract them were the *Evenings at Home*[31] and Miss Edgeworth's *Tales for Young and Old*.[32]

The only cloud on my young life was the gloomy religion, which made me doubt of my own salvation and despair of the salvation of any but a very small proportion of the people in the world. Thus the character of God appeared unlovely, and it was wicked not to love God; and this was my condemnation. I had learned the shorter catechism with the proofs from Scripture, and I understood the meaning of the dogmatic theology. Watts's[33] hymns were much more easy to learn, but the doctrine was the same. There was no getting away from the feeling that the world was under a curse ever since that unlucky apple-eating in the garden of Eden. Why, oh! why had not the sentence of death been carried out at once, and a new start made with more prudent people? The school in which as a day scholar I passed nine years of my

30 The Shorter Catechism, setting out the Christian religion in question and answer form, approved by the General Assembly of the Church of Scotland in 1648, continued to be used in Scotland and as a school text book well into the nineteenth century.

31 *Evenings at home, or, The juvenile budget opened: consisting of a variety of miscellaneous pieces for the instruction and amusement of youth*, by Dr Aikin and his sister Mrs Barbauld. First published 1792–6 and often reprinted. It contains stories, essays and poems for children, grouped for amusement for thirty evenings.

32 Maria Edgeworth (1767–1849), influential Anglo-Irish writer for children and adults, did not publish a volume of stories with the title *Tales for Young and Old*. There were many volumes of Edgeworth's stories in the Unitarian Christian Church Children's Library with which Spence had a great deal to do. She may be remembering *Popular Tales* (1804) or *Moral Tales* (1801) which were frequently republished; or perhaps volumes of the collected tales and novels which were published in eighteen volumes in the 1830s and nine volumes in the 1840s.

33 Isaac Watts (1674–1748), English nonconformist clergyman and hymn writer. His *Divine and moral songs: for the use of children* were very popular. Indeed, they were parodied by Lewis Carroll.

life was more literary than many which were more pretentious. Needlework was of supreme importance, certainly, but during the hour and a half every day, Saturday's half-holiday not excepted, which was given to it by the whole school at once (odd half-hours were also put in), the best readers took turns about to read some book selected by Miss Phin. We were thus trained to pay attention. History, biography, adventures, descriptions, and story books were read. Any questions or criticism about our sewing, knitting, netting etc., were carried on in a low voice, and we learned to work well and quickly, and good reading aloud was cultivated. First one brother then another had gone to Edinburgh for higher education than could be had at Melrose Parish School, and I wanted to go to a certain institution, the first of the kind, for advanced teaching for girls, which had a high reputation. I was a very ambitious girl at 13. I wanted to be a teacher first, and a great writer afterwards. The qualifications for a teacher would help me to rise to literary fame, so I obtained from my father a promise that I should go to Edinburgh next year; but he could not keep it. He was a ruined man.

CHAPTER 2

TOWARDS AUSTRALIA

Although my mother's family had lost heavily by him, her mother gave us £500 to make a start in South Australia. An eighty-acre section was bought for £80, and this entitled us to the steerage passage of four adults. This helped for my elder sister and two brothers (my younger brother David was left for his education with his aunts in Scotland), but we had to have another female, so we took with us a servant girl – most ridiculous, it seems now. I was under the statutory age of 15. The difference between steerage and intermediate fares had to be made up, and we sailed from Greenock in July 1839, in the barque *Palmyra*, 400 tons, bound for Adelaide, Port Phillip, and Sydney.[1] The *Palmyra* was advertised to carry a cow and an experienced surgeon. Intermediate passengers had no more advantage of the cow than steerage folks, and except for the privacy of separate cabins and a pound of white biscuit per family weekly, we fared exactly as the other immigrants did, though the cost was double. Twice a week we had either fresh meat or tinned meat, generally soup and bouille,[2] and the biscuit seemed half bran, and sometimes it was mouldy. But our mother thought it was very good for us to endure hardship, and so it was.

There were 150 passengers, mostly South Australian immigrants, in the little ship. The first and second class passengers were bound for Port Phillip and Sydney in greater proportion than for Adelaide. There was in the saloon the youthful William Milne, and in the intermediate was Miss Disher, his future wife.[3] He became President of the Legislative Council, and was knighted. There was my brother, J.B. Spence, who also sat in the Council, and

---

1 Spence's father, David Spence, did not travel with his family but left a fortnight earlier in the *Dumfries*. He arrived in South Australia on 13 October 1839.
2 Spence means bouilli, boiled beef. The words were later corrupted to 'bully beef'.
3 William Milne, later Sir William (1822–1895), Adelaide wine merchant, business man and politician. He married Eliza Disher in 1842.

was at one time Chief Secretary. There was George Melrose, a successful South Australian pastoralist;[4] there was my father's valued clerk, Thomas Laidlaw, who was long in the Legislative Council of New South Wales and the leading man in the town of Yass. 'Honest Tom of Yass' was his soubriquet. Bound for Melbourne there were Mr and Mrs Duncan, of Melrose, and Charles Williamson, from Hawick, who founded a great business house in Collins Street. There were Langs from Selkirk, and McHaffies, who became pastoralists. Our next cabin mate, who brought out a horse, had the Richmond punt when there was no bridge there. All the young men were reading a thick book brought out by the Society for Promoting Useful Knowledge about sheep, but they could dance in the evenings to the strains of Mr Duncan's violin, and although I was not 14, I was in request as a partner, as ladies were scarce. Jessie Spence and Eliza Disher, who were grown up, were the belles of the *Palmyra*. Of all the passengers in the ship the young doctor, John Logan Campbell, has had the most distinguished career.[5] Next to Sir George Grey he has had most to do with the development of New Zealand. He is now called the Grand Old Man of Auckland. He had his twenty-first birthday, this experienced surgeon (!) in the same week as I had my fourteenth, while the *Palmyra* was lying off Holdfast Bay (now Glenelg) before we could get to the old Port Adelaide to discharge. My brother saw him in 1883, but I have not set eye on him since that week in 1839. We have corresponded frequently since my brother's death. In his book *Poenamo*, written for his children, there is a picture of the *Palmyra*, with an account of the voyage and the only sensational incident in it. We had a collision in the Irish Sea, and our foremast was broken, so that we had to return to Greenock for repairs, and then obtained the concession of white biscuit for the second class for one day in the week. Sir John Campbell's gift of a beautiful park to the citizens of Auckland was made while my brother John was alive. Just recently he has given money and plans for building and equipping the first free kindergarten in Auckland – perhaps in New Zealand – and as this includes a training college for the students it is very complete. These *Palmyra* passengers have made their mark on the history of Australia and New Zealand. It is surprising what a fine class of people immigrated to Australia in these days to face all the troubles of a new country.

The first issue of the *Register*[6] was printed in London, and gave a glowing

4   George Melrose (1806–1894), pastoralist, who settled at Rosebank, Mt Pleasant.
5   John Logan Campbell (1817–1912) settled in Auckland in 1840 and established the firm of Brown & Campbell. Campbell's *Poenamo*, (Williams and Norgate) London, 1881, is an account of his early life in Auckland.
6   South Australia's first newspaper, to be called the *South Australian Gazette and Colonial Register*, was planned in England. The first part, the *South Australian Gazette*, was to be

account of the province that was to be – its climate, its resources, the sound principles on which it was founded. It is sometimes counted as a reproach that South Australia was founded by doctrinaires[7] and that we retain traces of our origin; to me it is our glory. In the land laws and the immigration laws it struck out a new path, and sought to found a new community where the sexes should be equal, and where land, labour, and capital should work harmoniously together. Land was not to be given away in huge grants, as had been done in New South Wales and Western Australia, to people with influence or position, but was to be sold at the high price of twenty shillings an acre. The price should be not too high to bring out people to work on the land. The Western Australian settlers had been well-nigh starved, because there was no labour to give real value to the paper or parchment deeds. The cheapest fare third class was from £17 to £20, and the family immigration, which is the best, was quite out of the reach of those who were needed. The immigrants[8] were not bound to work for any special individual or company, unless by special contract voluntarily made. They were often in better circumstances after the lapse of a few years than the landbuyers, and, in the old days, the owner of an eighty-acre section worked harder and for longer hours than any hired man would do, or could be expected to do.

In the South Australian Public Library[9] there is a curious record – the minutes and proceedings of the South Australian Literary Society, in the years 1834–5.[10] As the province was non-existent at that time, this cultivation of literature seems premature, but the members, 40 in number, were its founders, and pending the passage of the Bill by the Imperial Parliament, they met fortnightly in London to discuss its prospects, and to read papers on exploration and on matters of future development and government. The first paper was on education for the new land, and was read by Richard Davies Hanson.[11]

devoted to official announcements. The first issue was printed in London, 18 June 1826, the second in Adelaide on 3 June 1837.

7 The rest of this paragraph outlines the plan envisaged by Edward Gibbon Wakefield (1796–1862) whose radical ideas for colonisation put forward in *A Letter From Sydney* (1829) and supported by Robert Gouger were incorporated in the Act to establish the Colony of South Australia.

8 To South Australia.

9 Now the State Library of South Australia.

10 This document is now in State Records of South Australia. GRG 44/83. The signatories were all men who intended to emigrate to South Australia, although not all did.

11 Richard, later Sir Richard, Davies Hanson (1805–1876), nonconformist lawyer who was an associate of Edward Gibbon Wakefield and Robert Gouger. He arrived in South Australia in 1846 and had a distinguished career, becoming Advocate-General, Attorney-General and

The South Australian Company and Mr George Fife Angas[12] came to the rescue by buying a considerable area of land and making up the amount of capital which was required. It is interesting to note that the casting vote in the House of Lords which decided that the province of South Australia should come into existence was given by the Duke of Wellington. Adelaide was to have been called Wellington, but somehow the Queen Consort's name carried the day. The name of the conqueror of Waterloo is immortalised in the capital of the Dominion of the New Zealand, in the North Island, which, like South Australia, was founded on the Wakefield principle of selling land for money to be applied for immigration. The 40 signatures in the records of the South Australian Literary Society are most interesting to an old colonist like myself, and the names of many of them are perpetuated in those of our rivers and our streets: – Torrens, Wright, Brown, Gilbert, Gouger, Hanson, Kingston, Wakefield, Morphett, Childers, Hill (Rowland), Stephens, Mann, Finniss, Symonds.[13] The second issue of the *Register* was printed in Adelaide. It was also the *Government Gazette*. It gave the proclamation of the province, which was made under the historic gum tree near Holdfast Bay, now Glenelg. It also records the sales of the town acres which had not been allotted to the purchasers

    Premier. He also served as Chief Justice. He worked for the establishment of the University of Adelaide and was elected its first Chancellor in 1874.

12 George Fife Angas (1789–1879), banker and politician, was interested in the Colony from its beginnings. He joined the South Australian Colonization Commission in 1835, and rescued the Commission's land–sales project with his own funds. He helped establish the South Australian Company and encouraged immigration of German Lutherans. When he arrived in 1852 and settled at Lindsay Park near Angaston he was the state's largest individual landowner. An influential colonist, he served on the Board of Education and the Legislative Council.

13 These men all contributed to the establishment and early development of the colony. Their names are commemorated as follows: Colonel Robert Torrens (1780–1864), economist, member of the British House of Commons: River Torrens. Edward Wright, surgeon, member of the South Australian Colonization Commission, signed the minute book (but it is likely that the street was named after John Wright, financier, who was appointed as a Colonization Commissioner in 1835): Wright Street, Adelaide. John Brown (1801?–1879), first Commissioner for Immigration and Auditor-General, editor of the *Adelaide Times*: Brown Street, Adelaide, now replaced as the continuation of Morphett Street. Thomas Gilbert (1787?–1873), first Colonial Storekeeper and first Postmaster: Gilbert Street, Gilbert Place, Adelaide. Robert Gouger (1802–1846), secretary of the South Australian Association and first Colonial Secretary. He gave many books to the South Australian Literary Association which later became part of the collection of the South Australian Institute Library: Gouger Street, Adelaide. Richard Davies Hanson (1805–1876), lawyer, who served as Advocate-General, Attorney-General and Premier: Hanson Street, Adelaide, now

of preliminary sections. These were of 134 acres, and a town acre at the price of 12s.6d an acre. This was a temptation to invest at the very first, because afterwards the price was 20s an acre, without any city lot. From this cheap investment came the frequent lamentation, 'Why did not I buy Waterhouse's corner for 12s.6d½'[14] But there was more than 12s.6d needed. The investment was of £80, which secured the ownership of the corner block facing King William Street and Rundle Street, and besides 134 acres of valuable suburban land.

There were connected with the *Register* from the earliest days the enterprising head of the house, Robert Thomas, who must have been well aided by his intelligent wife.[15] The sons and daughters took their place in colonial

    replaced as the continuation of Pulteney Street; Hanson Bay, Lake Hanson. George Strickland Kingston (1807–1880), architect and Deputy Surveyor to Colonel William Light: Kingston Terrace, North Adelaide; Kingston Street, Adelaide; Kingston in South East. Daniel Wakefield (1798–1858), barrister, drafted the Act of Parliament which founded South Australia: Wakefield Street, Adelaide and Kent Town; Wakefield Road, Adelaide; Port Wakefield, River Wakefield. The streets are named after him, and not, as we might expect, after his brother, Edward Gibbon Wakefield. The brothers had a disagreement with Robert Gouger and emigrated instead to New Zealand. John Morphett (1809–1892), supporter of Wakefield and investor in the South Australian Company, assisted in the survey of Adelaide: Morphett Street, Adelaide; Morphett Vale, Morphettville. J. Wallbanke Childers, member of the British Parliament, served on the provisional committee of the South Australian Association and on the first Board of Colonization Commissioners: Childers Street; Childers Crescent, North Adelaide. Rowland, later Sir Rowland, Hill (1795–1879), originator of the penny postal system, member of the provisional committee of the South Australian Association, first Secretary to the first Board of Commissioners: Hill Street, North Adelaide. Samuel Stephens (1808–1840), first manager of the South Australian Company: Stephens Place; Stephens Street, Adelaide; Stephens Street, North Adelaide; Charles Mann (1799–1860), lawyer, first Advocate-General and Crown Solicitor, councillor on Adelaide's first municipal council, editor of South Australia's second newspaper, the *Southern Australian*: Mann Street; Mann Terrace, North Adelaide. Boyle Travers Finniss (1807–1893), deputy-Surveyor to Colonel William Light, appointed colonial treasurer and registrar-general in 1847: Finniss Street; Finniss Crescent, North Adelaide; River Finniss. R.G. Symonds (1810–1896), assistant-Surveyor to Colonel William Light: Symonds Place, Adelaide.

14 South east corner of Rundle Mall and King William Street, famous at the time because it was the site of Adelaide's first three story building. It is still there.

15 Robert Thomas, (1782–1860), London law-stationer and bookseller, and first Government printer. He entered into a partnership with George Stevenson to establish a printery in South Australia and to publish a newspaper, the *South Australian Gazette and Colonial Register*, with Stevenson as editor. His wife Mary Thomas is remembered for *The Diary and Letters of Mary Thomas (1836–1866)* edited by Evan Kyffin Thomas, Adelaide, 1915.

society. Mr George Stevenson left the staff of the *Globe and Traveller*, a good old London paper, to try his fortunes in the new province founded on the Wakefield principle, as Private Secretary to the first Governor (Capt. John Hindmarsh, R.N.).[16] It is matter of history how the Governor and the Commissioner of Lands differed and quarrelled, the latter having the money and the former the power of government, and it was soon found that Mr Stevenson could wield a trenchant pen. He had been on the *Traveller* branch of the London paper – what would be called now a travelling correspondent. The Governor was replaced by Col. Gawler, and Mr Stevenson went on the *Register* as editor. Mrs Stevenson was a clever woman, and could help her husband. She knew Charles Dickens, and still better, the family of Hogarth, into which he married. My father and mother were surprised to find so good a paper and so well printed in the infant city. Then there were A.H. Davis, of the Reedbeds,[17] and Nathaniel Hailes, who wrote under the cognomen of 'Timothy Short', who had been publisher and bookseller.[18] There was first Samuel Stephens,[19] who came out in the first ship for the South Australian Company, and married a fellow passenger, Charlotte Hudson Beare, and died two years after, and then Edward,[20] manager of the South Australian Bank, and later, John Stephens,[21] who founded the *Weekly Observer*, and afterwards bought the *Register*. These all belonged to a literary family.

16 George Stevenson (1799–1856), journalist and editor of the London *Globe* which was owned by Colonel Robert Torrens, secretary to Governor Hindmarsh and first editor and co-proprietor of the *South Australian Gazette and Colonial Register*. Later editor of his own *South Australian Gazette and Colonial Register*, which was renamed *South Australian Gazette and Mining Journal*. An ardent and successful gardener. His wife, Margaret Stevenson, née Gorton, daughter of a former editor of the *Globe*, was herself a writer.

17 Abraham Hopkins Davis (1795–1866), merchant, farmer, literary man (he established a weekly journal, the *Thursday Review*), and campaigner for representative government.

18 Nathaniel Hailes (1802–1879), auctioneer, poet, literary man and journalist. As 'Timothy Short' he edited the *Wanderer: a monthly periodical of original literature* in 1853. He published some long poems and contributed to local periodicals. He was secretary of the South Australian Institute 1856–59.

19 Samuel Stephens (1808–1840), colonial manager of the South Australian Company, married Charlotte Hudson Beare shortly after their arrival on Kangaroo Island in *Duke of York*, July 1836.

20 Edward Stephens, accountant, arrived under the auspices of the South Australian Company in January 1837 and became the first manager of the South Australian Bank.

21 John Stephens (1806–1850), editor, journalist and newspaper man, had edited the *Christian Advocate* in England. He worked in Adelaide on the *South Australian Gazette and Colonial Register*, then left to found the weekly paper, the *Observer*, which continued until 1931.

People came out on the smallest of salaries with big families – H.T.H. Beare[22] on £100 a year as architect, for the South Australian Company, and he had eighteen children by two wives. I do not know what salary Mr William Giles[23] came out on with nine children and a young second wife, but I am sure it was less than £300. His family in all counted 21. But things were bad in the old country before the great lift given by railways, and freetrade, which made England the carrier for the world; and the possibilities of the new country were shown in that first issue of the *Register* in London in the highest colours. Not too high by any means in the light of what has been accomplished in 73 years, but there was a long row to hoe first, and few of the pioneers reaped the prizes. But, in spite of hardships and poverty and struggle, the early colonial life was interesting, and perhaps no city of its size at the time contained as large a population of intelligent and educated people as Adelaide.

Mrs Oliphant,[24] writing in 1885 at the age of 57, says that reading the *Life of George Eliot* made her think of an autobiography, and this was written at the saddest crisis of her life. She survived her husband and all her children, and had just lost the youngest, the posthumous boy. For them and for the family of a brother she had carried on the strenuous literary work – fiction, biography, criticism, and history – and when she died at the age of 69 she had not completed the history of a great publishing house – that of Blackwood. Her life tallies with mine on many points, but it is not till I have completed my 84 years that her sad narrative impels me to set down what appears noteworthy in a life which was begun in similar circumstances, but which was spent mainly in Australia. The loss of memory which I see in many who are younger than myself makes me feel that while I can recollect I should fix the events and the ideals of my life by pen and ink. Like Mrs Oliphant, I was born (three years

> Eventually he bought the *Register* which was taken over by John Taylor after Stephens's death. He published *The Land of Promise: being an authentic and impartial history of the rise and progress of the new British province of South Australia* (1839) by 'One Who Is Going' and its second edition *The Rise and Progress of the New British Province of South Australia* (1839).
> 22 Thomas Hudson Beare (1792–1861), second in command in the service of the South Australian Company, arrived on *Duke of York*, July 1836, with his wife and four of his children. He and William Giles were partners in the cutter *Mary Anne*.
> 23 William Giles (1791–1862) was sent to run the lonely Kangaroo Island station of the South Australian Company. He arrived with his wife and eleven children. He moved to Adelaide in 1841 and became manager of the South Australian Company. He later became a sheep farmer, accountant and railway paymaster.
> 24 Margaret Oliphant, née Wilson, (1828–1897), prolific and popular Scottish novelist, biographer and compiler, author of nearly one hundred separate publications. Her *Autobiography* was published in 1899.

earlier) in the south of Scotland. Like her I had an admirable mother, but she lost hers at the age of 60, while I kept mine till she was nearly 97. Like Mrs Oliphant, I was captivated by the stand made by the Free Church as a protest against patronage, and like her I shook off the shackles of the narrow Calvinism of Presbyterianism, and emerged into more light and liberty. But unlike Mrs Oliphant, I have from my earliest youth taken an interest in politics, and although I have not written the tenth part of what she has done, I have within the last 20 years addressed many audiences in Australia and America, and have preached over 100 sermons. My personal influence has been exercised through the voice more strongly than by the pen, and in the growth and development of South Australia, to which I came with my parents and brothers and sisters when I was just 14, and the province not three years old, there have been opportunities for usefulness which might not have offered if I had remained in Melrose, in Sir Walter Scott's country.

Chapter 3

A Beginning at Seventeen

Perhaps my turn for economics was partly inherited from my mother, and emphasised by my father having been an unlucky speculator in foreign wheat, tempted thereto by the sliding scale, which varied from 33s. a quarter, when wheat was as cheap as it was in 1837, to 1s. a quarter when it was 70s. in 1839. It was supposed that my father had made his fortune when he took his wheat out of bond but losses and deterioration during seven years, and interest on borrowed money – credit having been strained to the utmost – brought ruin and insolvency, and he had to go to South Australia, followed by his wife and family soon after. It seems strange that this disaster should be the culmination of the peace, after the long Napoleonic war. When my father married in 1815 he showed he was making £600 a year, with £2,000 book debts, as a writer or attorney and as agent for a bank. But the business fell off; the bank called up the advances; and for 24 years there was a struggle. My mother would not have her dowry of £1,500 and other money left by an aunt settled on herself – neither her father nor herself approved of it – the wife's fortune should come and go with her husband's. My father first speculated in hops, and lost heavily. He took up unlucky people, whom other business men had drained. I suppose he caught at straws. He had the gentlest of manners – 'the politest man in Melrose', the old shoemaker called him. My paternal grandfather was Dr William Spence, of Melrose. His father was minister of the Established Church at Cockburn's Path, Berwickshire. His grandfather was a small landed proprietor, but he had to sell Spence's mains,[1] and the name was changed to Chirnside. So (as my father used to say) he was sprung from the tail of the gentry; while my mother was descended from the head of the commonalty. The Brodies had been tenant farmers in East Lothian for six or seven generations, though they originally came from the north. My

---

1 The home farm of an estate, cultivated by or for the proprietor. It was used as part of the farm name.

grandfather Brodie thought abrogation of the Corn Laws meant ruin for the farmers, who had taken 19 years' leases at war prices. But during the war times both landlords and farmers coined money, while the labourers had high prices for food and very little increase in their wages. I recollect both grandfathers well, and through the accurate memory of my mother I can tell how middle-class people in lowland Scotland lived and dressed and travelled, entertained visitors, and worshipped God. She told me of the 'Dear Years' 1799 and 1800, and what a terrible thing a bad crop was, when the foreign ports were closed by Napoleon. She told me that but for the shortlived Peace of Amiens she never heard of anything but war till the Battle of Waterloo settled it three months before her marriage.

From her own intimate relations with her grandmother, Margaret Fernie Brodie, who was born in 1736, and died in 1817, she knew how two generations before her people lived and thought. So that I have a grasp on the past which many might envy, and yet the present and the future are even more to me, as they were to my mother. On her death in 1887 I wrote a quatrain for her memorial, and which those who knew her considered appropriate –

HELEN BRODIE SPENCE
Born at Whittingham, Scotland, 1791.
Died at College Town, Adelaide, South Australia, 1887.
Half a long life 'mid Scotland's heaths and pines,
And half among our South Australian vines;
Though loving reverence bound her to the past,
Eager for truth and progress to the last.

Although my mother had the greatest love for Sir Walter Scott, and the highest appreciation of his poems and novels, she never liked Melrose. She liked Australia better after a while. Indeed, when we arrived in November 1839, to a country so hot, so dry, so new, we felt like the good old founder of the *Adelaide Register*, Robert Thomas, when he came to the land described in his own paper as 'flowing with milk and honey'. Dropped anchor at Holdfast Bay. 'When I saw the place at which we were to land I felt inclined to go and cut my throat.' When we sat down on a log in Light Square,[2] waiting till my father brought the key of the wooden house in Gilles Street, in spite of the dignity of my 14 years just attained, I had a good cry. There had been such a drought that they had a dearth, almost a famine. People like ourselves with

---

2   In the South Australian sesqui-centenary year (1986) a life-size bronze statue by Ieva Pocius representing Catherine Spence, commemorating her life and work, was erected in Light Square, the scene of her despair.

eighty-acre land orders were frightened to attempt cultivation in an unknown climate, with seed wheat at 25 shillings a bushel or more, and stuck to the town. We lived a month in Gilles Street, then we bought a large marquee, and pitched it on Brownhill Creek, above where Mitcham now stands, bought 15 cows and a pony and cart, and sold the milk in town at a shilling a quart. But how little milk the cows gave in those days! After seven months' encamping, in which the family lived chiefly on rice – the only cheap food, of which we bought a ton[3] – we came with our herd to West Terrace, Adelaide. My father got the position of Town Clerk at £150 a year twelve months after our arrival, and kept it till the municipal corporation was ended, as the City of Adelaide was too poor to maintain the machinery; but £75 was the rent of the house and yards. We sold the cows, and my brothers went farming, and we took cheaper quarters in Halifax Street.

The Town Clerkship, however, was the means of giving me a lesson in electoral methods. Into the Municipal Bill, drawn up under the superintendence of Rowland Hill (afterward the great post office reformer, but then the Secretary of the Colonization Commissioner for South Australia), he had introduced a clause providing for proportional representation at the option of the ratepayers. The twentieth part of the Adelaide ratepayers by uniting their votes upon one man, instead of voting for eighteen, could on the day before the ordinary election appear and declare this their intention, and he would be a Councillor on their votes. In the first election, November 1840, two such quorums elected two Councillors. The workmen in Borrow and Goodear's building elected their foreman, and another quorom of citizens elected Mr William Senden; and this was the first quota representation in the world. My father explained this unique provision to me at the time, and showed its bearings for minority representation.

After the break up of the municipality and the loss of his income my father lost health and spirits. The brothers did not succeed in the country. My sister had married Andrew Murray,[4] an apparently prosperous man, in 1841, but the protecting of the Government bills bought for remitting to England,

---

3   1 ton weighs 1.016 tonnes.

4   Andrew Murray (1813–1880) arrived from Scotland January 1839. He started a drapery business, Murray, Greig & Co., which failed in 1842. He then edited and later owned two newspapers in Adelaide, the *South Australian* 1843–51 and the *Adelaide Morning Chronicle* 1852–53. In 1852 he moved to Melbourne and became commercial editor and political writer, later editor, of the *Argus*, 1852–56. He owned and edited *Murray's Prices Current* 1862–67 and *Bear's Circular and Rural Economist* 1862–75. He married Jessie Spence in 1841, and predeceased her. They had ten children of whom five died young; see Appendix A, Family Tree.

and other causes, brought down every mercantile firm in Adelaide except A.L. Elder,[5] who had not been long established; and Murray & Greig came down too. Mr Murray was a ready writer, and got work on the *South Australian*, the newspaper which supported Capt. Grey's policy of retrenchment and stoppage of public work;[6] so, with a small salary, he managed to live. When I left Scotland I brought with me a letter of recommendation from my teacher, Miss Sarah Phin, concerning my qualifications and my turn for teaching. I don't know if it really did me any good, for the suspicious look and the question about how old I was at the time embarrassed me. Of course I was only 13$\frac{1}{2}$, and probably my teacher over-estimated me a little, but here is the letter, yellow with the dust of over 70 years.

> Melrose, June 20, 1839.
>
> My dearest Catherine – Our mutual friend, Mrs. Duncan, told me that you were not to sail for Australia till next month, and I have been thinking if my poor testimonial to your worth and abilities could be of any service to you I ought to give it – but how can I trust myself? – for could any one read what I feel my heart dictates it would be thought absurd. You were always one of the greatest ornaments of my school, best girl and the best scholar, and from the time you could put three letters together you have evinced a turn for teaching – so clear-headed and so patient, and so thoroughly upright in word and deed, and your knowledge of the Scriptures equal to that of many students of Divinity, so should you ever become a teacher you have nothing to fear. You will be able to undertake both the useful and the ornamental branches of education – French, Italian, and music you thoroughly understand. I feel conscious that you will succeed. Please to remember me to your excellent mother, and with love to Miss Spence and my darling Mary, believe me, my beloved Catherine, your affectionate friend and teacher, Sarah Phin.

My knowledge of music was not great, even in those days, but I could teach beginners for two or three years with fair success. We thought that my mother and the two eldest girls could start a school, and brought out with us a good selection of schoolbooks, bought from Oliver J. Boyd, Edinburgh,

---

5   Alexander Lang Elder (1815–1885) who arrived in 1839 was the first of the distinguished Elder family of traders, ship owners and business men to come to South Australia. He retired to England in 1853.

6   George Grey, later Sir, (1812–1898), soldier and explorer was appointed third Governor of South Australia in 1841. He implemented retrenchments and wage reductions for Government workers.

superior to the English books obtainable here, which we used up in time; but we dared not launch out into such a venture in 1840, and my sister Jessie had no desire to teach at all.

The years at Brownhill Creek and West Terrace were the most unhappy of my life. I suffered from the want of some intellectual activity, and from the sense of frustrated ambition and religious despair. The few books we had, or which we could borrow, I read over and over again. Aikin's *British Poets*,[7] a gift from Uncle John Spence, and Goldsmith's complete works,[8] a school prize of my brother William's, were thoroughly mastered, and the Waverley novels down to *Quentin Durward* were well absorbed.[9] I read in Chamber's Journal[10] of daily governesses getting a shilling an hour, and I told my friend, Mrs Haining,[11] that I would go out for sixpence an hour. Although she disliked that way of putting it, it was really on that basis that I had made my beginning when I reached the age of 17. In the meantime I had taught my younger sister Mary (afterwards Mrs W.J. Wren)[12] all I knew, and in the columns of the *South Australian* I wrote an occasional letter or a few verses. Through Mr George Tinline[13] we made the acquaintance of Mrs Samuel Stephens, her brother, Thomas Hudson Beare, and his

---

7 *Select Works of the British Poets*, with biographical and critical prefaces, by Dr John Aikin (1747–1822). 807 pages. First published 1820 and frequently reprinted.

8 Oliver Goldsmith (1730–1774), Irish poet, playwright, essayist and novelist.

9 The first 17 of Sir Walter Scott's *Waverley* novels were *Waverley* (1814), *Guy Mannering* (1815), *The Antiquary* (1816), *Old Mortality* (1816), *The Black Dwarf* (1816), *The Heart of Midlothian* (1818), *Rob Roy* (1818) *A Legend of Montrose* (1819), *The Bride of Lammermoor* (1819), *Ivanhoe* (1819), *The Monastery* (1820), *The Abbot* (1820), *Kenilworth* (1821), *The Pirate* (1822), *The Fortunes of Nigel* (1822), *Peveril of the Peak* (1823), *Quentin Durward* (1823).

10 *Chambers's Edinburgh Journal* (1832–1853), a periodical produced by William and Robert Chambers, Edinburgh publishers, later became *Chambers's Journal of Popular Literature, Science and the Arts* (1854–1898).

11 Jessie Haining, née Grant, (d. 1890), daughter of an Edinburgh bookseller, arrived 1841 with her husband, Rev. Robert Haining (1792–1872), who had been appointed as Church of Scotland minister in Adelaide. Spence attended his church until she joined the Unitarian Church in 1856.

12 Mary Spence married in 1855 William John Wren who had arrived in Adelaide in 1851. Wren was a lawyer who was in partnership with James Edward Martin in 1862 and later with James, later Sir James, Boucaut, lawyer, politician and Premier. Wren was a Unitarian with literary interests.

13 George Tinline (c.1915–1895), manager of the Bank of South Australia, played an important role in the establishment of the Bullion Act which rescued South Australian finances during the gold rush. He later became a pastoralist.

family,[14] who had all come out in the *Duke of York*, and lived six months on Kangaroo Island before South Australia was proclaimed a British province. I have been mixed up so much with this family that it is often supposed that they were relatives, but it was not so. Samuel Stephens had died from an accident two years after his marriage to a lady much older and much richer than himself, and she was living on two acres in North Adelaide, bought with her money at the first sale of city lands in 1837, and Mr Tinline boarded with her till his marriage. The nephews, and especially the nieces, of the old lady interested me – Lucy, the eldest, a handsome girl, was about two years younger than myself; Arabella, about the age of my sister Mary; Elizabeth, the baby Beare, who was the first white person to set foot on South Australian soil after the foundation of the province, died from a burning accident when quite young. The only survivor of that first family now is William L. Beare (84), held in honour as one of our earliest pioneers. By a second marriage there were nine more children. Several died young, but some still survive.

It was not till 1843 that I went as a daily governess at the rate of sixpence an hour, and gave two hours five days a week to the families of the Postmaster-General,[15] the Surveyor-General,[16] and the Private Secretary.[17] Thus I earned three guineas a month. I don't recollect taking holidays, except a week at Christmas. I enjoyed the work, and I was proud of the payment. My mother said she never felt the bitterness of poverty after I began to earn money, and the shyness which, in spite of all her instructions and encouragement, I had felt with all strangers, disappeared when I felt independent. When a girl is very poor, and feels herself badly dressed, she cannot help being shy, especially if she has a good deal of Scotch pride. I think mother felt more sorry for me in

---

14 Formerly Charlotte Hudson Beare, Mrs Samuel Stephens lived to be 93, dying in 1875. Lucy Ann Beare, the first wife of Mrs Stephens' brother, Thomas Hudson Beare, died in September 1837, on Kangaroo Island. Her niece Lucy Beare married Francis Duval and died young leaving five children, three of whom became Spence's wards. Eliza Beare was accidentally burned to death in 1842. William Loose Beare (1825–1810) became a manager of pastoral properties and a pastoralist himself.

15 Captain John Cliffe Watts (1786–1873), architect, and Postmaster General from 1841–1861.

16 Captain Edward Charles Frome (1802–1890), soldier, artist, Surveyor General and Colonial Engineer. He left the colony in 1849.

17 Secretary to Governor Grey. Alfred Miller Mundy (1809–1877) was Private Secretary at the beginning of 1843. In June he became Colonial Secretary. He had married Governor Hindmarsh's second daughter Jane in June 1841, and his first child was not born until 1843. Spence may have given lessons to someone in his household – she says 'families', not 'children'. The Private Secretary who replaced Mundy, William Littlejohn O'Halloran (1806–1885), did not marry until 1851.

those early days than for the others, because I was so ambitious, and took religious difficulties so hard. How old I felt at 17. Indeed, at 14 I felt quite grown up. In 1843 I felt I had begun the career in Australia that I had anticipated in Scotland. I was trusted to teach little girls, and they interested me, each individual with a difference. I had seen things I had written in print. If I was one of the oldest feeling of the young folk in South Australia in my teens, I am the youngest woman in feeling in my eighties; so I have had abundant compensation.

Catherine Helen Spence, reproduced from photograph in Jeanne F. Young, *Catherine Helen Spence: A Study and an Appreciation* (Lothian Publishing Co. Pty. Ltd.), Melbourne, 1937, facing page 42.

CHAPTER 4

LOVERS AND FRIENDS

It is always supposed that thoughts of love and marriage are the chief concerns in a girl's life, but it was not the case with me. I had only two offers of marriage in my life, and I refused both. The first might have been accepted if it had not been for the Calvinistic creed that made me shrink from the possibility of bringing children into the world with so little chance of eternal salvation, so I said 'No' to a very clever young man, with whom I had argued on many points, and with whom, if I had married him, I should have argued till one of us died! I was 17, and had just begun to earn money. I told him why I had refused him, and that it was final. In six weeks he was engaged to another woman.[1] My second offer was made to me when I was 23 by a man aged 55, with three children.[2] He was an artist,[3] whose second wife and several children had been murdered by the Maoris near Wanganui during the Maori insurrection of

1   Adelaide residents whose forebears knew Catherine Spence believe that this young man was James Allen (c.1816–1881) who was the cabin-mate on the journey to Australia in 1839 of Catherine's father David Spence. He associated with the family when they lived at Brown Hill Creek. He became a chemist in Hindley Street, Adelaide. He was listed among the seatholders and subscribers of the Unitarian Christian Church in 1865; his daughter, Lavinia, married A.M. Simpson, of A. Simpson and Son, ironworkers, also a Unitarian, who would become a Justice of the Peace. He later lived at Unley and was active in political movements.
2   John Alexander Gilfillan, (1793–1864), artist. He was born in the Channel Islands, was Professor of painting and drawing at the Andersonian University in Glasgow and emigrated to New Zealand in 1841 and to Australia after the massacre of his wife and four of his children. He married Matilda Witt in Adelaide in 1852 and had a second family. There are five of his oil paintings in the Art Gallery of South Australia but there is no record of sketches. His rare historical watercolours of Maori rural life in the 1840s are displayed in exhibitions in New Zealand.
3   A further comment on Gilfillan was cut by the original editor. The words which follow

the forties, and he had come to Adelaide with the three survivors. The massacre of that family was only one of the terrible tragedies of that time, but it was not the less shocking. The Maoris had never been known to kill a woman, and when the house was attacked, Mr Gilfillan got out of a back window to call the soldiers to their help. Though struck on the back of the head and the neck and scarred for life – owing to which he was always compelled to wear his hair long – he succeeded in his mission. His wife put her own two children through the window, and they toddled off hand in hand until they met their father returning with the soldiers. The eldest daughter, a girl of 13, escaped with a neighbour's child, a baby in arms. She was seen by the Maoris, struck on the forehead with a stone axe, and left unconscious. The crying of the baby roused her, and she went to the cowyard and milked a cow to get milk for the hungry child, and there she was found by the soldiers. She was queer in her ways and thoughts afterwards, and, it was said, always remained 13 years old. She died in November last, aged 74. Her stepmother and the baby and her own brother and sister were murdered one by one as they tried to escape by the same window that had led the rest of the family to safety. One of the toddling survivors still lives in New Zealand. Now, these are all the chances of marriage I have had in my life. Dickens,[4] in *David Copperfield*, speaks of an old maid who keeps the remembrance of some one who might have made her an offer, the shadowy Pidger, in her heart until her death. I cannot forget these two men. I am constantly meeting with the children, grandchildren, and even great-grandchildren of the first. As for the other, Andrew Murray gave me a fine landscape painted by John A. Gilfillan as a slight acknowledgment of services rendered to his newspaper when he left it to go to Melbourne, and it hangs up in my sitting room for all to see. Mr Gilfillan had a commission to paint 'The Landing of Capt. Cook' with the help of portraits and miniatures of the principal personages, and some sketches of his of Adelaide in 1849 are in the Adelaide Art Gallery. If the number of lovers had been few, no woman in Australia has been richer in friends. This narrative will show what good friends – men as well as women – have helped me and sympathised in my work and my aims. I believe that if I had been in love, especially if I had been disappointed in love, my novels would have been stronger and more interesting; but I kept a watch over myself, which I felt I knew I needed, for I was both imaginative and affectionate. I did not want to give my heart away. I did not desire a love disappointment, even for the sake of experience. I was 30 years old before the dark veil of religious despondency

'artist' in Spence's handwritten manuscript are 'but a man of no refinement. I think he thought I would make a good stepmother but I thought him most presumptuous.'

4   Charles Dickens (1812–1870), English novelist, published *David Copperfield*, 1849–50.

was completely lifted from my soul, and by that time I felt myself booked for a single life. People married young if they married at all in those days. The single aunts put on caps at 30 as a sort of signal that they accepted their fate; and, although I did not do so, I felt a good deal the same.

I went on with daily teaching for some years, during which my father's health declined, but before his death two things had happened to cheer him. My brother John left Myponga and came to town, and obtained a clerkship in the South Australian Bank at £100 a year. It was whilst occupying a position in the bank that he had some slight connection with the notorious Capt. Starlight, afterwards the hero of *Robbery Under Arms*, for through his hands much of the stolen money passed. In 1900, when Mrs Young and I were leaving Melbourne on our visit to Sydney, we were introduced to 'Rolf Boldrewood', the author of that well-known story. His grave face lit up with a smile when my friend referred to the author of her son's hero. 'Ah!' and he shook his head slowly. 'I'm not quite sure about the wisdom of making heroes of such sorry stuff,' he replied.[5] I thought I could do better with a school. I was 20, and my sister Mary nearly 16, and my mother could help. My school opened in May, 1846, a month before my father's death, and he thought that our difficulties were over. My younger brother, David Wauchope, had been left behind for his education with the three maiden aunts, but he came out about the end of that year, and began life in the office of the Burra Mine at a small salary. My eldest brother William, was not successful in the country, and went to Western Australia for some years, and later to New Zealand, where he died in his eightieth year, soon after the death of my brother John in his seventy-ninth, leaving me the only survivor of eight born and of six who grew to full age. My eldest sister Agnes died of consumption at the age of 16; and, as my father's mother and four of his brothers and sisters, had died of this malady, it was supposed to be in the family. The only time I was kept out of school during the nine years at Miss Phin's was when I was 12, when I had a cough and suppuration of the glands of the neck. As this was the way in which Agnes's illness had begun, my parents were alarmed, though I had no idea of it. I was leeched and blistered and drugged; I was put into flannel for the only time in my life; I was sent away for change of air; but no one could discover that the cough was from the lungs. It passed away with the cold weather, and I cannot say that I have had any illness since. My father died of decline; but, if he had been more fortunate, I think he would have lived much longer. Probably my mother's life was prolonged beyond that of a long-lived family by her coming to Australia

---

5   'Rolf Boldrewood' was the pseudonym of Thomas Alexander Browne (1826–1915), sheep station owner, goldfields commissioner, police magistrate and author. *Robbery Under Arms*, his most famous novel, was serialised in the *Sydney Mail* in 1882–1883.

in middle life; and, if I ever had any tendency to consumption, the climate must have helped me. There were no special precautions against infection in those days; but no other member of the family took it, and the alarm about me was three years after Agnes's death.

But to go on to those early days of the forties. There were two families with whom we were intimate. Mr George Tinline (who had been clerk to my fathers' old friend, William Rutherford, of Jedburgh), who was in the bank of South Australia when, in 1839, my father went to put our small funds in safety, introduced us to a beautiful young widow, Mrs Sharpe, and her sisters Eliza and Harriet, and her brother, John Taylor.[6] Harriet afterwards married Edward Stirling,[7] a close friend of my brother-in-law, Andrew Murray, and I was a great deal interested in the Stirlings and their eight children. Mr William Bakewell,[8] of Bartley & Bakewell, solicitors, married Jane Warren, of Springfield, Barossa, and I was familiar friend of their five children. In one house I was 'Miss Spence, the storyteller', in the other 'Miss Spence, the teller of tales'. Some of the tales appeared long after as Christmas stories[9] in the *Adelaide Observer*, but my young hearers preferred the oral narrative, with appropriate gestures and emphasis, and had no scruple about making faces, to anything printed in books. I took great liberties with what I had read, and sometimes invented all. It was a part of their education, probably – certainly, it was a part of mine, and it gave me a command of language which helped me when I became a public speaker. My brother-in-law's newspaper furnished an occasional opportunity to me, though no doubt he considered that he could fill his twice-a-week journal without my help. He was, however, helpful in other ways. He was one of the subscribers to a Reading Club, and through him I had

6   John Taylor (1823–1865), a former employee of the Bank of South Australia, became an enterprising pastoral pioneer with many mining interests. He took over the management of the *Register* and the *Observer* after the death of John Stephens until the paper was sold to C.H. Hussey. He was highly respected in financial and commercial circles. He became one of Spence's most treasured friends and was her model for Mr Reginald in her first novel *Clara Morison*.

7   Edward Stirling (1804–1873) a pioneer pastoralist, was in partnership with Thomas Elder, Robert Barr Smith and John Taylor in mining ventures. He became a member of the Legislative Council. He married Taylor's sister Harriet in 1847. His eight children were born between 1848 and 1863.

8   William Bakewell (1817–1870) arrived in South Australia in 1839, solicitor, member of Parliament, and Crown Solicitor. He married Jane Warren in 1844. Their five children were born between 1845 and 1854. He spent much time in England.

9   Dates and details of Spence's stories in newspapers can be found in the bibliography of Spence on the website of the State Library of South Australia. www.slsa.sa.gov.au/spence.

access to newspapers and magazines. The South Australian Institute[10] was a treasure to the family. I recollect a newcomer being astonished at my sister Mary having read Macaulay's *History*.[11] 'Why, it was only just out when I left England,' said he. 'Well, it did not take longer to come out than you did,' was her reply. We were all omnivorous readers, and the old-fashioned accomplishment of reading aloud was cultivated by both brothers and sisters. I was the only one who could translate French at sight, thanks to Miss Phin's giving me so much of Racine and Molière and other good French authors in my school days.

But more important than all this was the fact that we took hold of the growth and development of South Australia, and identified ourselves with it. Nothing is insignificant in the history of a young community, and – above all – nothing seems impossible. I had learned what wealth was, and a great deal about production and exchange for myself in the early history of South Australia – of the value of machinery, of roads and bridges, and of ports for transport and export. I had seen the four pound loaf at 4s and at 4d. I had seen Adelaide the dearest and the cheapest place to live in. I had seen money orders for 2s.6, and even for 6d, current when gold and silver were very scarce. Even before the discovery of copper South Australia had turned the corner. We had gone on the land and become primary producers, and before the gold discoveries in Victoria revolutionised Australia and attracted our male population across the border, the Central State was the only one which had a large surplus of wheat and hay to send to the goldfields.

Edward Wilson,[12] of the *Argus*, riding overland to Adelaide about 1848, was amazed to see from Willunga onward fenced and cultivated farms, with decent homesteads and machinery up to date. The Ridley stripper[13] enabled our people to reap and thresh the corn when hands were all too few for the sickle. He said he felt as if the garden of Paradise must have been in King

10   The South Australian Institute evolved in stages from the South Australian Literary Association which arrived in Australia with a collection of books. It later became the South Australian Library and Mechanics Institute. The South Australian Institute was founded by Act of Parliament in 1856 to promote culture and learning in the colony. Many of the original books are now in the State Library of South Australia.

11   Thomas Babington Macauley (1800–1859), man of letters and parliamentarian. He wrote *History of England*, volumes I and II, 1848, volumes III and IV, 1855.

12   Edward Wilson (1814–1878) emigrated from England to Melbourne. He bought the Melbourne *Argus* for which Spence's brother-in-law Andrew Murray worked and to which Spence contributed. He was a strenuous political and social campaigner who contributed to the establishment of responsible government in Victoria.

13   A reaping machine invented in 1843 by John Ridley of Hindmarsh, a suburb of Adelaide. His claim to the invention has been in dispute.

William Street,[14] and that the earliest difference in the world – that between Cain and Abel – was about the advantages of the eighty-acre system. Australia generally had already to realise the fact that the pastoral industry was not enough for its development, and South Australia had seemed to solve the problem through the doctrinaire founders, of family immigration, small estates, and the development of agriculture, horticulture, and viticulture. We owed a great deal in the latter branches to our German settlers – sent out originally by Mr G.F. Angas, whose interest was aroused by their suffering persecution for religious dissent – who saw that Australia had a better climate than that of the Fatherland. We owed much to Mr George Stevenson, who was an enthusiastic gardener and fruitgrower, and lectured on these subjects, but the contrast between the environs of Adelaide and those of Sydney and Melbourne were striking, and Mr Wilson never lost an opportunity of calling on the Victorian Legislature and the Victorian public to develop their own wonderful resources. When you take gold out of the ground there is less gold to win. When you grow golden grain or ruddy grapes this year you may expect as much and as good next year. My brother David went with the thousands to buy their fortunes at the diggings, but my brother John stuck to the Bank of South Australia. My brother-in-law's[15] subscribers and his printers had gone off and left him woefully embarrassed. He went to Melbourne. My friend John Taylor left his sheep in the wilderness and came to Adelaide to the aid of the *Register*. He had been engaged to Sophia Stephens, who died, and her father John Stephens also died soon after; and Mr Taylor shouldered the management of the paper until the time of stress was over.

When Andrew Murray obtained employment on the *Argus* as commercial editor, he left his twice-a-week newspaper in the charge of Mr W.W. Whitridge,[16] my brother John, and myself. If anything was needed to be written on State aid to religion[17] I was to do it, as Mr Whitridge was opposed to it. This lasted three months. The next quarter there were no funds for the editor, so John and I carried it on, and then let it die. At that time I believed in State aid, which had been abolished by the first elected Parliament of South Australia, although that Parliament consisted of one-third nominees pledged to vote for its continuance.

14 The main street of the city of Adelaide. It runs north and south.
15 Andrew Murray.
16 William Whitridge Roberts Whitridge (1824–1861) farmer, literary man and editor. With Andrew Garran he started the *Austral Examiner* in 1851. It was not successful. He became editor of the *Register* in 1856.
17 The South Australian Association had wanted to found a colony without an established church and without state aid to religion, always a contentious topic in the colony.

CHAPTER 5

NOVELS AND A POLITICAL INSPIRATION

It was the experience of a depopulated province which led me to write my first book, *Clara Morison – A Tale of South Australia during the Gold Fever*.[1] I entrusted the MS to my friend John Taylor, with whom I had just had the only tiff in my life. He, through his connection with the *Register*, knew that I was writing in the *South Australian*, trying to keep it alive, till Mr Murray decided to let it go, and he told this to other people. At a subscription ball to which my brother John took me and my younger sister Mary, she found she had been pointed out and talked of as the lady who wrote for the newspapers. I did not like it even to be supposed of myself, but Mary was indignant, and I wrote an injured letter to my friend. He apologised, and said he thought I would be proud of doing disinterested work, and he was sorry the mistake had been made regarding the sister who did it. Of course I forgave him. He was the last man in the world to give pain to anyone, and I highly admired him for his disinterested work on the *Register*. He reluctantly accepted £1,000 when the paper was sold. He must have lost much more through neglect of his own affairs at such a critical time. He was taking a holiday with his sister Eliza in England and France, where the beautiful widowed sister was settled as Madam Dubois, and I asked him to take *Clara Morison* to Smith, Elder and Co.'s, in London, and to say nothing to anybody about it; but before it was placed he had to return to Adelaide, and in pursuance of my wishes, left it with my other good friend, Mr Bakewell, who also happened to be visiting England with his family at the time – 1853–54. I had an idea that, as there was so much interest in Australia and its gold, I might get £100 for the novel. Mr Bakewell wrote a preface from which I extract a passage:

1   Catherine Helen Spence, *Clara Morison: A Tale of South Australia during the Gold Fever*, (John W. Parker & Son) London, 1854, 2 vols. Facsimile edition, with introduction and notes by Susan Magarey, (Wakefield Press) Netley, 1986.

The writer's aim seems to have been to present some picture of the state of society in South Australia in the years 1851–52, when the discovery of gold in the neighbouring province of Victoria took place. At this time, the population of South Australia numbered between seventy and eighty thousand souls, the greater part of whom were remarkable for their intelligence, their industry, and their enterprise, which, in the instance of the Burra Burra, and other copper mines had met with such signal success. When it became known that gold in vast quantities could be found within 300 miles of their own territory, they could not remain unmoved. The exodus was almost complete, and entirely without parallel. In those days there was no King in Israel, and every woman did what was right in her own sight.[2]

Another reason I had for writing the book. Thackeray had written about an emigrant vessel taking a lot of women to Australia, as if these were all to be gentlemen's wives – as if there was such a scarcity of educated women there, that anything wearing petticoats had the prospect of a great rise in position.[3] I had hoped that Smith, Elder and Co. would publish my book, but their reader – Mr Williams,[4] who discovered Charlotte Brontë's[5] genius when she sent them *The Professor*, and told her she could write a better, which she did (*Jane Eyre*) – wrote a similar letter to me, declining *Clara Morison*, as he had declined *The Professor*, but saying I could do better. J.W. Parker and Son published it in 1854, as one of the two-volume series, of which *The Heir of Redcliffe*[6] had been most successful. The price was to be £40; but, as it was too long for the series, I was charged £10 for abridging it. It was very fairly received and reviewed. I think I liked best Frederick Sinnett's[7] notice in the *Argus* – that it was the work of an observant woman novelist who happened to

2   *Judges* 17.
3   William Makepeace Thackeray (1811–1863) using the pseudonym 'Spec', published in *Punch*, 9 March 1850, a piece called 'Waiting at the Station' which caused Spence to wish to show the real situation in Australia.
4   William Smith Williams (d. 1875), chief reader for the Smith, Elder publishing company. He is remembered for the encouragement and assistance he gave Charlotte Brontë.
5   Charlotte Brontë, later Nicholls (1816–1855), English novelist; *Jane Eyre* (1847), *The Professor*, (Smith Elder) London, 1857.
6   *The Heir of Redclyffe* (1853), by English novelist Charlotte Mary Yonge (1823–1901).
7   Frederick Sinnett (1831–1866) engineer and journalist, arrived in Australia 1849 and went to the Victorian goldfields. Worked for the Melbourne *Argus*, then became manager of the Adelaide Iceworks and editor of the *Daily Telegraph* in Adelaide from 1859–1865. He then returned to Melbourne to work on the *Argus*. His appreciation of *Clara Morison* can be read in Frederick Sinnett, 'Fiction Fields of Australia', *Journal of Australasia*, no. 1, July–December 1856.

live in Australia, but who did not labour to bring in bushrangers and convicts, and specially Australian features. While I was waiting to hear the fate of my first book, I began to write a second, *Tender and True*, of which Mr Williams thought better, and recommended it to Smith, Elder and Co., who published it in two volumes in 1856, and gave me £20 for the copyright. This is the only one of my books that went through more than one edition. There were two or three large editions issued, but I never got a penny more. I was told that nothing could be made out of shilling editions; but that book was well reviewed and now and then I have met elderly people who read the cheap edition and liked it. The motif of the book was the jealousy which husbands are apt to feel of their wives' relations. As if the most desirable wife was an amiable orphan – if an heiress, so much the better. But the domestic virtues which make a happy home for the husband are best fostered in a centre where brothers and sisters have to give and take; and a good daughter and sister is likely to make a good wife and mother. I have read quite recently that the jokes against the mother-in-law which are so many and so bitter in English and American journalism are worn out, and have practically ceased; but Dickens and Thackeray set the fashion, and it lasted a long time.

While *Clara Morison* was making her debut, I paid my first visit to Melbourne. I went with Mr and Mrs Stirling in a French ship consigned to him, and we were 12 days on the way, suffering from the limited ideas that the captain of a French merchantman had of the appetites of Australians at sea. I intended to pay a six weeks' visit to my sister and her family, but she was so unwell that I stayed for eight months. I found that Melbourne in the beginning of 1854 was a very expensive place to live in, and consequently a very inhospitable place. Mr Murray's salary sounded a good one, £500 a year, but it did not get much comfort. His sister was housekeeper at Charles Williamson and Co.'s, and that was the only place where I could take off my bonnet and have a meal. From the windows I watched the procession that welcomed Sir Charles Hotham, the first Governor of the separated colony of Victoria. He was received with rejoicing, but he utterly failed to satisfy the people. He thought anything was good enough for them. One festivity I was invited to – a ball given on the opening of the new offices of the *Argus* in Collins Street – and there I met Mr Edward Wilson, a most interesting personality, the giver of the entertainment. He was then vigorously championing the unlocking of the land and the developing of other resources of Victoria than the gold. It had surprised him when he travelled overland to Adelaide to see from Willunga 30 miles of enclosed and cultivated farms, and it surprised me to see sheepruns close to Melbourne. With a better rainfall and equally good soil, Victoria had neither the farms nor the vineyards nor the orchards nor the gardens that had sprung up under the eighty-acre section and immigration system of South

Australia. It had been an outlying portion of New South Wales, neglected and exploited for pastoral settlement only. The city, however, had been well planned, like that of Adelaide, but the suburbs were allowed to grow anyhow. In Adelaide the belt of park lands kept the city apart from all suburbs. Andrew Murray was as keen for the development of Victoria agriculturally and industrially as Mr Wilson, and they worked together heartily. Owing to the state of my sister's health I was much occupied with her and her children; but in August she was well, and I returned with Mr Taylor and his sister in the steamer *Bosphorus*, when it touched at Melbourne on the way home. He brought me £30 for my book, and the assurance that it would be out soon, and that I should have six copies to give to my friends. Novel writing had not been to me a lucrative occupation. I had given up teaching altogether at the age of twenty-five, and I felt that though Australia was to be a great country, there was no market for literary work, and the handicap of distance from the reading world was great.

My younger sister married in 1855 William J. Wren, then an articled clerk in Bartley and Bakewell's office, and afterwards a partner with the present Sir James Boucaut.[8] Mr Wren's health was indifferent, and caused us much anxiety. My brother John married Jessie Cumming in 1858, and they were spared together for many years.[9] As the Wrens went on a long voyage to Hong-kong and back for the sake of my brother-in-law's health, my mother and I had the charge of their little boy.[10] But in that year, 1859, my mind received its strongest political inspiration, and the reform of the electoral system became the foremost object of my life. John Stuart Mill's[11] advocacy of Thomas Hare's[12] system of proportional representation brought back to my mind Rowland Hill's clause in the Adelaide Municipal Bill with wider and larger issues. It also showed me how democratic government could be made real, and safe, and progressive. I confess that at first I was struck chiefly by its conservative side, and I saw that its application would prevent the political association, which corresponded roughly with the modern Labour Party, from

---

8 Sir James Penn Boucaut (1831–1916) barrister, politician and judge. He became South Australia's youngest premier.

9 Further comment cut by the original editor: 'We tried hard to get David back from the diggings, and took up house with him for six months but he could not be kept in an office.'

10 Charles William Wren, born 15 November 1856.

11 John Stuart Mill (1806–1873), English philosopher and economist, member of Parliament, supporter of proportional representation and of rights for women.

12 Thomas Hare (1806–1891), English barrister and member of Parliament who developed the system of proportional representation, sometimes called single transferable voting, which is named after him.

returning five out of six members of the Assembly for the City of Adelaide. But for blunders on ballot papers the whole ticket of six would have been elected. They also elected the three members for Burra and Clare. I had then no footing on the Adelaide press, but I was Adelaide correspondent for the *Melbourne Argus* – that is to say, my brother was the correspondent, but I wrote the letters – he furnished the news. I read Mill's article one Monday night, and wrote what was meant for a leader on Tuesday morning, and went to read it to my brother at breakfast time, and posted it forthwith. I knew the *Argus* had been dissatisfied with the recent elections, and fancied that the editor would hail with joy the new idea; but I received the reply that the *Argus* was committed to the representation of majorities; and, though the idea was ingenious, he did not even offer to print it as a letter. About two years later Mr Lavington Glyde, MP,[13] brought forward in the Assembly Mr Fawcett's abstract[14] of Hare's great scheme, and I seized the opportunity of writing a series of letters to the *Register*, signed by my initials. Mr Glyde, seeing the House did not like his suggestions, dropped the matter, but I did not. I was no longer correspondent to the *Argus* – the telegraph stopped that altogether.[15] My wonderful maiden aunts made up to me and my mother the £50 a year that I had received as correspondent, and did as much for their brother, Alexander Brodie,[16] of Morphett Vale, from £1,000 they had sent to invest in South Australia. It was as easy to get ten per cent then as to get four per cent now; indeed I think the money earned twelve per cent at first. My brother John was accountant to the South Australian Railways, then not a very great department – I think the line stretched as far as Kapunda to the north from Port Adelaide. He was as much captivated by Mr Hare's idea as I was, and he said that if I would write a pamphlet he would pay for the printing of 1000 copies, to be sent to all the members of Parliament and other leading people in city and country. I called my pamphlet *A Plea for Pure Democracy*,[17] and when writing it I felt the democratic strength of the position as I had not felt it in reading Hare's own book. It cost my brother £15, but he never grudged it.

13 Lavington Glyde, (1825–1890) Commissioner of Crown Lands in South Australia, member of every Parliament from the first to the tenth.

14 *Mr Hare's Reform Bill Simplified and Explained*. By Right Hon. Henry Fawcett. London, 1861.

15 The first Australian telegraph line, enabling quick communications and business transactions, was built from Melbourne to Williamstown in Victoria in 1853–4. The line from Melbourne to Adelaide was completed in July 1858.

16 Alexander Brodie and his family emigrated from Scotland in 1839 a fortnight after Spence.

17 Pamphlet by C.H. Spence, *A Plea for Pure Democracy: Mr Hare's reform bill applied to South Australia*, (W.C. Rigby) Adelaide and (George Robertson) Melbourne, 1861, 24p. This pamphlet was reprinted by the Electoral Reform Society of South Australia in 1986.

While the pamphlet was in the press, I heard of the dangerous illness of my friend Lucy Anne Duval (née Beare),[18] one of the original passengers in the *Duke of York*, the first ship which arrived here. I went to consult Mr Taylor and Mr Stirling at their office. I saw only Mr Stirling. I said, 'I should like to go and nurse her,' and he said, 'If you will go, I'll pay your expenses;' and I went and stayed with her for three weeks, till she died, and left five children, three of them quite young. There were Duvals in England in good circumstances, and I wrote pleading for the three little ones, though every one said it was quite useless; but an uncle by marriage was touched, and sent £100 a year for the benefit of the three children, and I was constituted the guardian. The youngest died within two years, but the allowance was not decreased, and I was able to get some schooling for an elder boy. This was my first guardianship.

My pamphlet did not set the Torrens on fire. It did not convert the *Register*, but Mr Fred Sinnett, who was conducting the *Telegraph*,[19] was much impressed, especially as he had the greatest reverence for John Stuart Mill, and thought him a safe man to follow. I had another novel under way at the time, and Mr Sinnett thought it would help the *Telegraph* to bring it out as a serial story in the weekly edition; and I seized my opportunity to bring in Mr Hare and proportional representation. In England Mr Hare, Mr Mill, Rowland Hill, and his brother, and Professor Craik,[20] all considered my *Plea for Pure Democracy* the best argument from the popular side that had appeared. I got the kindest of letters from them, and my brother considered my labour and his money well spent. Professor Craik, writing to Miss Florence Davenport Hill about the *Plea for Pure Democracy*, says – 'It is really a pity that the pamphlet should not be reproduced in this country – modified, of course, to the slight extent that would be necessary. It is really a very remarkable piece of exposition – the best for popular effect by far on this subject that has come in my way. I rejoice to hear that there is a chance of Mr Hare's plan being adopted in South Australia.' I may be allowed to observe that there is still a chance, but not yet a reality. My aunts at Thornton Loch were applied to by my English admirers to see if they would be at the cost of an English edition; but, though

18 Lucy Ann Beare had married Francis Duval in December 1843. He died in October 1856, leaving four children (two others had died) and his wife pregnant. His youngest son was born in June 1857. Lucy died 1861, leaving five children, Lewis aged 17, Frederic 13, Lucy Alice Rose 7, William 5, and Francis 2. Francis died in 1863.

19 Frederick Sinnett was editing the *Daily Telegraph*. An advertisement announcing that 'A New Tale by Miss Spence' would be published serially in the *Weekly Mail* appeared in the *Telegraph* on 15 February 1864. Unfortunately the *Weekly Mail* has not survived.

20 Professor George Lillie Craik (1798–1866), English man of letters, Professor of History and English Literature at Queen's College, Belfast.

they were goodness itself to our material needs, they thought it was throwing money away to bring out a pamphlet on an unpopular subject that would not sell. Why, even in South Australia, though the price was marked at one shilling, not a single shilling had been paid for a single copy; and in South Australia I was known! Not so well known, however. I wrote under initials only, and many thought my letters and pamphlets were the work of Charles Simeon Hare,[21] one of the tallest talkers in South Australia, who said Mr Thomas Hare was his cousin. My novels were anonymous up to the third, which was not then written. If my name would have done the cause any good it would have been given, but it was too obscure then.

The original title of my third book was *Uphill Work*, and it took up the woman question as it appeared to me at the time – the difficulty of a woman earning a livelihood, even when she had as much ability, industry, and perseverance as a man. My friend Mrs Graham, who had been receiving £100 a year and many presents and much consideration from the Alstons, of Charles Williamson & Co., had to return to Scotland to cheer her father's last years. After his death she became housekeeper to the Crichton Asylum for the Insane, with 600 or 700 patients, at a salary of £30 a year. This started me on the story of two girls educated well and soundly by an eccentric uncle, but not accomplished in the showy branches, who, fearing that the elder and favourite niece would marry a young neighbour, and that the other might be a confirmed invalid, disinherited them, and left his estate to a natural son with a strict proviso against his marrying either of his cousins. In that case the property was to go to a benevolent institution named. Jane Melville applied for the situation of housekeeper to this institution at £30 a year, but was refused because she was too young and inexperienced. After all sorts of disappointments she took a situation to go out to Australia, and her sister accompanied her as a lady's maid in the same family. You may wonder how I brought in proportional representation, but I managed it. I think, on the whole, it is a stronger book than either of the others. The volume has two interesting associations, one which connects it with Mrs Oliphant. My friend Mrs Graham knew I had sent it to England for publication, and when she read the anonymous *Doctor's Family*[22] she was sure it was mine, and was delighted with it. When I read of the brave Australian girl Nettie, taking on herself the burden of the flabby sister and her worthless husband and their children, I wished that

---

21　Charles Simeon Hare (1808–1882) arrived in South Australia 1836. He was employed by the South Australia Company and later entered Parliament. He took a prominent part in the 'burning questions' of the day.

22　*The Rector and The Doctor's Family* (1863) and *In Trust: The Story of a Lady and her Lover* (1882) by Margaret Oliphant.

I had written such a capital story. In a subsequent tale of Mrs Oliphant's, *In Trust*, a father disinherits the elder girl from a fear of an unworthy marriage, but he leaves a letter to be opened when Rosy is 21, which – should Anne not marry Cosmo Douglas – restores her to her own mother's fortune, which was in his power. There was no saving clause in my book. The nieces were left only £20 a year each. Mr Williams did not think *Uphill Work* as good as *Tender and True*, and it was hung up till circumstances most unexpectedly brought me to England, and I tried Bentley, and found that his reader approved, but wished me to change the name, as the first critic would say it was uphill work to read it. 'Then let it be "Mr. Haliburton's Will."' '"That would clash with 'Mrs. Haliburton's [sic] Troubles."[23]' So the name was changed to Hogarth, and the title became *Mr Hogarth's Will*. It was well reviewed, and I got £35 as my half-share of the profits on a three-volume edition, besides £50 from the *Telegraph*. But the book was to have more effect in unexpected quarters than I could imagine. When staying with my aunts in Scotland I had a letter from Mr Edward Wilson's secretary, saying that he had wished to write an article for the *Fortnightly* on 'The Representation of Classes', which was his cure for the excesses of democracy; but, as he could not see, and his doctor had forbidden him even to dictate, he had reluctantly abandoned the idea. He had, however, heard that I was in Scotland, and, though my idea was different from his, he believed that I could write the article from some letters reprinted from the *Argus* and a few hints from himself, and that I could adapt them to English conditions. I gladly undertook the work, and satisfied Mr Wilson. Just before I left for Australia I went to Mr Wilson's, and we went through the proofs together. Mr Wilson, being a wealthy man, did not ask any payment from the *Fortnightly*,[24] but he gave me £10 and thanked me for stepping in to his assistance when he needed it. He said that my novel had been the subject of a great deal of discussion in his house. I asked, 'Why?' He replied, 'The uncle and the nieces, of course.' I thought no more of it till the death of Mr Wilson revealed that he had left his estate to the charities of Melbourne. Then my brother told me that when he was in England in 1877 Mr Wilson had told him that it was seldom that a novel had any influence over a man's conduct, but that reading his sister's novel had set him thinking, and had made him alter his will. He did not think it to the advantage of his nieces to be made rich, and he would leave his money to Victoria and Melbourne, where he had made it. I was the innocent cause of disappointing the nieces, for I think I made it clear

23   *Mrs Halliburton's Troubles*. A novel by Mrs Henry Wood, née Ellen Price (1814–1887).
24   *Fortnightly Review*, periodical edited originally by G.H. Lewes and published by Chapman & Hall, London. It ran from 1865 to 1934. 'Principles of Representation' appeared in 1866 in Volume 4, no. XXII, pp. 421–436.

that the uncle did very wrongly. But when I see £5,000 a year distributed among Melbourne charities, and larger gifts for the building of a new hospital, I cannot help thinking that these are the results of Mr Wilson reading *Mr Hogarth's Will*; and it may be that other similar trusts are the results of Mr Wilson's action.

Another literary success I had during that visit to England. I went to Smith, Elder, & Co. to ask if I could not get anything for the shilling edition of *Tender and True*, and was answered in the negative; but I had not talked ten minutes with Mr Williams before he said that if I would put these ideas into shape, he thought he could get an article accepted by the *Cornhill Magazine*.[25] 'An Australian's Impressions of England' was approved by the editor, and appeared in the *Cornhill* for January 1866; and for that I received £12, the best-paid work I had ever had up to that time. The *Saturday Review*[26] said of *Mr Hogarth's Will* that there was no haziness about money matters in it such as is too common among lady writers. Mr Bentley advised me to give my name, and not to sell my copyright; but the latter has been of no value to me; 500 copies of a three-volume novel exhausted the likely demand. I got 12 copies to give to friends, and one copy I gave to Mr Hare. His daughters were a little amused to see their father in a novel, and as the book was in the circulating library their friends and acquaintances used to ask, 'Is that really your papa that it is intended for?' I did not at the time think of facing anybody in England, but I had been both amused and annoyed with the portraits I was supposed to have drawn from real people in and about Adelaide – often people I had never seen and had not heard of. 'But Harris is Ellis to the life,' said my old Aunt Brodie of Morphett Vale. 'Miss Withing [sic] is my sister-in-law,' said another.[27] Neither of these people had I seen. Of course, Mr Reginald was Mr John Taylor, the only squatter I knew, but I myself was not identified with my heroine Clara Morison. I was Margaret Elliott, the girl who was studying law with her brother Gilbert; but my brother and my cousin Louisa Brodie were supposed to be figuring in my book as lovers. In a small society it was easy to affix the characteristics to some one whom it was possible the author might have met; but I shrank from the idea that I was capable of 'taking off' people of my acquaintance, and for many reasons would have liked it if the book had not been known to be mine in South Australia. There must,

---

25 *Cornhill Magazine*, periodical edited originally by William Makepeace Thackeray, and published London, Smith, Elder & Co. It ran from 1860 to 1975. 'An Australian's Impression of England appeared in Volume XIII, pp. 110–120.

26 *The Saturday Review of Politics, Literature Science and Art* was published in London and ran from 1856 to 1938.

27 The character in *Clara Morison* is actually called 'Miss Withering', and lives up to her name.

however, have been some lifelike presentment of my characters, or they could not have been recognised. About this time I read and appreciated Jane Austen's novels[28] – those exquisite miniatures, which no doubt her contemporaries identified with as much interest. Her circle was as narrow as mine – indeed, narrower. She was the daughter of a clergyman in the country. She represented well-to-do grown-up people, and them alone. The humour of servants, the sallies of children, the machinations of villains, the tricks of rascals, are not on her canvas; but she differentiated among equals with a firm hand, and with a constant ripple of amusement. The life I led had more breadth and wider interests. The life of Miss Austen's heroines, though delightful to read about, would have been deadly dull to endure. So great a charm have Jane Austen's books had for me that I have made a practice of reading them through regularly once a year.

As we grew to love South Australia, we felt that we were in an expanding society, still feeling the bond to the mother-land, but eager to develop a perfect society in the land of our adoption.

---

28 Jane Austen (1775–1817) English novelist, author of six novels of which *Pride and Prejudice*, 1813, is the most famous.

CHAPTER 6

A TRIP TO ENGLAND

I have gone on with the story of my three first novels consecutively, anticipating the current history of myself and South Australia. There were three great steps taken in the development of Australia. The first was when Macarthur introduced the merino sheep; the second when Hargreaves and others discovered gold; and the latest when cold-storage was introduced to make perishable products available for the European markets. The second step created a sudden revolution; but the others were gradual, and the area of alluvial diggings in Victoria made thousands of men without capital or machinery rush to try their fortunes – first from the adjacent colonies, and afterwards from the ends of the earth. Law and order were kept on the gold fields of Mount Alexander, Bendigo, and Ballarat by means of a strong body of police, and the high licence fees for claims paid for their services, so that nothing like the scenes recorded of the Californian diggings could be permitted. But for the time ordinary industries were paralysed. Shepherds left their flocks, farmers their land, clerks their desks, and artisans their trades. Melbourne grew apace in spite of the highest wages known being exacted by masons and carpenters. Pastoralists thought ruin stared them in the face till they found what a market the goldfields offered for their surplus stock. Our South Australian farmers left their holdings in the hands of their wives and children too young to take with them, but almost all of them returned to grow grain and produce to send to Victoria. It was astonishing what the women had done during their absence. The fences were kept repaired and the stock attended to, the grapes gathered, and the wine made. In these days it was not so easy to get 80 acres or more in Victoria; so, with what the farmers brought from their labours on the goldfields, they extended their holdings and improved their homes. For many years the prices in Melbourne regulated prices in Adelaide, but when the land was unlocked and the Victorian soil and climate were found to be as good as ours it was Mark Lane[1] that fixed prices over all Australia for primary products. After the return of most of the diggers there was a great deal of marrying and giving in marriage. The miners who had left the Burra for goldseeking gradually came back, and the nine remarkable copper mines of Moonta and Wallaroo attracted the Cornishmen, who preferred steady wages and homes to the diminishing chances of Ballarat and Bendigo, where machinery and deep sinking demanded capital, and the miners were paid by the week. These new copper mines were found in the Crown leases held by Captain (afterwards Sir Walter) Hughes.[2] He had been well dealt with by Elder, Smith and Co., and gave them the opportunity of supporting him. At that time my friends Edward Stirling and John Taylor were partners in that firm, and they shared in the success. Mr Bakewell belonged to the legal firm which did their business, so that my greatest friends seemed to be in it. I think my brother John profited less by the great advance of South Australia than he deserved for sticking to the Bank of South Australia. He got small rises in his salary, but the cost of living was so enhanced that at the end of seven years it did not buy much more than the £100 he had begun with. My eldest maiden aunt died, and left to her brother and sister in South Australia all she had in her power. My mother bought a brick cottage in Pulteney Street and a Burra share with her legacy – both excellent investments – and my brother left the bank and went into the aerated water business with James Hamilton Parr.[3]

We made the acquaintance of the family of Mrs Francis Clark, of Hazelwood, Burnside.[4] She was the only sister of five clever brothers – Matthew Davenport, Rowland, Edwin, Arthur, and Frederick Hill. Rowland is best known, but all were remarkable men. She was so like my mother in her sound judgment, accurate observation, and kind heart, that I was drawn to her

1 The Corn Exchange was situated in Mark Lane, City of London.
2 Walter Watson Hughes (1803–1887), pastoralist, mine-owner and public benefactor. Born in Scotland, he arrived in Adelaide in 1840. His gift enabled the foundation of the University of Adelaide.
3 James Hamilton Parr, auctioneer, whose mining ventures and extravagance later led to insolvency.
4 Francis Clark (1799–1853) and his wife Caroline Clark née Hill were Unitarians who arrived in Adelaide in 1850. He established an importing and accounting firm. They had nine children of whom two became close friends of Catherine Spence: Caroline Emily Clark (1825–1911) initiated the movement for boarding out children for whom the state was responsible and introduced Spence to the work; John Howard Clark (1830–1878) accountant, and proprietor and editor of the *Register* from 1865, was a brilliant literary man, influential in Adelaide, who helped Spence to establish herself as a speaker and writer.

Unitarian Christian Church, Wakefield Street, Adelaide,
photograph courtesy of the State Library of South Australia

at once. But it was Miss Clark[5] who sought an introduction to me at a ball, because her uncle Rowland had written to her that *Clara Morison*, the new novel, was a capital story of South Australian life. She was the first person to seek me out on account of literary work, and I was grateful to her. I think all the brothers Hill wrote books, and Rosamund and Florence Davenport Hill had just published *Our Exemplars*.[6] My friendship with Miss Clark led to much work together, and the introduction was a great widening of interests for me. There were four sons and three daughters – Miss Clark and Howard were the most literary, but all had great ability and intelligence. They were Unitarians, and W.J. Wren, my brother-in-law, was also a Unitarian, and had been one of the 12 Adelaide citizens who invited out a minister and guaranteed his salary. I was led to hear what the Rev. J. Crawford Woods[7] had to say for that faith, and told my old minister (Rev. Robert Haining) that for three months I would hear him in the morning and Mr Woods in the evening, and read nothing but the Bible as my guide; and by that time I would decide. I had been induced to go to the Sacrament at 17, with much heart searching, but when I was 25 I said I could not continue a communicant, as I was not a converted Christian. This step greatly surprised both Mr and Mrs Haining, as I did not propose to leave the church. The result of my three months' enquiry was that I became a convinced Unitarian, and the cloud was lifted from the universe. I think I have been a most cheerful person ever since. My mother was not in any way distressed, though she never separated from the church of her fathers. My brother was as completely converted as I was, and he was happy in finding a wife like minded. My sister, Mrs Wren also was satisfied with the new faith; so that she and her husband saw eye to eye. It was a very live congregation in those early days. We liked our pastor, and we admired his wife, and there were a number of interesting and clever people who went to the Wakefield Street church.

It was rather remarkable that my sister's husband[8] and my brother's wife[9] arrived on the same day in two different ships – one in the *Anglier* from England, and the other in the *Three Bells* from Glasgow – in 1851; but I did not

---

5 Caroline Emily Clark.
6 Rosamond and Florence Davenport Hill (1829–1919) were daughters of Matthew Davenport Hill, Recorder of Birmingham (1742–1872) and brother of Caroline Clark. He edited *Our Exemplars, poor and rich: biographical sketches of men and women who have, by an extraordinary use of their opportunities, benefited their fellow-creatures*, London, 1860.
7 Reverend John Crawford Woods (1824–1906) arrived in South Australia in 1855 and became the first minister of the Unitarian Church in Adelaide. He retired in 1889.
8 Andrew Murray.
9 Jessie Cumming.

make the acquaintance of either till 1854 and 1855. Jessie Cumming and Mary Spence shook hands and formed a friendship over Carlyle's *Sartor Resartus*.[10] My brother-in-law (W.J. Wren) had fine literary tastes, especially for poetry. The first gift to his wife after marriage was Elizabeth Browning's poems in two volumes and Robert Browning's *Plays and Dramatic Lyrics* in two volumes,[11] and Mary and I delighted in them all. In those days I considered my sister Mary and my sister-in-law the most brilliant conversationalists I knew. My elder sister, Mrs Murray, also talked very well – so much so that her husband's friends and visitors fancied she must write a lot of his articles; but none of the three ladies went beyond writing good letters. I think all of them were keener of sight than I was – more observant of features, dress, and manners; but I took in more by the ear. As Sir Walter Scott says, 'Speak that I may know thee'. To my mind, dialogue is more important for a novel than description; and, if you have a firm grasp of your characters, the dialogue will be true. With me the main difficulty was the plot; and I was careful that this should not be merely possible, but probable. I have heard scores of people say that they have got good plots in their heads, and when pressed to tell them they proved to be only incidents. You need much more than an incident, or even two or three, with which to make a book. But when I found my plot the story seemed to write itself, and the actors to fit in.

When the development of the Moonta Mine made some of my friends rich they were also liberal. Edward Stirling said that if I wanted a trip to England I should have it at his cost, but it seemed impossible. After the death of Mr Wren my mother and I went to live with my sister, and put two small incomes together, so as to be able to bring up and educate her two children, a boy and a girl.[12] My brother John had left the railway, and for nine years had been Official Assignee and Curator of Intestate Estates; and in 1863 he had been appointed manager of the new Adelaide branch of the English, Scottish, and Australian Bank. My friend, Mr Taylor, had helped well to get the position for one he thought the fittest man in the city. He had lost his wife, Miss Mary Ann Dutton, when on a visit to England, and at this time was engaged to Miss Harriet McDermott. His sisters both were very cold about the engagement. They did not like second marriages at all, and considered it a disrespect to the first wife's memory, even though a decent interval had elapsed.

10 Thomas Carlyle (1795–1881) Scottish writer and author of *Sartor Resartus* 1833–4, a romantic philosophical semi-autobiographical work that was very popular and influential in its day.
11 Elizabeth Barrett Browning (1806–1861); Robert Browning (1812–1889).
12 William John Wren died in February 1864, leaving Mary and two small children, Charles William Wren (1856–1934) and Eleanor Brodie Wren (1862–1948), see Appendix 4.

When he wrote to me about it I took quite a different view. He said it was the kindest and the wisest letter I had ever written in my life, and he knew I had loved his late wife very much. He came to thank me, and to tell me that he had always wished that I should be in England at the time he was there, and that he was going in a P & O boat immediately after his marriage. Although Mr Stirling had promised to pay my passage, I hesitated about going. There were my mother, who was 72, and my guardianship of the Duvals to think about. I had also undertaken the oversight of old Mrs Stephens,[13] the widow of one of the early proprietors of the *Register*. These objections were all overruled. I still hesitated. 'I cannot go unless I have money to spend,' I urged. 'Let me do that,' was the generous reply. 'I have left you £500 in my will. Let me have the pleasure of giving you something while I live.' I was not too proud to owe that memorable visit to England to my two good friends. John Taylor had put into my hands on board the *Goolwa*, in which I sailed, a draft for £200 for my spending money, and in the new will he made after his marriage he bequeathed me £300. I said 'Goodby' to him, with good wishes for his health and happiness. I never saw him again. He took a sickly looking child on his knee when crossing the Isthmus of Suez – there was no canal in 1864 – to relieve a weary mother. The child had smallpox, and my friend took it and died of it. He was being buried beside his first wife at Brighton when the *Goolwa* sailed up the Channel after a passage of 14 weeks – as long as that of the *Palmyra* 25 years before – and the first news we heard was that Miss Taylor had lost a brother, the children a favourite uncle, and I, a friend. It was a sad household, but the Bakewells were in London on business connected with some claims of discovery of the Moonta Mines, and they took me to their house in Palace Gardens, Kensington, till I could arrange to go to my aunt's in Scotland. All our plans about seeing people and places together were, of course, at an end. I was to go 'a lone hand'. Mrs Taylor had a posthumous son, who never has set foot in Australia. She married a second time, an English clergyman named Knight, and had several sons, but she has never revisited Adelaide, although she has many relatives here. So the friend who loved Australia, and was eager to do his duty by it – who thoroughly approved of the Hare system of representation, and thought I did well to take it up, was snatched away in the prime of life. I wonder if there is any one alive now to whom his memory is as precious. The *Register* files may preserve some of his work.

At Palace Gardens the Bakewell family were settled in a furnished house belonging to Col. Palmer, one of the founders of South Australia, though never a resident.[14] Palmer Place, North Adelaide, bears his name. Thackeray's

---

13 Widow of John Stephens, see Chapter II, note 21.
14 Colonel G. Palmer, one of the Colonization Commissioners gazetted in 1835.

house we had to pass when we went out of the street in the direction of the city. His death had occurred in the previous year. I had an engagement with Miss Julia Wedgwood,[15] through an introduction given by Miss Sophia Sinnett, an artist sister of Frederick Sinnett's. I was called for and sent home. I was not introduced to the family. It was a fine large house with men servants and much style. Miss Wedgwood, who was deaf, used an ear trumpet very cleverly. I found her as delightful as Miss Sinnett had represented her to be, and I discovered that Miss Sinnett had been governess to her younger sisters, but that there was real regard for her. I don't know that I ever spent a more delightful evening. She had just had Browning's *Dramatis Personae*, and we read together *Rabbi Ben Ezra* and *Prospice*.[16] She knew about the Hare scheme of representation, supported by Mill and Fawcett and Craik. She was a good writer, with a fine critical faculty. Everything signed by her name in magazines or reviews was thenceforward interesting to me. I promised her a copy of *Plea for Pure Democracy*, which she accepted and appreciated. By the father's side she was a granddaughter of Josiah Wedgwood, the founder of British pottery as a fine art. Her mother was a daughter of Sir James Mackintosh.[17] Mrs Wedgwood was so much pleased with my pamphlet that she wanted to be introduced to me, and when I returned to London I had the pleasure of making her acquaintance. Miss Wedgwood gave me a beautifully bound copy of *Men and Women*,[18] of which she had a duplicate, which I cherish in remembrance of her.

During my stay I was visited by Mr Hare. I had to face up to the people I had written to with no idea of any personal communication, and I must confess that I felt I must talk well to retain their good opinion. I promised to pay a visit to the Hares when I came to London for the season. He was a widower with eight children, whom he had educated with the help of a governess, but he was the main factor in their training. The two eldest daughters were married – Mrs Andrews, the eldest, had helped him in his calculations for his great book on 'Representation'. His second daughter was artistic, and was married to John Westlake,[19] an eminent lawyer, great in international law, a

---

15 Frances Julia Wedgwood (1833–1913), English novelist and writer on moral and religious ideas, biographer of her great grand-father Josiah Wedgwood (1730–1795).
16 Robert Browning's *Dramatis Personae* was published in 1864.
17 Sir James Mackintosh (1765–1832), philosopher, judge, member of Parliament.
18 Robert Browning's *Men and Women* was published in 1855.
19 John Westlake (1828–1913) English jurist, Professor of International Law at Cambridge University, liberal thinker on social and political questions and a strong supporter of the enfranchisement of women. He married Alice, second daughter of Thomas Hare in 1864, also a reformer who was for 12 years a member of the London School Board.

pupil of Colenso,[20] who was then in London, and who was the best-abused man in the church. Another visitor was George Cowan, a great friend of my late brother-in-law, Mr W.J. Wren, who wrote to him till his death, when the pen was taken up by my sister Mary till her death, and then I corresponded with him till his death. He came to London a raw Scotch lad, and met Mr Wren[21] at the Whittington Club. Both loved books and poetry, and both were struggling to improve themselves on small salaries.[22] George Cowan had been entrusted with the printed slips of *Uphill Work*, and had tried it at two publishers without success. I had to delay any operations till I returned to London, and promised to visit the Cowans there.

20 John Colenso (1814–1863), controversial English liberal Anglican clergyman who became Bishop of Natal. He was attacked for his expression of doubts about the historical accuracy of the Bible.
21 Further comment cut by the original editor: 'who was a Cockney with some need of culture.'
22 Further comment cut by the original editor: 'Cowan said Wren taught him to speak English. Wren said he was taught by Cowan to place his h's aright and the value of the letter r.'

CHAPTER 7

MELROSE REVISITED

Jack Bakewell[1] and Edward Lancelot Stirling[2] went to see me off by the night train to Dunbar Station, five miles from Thornton Loch, and I got there in time for breakfast. The old house was just the same except for an oriel window in the drawing room looking out on the North Sea, and the rocks which lay between it and Colhandy path (where my great-grandfather Spence had preached and his wife had preferred Wesley), and Chirnside, or Spence's Mains in the same direction. All the beautiful gardens, the farm village, where about 80 souls lived, the fields and bridges were just as I remembered them. My aunt Margaret was no longer the vigorous business-like woman whom I recollected riding or driving in her little gig all over the farm of 800 English acres which my great-grandfather had rented since 1811. Not the Miss Thompson whom I had introduced into *Uphill Work*. She had had a severe stroke of paralysis, and was a prisoner to the house, only being lifted from her bed to be dressed, and to sit in a wheeled chair and be taken round the garden on fine days. The vigorous intellect was somewhat clouded, and the power of speech also; but she retained her memory. She was always at work with her needle (for her hands were not affected) for the London children, grand-nieces, and nephews, who called her grand-mamma, for she had had the care of their parents during 11 years of her brother Alexander's widowhood. But Aunt Margaret could play a capital game of whist – long whist. I could see that she missed it much on Sunday. It was her only relaxation. She had given up the farm to James Brodie, who had married her cousin Jane, the eldest of the two children she had mothered, and he had to come to the farm once or twice

1 John Warren Bakewell, oldest son of Spence's friend William Bakewell.
2 Presumably Edward Charles Stirling, oldest son of Edward Stirling. It seems that Spence added the second name to distinguish him from his father, but it was the second son John whose second name was Lancelot.

a week, having a still larger farm of his own in East Lothian, and a stock farm in Berwickshire also to look after. The son of the old farm steward, John Burnet, was James Brodie's steward, and I think the farm was well managed, but not so profitable as in old times. Aunt Mary said, in her own characteristic way, 'she always knew that her sister was a clever woman, but that the cleverest thing she had done was taking up farming and carrying it on for 30 years when it was profitable, and turning it over when it began to fall off.' But she turned it over handsomely, and did not interfere in the management. My Aunt Mary deserves a chapter for herself. She was my beau ideal of what a maiden aunt should be, though why she was never married puzzles more than me. Between my mother and her there was a love passing the love of sisters – my father liked her better than his own sisters. When my letter announcing my probable visit reached her she misread it, and thought it was Helen herself who was to come; and when she found out her mistake she shed many tears. I was all very well in my way, but I was not Helen. It was not the practice in old times to blazon an engagement, or to tell of an offer that had been declined; but my mother firmly believed that her sister Mary, the cleverest and, as she thought, the handsomest of the five sisters, had never in her life had an offer of marriage, although she had a love disappointment at 30. She had fixed her affections on a brilliant but not really worthy man, and she had to tear him out of her heart with considerable difficulty. It cost her a severe illness, out of which she emerged with what she believed to be a change of heart. She was a converted Christian. I myself don't think there was so much change. She was always a noble, generous woman, but she found great happiness in religion. Aunt Mary's disappointment made her most sympathetic to all love stories, and without any disappointment at all, I think I may say the same of myself. She was very popular with the young friends of her youngest brother, who might have experienced calf love, so very real, but so very ineffectual. One of these said to her: – 'Oh, Miss Mary, you're just a delight, you are so witty.' Another, when she spoke of some man who talked such delightful nonsense, said, 'If you would only come to Branxholme I'd talk nonsense to you the haill (whole) day.' When I arrived at the old home I found Aunt Mary vigorously rubbing her hand and wrist (she had slipped downstairs in a neighbour's house, and broken her arm, and had to drive home before she could have it set). No one from the neighbour's house went to accompany her; no one came to enquire; no message was sent. When she recovered so far as to be able to be out, she met at Dunbar the gentleman and lady also driving in their conveyance. They greeted each other, and aunt could not resist the temptation to say: – 'I am so glad to see you, and so glad that you have spoken to me, for I thought you were so offended at my taking the liberty of breaking my arm in your house that you did not mean to speak to me again.' This little expression of what the French call malice, not the English meaning, was the only instance I can recollect of Aunt Mary's not putting the kindest construction on everybody's words and actions. But when I think of the love that Aunt Mary gathered to herself from brothers, sisters, nephews, nieces, cousins, and friends – it seems as if the happiest wife and mother of a large family could not reckon up as rich stores of affection. She was the unfailing correspondent of those members of the family who were separated by land and ocean from the old home, the link that often bound these together, the most tolerant to their failings, the most liberal in her aid – full of suggestions, as well as of sympathy. Now, in my Aunt Margaret's enfeebled state, she was the director of all things. Although she had differed from the then two single sisters and the family generally at the time of the disruption of the Church of Scotland, and gone over to the Free Church, the more intensely Calvinistic of the two, though accepting the same standards – the Westminster Confession and the Shorter Catechism – all the harsher features fell off the living texture of her faith like cold water off a duck's back. From natural preference she chose for her devotions those parts of the Bible which I selected with deliberate intention. She wondered to find so much spiritual kinship with me, when I built on such a different foundation. When I suggested that the 109th Psalm, which she read as the allotted portion in *Fletcher's Family Devotions*,[3] was not fit to be read in a Christian household, she said meekly – 'You are quite right, I shall mark it, and never read it again.'

My mother always thought me like her sister Mary, and when I asked Mr Taylor if he saw any resemblance between us, he said, with cruel candour – 'Oh, no. Your Aunt Mary is a very handsome woman.' But in ways and manners, both my sister Mary and myself had considerable resemblances to our mother's favourite sister; and I can see traces of it in my own nieces. There can be no direct descent from maiden aunts, though the working ants and bees do not inherit their industrious habits from either male or female parents, but from their maiden aunts. Galtons' theory,[4] that potentialities not utilised by individuals or by their direct descendants may miss a generation or two, opens a wide field of thought, and collaterals may draw from the original source what was never suspected. And the Brodies intermarried in such a way as to shock modern ideas. When my father was asked if a certain Mr Dudgeon, of Leith, was related to him, he said – 'He is my mother's cousin

---

3   Alexander Fletcher (1787–1860), *A Guide to Family Devotion: containing a hymn, a portion of Scripture with reflections, and a prayer, for the morning and evening of every day in the year*, London, 1834.
4   Francis Galton (1822–1911) 'The great man of measurement', English explorer and anthropologist, known for his pioneering studies of heredity and human intelligence.

and my stepmother's cousin, and my father-in-law's cousin, and my mother-in-law's cousin.' Except for Spences and Wauchopes there was not a relative of my father that was not related to my mother. Grandfather Brodie married his cousin, and Grandfather Spence married his late wife, Janet Park's cousin Katherine Swanston. I cannot see that these close marriages produced degenerates, either physical or mental, in the case of my own family.

Of the twelve months I spent in the old country, I spent six with the dear old aunts. How proud Aunt Mary was of my third novel, with the sketch of Aunt Margaret in it, of the *Cornhill* article, and the request from Mr Wilson to write for the *Fortnightly*. I introduced her to new books, and especially new poets; she had never heard of Browning and Jean Ingelow.[5] She was so much cleverer than her neighbours that I often wondered how she could put up with them. How conservative these farmers and farmers' wives and daughters were, to be sure. These big tenants considered themselves quite superior to tradesmen, even to merchants, unless they were in a big way. There was infinitely more difference between their standard of living and that of their labourers than between theirs and that of the aristocratic landlords. James Burnet, the farm steward, said to me – 'You have brought down the price of wheat with your Australian grain, and you do big things in wool, but you can never touch us in meat.' This was quite true in 1865. I expected to see some improvement in the farm hamlet, but the houses built by the landlord were still very poor and bare. The wages had risen a little since 1839, but not much. The wheaten loaf was cheaper, and so was tea and sugar, but the poor were still living on porridge and bannocks of barley and pease meal instead of tea and white bread. It was questionable if they were as well nourished. There were 100 souls living on the farms of Thornton and Thornton Loch.

A short visit from Mrs Graham to me at Thornton Loch opened up to Aunt Mary some of my treasures of memory. She asked me to recite 'Bertha in the Lane',[6] Hood's 'Tale of a Trumpet',[7] *Locksley Hall*,[8] *The Pied Piper*,[9] and Jean Ingelow's 'Songs of Seven'. She made me promise to go to see her, and find out how much she had to do for her magnificent salary of £30 a year; but she impressed Aunt Mary much. Mrs Graham had found that the Kirkbeen folks, among whom she lived, were more impressed by the six months' experiences of two maiden ladies, who had gone to Valparaiso to join a brother who died, than with her fresh and racy descriptions of four young Australian

5   Jean Ingelow (1820–1897), English poet, novelist and writer of stories for children.
6   Poem by Elizabeth Browning.
7   Thomas Hood (1799–1845), English author, editor and poet.
8   Alfred Tennyson (1809–1892), *Locksley Hall*, 1842.
9   Robert Browning (1812–1889), *The Pied Piper of Hamelin*.

colonies. She had seen Melbourne from 1852 to 1855 – a wonderful growth and development. The only idea the ladies from Valparaiso formed about Australia was that it was hot and must be Roman Catholic, and consequently the Sabbath must be desecrated. It was in vain that my friend spoke of the Scots Church and Dr Cairns's[10] Church. Heat and Roman Catholicism were inseparably connected in their minds.

Visiting Uncle and Aunt Handyside and grown-up cousins, whom I left children, I saw a lot of good farming and the easy circumstances which I always associated with tenants' holdings in East Lothian. Next farm to Fenton was Fentonbarns, a show place, which was held by George Hope,[11] a cousin of my grandmother's. He was an exceptional man – a radical, a free-trader, and a Unitarian. Cobden died that year.[12] Uncle Handyside was surprised that George Hope did not go into mourning for him. John Bright[13] still lived, and he was the bête noire of the Conservatives in that era; and the abolition of the corn laws was held to be the cause of the agricultural distress – not the high rent of agricultural land. George Hope was a striking personality. When my friend J.C. Woods was minister at St Mark's Unitarian Church, Edinburgh, Mr Hope used to be called the Bishop, though he lived 16 miles off. When the first Mrs Woods died, leaving an infant son, it was Mrs Hope who cared for it till it could go to his relatives in Ireland. Later he stood for Parliament himself. In the paper I wrote over the name of Edward Wilson for the *Fortnightly* I noted how the House of Commons represented the people – or misrepresented them. The House consisted of peers and sons of peers, military and naval officers, bankers, brewers, and landownership was represented enormously, but there were only two tenant farmers in the House. It was years after my return to Australia that I heard of his unsuccessful candidature, and that when he sought to take another lease of Fentonbarns, he was told that under no circumstances would his offer be entertained. Fentonbarns had been farmed by three generations of Hopes for 100 years, and to no owner by parchment titles could it have been more dear. George Hope's friend, Russell, of the *Scotsman*,[14] fulminated against the injustice of refusing a lease to the

---

10 Adam Cairns (1802–1881), Scottish Presbyterian and theologian who emigrated 1853 to Melbourne and founded the Presbyterian Church there.
11 George Hope (1811–1876), agriculturist. His farm, Fenton Barns, was known in America and Europe as a model of what a farm should be.
12 Richard Cobden (1804–1865), economist and politician, 'the apostle of free trade,' part founder and most prominent member of the Anti-Corn-Law League.
13 John Bright (1811–1889), English orator, politician and political agitator. Prominent member of the Anti-Corn-Law League.
14 Edinburgh daily newspaper.

foremost agriculturist in Scotland – and when you say that you may say of the United Kingdom – because the tenant held certain political opinions and had the courage to express them. My uncle Handyside, however, always maintained that his neighbour was the most honourable man in business that he knew, and far from being an atheist or even a deist, he had family prayers, and on the occasion of a death in the family, the funeral service was most impressive. He was one of the salt of the earth, and the atmosphere was clearer around him for his presence.

But I must give some space to my visit to Melrose, my childhood's home. My father's half-sister Janet Reid was alive, and though her two sons were, one at St Kitts and the other at Grand Canary, she lived with an old husband and her only daughter in Melrose still. I can never forget the look of tender pity cast on me as I was sitting in our old seat in church, looking at seats filled by another generation. The paterfamilias, so wonderfully like his father of 1839, and sons and daughters, sitting in the place of uncles and aunts settled elsewhere. They grieved that I had been banished from the romantic associations and the high civilisation of Melrose to rough it in the wilds, while my heart was full of thankfulness that I had moved to the wider spaces and the more varied activities of a new progressive colony. My dear old teacher was still alive, though the school had been closed for many years. She lived at St Mary's with her elder sister, who had taught me sewing and had done the housekeeping, but she herself was almost blind, and a girl came every day to read to her for two or three hours. She told me what a good thing it was that she knew all the Psalms in the prose version by heart, for in the sleepless nights which accompany old age so often they were such comfort to her in the night watches. I had sent her my two novels when they were published, *Clara Morison* and *Tender and True*. She would have been glad if they had been more distinctly religious in tone. Indeed, the novel I began at 19 would have suited her better, but my brother's insistence on reading it every day as I wrote it somehow made me see what poor stuff it was, and I did not go far with it. But Miss Phin was, on the whole, pleased with my progress, and glad that I was able to go to see her and talk of old times. How very small the village of Melrose looked! How little changed! The distances to the neighbouring villages of Darnick and Newstead, and across the Tweed to Gattonsville, seemed so shrunken. It was not so far to Abbotsford as to Norwood.[15] The very Golden Hills looked lower than my childish recollection of them. Aunt Janet Reid rejoiced over me sufficiently. 'You are not like your mother in the face, but, oh, Katie, you are like dear Mrs David in your ways. How I was determined to hate her when she came to Melrose first. I was not 13, and she

---

15 A suburb of Adelaide, not far from where Spence was living in Stepney.

was taking away the best of my brothers, the one that I liked best; but it did not take long before I was as fond of her as of David himself.'

I also had the pleasure of visiting Mr Murray, the parish schoolmaster, who taught my three brothers, then retired, living with his daughter, Louisa, an old schoolfellow at Miss Phin's. There was an absurd idea current in 1865 that all visiting Australians were rich, and I could not disabuse people of that notion. Of all the two families of Brodies and Spences who came out in 1839 there was only my brother John who could be called successful. He was then manager of the Adelaide branch of the English, Scottish, and Australian Bank. If it had not been for help from the wonderful aunts from time to time both families would have been stranded. I had the greatest faith in the future of Australia, but I felt that for such gifts as I possessed there was no market at home. Possibly I should have tried literature earlier if I had remained in Scotland, but I am not at all sure that I could have succeeded as well. For the first time in my life I had as much money as I wanted. I am surprised now that I spent that £200 when I had so much hospitality. In fact, except for a week in Paris, I never had any hotel expenses. I had got the money to enjoy it, and I did. This was what my friend wished. I made a few presents. I bought some to take home with me. I spent money on dress freely, so as to present a proper appearance when visiting. I was liberal with veils [sic], though I hate the practice.[16] To a woman who had to look on both sides of a shilling since 1839 this experience was new and delightful. Among other people I went to see was Mrs C——, the widow of the Tory writer and branch bank manager, who was my father's successful rival. He was not speculative like my father. He was a keen business man, and had a great hunger for land.

On the gravestones around Melrose Abbey are many names with the avocation added – John Smith, builder; William Hogg, mason – but many with the word portioner. They were small proprietors, but they were not distinguished for the careful cultivation which in France is known as 'la petite culture'. No; the portions were most carelessly handled, and in almost every instance they were 'bonded' or mortgaged. I recollect in old days these portioners used to make moonlight flittings and disappear, or they sold off their holdings openly and went to America, meaning the United States. The tendency was to buy up these portions, and a considerable estate could be built up by any shrewd man who had money, or the command of it. Before we left Melrose in 1839, Mr C—— had possession of a good deal of land. When he died he left property of the value of £90,000, an unheard-of estate for a country writer before the era of freetrade and general expansion. He had asked so much revenue from the railway company when the plan was to cut through

---

16 'Veils' or 'vailes' or 'vales': tips.

the gardens we as children used to play in, that the company made a deviation and left the garden severely alone. The eldest daughter had married a landed proprietor, the second was single, the third married to a wealthy man in the west, the fourth the richest widow in Scotland. One son had land, and the other son land, and another business training. All was material success, and I am sure I did not grudge it to them, but when I took stock of real things I had not the least glimmering of a wish to exchange. One generally desires a little more money than one has; but even that may cost too much. I think my dear old Aunt Reid felt that the Spences had gone down in my father's terrible smash in 1839, and the C—— family had steadily gone up, and she was pleased that a niece from Australia, who had written two books and a wonderful pamphlet, and, more important still in the eyes of Mrs Grundy, had money to spend and to give, was staying with her in Melrose, and wearing good and well made clothes. Old servants – the old laundress – old schoolfellows were visited. My father's old clerk, Allan Freer, had a good business in Melrose, though not equal to that of the Tory firm. I think the portioners were all sold out before he could enter the field, and the fate of these Melrose people has thoroughly emphasised for me the importance of having our South Australian workmen's blocks, the glory of Mr Cotton's[17] life, maintained always on the same footing of perpetual lease dependent on residence. If the small owner has the freehold, he is tempted to mortgage it, and then in most instances the land is lost to him, and added to the possessions of the man who has money. With a perpetual lease, there is the same security of tenure as in the freehold – indeed, there is more security, because he cannot mortgage. I did not see the land question as clearly on this 1865 visit, as I did later; but the extinction of the old portioners and the wealth acquired by the moneyed man of Melrose gave me cause for thinking.

---

17 George Witherage Cotton (1821–1892), arrived South Australia 1848, entered Parliament 1862 and helped with the formation of the Homestead League, which set out to rescue working men from unemployment by allowing them to lease land from the state at an affordable rent.

CHAPTER 8

I Visit Edinburgh and London

A visit to Glasgow and to the relatives of my sister-in-law opened out a different vista to me. This was a great manufacturing and commercial city, which had far outgrown Edinburgh in population and wealth; but the Edinburgh people still boasted of being the Athens of the north, the ancient capital with the grandest historic associations. In Glasgow I fell in with David Murray and his wife (of D.&W. Murray, Adelaide)[1] – not quite so important a personage as he became later. Not a relative of mine; but a family connection, for his brother William married Helen Cumming, Mrs J.B. Spence's sister. David Murray was always a great collector of paintings, and especially of prints, which last he left to the Adelaide Art Gallery. He was a close friend of my brother John's until the death of the latter. One always enjoys meeting with Adelaide people in other lands, and comparing the most recent items of news. I went to Dumfries according to promise, and spent many days with my old friend Mrs Graham, but stayed the night always with her sister, Mrs Maxwell, wife of a printer and bookseller in the town. Dumfries was full of Burns's relics and memorials.[2] Mr Gilfillan had taken the likeness of Mrs Burns and her granddaughter when he was a young man, and Mrs Maxwell corresponded with the grandaughter. It was also full of associations with Carlyle.[3] His youngest sister, Jean the Craw, as she was called on account of her dark hair

---

1   David Murray (1829–1907), merchant and member of Parliament, arrived from Scotland in 1853 and with his brother William established D&W Murray Ltd, a clothing and footwear manufacturing and trading business.
2   Robert Burns (1759–1796), Scottish poet who wrote in native Scots as well as in correct eighteenth-century English.
3   Thomas Carlyle (1795–1881), Scottish lecturer and historian, very influential in his day. His sister Jean became Mrs Aitkin. Carlyle married a Scot, Jane Baillie Welsh (1801–1866), in 1826.

and complexion was Mrs Aitkin, a neighbour and close friend of Mrs Maxwell. I was taken to see her, and I suppose introduced as a sort of author, and she regretted much that this summer Tom was not coming to visit her at Dumfries. She was a brisk, cheery person, with some clever daughters, who were friends of the Maxwell girls. When the Froude[4] memorials came out no one was more interested than Jean the Craw – 'Tom and his wife always understood each other. They were not unhappy, though after her death he reproached himself for some things.'

I found that my friend had just as much to do from morning to night as she could do, and I hoped with a great hope that *Uphill Work* would be published, and all the world would see how badly capable and industrious women were paid. I fancied that a three-volume novel would be read, marked, and inwardly digested by everybody! But Mrs Graham was appreciated by the matron, the doctors, and by the people of Dumfries, as she had not been in the village of Kirkbeen. Her picturesque descriptions of life in the various colonies interested home-staying folk, for she had the keenest observing faculties. There was an old cousin of Uncle Handyside's who always turned the conversation on to Russia, where he had visited successful brothers; but his talk was not incisive. My cousin Agnes asked me when I supposed this visit was paid, and I said a few years ago, probably, when she laughed and said – 'Nicol Handyside spent six weeks in Russia 30 years ago, and he has been talking about it ever since.' One visit I paid in Edinburgh to an old lady from Melrose, who lived with a married daughter. She had always been very deaf, and the daughter was out. With great difficulty I got her to see by my card that my name was Spence. 'Are you Jessie Spence?' I shook my head. 'No; Katie.' 'Are you Mary Spence?' Another headshake, 'No; I am Katie.' 'Then who are you?' She could understand the negative by the headshaking, but not anything else. I wanted a piece of paper or a slate badly, but the daughter came in and made her mother understand that I was the middle Spence girl, and then the old lady said, 'It is a very hot country you come from,' her only idea apparently of wonderful Australia. And to think that in times long past some intriguing aunts tried very hard to arrange a marriage between my father and the deaf young lady who had about £600 a year in land in and near Melrose. She might have been my mother! The idea was appalling! None of her children inherited the deafness, and they took a fair proportion of good looks from their father, for the mother was exceedingly homely. A bright-looking grandson was on the

---

4   James Anthony Froude (1818–1894) English historian who edited *Reminiscences* by Thomas Carlyle, (Longmans, Green) London, 1881, and *Letters and Memorials of Jane Welsh Carlyle prepared for publication by Thomas Carlyle*, (Longmans, Green) London, 1883. He published a four volume biography of Carlyle 1882–4. His revelations caused a great stir.

rug looking through a bound volume of *Punch*, as my nephew in Australia loved to do. The two mothers were school companions and playmates.

My return to London introduced me to a wider range of society. I had admissions to the Ladies' Gallery of the House of Commons from Sir Charles Dilke,[5] Professor Pearson's[6] friend, and I had invitations to stay for longer or shorter periods with people various in means, in tastes, and in interests. To Mr Hare I was especially drawn and I should have liked to join him and his family in their yearly walking tour, which was to be through the Tyrol and Venice; but Aunt Mary protested for two good and sufficient reasons. The first was that I could not walk 16 or 20 miles a day, even in the mountains, which Katie Hare said was so much easier than on the plains; and the second was that to take six weeks out of my visit to the old country was a great deal too much. If it could have done any good to proportional representation I might have stood out; but it could not. For that I have since travelled thousands of miles by sea and by land; and, though not on foot, I have undergone much bodily fatigue and mental strain, but in these early days of the movement it had only entered the academic stage. My *Plea for Pure Democracy* had been written at a white heat of enthusiasm. I do not think I ever before or since reached a higher level. I took this reform more boldly than Mr Mill, who sought by giving extra votes for property and university degrees or learned professions to check the too great advance of democracy. I was prepared to trust the people; and Mr Hare was also confident that, if all the people were equitably represented in Parliament, the good would be stronger than the evil. The wise would be more effectual than the foolish. I do not think any one whom I met took the matter up so passionately as I did; and I had a feeling that in our new colonies the reform would meet with less obstruction than in old countries bound by precedent and prejudiced by vested interests. Parliament was the preserve of the wealthy in the United Kingdom. There was no property qualification for the candidate in South Australia, and we had manhood suffrage.

South Australia was the first community to give the secret ballot for political elections. It had dispensed with Grand Juries.[7] It had not required a

5   Sir Charles Wentworth Dilke (1843–1911), radical English statesman.
6   Charles Henry Pearson (1830–1894), historian, politician and education reformer, professor of modern history at King's College, London, when he emigrated to Australia. After a short time in South Australia he went to Melbourne where he lectured in history at Melbourne University, became the first headmaster of Melbourne's Presbyterian Ladies College and then a member of Parliament. He advocated reform in education and women's rights. He was one of Spence's friends.
7   A jury of enquiry, accusation or presentment which enquires into indictments before they are submitted to a trial jury.

member of either House to stand a new election if he accepted ministerial office. Every elected man was eligible for office. South Australia had been founded by doctrinaires, and occasionally a cheap sneer had been levelled at it on that account; but, to my mind, that was better than the haphazard way in which other colonies grew. When I visited Sir Rowland Hill[8] he was recognised as the great post office reformer. To me he was also one of the founders of our province, and the first pioneer of quota representation. When I met Matthew Davenport Hill[9] I respected him, because he tried to keep delinquent boys out of gaol, and promoted the establishment of reform schools; but I also was grateful to him for suggesting to his brother the park lands which surround Adelaide, and give us both beauty and health. To Colonel Light, who laid out the city so well, we owe the many open spaces and squares; but he did not originate the idea of the park lands. Much of the work of Mr Davenport Hill and of his brother Frederick I took up later with their niece (Miss C.E. Clark), and their ideas have been probably more thoroughly carried out in South Australian than anywhere else; but in 1865 I was learning a great deal that bore fruit afterwards.

I fear it would make this narrative too long if I went into detail about the interesting people I met. Florence and Rosamund Davenport Hill[10] introduced me to Miss Frances Power Cobbe, whose *Intuitive Morals* I admired so much.[11] At Sir Rowland Hill's I met Sir Walter Crofton,[12] a prison reformer;

---

8 Rowland Hill, later Sir Rowland (1795–1879) originator of the penny postal system, member of the provisional committee of the South Australian Association, First Secretary to the first Board of Commissioners. Brother of Mrs Caroline Clark, mother of Caroline Emily Clark and John Howard Clark.

9 Matthew Davenport Hill (1792–1872), Recorder of Birmingham, another brother of Mrs Clark, pioneered the use of probation with young offenders; see also, above, Chapter VI, n. 6.

10 Rosamond and Florence Davenport Hill, daughters of Matthew Davenport Hill, cousins of Caroline Emily Clark and John Howard Clark, became friends of Spence and later visited Australia. In Adelaide in 1873, they looked at social problems and were critical of the treatment of destitute children. They published *What We Saw in Australia* in 1875.

11 Frances Power Cobbe (1822–1908), philanthropist, feminist, and author of works on religious and social questions. *An Essay on Intuitive Morals: being an attempt to popularise ethical science* was published in 1855. Her article 'The Philosophy of the Poor Laws and the Report of the Committee of Poor Relief', published in *Fraser's Magazine*, volume 80, September 1864, had a great influence on Spence.

12 Rt. Hon. Sir Walter Crofton (1815–1897), prison reformer, became administrator of the Irish prison system in 1854 and was first chairman of the Irish Convict Prisons Board. He was one of the developers of the early parole system.

Mr Wells, editor of *All the Year Round*;[13] Charles Knight, who had done so much for good and cheap literature;[14] Madame Bodichon (formerly Barbara Smith),[15] the great friend and correspondent of George Eliot,[16] who was interesting to me because by introducing the Australian eucalyptus to Algeria she had made an unhealthy marshy country quite salubrious. She had a salon, where I met very clever men and women – English and French – and which made me wish for such things in Adelaide. The kindness and hospitality that were shown to me – an absolute stranger – by all sorts of people were surprising. Mr and Mrs Westlake[17] took me on Sunday to see Bishop Colenso.[18] He showed me the photo of the enquiring Zulu who made him doubt the literal truth of the early books of the Bible, and presented me with the people's edition of his work on the Pentateuch.

In all my travels and visits I saw little of the theatre or concert room, and some of the candid confessions of Mrs Oliphant might stand for my own. I had read so many plays before I saw one that the unreality of much of the acted drama impressed me unfavourably. The asides in particular seemed impossible, and I think the more carefully the pieces are put on the stage the more critical I become concerning their probability; and when I hear the praise of the beautiful and expensive theatrical wardrobes which, in the case of actresses seem to set the fashion for the wealthy and well-born, I feel that it is a costly means of making the story more unlikely. I seem to lose the identity of the heroine who in two hours wears three or four different toilettes complete. As Mrs Oliphant did not identify the 'nobody in white tights' who rendered from *Twelfth Night*[19] the lovely lines beginning 'That strain again; it had a dying fall' with the Orsino she had imagined when reading the play, so I, who knew *She Stoops to Conquer*[20] almost by heart, was disappointed when I saw it

---

13 *All the Year Round*, a weekly journal, conducted by Charles Dickens, and left to his son, which ran from 1859–1895.

14 Charles Knight (1791–1873), author and publisher of a series of cheap books which condensed the information found in voluminous works.

15 Barbara Leigh Bodichon née Smith (1827–1890), English advocate for women's rights, especially working for university education for women. Although she spent much time in Algeria she was very influential in the women's movement in England.

16 George Eliot (1819–1880), pseudonym of Mary Ann, later Marian, Evans, considered by many in her time to be the greatest living English novelist. Her work was much admired by Spence.

17 John Westlake (1828–1913), see above, Chapter VI, n. 19.

18 John Colenso (1814–1863), see above, Chapter VI, n. 20. Spence's comment that Bishop Colenso was 'the very handsomest man I met in England' was cut by the original editor.

19 William Shakespeare.

20 *She Stoops to Conquer, or The Mistakes of a Night*, 1773, a play by Oliver Goldsmith (1730–1774).

on the stage. I was taken to the opera once by Mr and Mrs Bakewell, and heard Patti[21] in *Don Giovanni*,[22] at Covent Garden, but opera of all kinds is wasted on me. I liked some of the familiar airs and choruses, but all opera needs far more make-believe than I am capable of. It is a pity that I am so insensible to the youngest and the most progressive of the fine arts. I am, however, in the good company of Mrs Oliphant, who, speaking of the musical parties in Eton, where she lived so long, for the education of her boys, writes in words that suit me perfectly:

> In one of these friends' houses a family quartet played what were rather new and terrible to me – long sonatas and concerted pieces which filled my soul with dismay. It is a dreadful confession to make, and proceeds from want of education and instruction, but I fear any appreciation of music I have is purely literary. I love a song and a 'tune'; the humblest fiddler has sometimes given me the greatest pleasure, and sometimes gone to my heart; but music, properly so called, the only music that many of my friends would listen to, is to me a wonder and a mystery. My mind wanders through adagios and andantes, gaping, longing to understand. Will no one tell me what it means? I want to find the old unhappy far off things which Wordsworth imagined in the Gaelic song of the "Highland Lass".[23] I feel out of it, uneasy, thinking all the time what a poor creature I must be. I remember the mother of the sonata players approaching me with beaming countenance on the occasion of one of these performances, expecting the compliment which I faltered forth, doing my best not to look insincere. "And I have this every evening of my life," cried the triumphant mother. "Good heavens, and you have survived it all" was my internal response.

But the worst thing is when you do not expect a musical evening and this superior music is sprung on you. Mrs Webster[24] and I were once invited to

---

21 Adelina Patti (1843–1919), Italian soprano, one of the greatest coloratura singers of the nineteenth century.
22 *Don Giovanni*, opera by Wolfgang Amadeus Mozart (1756–1791).
23 William Wordsworth (1770–1850), English poet. 'The Solitary Reaper', 1807.
24 Mrs Webster, formerly Martha Turner, sister of Melbourne identity, H.G. Turner, prominent in Melbourne banking and commerce, and in literature; he was one of the founders of the *Melbourne Review*. Martha Turner came to Australia in 1870 to visit her brother, and stayed. Both were members of the Melbourne Unitarian Church and Martha Turner became the recognised pastor of the church, licensed to solemnize marriages and to consecrate children. She was the first woman to become the minister of a church in Australia. Her preaching encouraged Spence to preach herself. They became friends.

meet some very interesting people, some of the best conversationalists in Melbourne, and we were given high-class music instead, and scarcely could a remark be exchanged when a warning finger was held up and silence insisted on. I could not sing, but sometimes I attempted to hum a tune. I recollect during my first visit to Melbourne, my little nephew Johnnie,[25] delighted in the rhymes and poems which I recited; but one day when I was ironing I began to sing, and he burst out with 'Don't sing, auntie; let me hear the voice of your words.' So for my own delectation I began Wordsworth's 'Leechgatherer'[26] –

> There was a roaring in the wind all night,
> The rain came heavily and fell in floods;
> But now the sun is rising calm and bright,
> The birds are singing in the distant woods;
> Over his own sweet voice the stock dove broods,
> The jay makes answer as the magpie chatters,
> And all the air is filled with pleasant noise of waters.

'Oh, that's pretty, auntie; say it again,' I said it again, and yet again, at his request, till he could almost repeat it. And he was not quite four years old. He is still alive, and has not become a poet, which was what I expected in those early days. He could repeat great screeds of Browning's *Pied Piper of Hamelin*, which was his especial favourite. Music has often cheated me of what is to me the keenest pleasure in life. Like Samuel Johnson, I enjoy greatly 'good talk,' though I never took such a dominant part in it. There are two kinds of people who reduce me to something like silence – those who know too little and those who know too much. My brother-in-law's friend, Mr Cowan, was a great talker, and a good one, but he scarcely allowed me a fair share. He was also an admirable correspondent.

One predominant talker I met at Mr Edwin Hill's[27] – William Ellis,[28] a special friend of the Hills, and a noteworthy man. One needs to look back 60 years to become conscious of how much English education was in the hands of the church. Not only the public schools and the university were overshadowed by the Established Church, but what schools were accessible to the poor were a sort of appanage to the rectory, and the teachers were bound to work for the

---

25 John David Murray, born 1850.
26 William Wordsworth (1770–1850), English poet. 'Resolution and Independence', 1807.
27 Edwin Hill, a brother of Spence's friend Mrs Clark, and of Rowland, Matthew Davenport and Frederick Hill.
28 William Ellis (1800–1881), innovator in English education, who established the Birkbeck Schools.

good of the church and the convenience of the incumbent. The commercial schools, which were independent of the church, to which Non-conformists sent their boys, were satirised by Dickens, and they deserved the satire. The masters were generally incompetent, and the assistant teachers or ushers were the most miserable in regard to payment and status. William Ellis expended large sums of money, and almost all his leisure, in establishing secular schools that were good for something. He called them Birkbeck schools, thus doing honour to the founder of mechanics' institutes, and perhaps the founder of the first of these schools; and he taught what he called social science in them himself. He was the Senor Ferrer[29] of England; and, though he escaped martyrdom in the more enlightened country he was looked on suspiciously by those who considered education that was not founded on revealed religion and permeated by its doctrines as dangerous and revolutionary.

But there was one great personage who saw the value of those teachings on things that make for human happiness and intellectual freedom, and that was the Prince Consort.[30] He asked William Ellis to give some lessons to the eldest of the Royal children – the Princess Victoria, Prince Edward (our present King),[31] and Prince Alfred, afterwards Duke of Saxe-Coburg. Mr Ellis said all three were intelligent, and Princess Victoria exceptionally so. What a tragedy it was – more so than that of many an epic or drama – that the Princess Royal and the husband of her choice, who had educated themselves and each other to take the reins of the German Empire, and had drawn up so many plans for the betterment of the general conditions of the people, should, on their accession to power, have met death standing on the steps of the throne; and that only a powerless widow should have been left without much authority over her masterful son. But my firm belief is that in many of the excellent things that the Kaiser William[32] has done for his people, he is working on the plans that had been committed to writing by the Crown Prince and Princess. Her father's memory was so dear to the Crown Princess that anything he had

---

29 Francisco Ferrer (1859–1909), was an educational pioneer in Spain, who was wrongly arrested and executed for insurrection.
30 Prince Albert of Saxe-Coburg-Gotha married Queen Victoria, his cousin, in 1840. There were seven children. The eldest child, Princess Victoria, the Princess Royal, married the German Crown Prince, Frederick, who became Frederick III of Prussia in 1888. He died of cancer three months after his succession.
31 Edward VII (1841–1910), eldest son of Queen Victoria.
32 William II (Friedrich Wilhelm Victor Albrecht) (1859–1941), son of Frederick III of Germany and Victoria, Princess Royal of Great Britain and daughter of Queen Victoria, was King of Prussia and Emperor of Germany. He was known to the English as Kaiser William. Spence was writing before the first World War made his name hated in England.

suggested to her was cherished all her life; and I do not doubt that these early lessons on the right relation of human beings to each other – the social science which regards human happiness as depending on justice and toleration – is even now bearing fruit in the Fatherland. Shortsighted mortals see the immediate failures, but in the larger eye of the Infinite and the Eternal there is always progress towards better things from every honest attempt to remedy injustice, and to increase knowledge.

I arranged for a week in Paris with my young friends, Rosa and Symonds Clark,[33] of Hazelwood, and we travelled as far as Paris with the Hare family, who went on to the Tyrol. We enjoyed the week. Louis Napoleon[34] appeared then to be quite secure on his throne, and we saw the fetes and illuminations for his birthday. What a day and night of rain it was! But the thousands of people, joyful and good-humoured – under umbrellas or without them – gave us a favourable impression of Parisian crowds. In London I had been with Mr Cowan in the crush to the theatre. It was contrary to his principles to book seats, and I never was so frightened in my life. I thought a London crowd rough and merciless. I was the only one of the party who could speak any French, and I spoke it badly, and had great difficulty in following French conversation; but we got into a hotel where no English was spoken, and managed to pull through. But we did not know a soul, and I think we did not learn so much from our week's sight-seeing as we should have done if Miss Katie Hare had stayed the week with us.

I then paid a visit to Birmingham, and spent a week at the sittings of the British Association.[35] By subscribing a guinea I was made an Associate, and some of the sessions were very interesting, but much too deep for me. I sat out a lecture on the Higher Mathematics, by Professor Henry Smith,[36] to whom Professor Pearson gave me an introduction, in hopes that I might visit Oxford; but he was going abroad, and I could not go to Oxford if I knew nobody – especially alone. I went, however, to Carr's Lane Chapel, where a humble friend had begged me to go, because there she had been converted, and there the Rev. R.W. Dale[37] happened to preach on 'Where

---

33 Rosa Clark and Matthew Symonds Clark (1839–1920), younger siblings of Caroline Emily Clark.
34 Charles Louis Napoleon Bonaparte (1808–1873) known as Louis Napoleon, became Napoleon III, Emperor of the French, in 1852. He declared war on Prussia in 1870, was defeated and imprisoned.
35 British Association for the Advancement of Science.
36 Professor Henry Smith (1826–1883), classical scholar and professor of mathematics at Oxford University.
37 Robert William Dale (1829–1895), leading Congregationalist pastor in Birmingham, lecturer and writer of theological works.

prayer was wont to be made'. He said that consecration was not due to a Bishop or to any ecclesiastical ceremony, but to the devout prayers and praise of the faithful souls within it – that thousands over Scotland and England, and others in America, Australia, and New Zealand, look back to words which they had heard and praises and prayers in which they had joined as the holiest times in their lives. I thought of my good Mrs Ludlow, and thanked God for her. When Mr Cowan took me to the church in Essex place where he and his friend Wren used to hear Mr W.J. Fox,[38] M.P. for Oldham, preach, a stranger, a young American, was there. I found out afterwards he was Moncure Conway,[39] and he gave us a most striking discourse. There was going on in Birmingham at this time a controversy between the old Unitarians and the new. In the Church of the Messiah the old ministers gave a series of sermons on the absolute truth of the New Testament miracles. The Old Testament he was quite willing to give up, but he pinned his faith on those wrought by Christ and His apostles. Some of the congregation told me they had never thought of doubting them before, but the more Mr B. [sic] defended them as the bulwarks of Christianity, the more they felt that our religion rested on other foundations. I saw a good deal of the industrial life of Birmingham, and had a sight of the Black Country – by day and by night. Joseph Chamberlain[40] was then a young man; I believe he was a Sunday school teacher. The Unitarian Sunday Schools taught writing and arithmetic as well as reading. In the terrible lack of national day schools many of the poor had no teaching at all but what was given on Sundays, and no time on other days of the week to learn anything. I could not help contrasting the provision made by the parish schools of Scotland out of the beggarly funds or tithes given for church and schools out of the spoils of the Ancient Church by the Lords of the Congregation. Education was not free, but it was cheap, and it was general. Scotchmen made their way all over the world better than Englishmen mainly because they were better educated. The Sunday school was not so much needed, and was much later in establishing itself in Scotland. Good Hannah

38 William Johnson Fox (1786–1864), one of the founders of and minister of the South Place Ethical Society in London. A member of Parliament, he supported popular education and the repeal of the Corn Laws. He also wrote hymns.
39 Moncure Daniel Conway (1832–1907), American author and abolitionist. He moved to London and became influential in the South Place Ethical Society. He was a scholar of world religions and philosophies. Conway Hall, London, named in his honour in 1927, is a centre of intellectual, political and cultural life.
40 Joseph Chamberlain (1836–1914), English statesman with radical views who became an influential member of Parliament.

More[41] taught girls to read the Bible under a spreading tree in her garden because no church would give her a place to teach in. 'If girls were taught to read where would we get servants?' It was an early cry.

---

41 Hannah More (1745–1833), English writer of religious works, who was instrumental in the formation of the Religious Tract Society, publisher of tracts and many religious stories for children.

CHAPTER 9

MEETING WITH J.S. MILL AND GEORGE ELIOT

I leave to the last of my experiences in the old world in 1865–6 my interviews with John Stuart Mill and George Eliot. Stuart Mill's wife was the sister of Arthur[1] and of Alfred[2] Hardy, of Adelaide, and the former had given to me a copy of the first edition of Mill's *Political Economy*, with the original dedication to Mrs John Taylor, who afterwards became Mill's wife[3], which did not appear in subsequent editions; but, as he had two gift copies of the same edition, Mr Hardy sent it on to me with his most illegible handwriting: 'To Miss Spence from the author, not, indeed, directly, but in the confidence felt by the presenter that in so doing he is fulfilling the wish of the author – viz., circulating his opinions, more especially in such quarters as the present, where they will be accurately considered and tested.' I had also seen the dedication to Harriet Mill's beloved memory of the noble book on *Liberty*. Of her own individual work there was only one specimen extant – an article on the 'Enfranchisement of women',[4] included in Mill's collected essays – very good, certainly, but not so overpoweringly excellent as I expected. Of course, it was an early advocacy of the rights of women, or rather a revival of Mary Wollstonecraft's grand

---

1   Arthur Hardy (1817–1909), lawyer, pastoralist, land speculator with mining interests, and member of Parliament. He settled near the summit of Mount Lofty. One of the founders of the Unitarian Church in Adelaide.
2   Alfred Hardy (c.1814–1870), surveyor and pioneer of South Australia.
3   John Stuart Mill met Harriet Taylor, née Hardy, in 1831, when she was married to John Taylor (not Spence's friend John Taylor). They enjoyed an extremely close friendship for many years. Taylor died in 1849 and in 1851 Mill and Harriet Taylor married. Mill's *Principles of Political Economy* was published in 1848 and *On Liberty*, which he dedicated to Harriet, in 1859, the year after her death.
4   *Enfranchisement of Women* by Harriet Mill was published in 1868.

vindication of the rights of the sex;[5] and this was a reform which Mill himself took up more warmly than proportional representation, and advocated for years before Mr Hare's revelation. For myself, I considered electoral reform on the Hare system of more value than the enfranchisement of women, and was not eager for the doubling of the electors in number, especially as the new voters would probably be more ignorant and more apathetic than the old. I was accounted a weak-kneed sister by those who worked primarily for woman suffrage, although I was as much convinced as they were that I was entitled to a vote, and hoped that I might be able to exercise it before I was too feeble to hobble to the poll. I have unfortunately lost the letter Mr Mill wrote to me about my letters to the *Register*, and my *Plea for Pure Democracy*, but it gave him great pleasure to see that a new idea both of the theory and practice of politics had been taken up and expanded by a woman, and one from that Australian colony, of which he had watched and aided the beginnings, as is seen by the name of Mill Terrace, North Adelaide, today. Indeed, both Hare and Mill told me their first converts were women; and I felt that the absolute disinterestedness of my *Plea*, which was not for myself, but only that the men who were supposed to represent me at the polling booth should be equitably represented themselves, lent weight to my arguments. I have no axe to grind – no political party to serve; so that it was not until the movement for the enfranchisement of women grew too strong to be neglected that I took hold of it at all; and I do not claim any credit for its success in South Australia and the Commonwealth, further than this – that by my writings and my spoken addresses I showed that one woman had a steady grasp on politics and on sociology. In 1865, when I was in England, Mr Mill was permanently resident at Avignon, where his wife died, but he had to come to England to canvass for a seat in Parliament for Westminster as an Independent member, believed at that time to be an advanced Radical, but known to be a philosopher, and an economist of the highest rank in English literature. I had only one opportunity of seeing him personally, and I did not get so much out of him as I expected – he was so eager to know how the colony and colonial people were developing. He asked me about property in land and taxation, and the relations between employers and employés, and I was a little amused and a little alarmed when he said he was glad to get information from such knowledge; but he said he knew I was observant and thoughtful, and what I had seen I had seen well. He was particularly earnest about woman's suffrage, and Miss Taylor, his stepdaughter, said she thought he had made a mistake in asking for the vote for single women only and widows with property and wives who had a separate estate; it would have been more logical to have

---

5   Mary Wollstonecraft, later Godwin, (1759–1797), Anglo-Irish feminist writer, published *Vindication of the Rights of Women* in 1792.

asked for the vote on the same terms as were extended to men. The great man said meekly – 'Well, perhaps I have made a mistake, but I thought with a property qualification the beginning would awake less antagonism.' He said to me that if I was not to return to London till January we were not likely to meet again. He walked with me bareheaded to the gate, and it was farewell for both.

Wise man as Mill was he did not foresee that his greatest object, the enfranchisement of women, would be carried at the antipodes long before there was victory either in England or America. When I received, in 1869, from the publisher, Mr Mill's last book, *The Subjection of Women*, I wrote thanking him for the gift. The reply was as follows:

Avignon, November 28, 1869

Dear Madam

Your letter of August 16 has been sent to me here. The copy of my little book was intended for you, and I had much pleasure in offering it. The movement against women's disabilities generally, and for the suffrage in particular, has made great progress in England since you were last there. It is likely, I think, to be successful in the colonies later than in England, because the want of equality in social advantages between women and men is less felt in the colonies owing, perhaps, to women's having less need of other occupations than those of married life.

I am, dear Madam, yours very truly,
J. S. Mill

I have always held that, though the Pilgrim Fathers ignored the right of the Pilgrim Mothers to the credit of founding the American States – although these women had to take their full share of the toils and hardships and perils of pioneer and frontier life, and had in addition to put up with the Pilgrim Fathers themselves – Australian colonisation was carried out by men who were conscious of the service of their helpmates, and grateful for it. In New Zealand and South Australia, founded on the Wakefield system, where the sexes were almost equal in number, and the immigration was mainly that of families, the first great triumphs for the political enfranchisement of women were won, and through South Australia the women of the Commonwealth obtained the Federal vote for both Houses; whereas even in the sparsely inhabited western states in the United States which have obtained the state vote the Federal vote is withheld from them. But Mill died in 1873, 20 years before New Zealand or Colorado obtained woman's suffrage.

In treating of my one interview with Mr Mill I have carried the narrative down to 1869. With regard to my single meeting with George Eliot, I have to begin in 1865, and conclude even later. Before I left England Mr Williams, of

Smith, Elder and Co., offered me an introduction to George Henry Lewes,[6] and I expressed the hope that it might also include an introduction to George Eliot, whose works I so admired. Mr Lewes being away from home when I called, I requested that the introductory letter of Mr Williams should be taken to George Eliot herself. She received me in the big Priory drawing room, with the grand piano, where she held her receptions and musical evenings; but she asked me if I had any business relating to the article which Mr Williams had mentioned, and I had to confess that I had none. For once I felt myself at fault. I did not get on with George Eliot. She said she was not well, and she did not look well. That strong pale face, where the features were those of Dante or Savanarola, did not soften as Mill's had done. The voice, which was singularly musical and impressive, touched me – I am more susceptible to voices than to features or complexion – but no subject that I started seemed to fall in with her ideas, and she started none in which I could follow her lead pleasantly. It was a short interview, and it was a failure. I felt I had been looked on as an inquisitive Australian desiring an interview upon any pretext; and indeed, next day I had a letter from Mr Williams, in which he told me that, but for the idea that I had some business arrangement to speak of, she would not have seen me at all. So I wrote to Mr Williams that, as I had been received by mistake, I should never mention the interview; but that impertinent curiosity was not at all my motive in going that unlucky day to The Priory.

Years passed by. I read everything, poetry and prose that came from George Eliot's pen, and was so strong an admirer of her that Mr W.L. Whitham,[7] who took charge of the Unitarian Church while our pastor (Mr Woods) had a long furlough in England, asked me to lecture on her works to his Mutual Improvement Society, and I undertook the task with joy. Mr H.G. Turner[8] asked for the MS to publish in the second number of the *Melbourne Review*,[9] a very promising quarterly for politics and literature. I thought that, if I sent the review to George Eliot with a note it might clear me from the suspicion of being a mere vulgar lionhunter. Her answer was as follows:

6   George Henry Lewes (1817–1879), English writer, lived with Mary Ann Evans, who used the pseudonym 'George Eliot', from 1854 until his death.
7   Charles [not W.] Lawrence Whitham (1845–1908), Unitarian minister and educationist arrived in South Australia in 1874 and came to know Spence well. He became Inspector of Schools and was influential in South Australian education.
8   Henry Gyles Turner (1831–1920), Melbourne banker, historian and member of the group which established the *Melbourne Review*. He was a member of the original editorial committee and later editor. See also, above, Chapter VIII, n. 24.
9   *Melbourne Review* 1876–1885, a quarterly review, which dealt with serious topical subjects from a colonial standpoint, with articles by writers of colonial education and experience.

> The Priory,
> North Bank, Regent's Park,
> September 4, 1876.

Dear Madam

Owing to an absence of some months, it was only the other day that I read your kind letter of April 17; and, although I have long been obliged to give up answering the majority of letters addressed to me, I felt much pleased that you have given me an opportunity of answering one from you; for I have always remembered your visit with a regretful feeling that I had probably caused you some pain by a rather unwise effort to give you a reception which the state of my health at the moment made altogether blundering and infelicitous. The mistake was all on my side, and you were not in the least to blame. I also remember that your studies have been of a serious kind, such as were likely to render a judgment on fiction and poetry, or, as the Germans, with better classification, say, in 'Dichtung' in general, quite other than the superficial haphazard remarks of which reviews are generally made. You will all the better understand that I have made it a rule not to read writing about myself. I am exceptionally sensitive and liable to discouragement; and to read much remark about my doings would have as depressing an effect on me as staring in a mirror – perhaps, I may say, of defective glass. But my husband looks at all the numerous articles that are forwarded to me, and kindly keeps them out of my way – only on rare occasions reading to me a passage which he thinks will comfort me by its evidence of unusual insight or sympathy. Yesterday he read your article in *The Melbourne Review*, and said at the end – 'This is an excellently written article, which would do credit to any English periodical', adding the very uncommon testimony, 'I shall keep this'. Then he told me of some passages in it which gratified me by that comprehension of my meaning – that laying of the finger on the right spot – which is more precious than praise, and forthwith he went to lay *The Melbourne Review* in the drawer he assigns to any writing about me that gives him pleasure. For he feels on my behalf more than I feel on my own, at least in matters of this kind. If you come to England again when I happen to be in town I hope that you will give me the pleasure of seeing you under happier auspices than those of your former visit.

I am, dear madam, yours sincerely,
M. G. Lewes[10]

---

10 M.E. Lewes is given as the signature when this letter appears in the nine volume Yale edition of the George Eliot letters, edited by Gordon S. Haight, 1978.

The receipt of this kind and candid letter gave me much pleasure; and, although on the strength of that, I cannot boast of being a correspondent of that great woman, I was able to say that I had seen and talked with her, and that she considered me a competent critic of her work. Mrs Oliphant says that George Eliot's life impelled her to make an involuntary confession – 'How have I been handicapped in life? Should I have done better if I had been kept, like her, in a mental greenhouse and taken care of? I have always had to think of other people and to plan everything – for my own pleasure, it is true, very often, but always in subjection to the necessity which bound me to them. To bring up the boys – my own and Frank's – for the service of God was better than to write a fine novel, if it had been in my power to do so.' There might have been some points in which George Eliot might have envied Mrs Oliphant.

Chapter 10

Return from the Old Country

Before leaving Scotland I arranged that my friend, Mrs Graham of the strenuous life and £30 a year, should undertake the care of my aunts, to their mutual satisfaction. My last days in England were spent in either a thick London fog or an equally undesirable Scotch mist, which shrouded everything in obscurity, and made me long for the sunny skies and the clear atmosphere of Australia. I told my friends that in my country it either rained or let it alone. Indeed, the latest news from all Australia was that it had let it alone very badly, and that the overstocking of stations during the preceding good seasons had led to enormous losses. Sheepfarmers made such large profits in good seasons that they were apt to calculate that it was worth while to run the risk of drought; but experience has shown that overstocking does not really pay. The making of dams, the private and public provision of water in the underground reservoirs by artesian bores, and the facilities for travelling stock by such ways have all lessened the risks which the pioneer pastoralists ran bravely in the old days. An Australian drought can never be as disastrous in the twentieth century as it was in 1866; and South Australia, the Central State, has from the first been a pioneer in development as well as in exploration. The hum of the reaping machine first awoke the echoes in our wheatfields. The stump-jumping plough[1] and the mulleniser,[2] which beats down the scrub or low bush so that it can be burnt, were South Australian inventions, copied elsewhere, which have turned land accounted worthless into prolific wheat fields.

If South Australia was the first of the States to exhaust her agricultural

1 A plough designed to rise and fall over roots and stumps in newly cleared ground. Invented in South Australia by Richard Bower Smith in 1876.
2 To mullenise was to clear land covered in scrub by pushing down the undergrowth with a roller. It was developed by Charles Mullen, an Irish settler, near Adelaide in 1868.

soil, she was the first to restore it by means of fertilisers and the seed drill. When I see the drilled wheat fields I recollect my grandfather's two silver salvers – the prize from the Highland Society for having the largest area of drilled wheat in Scotland – and when I see the grand crops on the Adelaide Plains I recall the opinion that, with anything like a decent rainfall, that soil could grow anything. In 1866 the northern areas had not been opened. The farmers were continuing the process of exhausting the land by growing wheat – wheat – wheat, with the only variety, wheaten hay. I recollect James Burnet's[3] amazement when I said that our horses were fed on wheaten hay. 'What a waste of the great possibilities of a grain harvest!' He was doubtful when I said that with plenty of wheaten hay the horses needed no corn. South Australia, except about Mount Gambier, does not grown oats, though Victoria depends on oaten hay. The British agriculturist thinks that meadow hay is the natural forage for horses and cattle, and for winter turnips are the standby. It was a little amusing to me that I could speak with some authority to skilled and experienced agriculturists, who felt our rivalry at Mark Lane,[4] but who did not dream that with the third great move of Australia towards the markets of the world through cold storage we could send beef, mutton, lamb, poultry, eggs, and all kinds of fruit to the consumers of Europe, and especially of England and its metropolis. I did not see it, any more than the people to whom I talked. I still thought that for meat and all perishable commodities the distance was an insuperable obstacle, and that, except for live stock from America, or canned meat from Australia, the United Kingdom would continue self-supporting on these lines.

I returned to Australia, when this island continent was in the grip of one of the most severe and protracted droughts in its history. The war between Prussia and Austria had begun and ended;[5] the failure of Overend and Gurney[6] and others brought commercial disaster; and my brother, with other bankers, had anxious days and sleepless nights. Some rich men became richer; many poor men went down altogether. Our recovery was slow but sure. In the meantime I found life at home very dull after my interesting experiences abroad. There was nothing to do for proportional representation except to

---

3   James Burnet was James Brodie's steward, 'the son of the old farm steward, John Burnet', Chapter VII.
4   The Corn Exchange was situated in Mark Lane, City of London.
5   War between Prussia and Austria, the 'seven weeks war', took place in 1866. Austria was defeated at the battle of Sadowa.
6   In May 1866 Overend, Gurney & Co., Britain's leading discount company, which had engaged in unsound financial practices, collapsed taking many smaller banks and a railway construction firm with it.

write an occasional letter to the press. So I started another novel, which was published serially in the *Observer*.[7] Mr George Bentley; who published it subsequently in book form, changed its title from *Hugh Lindsay's Guest* to *The Author's Daughter*.[8] But my development as a public speaker was more important than the publication of a fourth novel. Much had been written on the subject of public speaking by men, but so far nothing concerning the capacities of women in that direction. And yet I think all teachers will agree that girls in the aggregate excel boys in their powers of expression, whether in writing, or in speech, though boys may surpass them in such studies as arithmetic and mathematics. Yet law and custom have put a bridle on the tongue of women, and of the innumerable proverbs relating to the sex the most cynical are those relating to her use of language. Her only qualification for public speaking in old days was that she could scold, and our ancestors imposed a salutary check on this by the ducking stool in public, and sticks no thicker than the thumb for marital correction in private. The writer of the Proverbs alludes to the perpetual dropping of a woman's tongue as an intolerable nuisance, and declares that it is better to live on the housetop than with a brawling woman in a wide house. A later writer, describing the virtuous woman, said that on her lips is the law of kindness, and after all this is the real feminine characteristic. As daughter, sister, wife, and mother – what does not the world owe to the gracious words, the loving counsel, the ready sympathy which she expresses? Until recent years, however, these feminine gifts have been strictly kept for home consumption, and only exercised for the woman's family and a limited circle of friends. In 1825, when I first opened my eyes to the world, there were indeed women who displayed an interest in public affairs. My own mother not only felt the keenest solicitude regarding the passing of the Reform Bill, but she took up her pen, and with two letters to the local press, under the signature of 'Grizel Plowter', showed the advantages of the proposed measure. But public speaking was absolutely out of the question for women, and though I was the most ambitious of girls, my desire was to write a great book – not at all to sway an audience.

When I returned from my first visit to England in 1866, I was asked by the committee of the South Australian Institute to write a lecture on my impressions of England,[9] different from the article which had appeared in *The Cornhill Magazine* under that title, but neither the committee nor myself

7   *Hugh Lindsay's Guest* was serialised in the Adelaide weekly newspaper, the *Observer*, from 4 May 1867 to 30 November 1867.
8   *The Author's Daughter*, (Richard Bentley) London, 1868.
9   Extracts from this lecture, 'Reminiscences of a visit to England' by Miss Spence, appeared in the *Register*, 23 October 1866, and the *Observer*, 27 October 1866.

thought of the possibility of my delivering it.[10] My good friend, the late Mr John Howard Clark, editor of the *Register*, kindly offered to read it. I did not go to hear it, but I was told that he had difficulty in reading my manuscript, and that, though he was a beautiful reader, it was not very satisfactory. So I mentally resolved that if I was again asked I should offer to read my own MS. Five years afterwards I was asked for two literary lectures by the same committee, and I chose as my subjects the works of Elizabeth Browning and those of her husband, Robert Browning.[11] Now, I consider that the main thing for a lecturer is to be heard, and a rising young lawyer (now our Chief Justice)[12] kindly offered to take the back seat, and promised to raise his hand if he could not hear. It was not raised once, so I felt satisfied. I began by saying that I undertook the work for two reasons – first, to make my audience more familiar with the writings of two poets very dear to me; and second, to make it easier henceforward for any woman who felt she had something to say to stand up and say it. I felt very nervous, and as if my knees were giving way; but I did not show any nervousness. I read the lecture, but most of the quotations I recited from memory. Not having had any lessons in elocution, I trusted to my natural voice, and felt that in this new role the less gesticulation I used the better. Whether the advice of Demosthenes[13] is rightly translated or not – first requisite, action; second, action; third, action – I am sure that English word does not express the requisite for women. I should rather call it earnestness – a conviction that what you say is worth saying, and worth saying to the audience before you. I had a lesson on the danger of overaction from hearing a gentleman recite in public 'The Dream of Eugene Aram',[14] in which he went through all the movements of killing and burying the murdered man. When a tale is crystallised into a poem it does not require the action of a drama. However little action I may use I never speak in public with gloves on. They interfere with the natural eloquence of the hand. After these lectures I occasionally was asked to give others on literary subjects.

10 Spence's memory is at fault here. An article by Carl Bridge published in *South Australiana*, volume 22, no. 1, March 1983 explains that the committee was anxious for her to give the talk but she declined saying that she was 'scarcely strong-minded enough for that'.
11 The lecture on Elizabeth Barrett Browning was given in the Institute Reading Room on 3 November 1871 and that on Robert Browning on 10 November 1871. Both lectures were reported in the local papers.
12 Sir Samuel James Way (1836–1916), barrister, member of Parliament, Attorney-General, Lieutenant Governor, Chief Justice 1876–1916.
13 Demosthenes (384BC–322BC), Athenian statesman, thought to be the greatest of the Greek orators.
14 'The Dream of Eugene Aram', Poem by Thomas Hood (1799–1845), British writer, editor and poet.

At this time I began to study Latin with my nephew, a boy of 14. He was then an orphan, my youngest and beloved sister Mary having recently died and left her two children to my care.[15] My teacher thought me the more apt pupil, but it was really due more to my command of English than to my knowledge of Latin that I was able to get at the meaning of Virgil and Horace. When it came to Latin composition I was no better than the boy of 14. Before the death of my sister the family invested in land in Trinity Street, College Town, and built a house. Mother had planned the house she moved into when I was six months old, and she delighted in the task, though she said it seemed absurd to build a house in her seventy-ninth year. But she lived in it from January, 1870, till December, 1887, and her youngest daughter lived in it for only ten months.[16] Before that time I had embarked with my friend, Miss Clark, on one of the greatest enterprises of my life – one which led to so much that my friends are apt to say that, if I am recollected at all, it will be in connection with the children of the State and not with electoral reform. But I maintain now, as I maintained then, that the main object of my life is proportional representation, or, to use my brother John's term, effective voting.

15 Charles and Eleanor Wren.
16 Further comment cut by the original editor: 'When the children grew up and wanted an addition it was the old lady who suggested how it was to be made and also that when we were about it it would be a good thing to add a little room for me to write in where I could have my books and my papers.'

CHAPTER 11

WARDS OF THE STATE

In a little book which the State Children's Council requested me to write as a memorial of the great work of Miss C.E. Clark on her retirement at the age of 80,[1] I have given an account of the movement from the beginning down to 1907, which had its origin in South Australia under the leadership of Miss Clark. When I was on my way out from England, Miss Clark wrote a letter to the *Register*, suggesting that the destitute, neglected, or orphaned children should be removed from the Destitute Asylum and placed in natural homes with respectable people; but the great wave which came over England about that time for building industrial schools and reformatories affected South Australia also, and the idea was that, though the children should be removed from the older inmates, it should be to an institution. Land was bought and plans were drawn up for an industrial school at Magill, five miles from Adelaide, when Miss Clark came to me and asked me to help her to take a different course. She enlisted Mrs (afterwards Lady) Colton[2] and Mrs (afterwards Lady) Davenport[3] in the cause, and we arranged for a deputation to the

---

1 *State Children in Australia: a history of boarding-out and its developments*, Adelaide, 1907. More information on this aspect of Spence's work can be found in Susan Magarey, *Unbridling the tongues of women: a biography of Catherine Helen Spence*, (Hale and Iremonger) Sydney, 1985, chapter 4.
2 Mary Colton née Cutting (1822–1898), philanthropist, and campaigner for the rights of women, children and the disadvantaged, president of the Women's Suffrage League and a founder of the Children's Hospital and the Young Women's Christian Association, member of the Boarding-Out Society and of the first State Children's Council. She married John Blacker Cotton, later Sir, in 1844.
3 Margaret Fraser Davenport, née Cleland (1819–1902), member of the Boarding-Out Society and of the first State Children's Council. Married Samuel Davenport, later Sir, in 1842.

Caroline Emily Clark, c.1885,
photograph courtesy of the State Library of South Australia, SLSA: B 47543

Minister; Howard Clark, Neville Blyth,[4] and Mr C.B. Young[5] joined us. We offered to find country homes and provide lady visitors, but our request was simply scouted. As we did not offer to bear any of the cost, it would be absurd to give us any share in the administration. Children would only be given homes for the sake of the money paid, and Oliver Twist's was held up as the sort of apprenticeship likely to be secured for pauper children. So we had to play the waiting game. The school built to accommodate 230 children was on four floors, though there were 40 acres of good land. It was so popular that, though only 130 went in at first, in two years it was so full that there was talk of adding a wing. This was our opportunity, and the same men and women went on another deputation, and this time we prevailed, and were allowed to place out the overflow as an experiment; and not only the Boarding-Out Committee, but the official heads of the Destitute Department, were surprised and delighted with the good homes we secured for five shillings a week, and with the improvement in health, in intelligence, and in happiness that resulted from putting children into natural homes. What distinguishes work for children in Australia from what is done elsewhere is that it is national, and not philanthropic. The State is in *loco parentis*, and sees that what the child needs are a home and a mother – that, if the home and the mother are good, the child shall be kept there; but that vigilant inspection is needed, voluntary or official – better to have both. Gradually the Magill School was emptied, and the children were scattered. Up to the age of 13 the home was subsidised, but when by the education law the child was free from school attendance, and went to service, the supervision continued until the age of 18 was reached. For nearly 14 years, from 1872 to 1886, the Boarding-Out Society pursued its modest labours as auxiliary to the Destitute Board. Our volunteer visitors reported in duplicate – one copy for the official board, and one for the unofficial committee. When the method was inaugurated, Mr T.S. Reed, Chairman of the Board, was completely won over.[6] We had nothing to do with the reformatories, except that our visitors went to see those placed out at service in their neighbourhood.

Our success attracted attention elsewhere. The late Dr Andrew Garran,[7]

---

4 Neville Blyth (1825–1890), ironmonger, member of Parliament, minister for Education, member of the Boarding-Out Society, brother of Sir Arthur Blyth.
5 Charles Burney Young (1824–1904), pastoralist, politician, vigneron, Governor of St Peter's College and member of the Board of Education.
6 Thomas Sadler Reed, chairman and chief executive of the Destitute Board.
7 Andrew Garran (1825–1901), journalist and politician. He arrived in Adelaide 1851 and was a preacher, tutor and co-editor of the *Register*. He moved to Sydney in 1856, later became editor of the *Sydney Morning Herald* and active in public affairs. He married Mary Isham Sabine in 1854.

who was on the *Register* when I went to England, had moved to Sydney in my absence, and was on the staff of the *Sydney Morning Herald*. When Miss Clark went to England in 1877, after her mother's death, Dr Garran wrote to me for some account of our methods, and of their success, physical, moral, and financial. Dr Garran came out with Mr G.F. Angas and the Australian Constitution in 1851 in search of health and work, both of which he found here. The first pages of my four volumes of newspaper cuttings are filled with two long articles, 'The Children of the State',[8] and this started the movement in New South Wales, led by Mrs Garran, née Sabine, and Mrs Jefferis, wife of the leading Congregational minister,[9] moved from Adelaide to Sydney. Professor Henry Pearson[10] asked me a year or two later to give similar information to the Melbourne *Age*. Subsequently I wrote on this subject, by request, to Queensland, New Zealand, and I think also Tasmania, where we were imitated first, but where there are still to be found children of the State in institutions. In Victoria and New South Wales a vigorous policy emptied these buildings, which were used for other public purposes, and the children were dispersed. The innovation which at first was scouted as utopian, next suspected as leading to neglect, or even unkindness – for people would only take these children for what they could make out of them – was found to be so beneficial that nobody in Australia would like to return to the barrack home or the barrack school. If the inspection had been from the first merely official, public opinion would have been suspicious and sceptical, but when ladies saw the children in these homes, and watched how the dull faces brightened, and the languid limbs became alert after a few weeks of ordinary life – when the cheeks became rosier, and the eyes had new light in them; when they saw that the foster parents took pride in their progress at school, and made them handy

---

8 Spence's writings at this time were 'Boarding-out system of South Australia', Parts I, II, III, *Sydney Morning Herald*, 25, 26, 27 March 1878; 'The Boarding-out system in South Australia', by one who assists in their management, *Age*, 2 September 1878; 'Children of the State in South Australia', unsigned leader, *Register*, 14 February 1881; 'Children of the State in South Australia', by one who takes part in their management, *Queenslander*, 26 November 1881.

9 Marian Jefferis, née Turner (d.1931), philanthropist, supporter of the boarding-out system. James Jefferis (1833–1917), leading Congregational minister. They moved from Adelaide to Sydney 1877, but returned to Adelaide in 1894.

10 Charles Henry Pearson (1830–1894), historian, politician and education reformer, professor of modern history at King's College, London. He emigrated to Australia and after a short time in South Australia went to Melbourne where he lectured in history at Melbourne University, became the first headmaster of Melbourne's Presbyterian Ladies College and a member of Parliament. He advocated reform in education and women's rights. He was one of Spence's friends.

about the house, as they could never be at an institution, where everything is done at the sound of a bell or the stroke of a clock – these ladies testified to what they knew, and the public believed them. In other English-speaking countries boarding-out in families is sometimes permitted; but here, under the Southern Cross, it is the law of the land that children shall not be brought up in institutions, but in homes; that the child whose parent is the State shall have as good schooling as the child who has parents and guardians; that every child shall have, not the discipline of routine and redtape, but free and cheerful environment of ordinary life, preferably in the country – going to school with other young fellow-citizens, going to church with the family in which he is placed, having the ordinary pleasures of common life; but guarded from injustice, neglect, and cruelty by effective and kindly supervision. This movement, originated in South Australia, and with all its far-reaching developments and expansions, is due to the initiative of one woman of whom the State is justly proud – Miss Caroline Emily Clark.

Even while we were only a Boarding-Out Committee it was found necessary to have one paid inspector; but there was great dissatisfaction with the Boys' Reformatory – which had been located in an old leaky hulk,[11] where the boys could learn neither seamanship nor anything else – and with some other details of the management of the destitute poor, and a commission with the Chief Justice as Chairman, was appointed to make enquiries and suggest reforms.[12] The result was the separation of the young from the old absolutely; and a new body, the State Children's Council, of 12 men and women of nearly equal proportions, had authority over the reformatories, as well as what was called the industrial school, which was to be reduced to a mere receiving home, and all the children placed out, either on subsidy or at service.[13] Most of the old committee were appointed; but, to my great joy, Dr Edward C. Stirling[14] and Mr James Smith,[15] the most enlightened man on the Destitute

---

11 The leaking wooden hulk *Fitzjames*, unseaworthy since 1866, was moored off the coast of Semaphore and used as a quarantine vessel and a boys' reformatory. It housed male juvenile offenders and destitute children.

12 Royal Commission into the Destitute Act, chaired by Chief Justice, Sir Samuel Way, 1883–1885.

13 The State Children's Council was set up in 1886.

14 Edward Charles Stirling, later Sir, (1848–1919), eldest son of Spence's friend Edward Stirling, surgeon, first professor of physiology at the University of Adelaide, member of Parliament, founder and president of South Australian Women's Suffrage League, and from 1884–1912, Director of the South Australian Museum.

15 James Smith (1820–1900), active in public affairs, one of the founders of the Executor, Trustee and Agency Company, member of the Destitute Board and State Children's Council.

Board, were among the new members. We had a paid staff, with a most able secretary – Mr. J.B. Whiting.[16]

Dr Stirling was unanimously voted in as President, and we felt we began our new duties under the most promising auspices. But, alas, in two years there was so much friction between the council and the Ministry that we all resigned in a body, except Mrs Colton (who was in England) and Mrs Farr.[17] We were fighting the battle of the unpaid boards, and we were so strong in the public estimation that we might have won the victory. The Government had relieved children on the petition of parents, contrary to the strong recommendation of the council. Although the commission had declared that the reformatory boys should be removed at once from the hulk *Fitzjames*, they were still kept there, and the only offer of accommodation given was to share the Magill Industrial School with the reformatory girls. Now, this the council would not hear of, for we felt that the Government plans for separate entrances and separate staircases were absolutely futile and ridiculous for keeping apart these two dangerous classes in a single building.[18] The Government gave way on the point of providing a separate building for the reformatory girls; and the committee, with the exception of Dr Stirling and Mr James Smith – our two strongest members – were reappointed. The official staff was increased by the appointment of clerks and inspectors, many of them women, who have always given every satisfaction, and who justify the claim made that women's work is conscientious and thorough.

More departments were gradually added to our sphere of action. The separate trial of juvenile delinquents was strongly advocated by the council. Miss Clark and Mr C.H. Goode[19] were particularly keen on the introduction of Children's Courts. In this reform South Australia led the world, and in the new Act of 1896, after six years of tentative work, it became compulsory to try

---

16 John Beeby Whiting, later secretary to the Agent General in London.

17 Julia Warren Farr née Ord (1825–1914), worker for the disadvantaged and founder of Farr House, a home for orphan girls and the Home for Incurables, now the Julia Farr Centre. Her husband, Rev. George Henry Farr, became Archdeacon of Adelaide and Headmaster of St Peter's College.

18 This sentence, before the original editing, read 'Now this the council would not hear of, and that was my main reason for resigning. Mrs Farr asked me to go up with Mr Owen Smyth, Superintendent of Public Buildings, to consider his plans of separate entrances, and separate staircases, and both I who had resigned, and Mrs Farr who had not, said it was absolutely futile and ridiculous to attempt to keep separate these two dangerous classes in a single building.'

19 Charles Henry Goode, later Sir, (1827–1922), merchant and philanthropist, with a special interest in young people.

offenders under 18 at the Children's Court in the city and suburbs, and in the Magistrate's room in the country. The methods of organisation and control vary in the different States of the Commonwealth, but on one point the six are all agreed – that dependent and delinquent children are a national asset and national responsibility, and any forward step anywhere has every chance of being copied. The result of Children's Courts and probation has been that, while the population of the State has greatly increased, the committals to the Gaol and for penal servitude have steadily decreased, and the Boys' Reformatory has been reduced to one-third of the number in earlier days. There are, of course, many factors in all directions of social betterment, but the substitution of homes for institutions, and of probation carefully watched for summary punishment, are, in my opinion, the largest factors in this State. The affection between children and their foster parents is often lifelong; and we see thousands who were taken from bad parents and evil environments taking their place in the industrial world, and filling it well. The movement in South Australia initiated by Miss Clark spread from State to State, and the happy thought of the President and Secretary of the Council that I should write an account of 'Boarding-out and its Developments' as a memorial of her great work bore fruit in the legislation of the United Kingdom itself. A letter I received from Mr Herbert Samuel, then Under-Secretary of State in the British Government, was gratifying, both to the council and to me:–

> Home Office, Whitehall, S.W.,
> August 5, 1907.

Dear Madam – I have just read your little book on 'State Children in Australia;' and, although a stranger to you, would venture to write to thank you for the very valuable contribution you have made to the literature on the subject. The present Government in England are already engaged in promoting the more kindly and more effective methods of dealing with destitute, neglected, or delinquent children, which are already so widely adopted in South Australia. We are passing through Parliament this year a Bill to enable a system of probation officers, both paid and voluntary, to be established throughout the country, for dealing not indeed with child offenders alone, but with adult offenders also, who may be properly amenable to that treatment. And next year we propose to introduce a comprehensive Children's Bill, which has been entrusted to my charge, in which we hope to be able to include some of the reforms you have at heart. In the preparation of that Bill the experience of your colony and the account of it which you have published will be of no small assistance.

> Yours sincerely,
> Herbert Samuel.

Another department of our work was for the protection of infant life, and this we took over from the Destitute Board, where some unique provisions had been initiated by Mr James Smith. The Destitute Asylum was the last refuge of the old and incapacitated poor, but it never opened its doors to the able bodied. In the Union Workhouse in England room is always found for friendless and penniless to come there for confinement, who leave as soon as they are physically strong enough to take their burden – their little baby – in their arms and face the world again. In Adelaide these women were in 1868 divided into two classes, one for girls who had made their first slip – girls weak, but very rarely wicked – so as to separate them from women who came for a second or third time, who were cared for with their infants in the general asylum. Mr James Smith obtained in 1881 legislation to empower the Destitute Board to make every woman sign an agreement to remain with her infant, giving it the natural nourishment, for six months. This has saved many infant lives, and has encouraged maternal affection. The Destitute Board kept in its hand the issuing of licences, and appointed a lady to visit the babies till they were two years old, and did good work; but when that department was properly turned over to the State Children's Council there was even more vigilance exercised, and the death rate among these babies, often handicapped before birth, and always artificially fed after, was reduced to something less than the average of all babies. We have been fortunate in our chief inspectress of babies. Her character has uplifted the licensed foster mothers, and the two combined have raised the real mothers. It is surprising how few such babies are thrown on the State. The department does not pay any board or find any clothing for these infants. It, however, pays for supervision and pays for a lady doctor, so that there need be no excuse for not calling in medical assistance if it is felt to be needed. Occasionally a visitor from other States or from England is allowed as a great favour to see, not picked cases, but the ordinary run, of the homes of foster mothers, and the question, 'Where and how do you get such women?' is asked. We have weeded out the inferiors, and our instructions with regard to feeding and care are so definite, and found to be so sound, that the women take a pride in the health and the beauty of the little ones; and besides they keep up the love of the real mother by the care they give them. A recent Act has raised the age of supervision of illegitimate babies from two to seven years, and this has necessitated the appointment of an additional inspectress. In South Australia baby farming has been extinguished, and in the other States legislation on similar lines has been won, and they are in process of gradually weeding out bad and doubtful foster mothers. And the foster fathers are often as fond of the babies as their wives – and as softhearted. 'Did you see that the poor girl had on broken boots this weather?' said he. 'Yes, it's a pity; but we are poor folks ourselves – we can't help it,' said she. 'Let her off the 6s for a fortnight, so as she can get a pair of sound boots for her feet, we'll worry through without it.' And they did. The extreme solicitude of the State Children's Department, as carried out by its zealous officers, for the life and the wellbeing of their babies serves them in public extenuation, and the children are often so pretty and engaging that they win love all round. A grown-up son in the home was very fond of little Lily. 'Mother, will you get Lily a cream coat, such as I see other babies wearing, and I will pay for it.'

A most pathetic story I can tell of a girl respectably connected in the country, who had been cast off in disgrace, and came to town to take a place, committing her infant to a good foster mother. When he was old enough to move about, and was just trying to walk, the mother was taken dangerously ill to the Adelaide Hospital. The foster mother thought the girl's father should be sent for, and wrote to him giving her own address, but not disclosing her connection with the patient. The father of the girl came, and was told that he had better be accompanied by his informant, who could prepare the sick woman for the interview. The little boy was running about, and the old man took him on his knee while the woman got ready to go out. 'You must come with us, Sonny,' said she. 'I can't leave you alone in the house.' 'A very fine little chap. Your youngest, I suppose. I can see he is a great pet.' 'No,' said the woman slowly, 'he is not my son, he is your grandson.' 'Good God, my grandson.' Then, clasping the little fellow to his heart, he said, 'I'll never part with him.' The mother recovered, and was taken home with her child and forgiven. Such is often the work of the good foster mother. In all the successes of the irresponsible committee and of the responsible State Children's Council the greatest factor has been the character of the good women who have been mothers to the little ones. The fears that only self-interest could induce them to take on the neglected and uncontrollable children were not borne out by experience, and in the case of these babies not really illegitimate – it is the parents who deserve that title, no infant can – the mother's instinct came out very strong. At a conference of workers among dependent children, held in Adelaide in May, 1909, when all six States were represented, a Western Australian representative said that the average family home was not so good for its natural circle that it could be depended on for strangers; but our answer was that, both for the children of the State and for the babies who were not State children, we insisted on something better than the average home, and through our inspection we sought to improve it still further. We have not reached perfection by any means. When we begin to think we have, we are sure to fall back. Another good office the State Children's Department fills is that of advice gratis. One of the most striking chapters in Gen. Booth's

Darkest England[20] dealt with the helplessness of the poor and the ignorant in the face of difficulties, of injustice, and of extortion. When I was in Chicago in 1893 I saw that the first university settlement, that of Hull House, presided over by Miss Jane Addams (St Jane some of her friends call her) was the centre to which the poor American, German, Italian, or other alien went for advice as well as practical help.[21] A word in season was often of more value than dollars. To be told what to do or what not to do at a crisis when decision is so important may be salvation for the pocket or for the character.

---

20 William Booth (1829–1912), founder in England of the Volunteer Army, which in 1878 became known as the Salvation Army, author of *In Darkest England and the Way Out*, London, 1890.

21 Hull House in Chicago was founded in 1889 by Jane Addams and Ellen Starr to encourage female college graduates in the United States of America to work with the poor and struggling. Addams (1860–1935), sociologist and author, became known as the founder of modern American settlement work. She shared the Nobel peace prize in 1931.

CHAPTER 12

PREACHING, FRIENDS, AND WRITING

My life now became more interesting and varied. A wider field for my journalistic capabilities was open to me, and I also took part in the growth of education, both spiritual and secular. The main promoters of the ambitious literary periodical the *Melbourne Review*, to which I became a contributor, were Mr Henry Gyles Turner (the banker),[1] Mr Alexander Sutherland, M.A. (author of *The History of Australia* and several other books),[2] and A. Patchett Martin (the litterateur).[3] It lived for nine years, and produced a good deal of creditable writing, but it never was able to pay its contributors, because it never attained such a circulation as would attract advertisements. The reviews and magazines of the present day depend on advertisements. They cheapen the price so as to gain a circulation, which advertisers cater for. I think my second article[4] was on the death of Sir Richard Hanson (one of the original South Australian Literary Society, which met in London before South Australia existed). At the time of his death he was Chief Justice. He was the author of two books of Biblical criticism[5] –

---

1   Henry Gyles Turner (1831–1920), Melbourne banker, historian and member of the group which established the *Melbourne Review*. He was a member of the original editorial committee and later editor. He was a founding member of the Melbourne Unitarian Church. His sister, Martha Turner, later Webster, greatly influenced Spence.
2   Alexander Sutherland (1852–1902), author, journalist and schoolmaster, Registrar at Melbourne University and lecturer in English Language and Literature. One of the editors of the *Melbourne Review*.
3   Arthur Patchett Martin (1851–1902), journalist, author and poet, one of the founders, and an editor, of the *Melbourne Review*.
4   'Sir Richard Hanson' by C.H. Spence, *Melbourne Review*, 1876, vol. 1, pp. 427–50.
5   Sir Richard Davies Hanson, *The Jesus of History*, (Williams & Norgate) London, 1869; Sir Richard Davies Hanson, *The Apostle Paul and the Preaching of Chrisianity in the Primitive Church*, (Williams & Norgate) London, 1875.

The Jesus of History and *Paul and the Primitive Church* – and I undertook to deal with his life and work. About that time there was one of those periodic outbursts of Imperialism in the Australian colonies – not popular or general, but among politicians – on the question of how the colonies could obtain practical recognition in the Legislature of the United Kingdom. Each of the colonies felt that Downing Street inadequately represented its claims and its aspirations, and there were several articles in the *Melbourne Review* suggesting that these colonies should be allowed to send members to the House of Commons. This, I felt, would be inadmissible; for, unless we were prepared to bear our share of the burdens, we had no right to sit in the taxing Assembly of the United Kingdom. The only House in which the colonies, small or great, could be represented was the House of Lords; and it appeared to me that, with a reformed House of Lords, this would be quite practicable. An article in *Fraser's Magazine*,[6] 'Why not the Lords, too?' had struck me much, and the lines on which it ran greatly resemble those laid down by Lord Rosebery[7] for lessening its number and improving in character the unwieldy hereditary House of Peers; but neither that writer nor Lord Rosebery grasped the idea that I made prominent in an article I wrote for the *Review*, which was that the reduction of the peers to 200, or any other number ought to be made on the principle of proportional representation, because otherwise the majority of the peers, being Conservative, an election on ordinary lines would result in a selection of the most extreme Conservatives in the body. My mother had pointed out to me that the 16 representative Scottish peers elected by those who have not a seat as British peers, for the duration of each Parliament, were the most Tory of the Tories, and that the same could be said of the 28 representative peers for Ireland elected for life. So, though the House of Lords contains a respectable minority of Liberals, under no system of exclusively majority representation could any of them be chosen among the 200. I had the same idea of life peers to be added from the ranks of the professions, of science, and of literature, unburdened by the weight and cost of an hereditary title, that Lord Rosebery has; and into such a body I thought that representatives of the great self-governing colonies could enter, so that information about our resources, our politics, and our sociology might be available, and might permeate the press. But, greatly to my surprise, my article was sent back, but was afterwards accepted by *Fraser's Magazine*.[8]

6   *Fraser's Magazine for Town and Country*. An influential London periodical. In various forms it ran from 1857–1905.
7   Sir Archibald John Primrose, fourth Earl of Rosebery (1783–1868), Privy Councillor, supporter of the Reform Bill of 1842.
8   'Australian Federation and Imperial Union', *Fraser's Magazine*, New Series, volume XVL, pp. 526–537. Article signed S.

This was better for me, for what would have been published for nothing in the *Melbourne Review* brought me £8 15s from a good English magazine. I continued to write for this review, until it ceased to exist, in 1885, literary and political articles. The former included a second one on 'George Eliot's Life and Work', and one on 'Honoré de Balzac', which many of my friends thought my best literary effort.[9]

It was through Miss Martha Turner[10] that I was introduced to her brother and to the *Melbourne Review*. She was at that time pastor of the Unitarian Church in Melbourne. She had during the long illness of Rev. Mr Higginson helped her brother with the services. At first she wrote sermons for him to deliver, but on some occasions when he was indisposed she read her own compositions. Fine reader as Mr H.G. Turner is he did not come up to her, and especially he could not equal her in the presentment of her own thoughts. The congregation on the death of Mr Higginson asked Miss Turner to accept the pastorate. She said she could conduct the services, but she absolutely declined to do the pastoral duties – visiting especially. She was licensed to conduct marriage services and baptised (or, as we call it, consecrated) children to the service of Almighty God and to the service of man. During the absence of our pastor[11] for a long holiday in England Mr C.L. Whitham, afterwards an education inspector, took his place for two years, and he arranged for an exchange of three weeks with Miss Turner. She was the first woman I ever heard in the pulpit. I was thrilled by her exquisite voice, by her earnestness, and by her reverence. I felt as I had never felt before that if women are excluded from the Christian pulpit you shut out more than half of the devoutness that is in the world. Reading George Eliot's description of Dinah Morris[12] preaching Methodism on the green at Hayslope had prepared me in a measure, but when I heard a highly educated and exceptionally able woman conducting the services all through, and especially reading the Scriptures of the Old and New Testaments with so much intelligence that they seemed to take on new meaning, I felt how much the world had been losing for so many centuries. She twice exchanged with Adelaide – the second time when Mr Woods had returned – and it was the beginning to me of a close friendship.

9   'George Eliot's Life and Works', *Melbourne Review*, vol. 10, no. 39, pp. 217–44, 1885; 'Honoré de Balzac: a psychological study', *Melbourne Review*, vol. 4, pp. 348–57, 1879.
10 Martha Turner, (born 1839), sister of Henry Gyles Turner, preacher in the Unitarian Church, and thought to be the first female preacher in Australia. She married Webster in 1878.
11 John Crawford Woods.
12 Dinah Morris in George Eliot's *Adam Bede*, (William Blackwood and Sons) Edinburgh and London, 1859.

Imitation, they say, is the sincerest flattery; and when a similar opportunity was offered to me during an illness of Mr Woods, when no layman was available, I was first asked to read a sermon of Martineau's,[13] and then I suggested that I might give something of my own. My first original sermon was on 'Enoch and Columbus', and my second on 'Content, discontent, and uncontent'. I suppose I have preached more than a hundred times in my life, mostly in the Wakefield Street pulpit; but in Melbourne and Sydney I am always asked for help; and when I went to America in 1893–94 I was offered seven pulpits – one in Toronto, Canada, and six in the United States. The preparation of my sermons – for, after the first one I delivered, they were always original – has always been a joy and delight to me, for I prefer that my subjects as well as their treatment shall be as humanly helpful as it is possible to make them. In Sydney particularly I have preached to fine audiences. On one occasion I remember preaching in a large hall, as the Unitarian Church could not have held the congregation. It was during the campaign that Mrs. Young[14] and I conducted in Sydney in 1900, and we had spent the day – a delightful one – with the present Sir George and Lady Reid[15] at their beautiful home at Strathfield, and returned in time to take the evening service at Sydney. I spoke on the advantages of international peace, and illustrated my discourse with arguments, drawn from the South African War,[16] which was then in progress. I seized the opportunity afforded me of speaking some plain home truths on the matter. I was afterwards referred to by the *Sydney Bulletin* as 'the gallant little old lady who had more moral courage in her little finger than all the Sydney ministers had in their combined anatomies.' For one of my sermons I wrote an original parable, which pleased my friends so much that I include it in the account of my life's work.

> And it came to pass after the five days of Creation which were periods of unknown length of time that God took the soul, the naked soul, with which He was to endow the highest of his creatures – into Eden to look with Him on the work which He had accomplished. And the Soul could see, could

---

13 James Martineau (1805–1900), English Unitarian minister and educator, influential theologian and philosopher, brother of Harriet Martineau.
14 Jeanne Forster Young (born Sarah Jane Forster) (1866–1955), close friend and ally of Spence, who accompanied Spence on tours for effective voting, and was secretary of Effective Voting League. She completed Spence's *Autobiography* after Spence's death, and published *Catherine Helen Spence: a study and an appreciation*, (Lothian) Melbourne, 1937.
15 Sir George Houston Reid (1845–1918), barrister, free trader, Premier of New South Wales, Prime Minister of Australia.
16 War between the Boers and the English in South Africa, 1899–1902.

hear, could understand, though there were neither eyes, nor ears, nor limbs, nor bodily organs to do its bidding. And God said, 'Soul, thou shalt have a body as these creatures that thou seest around thee have. Thou art to be king, and rule over them all. Thy mission is to subdue the earth, and make it fruitful and more beautiful than it is even now, in thus its dawn. Which of all these living creatures wouldst thou resemble?' And the Soul looked, and the Soul listened, and the Soul understood. The beauty of the birds first attracted him, and their songs were sweet, and their loving care of their young called forth a response in the Prophetic Soul. But the sweet singers could not subdue the earth – nay, even the strongest voice could not. Then the Soul gazed on the lion in his strength; on the deer in his beauty. He saw the large-eyed bull with the cow by his side, licking her calf. The stately horse, the huge elephant, the ungainly camel – could any of these subdue the earth? He looked down, and they made it shake with their heavy tread, but the Soul knew that the earth could not be subdued by them. Then he saw a pair of monkeys climbing a tree – the female had a little one in her arms. Where the birds had wings, and the beasts four legs planted on the ground, the monkeys had arms, and, at the end of each, hands, with five fingers; they gathered nuts and cracked them, and picked out the kernels, throwing the shells away – the mother caressed her young one with gentle fingers. The Soul saw also the larger ape with its almost upright form. 'Ah!' sighed the Soul, 'they are not beautiful like the other creatures, neither are they so strong as many of them. But their forelimbs, with hands and fingers to grasp with, are what I need to subdue the earth, for they will be the servants who can best obey my will. Let me stand upright and gaze upward, and this is the body that I choose.' And God said, 'Soul, thou hast chosen well, Thou shalt be larger and stronger than these creatures thou seest; thou shalt stand upright, and look upward and onward. And the Soul can create beauty for itself, when it shines through the body.' And it was so, and Adam stood erect and gave names to all other creatures.

In the seventies the old education system, or want of system, was broken up, and a complete department of public instruction was constructed. Mr J.A. Hartley,[17] head master of Prince Alfred College, was placed at the head of it, and a vigorous policy was adopted. When the Misses Davenport Hill came out to visit aunt and cousins, I visited with them and Miss Clark the Grote Street

---

17 John Anderson Hartley (1844–1896), educationist, headmaster of Prince Alfred College, later Inspector-General of Schools in South Australia from 1878 to 1895 and permanent head of the South Australian Education Department. Hartley became a personal friend of Spence who lived near him.

Model School, and I was delighted with the new administration. I hoped that the instruction of the children of the people would attract the poor gentlewomen who were so badly paid as governesses in families or in schools; but my hope has not been at all adequately fulfilled. The *Register* had been most earnest in its desire for a better system of public education. The late Mr John Howard Clark, its then editor, wanted some articles on the education of girls, and he applied to me to do them, and I wrote two leading articles on the subject, and another on the 'Ladder of Learning,' from the elementary school to the university, as exemplified in my native country where ambitious lads cultivated literature on a little oatmeal.[18] For an Adelaide University was in the air, and took form owing to the benefactions of Capt. (afterwards Sir Walter Watson) Hughes,[19] and Mr (afterwards Sir Thomas) Elder.[20] But the opposition to Mr Hartley, which set in soon after his appointment, and his supposed drastic methods, and autocratic attitude, continued. I did not know Mr Hartley personally, but I knew he had been an admirable head teacher, and the most valuable member of the Education Board which preceded the revolution. I knew, too, that the old school teachers were far inferior to what were needed for the new work, and that you cannot make an omelette without breaking eggs. A letter which I wrote to Mr Hartley, saying that I desired to help him in any way in my power, led to a friendship which lasted till his lamented death in 1896. I fancied at the time that my aid did him good, but I think now that the opposition had spent its force before I put in my oar by some letters to the press. South Australians became afterwards appreciative of the work done by Mr Hartley, and proud of the good position this State took in matters educational among the sister States under the Southern Cross.

It was due to Mrs Webster's[21] second visit to Adelaide to exchange with Mr Woods that I made the acquaintance of Mr and Mrs R. Barr Smith.[22] They went to the church and were shown into my seat, and Mrs Smith asked me to bring the eloquent preacher to Torrens Park to dine there. I discovered that they had long wanted to know me, but I was out of society. I recollect

18 Spence wrote a series of unsigned articles for the *Register* on education for girls early in 1877.
19 Walter Watson Hughes (1803–1887), pastoralist, mine-owner and public benefactor.
20 Sir Thomas Elder (1818–1897), mine owner, pastoralist, member of Parliament, and public benefactor. Elder Hall, Elder Conservatorium, and Elder Park, named after him, were supported by his gifts.
21 The married name of the preacher Martha Turner.
22 Robert Barr Smith (1824–1915), mine owner, pastoralist, public benefactor, married Thomas Elder's sister, Joanna (1835–1919). Seven of their thirteen children survived to adulthood. They were much travelled literary people. Torrens Park became their home in 1874. It is now part of Scotch College.

afterwards going to the office to see Mr Smith on some business or other, when he was out, and meeting Mr Elder instead. He pressed on me the duty of going to see Mrs Black, a lady from Edinburgh, who had come out with her sons and daughter. Mr Barr Smith came in, and his brother-in-law said, 'I have just been telling Miss Spence she should go and call on the Blacks.' 'Tom,' said Mr Barr Smith, 'we have been just 20 years making the acquaintance of Miss Spence. About the year 1899 Miss Spence will be dropping in on the Blacks.' What a house Torrens Park was for books. There was no other customer of the book shops equal to the Torrens Park family. Rich men and women often buy books for themselves, and for rare old books they will give big prices; but the Barr Smiths bought books in sixes and in dozens for the joy of giving them where they would be appreciated. On my literary side Mrs Barr Smith, a keen critic herself, fitted in with me admirably, and what I owed to her in the way of books for about ten years cannot be put on paper, and in my journalistic work she delighted. Other friendships, both literary and personal, were formed in the decade which started the elementary schools and the University. The first Hughes professor of English literature was the Rev. John Davidson,[23] of Chalmers Church, married to Harriet,[24] daughter of Hugh Miller, the self-taught geologist and journalist.

On the day of the inauguration of the University the Davidsons asked Miss Clark and myself to go with them, and there I met Miss Catherine Mackay (now Mrs Fred Martin), from Mount Gambier.[25] I at first thought her the daughter of a wealthy squatter of the south-east, but when I found she was a litterateur trying to make a living by her pen, bringing out a serial tale, 'Bohemian Born,' and writing occasional articles, I drew to her at once. So long as the serial tale lasted she could hold her own; but no one can make a living at occasional articles in Australia, and she became a clerk in the Education Office, but still cultivated literature in her leisure hours. She has published two novels — *An Australian Girl* and *The Silent Sea*[26] — which so good a judge as

23 John Davidson (1834–1881), minister of the Free Church of Scotland, was called to Chalmers Church in Adelaide, and later became Professor of English Literature and Mental and Moral Philosophy at the University of Adelaide.

24 Harriet Miller Davidson née Miller (1839–1883), poet, novelist and short story writer. She frequently contributed to the *Register* and *Observer*.

25 Catherine Edith Macauley Mackay (1847–1937) teacher, poet and novelist. Born in Scotland, she lived many years in the south east of South Australia. She married Frederick Martin 1882. 'A Bohemian Born' (1878), 'After Many Years' (1878) and 'Breaking the Law' (1879) were serialised in South Australian newspapers.

26 Catherine Martin, *An Australian Girl*, (Bentley and Sons) London, 1890; Catherine Martin, *The Silent Sea*, by Mrs Alick Macleod [pseud], (Bentley) London, 1892.

F.W.H. Myers[27] pronounced to be on the highest level ever reached in Australian fiction, and in that opinion I heartily concur. I take a very humble second place beside her, but in the seventies I wrote *Gathered In*, which I believed to be my best novel – the novel into which I put the most of myself, the only novel I wrote with tears of emotion.[28] Mrs Oliphant says that Jeanie Deans[29] is more real to her than any of her own creations, and probably it is the same with me, except for this one work. From an old diary of the fifties, when my first novels were written I take this extract: 'Queer that I who have such a distinct idea of what I approve in flesh-and-blood men, should only achieve in pen and ink a set of impossible people, with an absurd muddy expression of gloom, instead of sublime depth as I intended. Men novelists' women are as impossible creations as my men, but there is this difference – their productions satisfy them, mine fail to satisfy me.' But in my last novel – still unpublished – I felt quite satisfied that I had at last achieved my ambition to create characters that stood out distinctly and real. Miss Clark took the MS to England, but she could not get either Bentley or Smith Elder, or Macmillan to accept it.

On the death of Mr John Howard Clark, which took place at this time, Mr John Harvey Finlayson[30] was left to edit the *Register*, and I became a regular outside contributor to the *Register* and the *Observer*. He desired to keep up and if possible improve the literary side of the papers, and felt that the loss of Mr Clark might be in some measure made up if I gave myself wholeheartedly to the work. Leading articles were to be written at my own risk. If they suited the policy of the paper they would be accepted, otherwise not. What a glorious opening for my ambition and for my literary proclivities came to me in July 1878, when I was in my fifty-third year! Many leading articles were rejected, but not one literary or social article. Generally these last appeared in both daily and weekly papers. I recollect the second original social article I wrote was on 'Equality as an influence on society and manners',[31] suggested by Matthew Arnold.[32] The much-travelled

---

27 Frederic William Henry Myers (1843–1901), influential English poet and essayist, who was one of the founders of the Society for Psychical Research.
28 *Gathered In* was serialised September 1881–April 1882 in the *Queenslander* and the *Brisbane Courier*, and in South Australia in the *Observer*. It was first published in book form in 1977 by Sydney University Press.
29 *The Heart of Midlothian* by Sir Walter Scott 1818.
30 John Harvey Finlayson (1843–1915), South Australian born journalist who joined the *Register* shortly after leaving school and was later its editor for twenty years.
31 'Equality as an influence on society and manners', *Register*, 9 August 1878.
32 Matthew Arnold (1822–1888), Inspector of Schools, Professor of Poetry at Oxford, poet, essayist and critic of English social and political life.

Bay window in house at 8 Trinity Street, College Park, South Australia, photograph by Susan Magarey

Smythe,[33] then, I think, touring with Charles Clark,[34] wrote to Mr Finlayson from Wallaroo thus. 'In this dead-alive place, where one might fire a mitrailleuse down the principal street without hurting anybody, I read this delightful article in yesterday's *Register*. When we come again in Adelaide, and we collect a few choice spirits, be sure to invite the writer of this article to join us.' I felt as if the round woman had got at last into the round hole which fitted her; and in my little study, with my books and my pigeon holes, and my dear old mother sitting with her knitting on her rocking chair at the low window, I had the knowledge that she was interested in all I did. I generally read the MS to her before it went to the office. What is more remarkable, perhaps, is that the excellent maid who was with us for 12 years, picked out everything of mine that was in the papers and read it. A series of papers called 'Some Social Aspects of Early Colonial Life' I contributed under the pseudonym of 'A Colonist of 1839'.[35] From 1878 till 1893, when I went round the world via

---

33 Robert Sparrow Smythe (1833–1917), journalist and entrepreneur, explored and travelled with Rev. Charles Clark.
34 Charles Clark (1838–1903), Baptist minister, outstanding preacher and public lecturer, who travelled to many countries.
35 *Some Social Aspects of South Australian Life*, by a Colonist of 1839 – C.H. Spence. Adelaide, 1878. Pamphlet. Articles reprinted from the *Register*.

America, I held the position of outside contributor on the oldest newspaper in the state, and for these 14 years I had great latitude. My friend Dr Garran, then editor of the *Sydney Morning Herald*,[36] accepted reviews and articles from me. Sometimes I reviewed the same books for both, but I wrote the articles differently, and made different quotations, so that I scarcely think any one could detect the same hand in them; but generally they were different books and different subjects, which I treated.[37] I tried the *Australasian*[38] with a story, 'Afloat and Ashore', and with a social article on 'Wealth, Waste, and Want'.[39] I contributed to the *Melbourne Review*, and later to the *Victorian Review*, which began by paying well, but filtered out gradually. I found journalism a better paying business for me than novel writing, and I delighted in the breadth of the canvas on which I could draw my sketches of books and of life. I believe that my work on newspapers and reviews is more characteristic of me, and intrinsically better work than what I have done in fiction; but when I began to wield the pen, the novel was the line of least resistance. When I was introduced in 1894 to Mrs Croly, the oldest woman journalist in the United States,[40] as an Australian journalist, I found that her work, though good enough, was essentially woman's work, dress, fashions, functions, with educational and social outlooks from the feminine point of view. My work might show the larger questions which were common to humanity; and when I recall the causes which I furthered, and which in some instances I started, I feel inclined to magnify the office of the anonymous contributor to the daily press. And I acknowledge not only the kindness of friends who put some of the best new books in my way, but the large-minded tolerance of the editors of the *Register*, who gave me such a free hand in the treatment of books, of men, and of public questions.

---

36 *Sydney Morning Herald*, Australia's oldest surviving newspaper.
37 Dates of Spence's articles and reviews can be found in the bibliography of Spence on the website of the State Library of South Australia. www.slsa.sa.gov.au/spence.
38 The *Australasian*, formed by a merger of three Melbourne weeklies, became the weekend companion to the Melbourne *Argus*, 1864–1946.
39 'Afloat or Ashore' in the *Australasian*, 6 and 13 July 1878; 'Wealth and Waste' in the *Australasian*, 10 and 17 May 1879.
40 Jane Cunningham Croly (1829–1901), journalist and the driving force behind the American Club women's movement which inspired thousands of women into a wide range of social reform activities. She is now remembered in the United States of America as a reformer.

CHAPTER 13

MY WORK FOR EDUCATION

I was the first woman appointed on a Board of Advice under the Education Department, and found the work interesting.[1] The powers of the board were limited to an expenditure of £5 for repairs without applying to the department and to interviewing the parents of children who had failed to attend the prescribed number of days, as well as those who pleaded poverty as an excuse for the non-payment of fees. I always felt that the school fees were a heavy burden on the poor, and rejoiced accordingly when free education was introduced into South Australia.[2] This was the second state to adopt this great reform, Victoria preceding it by a few years. I objected to the payment of fees on another ground. I felt they bore heavily on the innocent children themselves through the notion of caste which was created in the minds of those who paid fees to the detriment of their less fortunate school companions. And again, education that is compulsory should be free. Other women have since become members of school boards, but I was the pioneer of that branch of public work for women in this state. It is a privilege that American women have been fighting for for many years – to vote for and to be eligible to sit on school boards. In many of the states this has been won to their great advantage. In this present year of 1910 Mrs Ella Flagg Young,[3] at the age of 65, has been elected by the Chicago Board, Directory of the Education of that great city of over

---

1   More information on this aspect of Spence's work can be found in Barbara Wall, 'Catherine Spence and the School Boards of Advice', *Journal of the Historical Society of South Australia*, no. 28, 2000.
2   1875.
3   Ella Flagg Young (1845–1918), American educator, identified with the Chicago Public School system for 53 years, Professor of Education at University of Chicago 1899–1905, Principal of the Chicago Normal School, (later Chicago Teachers College). A leader in woman-suffrage work and first woman president of the National Education Association 1910–11.

Advanced School for Girls, c.1885,
photograph courtesy of the State Library of South Australia, SLSA: B 25677/42

two millions of inhabitants at a salary of £2,000 a year, with a male university professor as an assistant. At an age when we in South Australia are commanding our teachers to retire, in Chicago, which is said by Foster Fraser[4] to cashier men at 40, this elderly woman has entered into her great power.

It is characteristic of me that I like to do thoroughly what I undertake to do at all, and when, on one occasion I had not received the usual summons to attend a board meeting, I complained of the omission to the Chairman. 'I do not want,' I said, 'to be a merely ornamental member of this board. I want to go to all the meetings.' He replied, courteously, 'It is the last thing that we would say of you, Miss Spence, that you are ornamental!' It was half a minute before he discovered that he had put his disclaimer in rather a different form from what he had

4   Sir John Foster Fraser (1868–1936), English traveller, adventurer and prolific writer.

intended, and he joined in the burst of laughter which followed. Another amusing contretemps occurred when the same gentleman and I were visiting the parents who had pleaded for exemption from the payment of fees. At one house there was a grown-up daughter who had that morning left the service of the gentleman's mother – a fact enlarged upon by my companion during the morning's drive. 'Why is your eldest daughter out of a place?' was the first question he put to the woman. 'She might be earning good wages, and be able to help you pay the fees.' 'Oh!' came the unexpected reply, 'she had to leave old Mrs —— this morning; she was that mean there was no living in the house with her!' Knowing her interlocutor only as the man in authority, the unfortunate woman scarcely advanced her cause by her plain speaking, and I was probably the only member of the trio who appreciated the situation. I am sure many people who were poorer than this mother paid the fees rather than suffer the indignity of such cross-questioning by the school visitors and the board – an unfortunate necessity of the system, which disappeared with the abolition of school fees.

It had been suggested by the Minister of Education[5] of that period that the children attending the state schools should be instructed in the duties of citizenship, and that they should be taught something of the laws under which they lived, and I was commissioned to write a short and pithy statement of the case. It was to be simple enough for intelligent children in the fourth class; eleven or twelve – it was to lead from the known to the unknown – it might include the elements of political economy and sociology – it might make use of familiar illustrations from the experience of a new country – but it must not be long. It was not very easy to satisfy myself and Mr Hartley – who was a severe critic – but when the book of 120 pages was completed he was satisfied.[6] A preface I wrote for the second edition – the first five thousand copies being insufficient for the requirements of the schools – will give some idea of the plan of the work: 'In writing this little book, I have aimed less at symmetrical perfection than at simplicity of diction, and such arrangement as would lead from the known to the unknown, by which the older children in our public schools might learn not only the actual facts about the laws they live under, but also some of the principles which underlie all law.' The reprinting gave me an opportunity to reply to my critics that 'political economy, trades unions, insurance companies, and newspapers' were outside the scope of the laws we live under. But I thought that in a new state where the optional duties of the Government are so numerous, it was of great importance for the young citizen

---

5   Neville Blyth (1825–1890).
6   Catherine Helen Spence, *The Laws We Live Under*, (Government Printing Office) Adelaide, 1880, second edition 1881.

to understand economic principles. As conduct is the greater part of life, and morality, not only the bond of social union, but the main source of individual happiness, I took the ethical part of the subject first, and tried to explain that education was of no value unless it was used for good purposes. As without some wealth, civilisation was impossible, I next sought to show that national and individual wealth depends on the security that is given by law, and on the industry and thrift which that security encourages. Land tenure is of the first importance in colonial prosperity, and consideration of the land revenue and the limitations as to its expenditure led me to the necessity for taxation and the various modes of levying it. Taxation led me to the power which imposes, collects, and expends it. This involved a consideration of those representative institutions which made the Government at once the master and the servant of the people. Under this Government our persons and our prosperity are protected by a system of criminal, civil, and insolvent law – each considered in its place. Although not absolutely included in the laws we live under, I consider that providence, and its various outlets in banks, savings banks, joint stock companies, friendly societies, and trades unions, were matters too important to be left unnoticed; and also those influences which shape character quite as much as statute laws – public opinion, the newspaper, and amusements. As the use of my little book was restricted solely to school hours, my hope that the parents might be helped and encouraged by its teaching was doomed to disappointment. But the children of 30 years ago, when *The Laws We Live Under* was first published, are the men and women of today, and who shall say but that among them are to be found some at least worthy and true citizens, who owe to my little book their first inspiration to 'hitch their wagon to a star'. Last year an enthusiastic young Swedish teacher and journalist was so taken with this South Australian little handbook of civics that he urged on me the duty of bringing it up to date, and embracing women's suffrage, the relations of the states to the Commonwealth, as well as the industrial legislation which is in many ways peculiar to Australia, but although those in authority were sympathetic no steps have been taken for its reproduction.

Identified as I had been for so many years with elementary education in South Australia, my mind was well prepared to applaud the movement in favour of the higher education of poorer children of both sexes by the foundation of bursaries and scholarships, and the opening up of the avenues of learning to women by admitting them to university degrees. Victoria was the first to take this step, and all over the Commonwealth the example has been followed. I am, however, somewhat disappointed that university women are not more generally progressive in their ideas. They have won something which I should have been very glad of, but which was quite out of reach. All opportunities ought to be considered as opportunities for service. As my brother David regarded the possession of honours and wealth as demanding sacrifice for the common good, so I regarded special knowledge and special culture as means for advancing the culture of all. It is said to be human nature when special privileges or special gifts are used only for egoistic ends; but the complete development of the human being demands that altruistic ideas should also be cultivated. We see that in China an aristocracy of letters – for it is through passing difficult examinations in old literature that the ruling classes are appointed – is no protection to the poor and ignorant from oppression or degradation. It is true that the classics in China are very old, but so are the literatures of Greece and Rome, on which so many university degrees are founded; and it ought to be impressed upon all seekers after academic honours that personal advantage is not the be-all and end-all of their pursuits. In our democratic Commonwealth, although there are some lower titles bestowed by the Sovereign on colonists more or less distinguished, these are not hereditary, so that an aristocracy is not hereditary. There may be an upper class, based on landed estate or one on business success, or one on learning, but all tend to become conservative as conservatism is understood in Australia. Safety is maintained by the free rise from the lower to the higher. But all the openings to higher education offered in high school and university do not tempt the working man's children who want to earn wages as soon as the law lets them go to work. Nor do they tempt their parents to their large share of the sacrifice which young Scotch lads and even American lads make to get through advanced studies. The higher education is still a sort of preserve of the well-to-do, and when one thinks of how greatly this is valued it seems a pity that it is not open to the talents, to the industry, to the enthusiasm of all the young of both sexes. But one exception I must make to the aloofness of people with degrees and professions from the preventable evils of the world, and that is in the profession that is the longest and the most exacting – the medical profession. The women doctors whom I have met in Adelaide, Melbourne, and Sydney have a keen sense of their responsibility to the less fortunate. That probably is because medicine as now understood and practised is the most modern of the learned professions, and is more human than engineering, which is also modern. It takes us into the homes of the poor more intimately than even the clergyman, and it offers remedies and palliatives as well as advice. The law is little studied by women in Australia, but in the United States there are probably a thousand or more legal practitioners. It is the profession that I should have chosen when I was young if it had been in any way feasible. I had no bent for the medical profession, and still less for what every one thinks the most womanly of avocations – that of the trained nurse. I could nurse my own relatives more or less well, but did not distinguish myself in that way, and I could not devote myself to strangers.

The manner in which penniless young men become lawyers in the United States seems impossible in Australia. Judge Lindsey,[7] son of a ruined southern family, studied law and delivered newspapers in the morning, worked in a lawyer's office through the day, and acted as janitor at night. The course appears to be shorter, and probably less Latin and Greek were required in a western State than here. But during the long vacation in summer, students go as waiters in big hotels at seaside or other health resorts, or take up some other seasonal trade. All the Columbian guards at the Chicago Exhibition[8] were students. They kept order, they gave directions, they wheeled invalids in bath chairs, and they earned all that was needed for their next winter's course. In the long high school holidays youths and maidens who are poor and ambitious work for money. I have seen fairly well-paid professors who went back to the father's farm and worked hard all harvest time – and students always did so. It appears easier in America to get a job for three months' vacation than in England or Australia, and the most surprising thing about an American is his versatility. Teaching is with most American men only a step to something better, so that almost all elementary and the far greater proportion of high school teaching is in the hands of women. In Australia our male teachers have to spend so many years before they are fully equipped that they rarely leave the profession. The only check on the supply is that the course is so long and laborious that the youth prefers an easy clerkship. Women, in spite of the chance of marriage, enter the profession in the United States in greater numbers, and as the scale of salaries is by no means equal pay for equal work, except in New York, money is saved by employing women. I think that it is the student of arts (that English title which is as vague and unmeaning as the Scottish one of humanities) – student of ancient classical literature – who, whether man or woman, has least perception of the modern spirit or sympathy with the sorrows of the world. With all honour to the classical authors, there are two things in which they were deficient – the spirit of broad humanity and the sense of humour. All ancient literature is grave – nay, sad. It is also aristocratic for learning was the possession of the few.

While writing this narrative I came upon a notable thing done by Miss Crystal Eastman,[9] a member of the New York Bar, and Secretary of the

7 Benjamin Barr Lindsey (1869–1943), lawyer, judge and reformer.
8 The Chicago World's Fair of 1893, also known as the World's Columbian Exposition, was an extremely popular and influential social and cultural event. It took place on the shores of Lake Michigan and lasted for six months.
9 Crystal Eastman (1881–1928), socialist feminist, member of the New York Bar, appointed first member of the Employer's Liability Commission in New York State. She drafted New York State's first worker's compensation law.

State Commission on Employers' Liability. It is difficult for us to understand how so many good things are blocked, not only in the Federal Government, but in the separate States, by the written constitutions. In Great Britain the Constitution consists of unwritten principles embodied either in Parliamentary statutes or in the common law, and yields to any Act which Parliament may pass, and the judiciary can impose no veto on it. This is one reason why England is so far ahead of the United States in labour legislation. Miss Eastman was the principal speaker at the annual meeting in January, 1910, of the New York State Bar Association. She is a trained economic investigator as well as a lawyer, and her masterly analysis of conditions under the present liability law held close attention, and carried conviction to many present that a radical change was necessary. The recommendations for the statute were to make limited compensation for all accidents, except those wilfully caused by the victim, compulsory on all employers. With regard to dangerous occupations the person who profits by them should bear the greatest share of the loss through accident. As for the constitutionality of such legislation Miss Eastman said – 'If our State Constitution cannot be interpreted so as to recognise such an idea of justice then I think we should amend our Constitution. I see no reason why we should stand in such awe of a document which expressly provides for its own revision every ten years.' The evils against which this brave woman lawyer contends are real and grievous. Working people in America who suffer from injury are unmercifully exploited by the ambulance-chasing lawyers. Casualty insurance companies are said to be weary of being diverted from their regular business to become a mere fighting force in the Courts to prevent the injured or the dependents from getting any compensation. The long-suffering public is becoming aware that the taxpayers are compelled to bear the burden of supporting the pitifully great multitude of incapacitated or rendered dependent because of industrial accident or occupational disease. Employers insure their liability, and the poor man has to fight an insurance company, and at present reform is blocked on the plea that it is unconstitutional. There are difficulties even in Australia, and to enquire into such difficulties would be good work for women lawyers.

CHAPTER 14

SPECULATION, CHARITY, AND A BOOK

In the meantime my family history went on. My nephew was sent to the Northern Territory to take over the branch of the English and Scottish Bank at Palmerston,[1] and he took his sister from school to go with him and stay three months in the tropics.[2] He was only 21 at the time. Four years after he went to inspect the branch, and took his sister with him again. I think she loved Port Darwin more than he did, and she always stood up for the climate. South Australia did a great work in building, unaided by any other Australian State, the telegraph line from Port Darwin to Adelaide,[3] and at one time it was believed that rich goldfields were to be opened in this great empty land, which the British Government had handed over to South Australia, because Stuart[4] had been the first to cross the island continent, and the handful of South Australian colonists had connected telegraphically the north and the south. The telegraph building had been contracted for by Darwent and Dalwood,[5] and my brother, through the South Australian Bank, was helping to finance them. That was in 1876–7. This was the first, but not the last by any means, of enterprises which contractors were not able to carry out in this State, either from taking a big enterprise at too low a rate or from lack of financial backing. The government, as in the recent cases of the Pinnaroo Railway and the Outer Harbour, had to complete the half-done work as the direct employer of labour and the direct purchaser of materials. A great furore for goldmining in the

1 The early name for Darwin.
2 Charles Wren took his sister Eleanor Wren to Darwin.
3 The overland telegraph from Adelaide to Darwin was completed in 1872.
4 John McDouall Stuart (1815–1866), explorer, crossed Australia from South to North in 1862, surveying parts of the overland telegraph route.
5 Darwent & Dalwood Overland Telegraph Construction Team completed part of the telegraph line but were dismissed by the Government.

Northern Territory arose, and people in England bought city allotments in Palmerston, which was expected to become the queen city of North Australia, Port Darwin is no whit behind Sydney Harbour in beauty and capacity. The navies of the world could ride safely in its waters. A railway of 150 miles in length, the first section of the great transcontinental line, which was to extend from Palmerston to Port Augusta, was built to connect Pine Creek, where there was gold to be found, with the seaboard. South Australia was more than ever a misnomer for this State. Victoria lay more to the south than our province, and now that we stretched far inside the tropics the name seemed ridiculous. My friend Miss Sinnett[6] suggested Centralia as the appropriate name for the State, which by this gift was really the central State; but in the present crisis, when South Australia finds the task of keeping the Northern Territory white too arduous and too costly, and is offering it on handsome terms to the Commonwealth, Centralia might not continue to be appropriate. Our northern possession has cost South Australia much. The sums of money sunk in prospecting for gold and other metals have been enormous, and at present there are more Chinese there than Europeans. In the early days, when the Wrens were there, Eleanor was surprised when their wonderful Chinese cook came to her and said, 'Missie, I go along a gaol to-morrow. You take Ah Kei. He do all light till I go out!' The cook had been tried and condemned for larceny, but he was allowed to retain his situation till the last hour. Instead of being kept in gaol pending his trial he earned his wages and did his work. He had no desire to escape. He liked Palmerston and the bank, and he went back to the latter when released. He was an incorrigible thief, and got into trouble again; but as a cook he was superlative.

That decade of the eighties was a most speculative time all over Australia and New Zealand. I was glad that leaving the English and Scottish Bank enabled my brother to go into political and official life, but it also allowed him to speculate far beyond what he could have done if he had been manager of a bank. Everybody speculated – in mines, in land, and in leases. I was earning by my pen a very decent income, and I spent it, sometimes wisely and sometimes foolishly. I could be liberal to church and to good causes. I was able to keep a dear little State child at school for two years after the regulation age, and I was amply repaid by seeing her afterwards an honoured wife and mother, able to assist her children and their companions with their lessons. I helped some lame dogs over the stile. One among them was a young American of brilliant scholastic attainments, who was the victim of hereditary alcoholism. His mother, a saintly and noble prohibitionist worker, whom I afterwards met in

---

6 Miss Sophia Sinnett, artist sister of Frederick Sinnett (1831–1866), engineer and journalist, who spent some time in Adelaide.

America, had heard of me, and wrote asking me to keep a watchful eye on her boy. This I did for about 12 months, and found him employment. He held a science degree, and was an authority on mineralogy, metallurgy, and kindred subjects. During this speculative period he persuaded me to plunge (rather wildly for me) in mining shares. I plunged to the extent of £500, and I owe it to the good sense and practical ability of my nephew that I lost no more heavily than I did, for he paid £100 to let me off my bargain.

My protégé continued to visit me weekly, and we wrote to one another once a week or oftener. The books I lent to him I know to this day by their colour and the smell of tobacco. I wrote to his mother regularly, and consulted with his good friend, Mr Waterhouse, over what was best to be done. One bad outburst he had when he had got some money through me to pay off liabilities. I recollect his penitent, despairing confession, with the reference to Edwin Arnold's[7] poem –

> He who died at Azun gave
> This to those who dug his grave.

The time came when I felt I could hold him no longer, although that escapade was forgiven, and I determined to send him to his mother – not without misgivings about what she might have still to suffer. He wrote to me occasionally. His health was never good, and I attribute the craving for drink and excitement a good deal to physical causes; but at the same time I am sure that he could have withstood it by a more resolute will. The will is the character – it is the real man. When people say that the first thing in education is to break the will, they make a radical mistake. Train the will to work according to the dictates of an enlightened conscience, for it is all we have to trust to for the stability of character. My poor lad called me his Australian mother. When I saw his real mother, I wondered more and more what sort of a husband she had, or what atavism Edward drew from to produce a character so unlike hers. I heard nothing from herself of what she went through, but from her friends I gathered that he had several outbreaks, and cost her far more than she could afford. She paid everything that he owed in Adelaide, except her debt to me, but that I was repaid after her death in 1905, and she always felt that I had been a true friend to her wayward son. I recollect one day my friend coming on his weekly visit with a face of woe to tell me he had seen a man in dirt and rags, with half a shirt, who had been well acquainted with Charles Dickens and other notables in London. My friend had fed him and clothed him, but he

---

7 Sir Edwin Arnold (1832–1904), English poet who had worked in India. *The Light of Asia*, 1879, is an epic poem, set in India, and dealing with the life and teaching of Buddha.

wanted to return to England to rich friends. I wrote to a few good folk, and we raised the money and sent the wastrel to the old country. How grateful he appeared to be, especially to the kind people who had taken him in; but he never wrote a line. We never heard from him again. Years afterwards I wrote to his brother-in-law, asking where the object of our charity now was, if he were still alive. The reply was that his ingratitude did not surprise the writer – that he was a hopeless drunkard, a remittance man, whom the family had to ship off as soon as possible when our ill-judged kindness sent him to England. At that time he was in Canada, but it was not worth while to give any address. When Mr Bowyear[8] started the Charity Organisation Society in Adelaide,[9] he said I was no good as a visitor; I was too credulous, and had not half enough of the detective in me. But I had not much faith in this remittance man.

I have been strongly tempted to omit altogether the next book which I wrote; but, as this is to be a sincere narrative of my life and its work, I must pierce the veil of anonymity and own up to *An Agnostic's Progress*.[10] I had been impressed with the very different difficulties the soul of man has to encounter nowadays from those so triumphantly overcome by Christian in the great work of John Bunyan in the first part of *The Pilgrim's Progress*.[11] He cannot now get out of the Slough of Despond by planting his foot on the stepping stones of the Promises. He cannot, like Hopeful, pluck from his bosom the Key of Promise which opens every lock in Doubting Castle when the two pilgrims are shut in it by Giant Despair, when they are caught trespassing on his grounds. Even assured Christians, we know, may occasionally trespass on these grounds of doubt; but the weapons of modern warfare are not of the seventeenth century. The Interpreter's House in the old allegory dealt only with things found in the Bible, the only channel of revelation to John Bunyan. To the modern pilgrim God reveals Himself in Nature, in art, in literature, and in story. The Interpreter's House in the old allegory dealt only with things found in the Bible, the only channel of revelation to John Bunyan. To the modern pilgrim God reveals Himself in Nature, in art, in literature and in

---

8 George John Shirreff Bowyear (c.1851–1923), Anglican clergyman, married to Lucy Howard Clark, daughter of John Howard Clark, Spence's friend.

9 The Charity Organisation Society was formed in 1884. In 1885 it amalgamated with the Adelaide Benevolent and Strangers' Friend Society, which ran from 1849–1990. In 1887 the name reverted to Adelaide Benevolent and Strangers' Friend Society. The societies were formed to provide assistance for needy people.

10 Catherine Helen Spence, *An Agnostic's Progress from the Known to the Unknown*, (Williams and Norgate) London, 1884.

11 John Bunyan (1628–1688), English author and preacher. *The Pilgrim's Progess from this World to that which is to come, An allegory*, 1678.

history. The Interpreter's Hand had to do with all these things. Vanity Fair is not a place through which all pilgrims must pass as quickly as possible, shutting their eyes and stopping their ears so that they should neither see nor hear the wicked things that are done and said there. Vanity Fair is the world in which we all have to live and do our work well, or neglect it. Pope and Pagan are not the old giants who used to devour pilgrims, but who can now only gnash their teeth at them in impotent rage. They are live forces, quite active, and with agents and supporters alert to capture souls. Of all the influences which affected for evil my young life I perhaps resented most Mrs Sherwood's *Infant's Progress*.[12] There were three children in it going from the City of Destruction to the Celestial City by the route laid down by John Bunyan; but they were handicapped even more severely than the good Christian himself with his heavy burden – for that fell off his back at the first sight of the Cross and Him who was nailed to it, accepted by the eye of Faith as the one Sacrifice for the sins of the world – for the three little ones, Humble Mind, Playful, and Peace, were accompanied always and everywhere by an imp called Inbred Sin, who never ceased to tempt them to evil.

The doctrine of innate human depravity is one of the most paralysing dogmas that human fear invented or priestcraft encouraged. I did not think of publishing *An Agnostic's Progress* at first. I wrote it to relieve my own mind. I wanted to satisfy myself that reverent agnostics were by no means materialists; that man's nature might or might not be consciously immortal, but it was spiritual; that in the duties which lay before each of us towards ourselves and towards our fellow-creatures, there was scope for spiritual energy and spiritual emotion. I was penetrated by Browning's great idea expressed over and over again – the expansion of Paul's dictum that faith is not certainty, but a belief without sufficient proof, a belief which leads to right action and to self-sacrifice. Of the 70 years of life which one might hope to live and work in, I had no mean idea. I asked in the newspaper, 'Is life so short?' and answered, 'No'. I expanded and spiritualised the idea in a sermon, and I again answered emphatically 'No'. I saw the continuation and the expansion of true ideas by succeeding generations. To the question put sometimes peevishly, 'Is life worth living?' I replied with equal emphasis, 'Yes'. My mother told me of old times. I recalled half a century of progress, and I hoped the forward movement would continue. I read the manuscript of *An Agnostic's Progress* to Mr and Mrs Barr Smith, and they thought so well of it that they offered to take it to England on one of their many visits to the old country, where they had no

---

12 Mary Martha Sherwood née Butt (1775–1851), English author of many fiercely didactic and moral tales for children. *The Infant's Progress: from the valley of instruction to everlasting glory*, 1821.

doubt it would find a publisher. Trübner's reader reported most favourably of the book, and we thought there was an immediate prospect of its publication; but Mr Trübner[13] died, and the matter was not taken up by his successor, and my friends did what I had expressly said they were not to do, and had it printed and published at their own expense. There were many printer's errors in it, but it was on the whole well reviewed, though it did not sell well. The *Spectator*[14] joined issue with me on the point that it is only through the wicket gate of Doubt that we can come to any faith that is of value; but I am satisfied that I took the right stand there. My mother was in no way disquieted or disturbed by my writing the book, and few of my friends read it or knew about it. I still appeared so engrossed with work on the *Register* and the *Observer* that my time was quite well enough accounted for. I tried for a prize of £100 offered by the *Sydney Mail*[15] with a novel called *Handfasted*,[16] but was not successful, for the judge feared that it was calculated to loosen the marriage tie – it was too socialistic, and consequently dangerous.

13 Nicholas (Nikolaus) Trübner (1817–1884), scholar, author and publisher with a great interest in philosophy, religion and oriental studies. He came to England from Germany in 1843 and became a leading publisher with connections to many American writers and publishers.
14 The *Spectator*, a weekly established in London in 1828, is the oldest continuously published magazine in the English language.
15 The weekly companion paper to the *Sydney Morning Herald* from 1860 to 1938.
16 *Handfasted* was submitted to the *Sydney Mail* in 1879 but not published until 1984 when it was edited with a preface and afterword by Helen Thomson and published by Penguin Books, Ringwood, Australia. Two comments about *Handfasted* were cut by the original editor. Spence added that it was 'copied for me by my neice [sic] Eleanor Wren as I thought her writing would give it more chance' of winning a prize and reflected that 'I do not think it is on the whole as good a novel as my others. It is rather overweighted with social and economic speculations and it was written before I had read *Progress and Poverty*.'

CHAPTER 15

JOURNALISM AND POLITICS

In reviewing books I took the keenest interest in the *Carlyle Biographies and Letters*, because my mother recollected Jeanie Welsh[1] as a child, and her father was called in always for my grandfather Brodie's illnesses. I was also absorbed in the *Life and Letters of George Eliot*. The Barr Smiths gave me the *Life and Letters of Balzac*,[2] and many of his books in French, which led me to write both for the *Register* and for the *Melbourne Review*. I also wrote 'A last word', which was lost by the *Centennial*[3] in Sydney when it died out. It was also from Mrs Barr Smith that I got so many of the works of Alphonse Daudet[4] in French, which enabled me to give a rejoinder to Marcus Clarke's[5] assertion that Balzac was a French Dickens. Indeed, looking through my shelves, I see so many books which suggested articles and criticisms which were her gifts that I always connect her with my journalistic career.

Many people have consulted me about publishing poems, novels, and essays. As I was known to have actually got books published in England, and to be a professional journalist and reviewer, I dare say some of those who applied to me for encouragement thought I was actuated by literary jealousy; but people are apt to think they have a plot when they have only an incident, or two or three incidents; and many who can write clever and even brilliant letters have no idea of the construction of a story that will arrest and sustain the

---

1 Jane Baillie Welsh who married Thomas Carlyle.
2 Honoré de Balzac (1799–1850), French novelist, author of the series of novels making up *La Comédie Humaine*.
3 A literary monthly magazine published in Sydney which ran from 1888 to 1890.
4 Alphonse Daudet (1840–1897), French novelist and short story writer.
5 Marcus Andrew Hislop Clarke (1846–1881), journalist and novelist, emigrated to Australia in 1863. He is remembered for his fictional portrait of convict life, *For the Term of His Natural Life*, published in book form in 1874, serialised 1870–72.

reader's attention. The people who consulted me all wanted money for their work. They had such excellent uses for money. They had too little. They were neither willing nor able to bear the cost of publication, and it was absolutely necessary that their work should be good enough for a business man to undertake it. I am often surprised that I found English publishers myself, and the handicap of distance and other things is even greater now. If stories are excessively Australian, they lose the sympathies of the bulk of the public. If they are mildly Australian, the work is thought to lack distinctiveness. Great genius can overcome these things, but great genius is rare everywhere. Except for my friend Miss Mackay (Mrs F. Martin),[6] I know no Australian novelist of genius, and her work is only too rare in fiction. Mrs Cross[7] reaches her highest level in *The Marked Man*. But she does not keep it up, though she writes well and pleasantly. Of course poetry does not pay anywhere until a great reputation is made. Poetry must be its own exceeding great reward. And yet I agree with Charles Kingsley[8] that if you wish to cultivate a really good prose style you should begin with verse. In my teens I wrote rhymes and tried to write sonnets. I encouraged writing games among my young people, and it is surprising how much cleverness could be developed. I can write verses with ease, but very rarely could I rise to poetry; and therefore I fear I was not encouraging to the budding Australian poet.

There was a column quite outside of the *Register* to which I liked to contribute for love. That was 'The Riddler',[9] which appeared in the *Observer* and in the *Evening Journal* on Saturdays. It brought me in contact with Mr William Holden,[10] long the oldest journalist in South Australia, who revelled in statistical returns and algebraical problems and earth measurements, but who also appreciated a good charade or double acrostic. I used to give some of the ingredients for his 'Christmas Mince Pie', and wrote many riddles of various sorts. My charades were not so elegant as some arranged by Miss Clark, and not so easily found out; and my double acrostics were not so subtle as those given in competition nowadays, but they were in the eighties reckoned excellent. My fame had reached the ears of Mrs Alfred Watts (née

---

6 The novelist Catherine Martin. See above, Chapter XII, n. 25.
7 Ada Cambridge (1844–1926), writer and novelist, was born in England and married Anglican clergyman George Frederick Cross in 1870. She lived in Victoria and published frequently in Australian newspapers. *The Marked Man*, 1890.
8 Charles Kingsley (1819–1875), English clergymen, social reformer, novelist, and writer of stories for children.
9 A column of puzzles which invited readers to send in solutions.
10 William Holden (1808–1897), the 'father of Australian journalism,' on the staff of the *Register* 1851–1896, known for his interest in art, music and mathematics.

Giles),[11] who spent her early colonial life on Kangaroo Island, and she asked me to write some double acrostics for the poor incurables. I stared at her in amazement. 'We want to be quite well to tackle double acrostics and to have access to books. Does not *Punch* speak of the titled lady, eager to win a guinea prize, who gave seven volumes of Carlyle's works to seven upper servants, and asked each to search one to find a certain quotation?' 'Oh,' said Mrs Watts, 'I don't mean for the incurables to amuse themselves with. I mean for the benefit of the home.'

In the end I prepared a book of charades and double acrostics, for the printing and binding of which Mrs Watts paid. It was entitled *Silver Wattle*,[12] and the proceeds from the sale of this little book went to help the funds of the home. For a second volume issued for the same purpose Mrs Strawbridge[13] wrote some poems, Mrs H.M. Davidson[14] a translation of Victor Hugo, Miss Clark her beautiful 'Flowers of Greece,' and her niece some pretty verses, which, combined with the double acrostics and acting charades supplied by me, made an attractive volume. Mrs Watts had something of a literary turn, which found expression in *Memories of Early Days in South Australia*, a book printed for private circulation among her family and intimate friends. Dealing with the years between 1837 and 1845 it was very interesting to old colonists, particularly when they were able to identify the people mentioned, sometimes by initials and sometimes by pseudonyms. The author was herself an incurable invalid from an accident shortly after her marriage, and felt keenly for all the inmates of the Fullarton home.

In 1877 my brother John – with whom I had never quarrelled in my life, and who helped and encouraged me in everything I did – retired from the English, Scottish, and Australian Bank, and decided to contest a seat for the Legislative Council. It was the last occasion on which the Council was elected with the State as one district. Although he announced his candidature only the night before nomination day, and did not address a single meeting, he was elected third on the poll. He afterwards became the Chief Secretary, and later

---

11 Jane Isabella Watts, née Giles (1824–1894), author of *Memories of Early Days in South Australia, an account of South Australian social life and customs 1836–1851*. Privately printed 1882.
12 *Silver Wattle: South Australian Acrostics. The proceeds to be devoted to the Home for Incurables, Fullarton*, (Kyffin Thomas) Adelaide, 1879.
13 Eliza Stockholm Strawbridge (c.1818–1897), teacher, poet and artist.
14 Harriet Miller Davidson née Miller (1839–1883), poet, novelist and short story writer. She frequently contributed to the *Register* and *Observer*. Her husband, minister of the Free Church of Scotland, was called to Chalmers Church in Adelaide, and became Professor of English Literature and Mental and Moral Philosophy at the University of Adelaide.

John Brodie Spence, c.1880,
photograph courtesy of the State Library of South Australia, SLSA: B 22103/80

Commissioner of Public Works. He was an excellent worker on committees, and was full of ideas and suggestions. Although not a good speaker, he rejoiced in my standing on platform or in pulpit. He was nearly as democratic as I was; and when he invented the phrase 'effective voting' it was from the sense that true democracy demanded not merely a chance, but a certainty, that the vote given at the poll should be effective for some one. My brother David inherited all the Conservatism of the Brodies for generations back. Greatly interested in all abtruse problems and abstract questions he had various schemes for the regeneration of mankind. Two opposing theories concerning the working of bi-cameral Legislatures supplied me with material for a *Review* article.[15] One theory was intensely Conservative, and emanated from my brother David, who was a poor man. The other was held by the richest man of my acquaintance, and was distinctly Liberal. My brother argued that the Upper House should have the power to tax its own constituents, and was utterly opposed to any extension of the franchise. My rich friend objected to the limited franchise, and desired to have the State proclaimed on electorate with proportional representation as a safeguard against unwise legislation and as a means to assist reforms. The great blot, he considered, on Australian Constitutions was the representation by districts, especially for the House that controlled the public purse. If districts were to be tolerated at all, they should be represented by men who had a longer tenure of office than our Assembly's three years, and who did not have so often to ask for votes, which frequently depended on a railway or a jetty or a Rabbit Bill. So long as Government depends for its existence on the support of local representatives it is tempted to spend public money to gratify them. Both men were Freetraders, and both believed strongly in the justice of land values taxation.

My friend the late Professor Pearson[16] had entered into active political life in Melbourne, and was a regular writer for the *Age*. Perhaps no other man underwent more obloquy from his old friends for taking the side of Graham Berry,[17] especially as he was a Freetrader, and the popular party was Protectionist. He justified his action by saying that a mistake in the fiscal policy of a country should not prevent a real Democrat from siding with the party which opposed monopoly, especially in land. He saw in 'lalifundia' – huge estates – the ruin of the Roman Empire, and its prevalence in the United Kingdom was the greatest danger ahead of it. In these young countries the tendency to build up large holdings was naturally fostered by what was the earliest of our industries. Sheepfarming is not greatly pursued in the United States or Canada, because of the rigorous winter – but Australia is the favourite home of the merino sheep. Originally there was no need to buy land, or even to pay rent to the Government for it; the land had no value till settlement gave it. The squatter leased it on easy terms, and bought it only when it had sufficient value to be desired by agriculturists or by selectors who posed as

---

15 'Two Theories for the Working of Bi-cameral Legislatures', *Melbourne Review*, vol. 4, 1879.

16 Charles Henry Pearson (1830–1894), historian, politician and education reformer.

17 Sir Graham Berry (1822–1904), politician, notorious as the Premier of Victoria who advised the Governor to dismiss many public servants, county court judges, coroners and police magistrates because the Legislative Council had refused to pass a Supply Bill.

agriculturists. When he bought it he generally complained of the price these selectors compelled him to pay, but it was then secure; and, with the growth of population and the railroads and other improvements, these enforced purchasers, even in 1877, had built up vast estates in single hands in every State in Australia. In the *Melbourne Review* for April 1877, Professor Pearson sketched a plan of land taxation, which was afterwards carried out, in which the area of land held was the test for graduated taxation. Henry George[18] had not then declared his gospel; and, although I felt that there was something very faulty in the scheme, I did not declare in my article on the subject that an acre in Collins Street might be of more value than fifty thousand acres of pastoral land five hundred miles from the seaboard, and was therefore more fitly liable to taxation for the advantage of the whole community, who had given to that acre this exceptional value. I did not declare it because I did not believe it. But I thought that the end aimed at – the breaking up of large estates – could be better and more safely affected, though not so quickly, by a change in the incidence of succession duties.

Some time after I saw a single copy of Henry George's *Progress and Poverty* on Robertson's[19] shelves, and bought it, and it was I who after reading this book opened in the three most important Australian colonies the question of the taxation of land values. An article I wrote went into the *Register*,[20] and Mr Liston, of Kapunda, read it, and spoke of it at a farmers' meeting. I had then a commission from the *Sydney Morning Herald* to write on any important subject, and I wrote on this. It appeared, like a previous article on Howell's 'Conflicts of Capital and Labour', as an unsigned article.[21] A new review, the

---

18 Henry George (1839–1897), American writer on political economy and sociology, an advocate of the nationalisation of land and of the 'single tax' on its increment value. *Progress and Poverty: An enquiry into the cause of industrial depressions, and of increase of want with increase of wealth. The remedy*, 1879.

19 George Robertson (1825–1898), bookseller, publisher and stationer based in Melbourne and later with branches in Sydney, Adelaide and Brisbane. His firm Robertson & Mullen was not the same as Angus and Robertson, which was started by another George Robertson (1860–1933).

20 'Progress and Poverty', *Register*, 10 May 1881. Unsigned review by Spence of Henry George's book.

21 'Progress and Poverty', *Sydney Morning Herald*, 2 May 1881. Article signed SPES, one of Spence's pseudonyms. 'Conflicts of Capital and Labour', *Sydney Morning Herald*, 8 January 1879. Review of Howell's book signed SPES. George Howell, *The conflicts of capital and labour: historically and economically considered. Being a history and review of the trade unions of Great Britain, showing their origin, progress, constitution, and objects, in their varied political, social, economical, and industrial aspects*, London, 1878.

Victorian,[22] had been started by Mortimer Franklyn, which paid contributors; and, now that I was a professional journalist, I thought myself entitled to ask remuneration. I sent to the new periodical, published in Melbourne, a fuller treatment of the book than had been given to the two newspapers, under the title of 'A Californian Political Economist'.[23] This fell into the hands of Henry George himself, in a reading room in San Francisco, and he wrote an acknowledgement of it to me. In South Australia the first tax on unimproved land values was imposed. It was small – only a halfpenny in the pound, but without any exemption; and its imposition was encouraged by the fact that we had had bad seasons and a falling revenue. The income tax in England was originally a war tax, and they say that if there is not a war the United States will never be able to impose an income tax. The separate states have not the power to impose such a tax. Henry George said to me in his home in New York: 'I wonder at you, with your zeal and enthusiasm, and your power of speaking, devoting yourself to such a small matter as proportional representation, when you see the great land question before you.' I replied that to me it was not a small matter. I cannot, however, write my autobiography without giving prominence to the fact that I was the pioneer in Australia in this as in the other matter of proportional representation.

---

22 A monthly magazine published in Melbourne 1879–1886, edited by H. Mortimer Franklyn.
23 'A Californian Political Economist', *Victorian Review*, vol. 4, no. xx, 1881.

Chapter 16

Sorrow and Change

In the long and cheerful life of my dear mother there at last came a change. At 94 she fell and broke her wrist. The local doctor (a stranger), who was called in, not knowing her wonderful constitution, was averse from setting the wrist, and said that she would never be able to use the hand. But I insisted, and in six weeks she was able to resume her knitting, and never felt any ill effects. At 95 she had a fall, apparently without cause, and was never able to stand again. She had to stay in bed for the last 13 months of her life, with a gradual decay of the faculties which had previously been so keen. My mother wanted me with her always. Her talk was all of times far back in her life – not of Melrose, where she had lived for 25 years, but of Scoryhall (pronounced Scole), where she had lived as a girl. I had been shown through the house by my aunt Handyside in 1865, and I could follow her mind wanderings and answer her questions. As she suffered so little pain it was difficult for my mother to realise the seriousness of her illness; and, tiring of her bedroom, she begged to be taken to the study, where, with her reading and knitting, she had spent so many happy hours while I did my writing. Delighted though she was at the change, a return to her bed – as to all invalids – was a comfort, and she never left it again. Miss Goodham – an English nurse and a charming woman, who has since remained a friend and correspondent of the family – was sent to help us for a few days at the last. Another sorrow came to us at this time in the loss of my ward's husband, and Rose Hood – née Duval – returned to live near me with her three small children.[1] Her commercial training enabled her to take a position as clerk in the State Children's Department, which she retained until

---

1 Lucy Alice Rose Duval (1854–1899), married Henry James Hood who died in April 1886. They had four children, one of whom died in early childhood. When their father died, George was three and a half, Catherine, sometimes spelled Katherine, was two and Charles was a baby.

Catherine Helen Spence and her mother, Helen Brodie Spence, c.1880, photograph courtesy of the State Library of South Australia, SLSA: B 7106

her death. The little ones were very sweet and good, but the supervision of them during the day added a somewhat heavy responsibility to our already overburdened household. In these days, when one hears so much of the worthlessness of servants, it is a joy to remember how our faithful maid – we kept only one for that large house – at her own request, did all the laundry work for the family of five, and all through the three years of Eleanor's illness[2] waited on her with untiring devotion.

An amusing episode which would have delighted the heart of my dear friend Judge Lindsey[3] occurred about this time. The fruit from our orange trees which grew along the wall bordering an adjoining paddock was an irresistible temptation to wandering juveniles, and many and grievous were the depredations. Patience, long drawn out, at last gave way, and when the milkman caught two delinquents one Saturday afternoon with bulging blouses of forbidden fruit it became necessary to make an example of some one. The trouble was to devise a fitting punishment. A Police Court, I had always maintained, was no place for children; corporal punishment was out of the question; and the culprits stood tremblingly awaiting their fate till a young doctor present suggested a dose of Gregory's powder. His lawyer friend acquiesced, and Gregory's powder it was. A moment's hesitation and the nauseous draught was swallowed to the accompaniment of openly expressed sympathy, one dear old lady remarking, 'Poor children – and not so much as a taste of sugar.' Probably, however, the unkindest cut of all was the carrying away by the milkman of the stolen fruit! The cure was swift and effective; and ever after the youth of the district, like the Pharisee of old, passed by on the other side.

My dear mother died about eight o'clock on the evening of 8 December 1887, quietly and painlessly. With her death, which was an exceedingly great loss to me, practically ended my quiet life of literary work. Henceforth I was free to devote my efforts to the fuller public work for which I had so often longed, but which my mother's devotion to and dependence on me rendered impossible. But I missed her untiring sympathy, for with all her love for the old days and the old friends there was no movement for the advancement of her adopted land that did not claim her devoted attention. But though I was now free to take up public work, the long strain of my mother's illness and death had affected my usually robust health, and I took things quietly. I had been asked by the University Shakespeare Society to give a lecture on Donnelly's

---

2 Eleanor Wren suffered from back problems which confined her to bed for three years.
3 Benjamin Barr Lindsey (1869–1943), American lawyer, judge and reformer, passionate about politics and social justice, founder of the Denver Juvenile Court. He contested the Govenorship of Colorado in 1906.

book, *The Great Cryptogram*;[4] and it was prepared during this period, and has frequently been delivered since. October of the year following my mother's death found me again in Melbourne, where I rejoiced in the renewal of a friendship with Mr and Mrs Thomas Walker, the former of whom had been connected with the construction of the overland railway.[5] They were delightful literary people, and I had met them at the hospitable house of the Barr-Smiths, and been introduced as 'a literary lady'. 'Then perhaps,' said Mr Walker, 'you can give us the information we have long sought in vain – who wrote *Clara Morison?*' Their surprise at my 'I did' was equalled by the pleasure I felt at their kind appreciation of my book, and that meeting was the foundation of a lifelong friendship. Before my visit closed I was summoned to Gippsland through the death by accident of my dear sister Jessie[6] – the widow of Andrew Murray, once editor of the *Argus* – and the year 1888 ended as sadly for me as the previous one had done. The following year saw the marriage of my nephew, Charles Wren, of the E.S. and A. Bank,[7] to Miss Hall, of Melbourne.[8] On his deciding to live on in the old home, I, with Ellen Gregory,[9] whom I had brought out in 1867 to reside with relations, but who has remained to be the prop and mainstay of my old age – and Mrs Hood and her three children, moved to a smaller and more suitable house I had in another part of East Adelaide.[10] A placid flowing of the river of life for a year or two led on to my being elected, in 1892, President of the Girls' Literary Society. This position I

4 Ignatius Donnelly (1831–1901), author of *The Great Cryptogram: Francis Bacon's cipher in the so-called Shakespeare plays*, (Sampson Low, Marston, Searle and Rivington) London, 1888. Spence was a Baconian.
5 Thomas Walker was a contractor. In 1881 Walker and Swan established a brickworks for railway contracts.
6 Jessie Murray died in 1888 at Balbrechan, Yarragon, Victoria from blood poisoning, after an injury when hit by a falling bough.
7 Charles William Wren (1856–1934), gained employment with the English, Scottish and Australian Chartered Bank in Adelaide in 1872. He became Branch Inspector in 1885, moved to Melbourne in 1888, became Resident Inspector in New South Wales in 1901 and was the bank's Australasian General Manager situated in Victoria from 1909 until his retirement in 1933. His sister Eleanor Brodie Wren (1862–1948) moved with him to Melbourne and remained there until her death.
8 Miss Eleanor Dora Hall of Melbourne married Charles Wren at St Stephen's Anglican Church, Elsternwick, Melbourne, on 6 March 1889.
9 Ellen Louisa Gregory accompanied Spence on her return from England in 1866 (not 1867). They arrived on the *Octavia* on June 20. Miss Gregory lived with Spence for many years. She died in Melbourne in 1927, aged 75.
10 'Eildon' on Walkerville Road (now Stephen Terrace), East Adelaide.

filled with joy to myself and, I hope, with advantage to others, until some years later the society ceased to exist.

Crowded and interesting as my life had been hitherto, the best was yet to be. My realisation of Browning's beautiful line from 'Rabbi Ben Ezra'[11] – 'The last of life, for which the first was made', came when I saw opening before me possibilities for public service undreamed of in my earlier years. For the advancement of effective voting I had so far confined my efforts to the newspapers. My brother John had suggested the change of name from proportional representation to effective voting as one more likely to catch the popular ear, and I had proposed a modification of Hare's original plan of having one huge electorate, and suggested instead the adoption of six-member districts. The state as one electorate returning 42 members for the Assembly may be magnificent, and may also be the pure essence of democracy, but it is neither commonsense nor practicable. 'Why not take effective voting to the people?' was suggested to me. No sooner said than done. I had ballot papers prepared and leaflets printed, and I began the public campaign which has gone on ever since. During a visit to Melbourne as a member of a charities conference[12] it was first discovered that I had some of the gifts of a public speaker. My friend, the Rev. Charles Strong,[13] had invited me to lecture before his working men's club at Collingwood, and I chose as my subject 'Effective Voting'.

When on my return Mr Barr Smith, who had long grasped the principle of justice underlying effective voting, and was eager for its adoption, offered to finance a lecturing tour through the state, I jumped at the offer. There was the opportunity for which I had been waiting for years. I got up at unearthly hours to catch trains, and sometimes succeeded only through the timely lifts of kindly drivers. Once I went in a carrier's van, because I had missed the early morning cars. I travelled thousands of miles in all weathers to carry to the people the gospel of electoral reform. Disappointments were frequent, and sometimes disheartening; but the silver lining of every cloud turned up somewhere, and I look back on that first lecturing tour as a time of the sowing of good seed, the harvest of which is now beginning to ripen. I had no advance agents to announce my arrival, and at one town in the north I found nobody at the station to meet me. I spent the most miserable two and a half hours of my life waiting Micawber-like for something to turn up; and it turned up in the person of the village blacksmith. I spoke to him, and explained my mission to

11 Robert Browning, 'Rabbi Ben Ezra' in *Dramatis Personae*, 1864.
12 The first Australasian Conference on Charity was held in Melbourne in November 1890.
13 Charles Strong (1844–1942), formerly a Presbyterian minister in Scotland, formed the Australian Church in Melbourne in 1884, espousing a loving rather than a punishing God. He served on the Council of the Working Men's College.

the town. He had heard nothing of any meeting. Incidentally I discovered that my correspondent was in Adelaide, and had evidently forgotten all about my coming. 'Well,' I said to the blacksmith, 'if you can get together a dozen intelligent men I will explain effective voting to them.' He looked at me with a dumbfounded air, and then burst out, 'Good G——, madam, there are not three intelligent men in the town.' But the old order has changed, and in 1909 Mrs Young addressed an enthusiastic audience of 150 in the same town on the same subject. The town, moreover, is in a parliamentary district, in which every candidate at the recent general election – and there were seven of them – supported effective voting. Far down in the south I went to a little village containing seven churches, which accounted (said the local doctor) for the extreme backwardness of its inhabitants. 'They have so many church affairs to attend to that there is no time to think of anything else.' At the close of this lecturing tour the *Register* undertook the public count through its columns, which did so much to bring the reform before the people of South Australia. Public interest was well aroused on the matter before my long projected trip to America took shape. 'Come and teach us how to vote,' my American friends had been writing to me for years; but I felt that it was a big order for a little woman of 68 to undertake the conversion to electoral reform of sixty millions of the most conceited people in the world. Still I went. I left Adelaide bound for America on 4 April 1893, as a Government Commissioner and delegate to the Great World's Fair Congresses in Chicago.

In Melbourne and Sydney on my way to the boat for San Francisco I found work to do. Melbourne was in the throes of the great financial panic, when bank after bank closed its doors; but the people went to church as usual. I preached in the Unitarian Church on the Sunday, and lectured in Dr Strong's Australian Church on Monday. In Sydney Miss Rose Scott[14] had arranged a drawing-room meeting for a lecture on effective voting. A strong convert I made on that occasion was Mr (afterwards Senator) Walker.[15] A few delightful hours I spent at his charming house on the harbour with his family, and was taken by them to see many beauty spots. Those last delightful days in Sydney left me with pleasant Australian memories to carry over the Pacific. When the boat sailed on April 17, the rain came down in torrents. Some interesting missionaries were on board. One of them, the venerable Dr Brown,[16] who had

---

14 Rose Scott (1847–1925), Sydney social reformer and campaigner for women's rights. She became one of Spence's friends and allies.
15 James Thomas Walker (1841–1923), Scottish born bank manager, and Senator for New South Wales, 1901–1913.
16 Dr George Brown (1835–1917), missionary in Samoa, general secretary of Australasian Overseas Mission and President of Methodist Church of Australasia.

been for 30 years labouring in the Pacific, introduced me to Sir John Thurston.[17] Mr Newell[18] was returning to Samoa after a two years' holiday in England. He talked much, and well about his work. He had 104 students to whom he was returning. He explained that they became missionaries to other more benighted and less civilised islands, where their knowledge of the traditions and customs of South Sea Islanders made them invaluable as propagandists. The writings of Robert Louis Stevenson,[19] had prepared me to find in the Samoans a handsome and stalwart race, with many amiable traits, and I was not disappointed. The beauty of the scenery appealed to me strongly, and I doubt whether 'the light that never was on sea or land' could have rivalled the magic charm of the one sunrise we saw at Samoa. During the voyage I managed to get in one lecture, and many talks on effective voting. Had I been superstitious my arrival in San Francisco on Friday, May 12, might have boded ill for the success of my mission, but I was no sooner ashore than my friend Alfred Cridge took me in charge, and the first few days were a whirl of meetings, addresses, and interviews.

17 Sir John Bates Thurston (1836–1897), British consul and colonial secretary for Fiji, appointed Governor of the Western Pacific in 1887.
18 James Edward Newell (1852–1910), missionary in Samoa and the South Pacific.
19 Robert Louis Stevenson (1850–1894), Scottish poet, essayist and novelist. He settled in Samoa in 1888 in the hope of improving his health.

Chapter 17

Impressions of America

Alfred Cridge,[1] who reminded me so much of my brother David that I felt at home with him immediately, had prepared the way for my lectures on effective voting in San Francisco. He was an even greater enthusiast than I. 'America needs the reform more than Australia', he used to say. But if America needs effective voting to check corruption, Australia needs it just as much to prevent the degradation of political life in the Commonwealth and States to the level of American politics. My lectures in San Francisco, as elsewhere in America, were well attended, and even better received. Party politics had crushed out the best elements of political life, and to be independent of either party gave a candidate, as an agent told Judge Lindsey[2] when he was contesting the governorship of Colorado, 'as much chance as a snowball would have in hell'. So that reformers everywhere were eager to hear of a system of voting that would free the electors from the tyranny of parties, and at the same time render a candidate independent of the votes of heckling minorities, and dependent only on the votes of the men who believed in him and his politics. I met men and women interested in public affairs – some of them well known, others most worthy to be known, and all willing to lend the weight of their character and intelligence to the betterment of human conditions at home and abroad. Among these were Judge Maguire,[3] a leader of the Bar in San Francisco and a member of the State Legislature, who had fought trusts,

---

1 Alfred Denton Cridge (1824–1902), San Francisco journalist, a strong supporter of proportional representation about which he published books and pamphlets.
2 Benjamin Barr Lindsey (1869–1943), lawyer, judge and reformer, passionate about politics and social justice, founder of the Denver Juvenile Court. He contested the Governorship of Colorado in 1906. See also above, Chapter XVI, p. 143.
3 James George Maguire (1853–1920), politician and Superior Court Judge.

'grafters', and 'boodlers'[4] through the whole of his public career, and Mr James Barry, proprietor of the *Star*.[5]

'You come from Australia, the home of the secret ballot?' was the greeting I often received, and that really was my passport to the hearts of reformers all over America. From all sides I heard that it was to the energy and zeal of the Single-taxers in the various states – a well-organised and compact body – that the adoption of the secret ballot was due. To that celebrated journalist, poetess, and economic writer, Charlotte Perkins Stetson,[6] who was a cultured Bostonian, living in San Francisco, I owed one of the best women's meetings I ever addressed. The subject was 'State children and the compulsory clauses in our Education Act', and everywhere in the States people were interested in the splendid work of our State Children's Department and educational methods. Intelligence and not wealth I found to be the passport to social life among the Americans I met. At a social evening ladies as well as their escorts were expected to remove bonnets and mantles in the hall, instead of being invited into a private room as in Australia – a custom I thought curious until usage made it familiar. The homeliness and unostentatiousness of the middle-class American were captivating. My interests have always been in people and in the things that make for human happiness or misery rather than in the beauties of Nature, art, or architecture. I want to know how the people live, what wages are, what the amount of comfort they can buy; how the people are fed, taught, and amused; how the burden of taxation falls; how justice is executed; how much or how little liberty the people enjoy. And these things I learned to a great extent from my social intercourse with those cultured reformers of America. Among these people I had not the depressing feeling of immensity and hugeness which marred my enjoyment when I arrived at New York. My literary lectures on the Brownings and George Eliot were much appreciated, especially in the East, where I found paying audiences in the fall or autumn of the year. These lectures have been delivered many times in Australia; and, as the result of the Browning lecture given in the Unitarian Schoolroom in Wakefield Street, Adelaide, I received from the pen of Mr J.B. Mather[7] a clever epigram. The room was large and sparsely filled, and to the modest back seat taken by my friend my voice scarcely penetrated. So he amused himself and me by writing:

4   Those who trade in political bribes and corruption.
5   *The California Star*, the oldest West Coast Weekly, established 1846.
6   Charlotte Perkins Stetson (1860–1935), usually remembered now as Charlotte Perkins Gilman, American feminist writer and thinker, struggling against notoriety at the time of Spence's visit for having left her husband. Spence found her an inspiration.
7   John Baxter Mather (1853–1940), Scottish emigrant, South Australian poet, journalist and landscape painter. He was for a time on the staff of the *Advertiser*.

> I have no doubt that words of sense
> Are falling from the lips of Spence.
> Alas! that Echo should be drowning
> Both words of Spence and sense of Browning.

I found the Brownings far better appreciated in America than in England, especially by American women. In spite of the fact that the *San Francisco Chronicle*[8] had interviewed me favourably on my arrival, and that I knew personally some of the leading people on the *Examiner*,[9] neither paper would report my lectures on effective voting. The *Star*, however, quite made up for the deficiencies of the other papers, and did all it could to help me and the cause. While in San Francisco I wrote an essay on 'Electoral Reform' for a Toronto competition, in which the first prize was $500. Mr Cridge was also a competitor; but, although many essays were sent in, for some reason the prize was never awarded, and we had our trouble for nothing. On my way to Chicago I stayed at a mining town to lecture on effective voting. I found the hostess of the tiny hotel a brilliant pianist and a perfect linguist, and she quoted poetry – her own and other people's – by the yard. A lady I journeyed with told me that she had been travelling for seven years with her husband and *Chambers's Encyclopedia*. I thought they used the encyclopaedia as a guide book until, in a sort of postscript to our conversation, I discovered the husband to be a book agent, better known in America as a 'book fiend'.

Nobody had ever seen anything like the World's Fair.[10] My friend Dr Bayard Holmes of Chicago,[11] whose acquaintance I made through missing a suburban train, expressed a common feeling when he said he could weep at the thought that it was all to be destroyed – that the creation evolved from the best brains of America should be dissolved. Much of our human toil is lost and wasted, and much of our work is more ephemeral than we think; but this was a conscious creation of hundreds of beautiful buildings for a six months' existence. Nowhere else except in America could the thing have been done, and nowhere else in America but in Chicago. At the Congress of Charity and

---

8 A weekly paper.
9 San Francisco morning paper.
10 The Chicago World's Fair of 1893, also known as the World's Columbian Exposition, was an extremely popular and influential social and cultural event. It took place on the shores of Lake Michigan and lasted for six months.
11 Bayard Taylor Holmes (1852–1924), professor of surgical pathology and bacteriology at the College of Physicians and Surgeons in Chicago, popular lecturer and social reformer with a strong interest in the education of the labouring classes, factory inspection and child welfare, one of the promoters of Hull House.

Miss C.H. Spence,
reproduced from the *Adelaide Observer*, 8 April 1893

Correction[12] I found everyone interested in Australia's work for destitute children. It was difficult for Miss Windeyer,[13] of Sydney, and myself – the only Australians present – to put ourselves in the place of many who believed in institutions where children of low physique, low morals, and low intelligence are massed together, fed, washed, drilled, taught by rule, never individualised, and never mothered. I spoke from pulpits in Chicago and Indianapolis on the subject, and was urged to plead with the Governor of the latter State to use his influence to have at least tiny mites of six years of age removed from the

12 Spence represented the South Australian State Children's Council at the International Conference on Charities and Correction held in conjunction with the World Fair.
13 Margaret Windeyer (1866–1939), campaigner for women's suffrage in Sydney, a commissioner to the Chicago exhibition in 1893, later a librarian in New South Wales, a member of the Free Kindergarten movement and a supporter of children's libraries.

reformatory, which was under the very walls of the gaol. But he was obdurate to my pleadings and arguments, as he had been to those of the State workers. He maintained that these tiny waifs of six were incorrigible, and were better in institutions than in homes. The most interesting woman I met at the conference was the Rev. Mrs Anna Garlin Spencer, pastor of Bell Street Chapel, Providence.[14] I visited her at home, in that retreat of Baptists, Quakers, and others from the hard persecution of the New England Orthodoxy, the founders of which had left England in search of freedom to worship God. Her husband was the Unitarian minister of another congregation in the same town. At the meetings arranged by Mrs Spencer, Professor Andrews,[15] one of the Behring Sea Arbitrators,[16] and Professor Wilson[17] were present; and they invited me to speak on effective voting at the Brown University.

In Philadelphia I addressed seven meetings on the same subject. At six of them an editor of a little reform paper was present. For two years he had lived on brown bread and dried apples, in order that he could save enough to buy a newspaper plant for the advocacy of reforms. In his little paper he replied to the critics, who assured me that it was no use worrying, as everything would come right in time. 'Time only brings wonders,' he wrote, 'when good and great men and women rise up to move the world along. Time itself brings only decay and death. The truth is "Nothing will come right unless those who feel they have the truth speak, and work, and strain as if on them alone rested the destinies of the world."' I went to see a celebrated man, George W. Childs, who had made a fortune out of the *Philadelphia Ledger*, and who was one of the best employers in the States. He knew everybody, not only in America but in Europe; and his room was a museum of gifts from great folks all over the world. But, best of all, he, with his devoted friend Anthony Drexel, had founded the Drexel Institute,[18] which was their magnificent educational legacy to the historic town. I saw the Liberty Bell in Chicago – the bell that rang out the Declaration of Independence, and cracked soon after – which is cherished

---

14 Anna Garlin Spencer (1851–1931), American educator, feminist and Unitarian minister, President of the Children's Section of the Charities and Correction Congress in Chicago.
15 Elisha Benjamin Andrews (1844–1917), President of Brown University 1889–1898.
16 In 1893 a court of arbitration ruled that the United States of America had no jurisdiction in the Behring Sea beyond the three mile limit, but regulations were made to prevent the wholesale slaughter of fur-bearing seals.
17 Thomas Woodrow Wilson (1856–1924), professor of jurisprudence and political economy at Princeton University 1890–1902, later President of the United States.
18 George William Childs (1829–1894), American philanthropist, and Anthony Joseph Drexel (1826–1893), banker, co-owners of the Philadelphian *Public Ledger* and co-founders of the Drexel Institute of Arts, Science and Literature in Philadelphia.

by all good Americans. It had had a triumphant progress to and from the World's Fair, and I was present when once again it was safely landed in Independence Hall, Philadelphia. I think the Americans liked me, because I thought their traditions reputably old, and did not, like European visitors, call everything crude and new.

The great war in America[19] strengthened the Federal bond, while it loosened the attachment to the special State in which the United States citizen lives. Railroads and telegraphs have done much to make Americans homogeneous, and the school system grapples bravely with the greater task of Americanising the children of foreigners, who arrive in such vast numbers. Canada allowed the inhabitants of lower Canada to keep their language, their laws, and their denominational schools; and the consequence is that these Canadian-British subjects are more French than the French, more conservative than the Tories, and more Catholic than Irish or Italians. Education is absolutely free in America up to the age of 18; but I never heard an American complain of being taxed to educate other people's children. In Auburn I met Harriet Tubman,[20] called the 'Moses of her people' – an old black woman who could neither read nor write, but who had escaped from slavery when young, and had made 19 journeys south, and been instrumental in the escape of 300 slaves. To listen to her was to be transferred to the pages of *Uncle Tom's Cabin*.[21] Her language was just like that of Tom and old Jeff. A pious Christian, she was full of good works still. Her shanty was a refuge for the sick, blind, and maimed of her own people. I went all over Harvard University under the guidance of Professor Ashley,[22] to whom our Chief Justice[23] had given me a letter of introduction. He got up a drawing-room meeting for me, at which I met Dr Gordon Ames, pastor of the Unitarian Church of the Disciples.[24] He invited me to preach his thanksgiving service for him on the following Thursday, which I was delighted to do. Mrs Ames was the factory inspector of women and children in Massachusetts, and was probably the wisest woman I met in my travels. She spoke to me of the evils of stimulating the religious sentiment too young, and said that the hushed awe with which most

---

19 The American Civil War, 1861–1865.
20 Harriet Tubman (1820–1913), American Negro abolitionist.
21 *Uncle Tom's Cabin: a tale of life among the lowly*, famous anti-slavery novel, published in 1852 by Harriet Beecher Stowe (1811–1890).
22 Professor of Historic Economics at Harvard. His wife was a cousin of Miss Emily Clark.
23 Sir Samuel Way (1836–1916).
24 Charles Gordon Ames (1828–1912), Unitarian minister devoted to social reform. Julia Frances (Fanny) Ames, née Baker (1840–1931), active in women's issues and other reform movements.

people spoke of God and His constant presence filled a child's mind with fear. She related an experience with her own child, who on going to bed had asked if God was in the room. The child was told that God was always besides us. After being left in darkness the child was heard sobbing, and a return to the nursery elicited the confession, 'Oh, mamma, I can't bear to be left with no one but God.' Better the simple anthropomorphism which makes God like the good father, the generous uncle, the indulgent grandfather, or the strong elder brother.

Such ideas as these of God were held by the heroines of the following stories: – A little girl, a niece of the beloved Bishop Brooks, had done wrong, and was told to confess her sin to God before she slept, and to beg His forgiveness. When asked next day whether she had obeyed the command, she said – 'Oh, yes! I told God all about it, and God said, "Don't mention it, Miss Brooks."' A similar injunction was laid upon a child brought up by a very severe and rather unjust aunt. Her reply when asked if she had confessed her sin was – 'I told God what I had done, and what you thought about it, and I just left it to Him.' The response of a third American girl (who was somewhat of a 'pickle' and had been reared among a number of boys) to the enquiry whether she had asked forgiveness for a wrong done was – 'Oh, yes; I told God exactly what I had done, and He said, "Great Scot, Elsie Murray, I know 500 little girls worse than you."' To me this was a much healthier state of mind than setting children weeping for their sins, as I have done myself.

On my second visit to Boston I spent three weeks with the family of William Lloyd Garrison, son of the famous Abolitionist.[25] The Chief Justice had given me a letter of introduction to him, and I found him a true-hearted humanitarian, as devoted to the gospel of single tax as his father had been to that of anti-slavery. They lived in a beautiful house in Brookline, on a terrace built by an enterprising man who had made his money in New South Wales. Forty-two houses were perfectly and equally warmed by one great furnace, and all the public rooms of the ground floor, dining, and drawing rooms, library, and hall were connected by folding doors, nearly always open, which gave a feeling of space I never experienced elsewhere. Electric lighting and bells all over the house, hot and cold baths, lifts, the most complete laundry arrangements, and cupboards everywhere ensured the maximum of comfort with the minimum of labour. But in this house I began to be a little ashamed of being so narrow in my views on the coloured question. Mr Garrison, animated with the spirit of the true brotherhood of man, was an advocate of the

---

25 William Lloyd Garrison (1838–1909), son of the great abolitionist William Lloyd Garrison, advocate of single tax, free trade, women's suffrage and the repeal of the Chinese Exclusion Act.

heathen Chinee,[26] and was continually speaking of the goodness of the negro and coloured and yellow races, and of the injustice and rapacity of the white Caucasians. I saw the files of his father's paper, the *Liberator*,[27] from its beginning in 1831 till its close, when the victory was won in 1865. Of the time spent in the Lloyd-Garrison household 'nothing now is left but a majestic memory', which has been kept green by the periodical letters received from this noble man up till the time of his death last year.[28] He showed me the monument erected to the memory of his father in Boston in the town where years before the great abolitionist had been stoned by the mob. Only recently it rejoiced my heart to know that a memorial to Lloyd Garrison the younger had been unveiled in Boston, his native city; at the same time that a similar honour was paid to his venerated leader, 'the prophet of San Francisco'.[29]

I account it one of the great privileges of my visit to America that Mrs Garrison introduced me to Oliver Wendell Holmes,[30] and by appointment I had an hour and a half's chat with him in the last year of his long life. He was the only survivor of a famous band of New England writers. Longfellow, Emerson, Hawthorn, Bryant, Lowell, Whittier, and Whitman were dead. His memory was failing, and he forgot some of his own characters; but Elsie Venner he remembered perfectly and he woke to full animation when I objected to the fatalism of heredity as being about as paralysing to effort as the fatalism of Calvinism. As a medical man (and we are apt to forget the physician in the author) he took strong views of heredity. As a worker among our destitute children, I considered environment the greater factor of the two, and spoke of children of the most worthless parents who had turned out well when placed early in respectable and kindly homes. Before I left, the author presented me with an autograph copy of one of his books – a much-prized gift. He was reading Cotton Mather's[31] *Memorabilia*, not for theology, but for gossip. It was the only chronicle of the small beer of current events in the days of the witch persecutions, and the expulsion of the Quakers, Baptists, and

26 'The Heathen Chinee' was the title of a poem by American poet Francis Bret Harte (1839–1902), published in 1870.
27 Abolitionist weekly (1831–1865), famous for its unswerving devotion to radical causes.
28 1909.
29 Henry George (1839–1897), American writer on political economy and sociology.
30 Oliver Wendell Holmes (1809–1894), Professor of Anatomy and Physiology at Harvard University from 1847 to 1882, poet, essayist and novelist. His novel *Elsie Venner* was published in 1861.
31 Cotton Mather (1663–1728), American divine and writer, who was involved in the Salem witch trials of 1692. He did not publish a book entitled *Memorabilia*, but he published many tracts and articles of which this may be one.

other schismatics. I have often felt proud that of all the famous men I have mentioned in this connection there was only one not a Unitarian, and that was Whittier, the Quaker poet of abolition; and his theology was of the mildest.[32]

Another notable man with whom I had three hours' talk was Charles Dudley Warner, the humorous writer.[33] I am not partial to American humorists generally, but the delicate and subtle humour of Dudley Warner I always appreciated. In our talk I saw his serious side, for he was keen on introducing the indeterminate sentence into his own State, on the lines of the Elmira and Concord Reformatories. He told me that he never talked in trains, but during the three hours' journey to New York neither of us opened the books with which we had provided ourselves, and we each talked of our separate interests, and enjoyed the talk right through. Mrs Harriet Beecher Stowe[34] I saw, but her memory was completely gone. With Mrs Julia Ward Howe,[35] the writer of *The Battle Hymn of the Republic*, I spent a happy time. She had been the President of the New England Women's Club for 25 years, and was a charming and interesting woman. I was said to be very like her, and, indeed, was often accosted by her name; but I think probably the reason was partly my cap, for Mrs Howe also wears one, and few other American ladies do. Whenever I was with her I was haunted by the beautiful lines from the closing verse of the 'Battle Hymn' –

> In the beauty of the lilies, Christ was born, across the sea,
> With a glory in His bosom that transfigures you and me;
> As He died to make men holy, let us die to make men free,
> While God is marching on.

At her house I met many distinguished women. Mrs J.T. Fields, the widow of the well-known author-publisher;[36] Madame Blanc-Bentzon,[37] a writer for

---

32 John Greenleaf Whittier (1807–1892), American editor, poet and abolitionist.
33 Charles Dudley Warner (1829–1900), American journalist, editor, essayist and novelist. Spence was a great admirer of his *Being a Boy* (1877), an account of boyhood on a New England farm in the 1840s.
34 Harriet Beecher Stowe (1811–1890), American author, teacher and activist in the movement to abolish slavery, author of *Uncle Tom's Cabin*, 1852.
35 Julia Ward Howe (1819–1910), prominent abolitionist, founder of New England Woman Suffrage Association.
36 Annie Adams Fields (1834–1915), writer and literary hostess with a wide circle of friends in the United States and England, widow of James Thomas Fields, American publisher of Dickens, among others.
37 Marie-Thérèse Bentzon (1840–1907), known as Madame Blanc-Bentzon, French novelist, critic, reviewer, translator and traveller. 'Blanc' was Madame Bentzon's writing name.

French reviews; Miss Sarah Orne Jewett,[38] one of the most charming of New England writers, and others.

My best work in Canada was the conversion to effective voting of my good friend Robert Tyson.[39] For years now he has done yeoman service in the cause, and has corresponded with workers all over the world on the question of electoral reform. I visited Toronto, at the invitation of Mr O.A. Howland,[40] with whom I had corresponded for years. I was invited to dinner with his father, Sir William Howland,[41] who was the first Lieutenant-Governor of Toronto after the federation of the Dominion. I found it very difficult to remember the names of the many interesting people I met there, although I could recollect the things they spoke about. Mr Howland took me on with him to an evening garden party – quite a novel form of entertainment for me – where there were other interesting people. One of these, a lady artist who had travelled all round the world, took me on the next afternoon to an at-home at Professor Goldwin Smith's.[42] In a talk I had with this notable man he spoke of his strong desire that Canada should become absorbed in the States; but the feeling in Canada was adverse to such a change. Still, you found Canadians everywhere, for many more men were educated than could find careers in the Dominion. Sir Sandford Fleming,[43] the most ardent proportionalist in Canada, left Toronto on his trip to New Zealand and Australia shortly after I arrived there. I spent a few hours with him, and owed a great deal of my success in the Dominion to his influence. I felt that I had done much good in Canada, and my time was so occupied that the only thing I missed was leisure.

Much of the time in New York was spent in interviews with the various papers. I had a delightful few days at the house of Henry George, and both he and his wife did everything in their power to make my visit pleasant. Indeed, everywhere in America I received the greatest kindness and consideration.

38 Sarah Orne Jewett (1849–1909), American novelist and short story writer, first president of Vassar College.
39 Robert Tyson, a Canadian who edited the Review published by the American Proportional Representation League from 1901–1913. He wrote an appendix to Alfred Cridge's *Proportional Representation, including its relation to the initiative and referendum* which was published as memorial to Cridge in 1904, with a biographical sketch.
40 Oliver Aiken Howland (1847–1905), barrister, Mayor of Toronto, one of the founders of the union of Canadian Municipalities, author of *The New Empire*, 1891, and advocate of proportional representation.
41 Sir William Holmes Howland (1844–1893), Canadian businessman, social reformer, philanthropist and politician.
42 Goldwin Smith (1823–1910), English born Canadian historian and publicist.
43 Sir Sandford Fleming (1827–1915), Canadian engineer and publicist.

I had been 11 months in the States and Canada, and lived the strenuous life to the utmost. I had delivered over 100 lectures, travelled thousands of miles, and met the most interesting people in the world. I felt many regrets on parting with friends, comrades, sympathisers, and fellow-workers. When I reflected that on my arrival in San Francisco I knew only two persons in America in the flesh, and only two more through correspondence, and was able to look back on the hundreds of people who had personally interested me, it seemed as if there was some animal magnetism in the world, and that affinities were drawn together as if by magic.

CHAPTER 18

BRITAIN, THE CONTINENT, AND HOME AGAIN

I went by steamer to Glasgow, as I found the fares by that route cheaper than to Liverpool. Municipal work in that city was then attracting world-wide attention, and I enquired into the methods of taxation and the management of public works, much to my advantage. The cooperative works at Shieldhall were another source of interest to me.[1] At Peterborough I stayed with Mr Hare's daughter, Katie,[2] who had married Canon Clayton.[3] Never before did I breathe such an ecclesiastical atmosphere as in that ancient canonry, part of the old monastery, said to be 600 years old. While there I spoke to the Guild of Co-operative Women on 'Australia'. In Edinburgh I had a drawing-room meeting at the house of Mrs Muir Dowie, daughter of Robert Chambers[4] and mother of Ménie Muriel Dowie,[5] who wrote *Through the Carpathians*, and another at the Fabian Society, both on effective voting. Mrs Dowie and Priscilla Bright McLaren,[6] sister of John Bright,[7] were both keen on the suffrage, and most interesting women. I had been so much associated with the

---

1 Shieldhall, near Glasgow, was the site of some of the factories of the Cooperative Wholesale Movement in Scotland, in which workers combined to overcome some of the problems and hardships caused by the industrial revolution.
2 Spence had met Katie Hare and her father when she was in England in 1865.
3 Lewis Clayton (c.1838–1917), Canon, suffragan Bishop of Peterborough and later Bishop of Leicester.
4 Robert Chambers (1802–1871), founder with his brother William of the Scottish publishing house W. and R. Chambers.
5 *A Girl in the Karpathians*, 1891, by Ménie Muriel Dowie, later Norman, (her husband was literary editor of the *Morning Chronicle*), later Fitzgerald.
6 A veteran leader of the woman's suffrage movement.
7 John Bright (1811–1889), English nonconformist politician and statesman, renowned for his oratory.

suffragists in America, with the veteran Susan B. Anthony[8] at their head, that English workers in the cause gave me a warm welcome.

London under the municipal guidance of the County Council was very different from the London I had visited 29 years earlier. Perhaps Glasgow and Birmingham have gone further in municipalising monopolies than Londoners have, but the vastness of the scale on which London moves makes it more interesting. Cr Peter Burt,[9] of Glasgow, had worked hard to add public-houses to the list of things under municipal ownership and regulation, and I have always been glad to see the increasing attention paid to the Scandinavian methods of dealing with the drink traffic.[10] I have deplored the division among temperance workers, which makes the prohibitionists hold aloof from this reform, when their aid would at least enable the experiment to be tried. But in spite of all hindrances the world moves on towards better things. It is not now a voice crying in the wilderness. There are many thousands of wise, brave, devoted men and women possessed with the enthusiasm of humanity in every civilised country, and they must prevail. Professor and Mrs Westlake, the latter of whom was Mr Hare's eldest daughter, arranged a most successful drawing-room meeting for me at their home, the River House, Chelsea, at which Mr Arthur Balfour[11] spoke. While he thought effective voting probably suitable for America and Australia, he scarcely saw the necessity for it in England. Party leaders so seldom do like to try it on themselves, but many of them are prepared to experiment on 'the other fellow'. In this State we find members of the Assembly anxious to try effective voting on the Legislative Council, Federal members on the State House, and vice versa. Other speakers who supported me were Sir John Lubbock (Lord Avebury),[12] Leonard (now Lord) Courtney,[13] Mr Westlake, and Sir John Hall,[14] of New Zealand. The

---

8 Susan Brownell Anthony (1820–1906), American teacher, reformer, abolitionist and campaigner for women's rights.
9 Councillor of the enterprising, wealthy and socialistic Glasgow Municipality.
10 The Gothenburg system was designed to abolish unlicensed distilling by handing over retail traffic to a non-commercial monopoly, the profits going to the state.
11 Arthur James Balfour, first Earl Balfour (1848–1930), British politician and statesman, born in Scotland, First Lord of the Treasury, later Prime Minister. For the Westlakes, see above, Chapter 6, n. 19.
12 Sir John Lubbock, first Baron Avebury (1834–1913), banker, natural historian, parliamentarian.
13 Leonard Henry Courtney, Baron Courtney (1836–1918), English politician and man of letters. An advocate of proportional representation and women's rights.
14 Sir John Hall (1824–1907), born in England, emigrated to New Zealand, run-holder, politician and Premier of New Zealand. He became the parliamentary leader of the female suffrage movement. He retired from parliament in 1893.

flourishing condition of the Proportional Representation Society in England at present is due to the earnestness of the lastnamed gentlemen, and its extremely able hon. secretary (Mr John H. Humphreys).[15]

A few days were spent with Miss Jane Hume Clapperton,[16] author of *Scientific Meliorism*, and we had an interesting time visiting George Eliot's haunts and friends. Through the Warwickshire lanes – where the high hedges and the great trees at regular intervals made it impossible to see anything beyond, except an occasional gate, reminding me of Mrs Browning's[17] –

> And between the hedgerows green,
> How we wandered – I and you;
> With the bowery tops shut in,
> And the gates that showed the view.

– we saw the homestead known as 'Mrs Poyser's Farm', as it answers so perfectly to the description in *Adam Bede*.[18] I was taken to see Mrs Cash,[19] a younger friend of George Eliot, and took tea with two most interesting old ladies[20] – one 82, and the other 80 – who had befriended the famous authoress when she was poor and stood almost alone. How I grudged the thousands of acres of beautiful agricultural land given up to shooting and hunting! We in Australia have no idea of the extent to which field sports enter into the rural life of England. People excused this love of sport to me on the ground that it was a safety valve for the energy of idle men. Besides, said one, hunting leads, at any rate, to an appreciation of Nature; but I thought it a queer appreciation

---

15 John H. Humphreys, for many years a writer on proportional representation, elections and constitutional reform.

16 Jane Hume Clapperton (1832–1914), Scottish-born novelist, writer on ethics, social conditions, women's rights and suffrage, and especially noted for an exposition of Malthusian population control proposals, *Scientific Meliorism and the Evolution of Happiness*, 1885. This work was the inspiration for Catherine Spence's last work of fiction, *A Week in the Future*, (Hale and Iremonger) Sydney, 1987, with an Introduction and Notes by Lesley Durrell Ljungdahl.

17 'Bertha in the Lane' by Elizabeth Barrett Browning. The first line should be 'Through the winding hedgerows green.'

18 Mrs Poyser is a character in George Eliot's *Adam Bede* (William Blackwood and Sons) London, 1859.

19 Mary Cash, née Sibree (1824–1895), then only 16, met and admired George Eliot in 1840. The friendship was renewed in Eliot's last years.

20 Sara Hennell (1812–1899) and her sister, Mrs Charles Bray, née Caroline [Cara] Hennell (1814–1905). These two women were longstanding friends and correspondents of George Eliot.

of Nature that would lead keen fox hunters to complain of the 'stinking' violets that throw the hounds off the scent of the fox. I saw Ascot and Epsom, but fortunately not on a race day. A horse race I have never seen. George Moore's realistic novel *Esther Waters*[21] does not overstate the extent to which betting demoralises not only the wealthier, but all classes. There is a great pauper school in Sutton, where from 1,600 to 1,800 children are reared and educated. On Derby Day the children go to the side of the railroad, and catch the coppers and silver coins thrown to them by the passengers, and these are gathered together to give the children their yearly treat. But this association in the children's minds of their annual pleasure with Derby Day must, I often think, have a demoralising tendency.

While in London I slipped in trying to avoid being run down by an omnibus, and dislocated my right shoulder. I was fortunate in being the guest of Mr and Mrs Petherick[22] at the time. I can never be sufficiently grateful to them for their care of and kindness to me. Only last year I went to Melbourne to meet them both again. It was the occasion of the presentation to the Federal Government of the Petherick Library,[23] and I went over to sign and to witness the splendid deed of gift.

I have left almost to the last of the account of my English visit all mention of the Baconians I met and from whom I gained valuable information in corroboration of the Baconian authorship. In some circles I found that, to suggest that Shakespeare did not write the plays and poems was equal to throwing a bombshell among them. As a Baconian I received an invitation to a picnic at the beautiful country house of Mr Edwin Lawrence,[24] with whom I had a pleasant talk. The house was built on a part of a royal forest, in which firs and pines were planted at the time of the great Napoleonic wars, when timber could not be got from the Baltic, and England had to trust to her own hearts of oak and her own growth of pine for masts and planks. Mr Lawrence had written pamphlets and essays on the Baconian theory, and I found my knowledge of the subject expanding and growing under his intelligent talk. His wife's father (J. Benjamin Smith)[25] had taught Cobden the ethics of free trade.

21   *Esther Waters*, a novel published in 1894 by Anglo-Irish novelist George Moore (1852–1933).
22   Edward Augustus Petherick (1847–1917), worked in Melbourne for George Robertson's bookselling and publishing business and became their London representative. His magnificent collection of Australiana eventually became part of the National Library of Australia.
23   The Petherick collection of Australiana.
24   Sir Edwin Durning-Lawrence (1837–1914), author of *Bacon is Shakespeare*, (Gay and Hancock) London, 1910; and *The Shakespeare Myth*, (Gay and Hancock) London, 1912.
25   John Benjamin Smith (1794–1879), president of the Manchester Chamber of Commerce.

It was through the kind liberality of Miss Florence Davenport Hill that a pamphlet, recording the speeches and results of the voting at River House, Chelsea, was printed and circulated.[26] When I visited Miss Hill and her sister and found them as eager for social and political reform as they had been 29 years earlier, I had another proof of the eternal youth which large and high interests keep within us in spite of advancing years. Miss Davenport Hill had been a member of the London School Board for 15 years, and was re-elected after I left England. Years of her life had been devoted to work for the children of the State, and she was a member of the Board of Guardians for the populous union of St Pancras. Everyone acknowledged the great good that the admission of women to those boards had done. I spent a pleasant time at Toynbee Hall,[27] a University centre, in the poorest part of London, founded by men. Canon and Mrs Barnett[28] were intensely interested in South Australian work for state children. Similar University centres which I visited in America, like Hull House,[29] in Chicago, were founded by women graduates. Mrs Fawcett[30] I met several times, but Mrs Garrett Anderson[31] only once. When the suffrage was granted to the women of South Australia I received a letter of congratulation from Dr Helen Blackburn,[32] one of the first women to take a medical degree. Nowadays women doctors are accepted as part of our daily life, and it is owing to the brave pioneers of the women's cause, Drs Elizabeth

---

26 This pamphlet, *Report on 'proportional representation' or effective voting held at River House, Chelsea, July 10, 1894*, was published in London in 1894.

27 Toynbee Hall, named after Arnold Toynbee (1852–1883), English social reformer and economist, was the first of many institutions built in the East End of London for the purpose of uplifting and brightening the lives of the poorer classes.

28 Samuel Augustus Barnett (1877–1914), English clergyman and social reformer, instituted University settlements like Toynbee Hall to bring university men into contact with poorer people in the cities. He became Warden of Toynbee Hall. He married Henrietta Octavia Rowland, philanthropist and charity worker.

29 Hull House in Chicago was founded in 1889 by Jane Addams and Ellen Starr to encourage female college graduates in the United States of America to work with the poor and struggling. It is now a museum.

30 Dame Millicent Fawcett, née Garrett (1847–1929), a leader in the movement for women's suffrage and higher education and independent employment for women.

31 Elizabeth Anderson, née Garrett (1836–1917), first English woman doctor, sister of Dame Millicent Fawcett,

32 Helen Blackburn (1842–1903), Irish social reformer, early leader in the movement for female emancipation in Britain. Secretary of the National Society for Women's Suffrage, 1874–1895. Blackburn did not study medicine. Young may have confused Blackburn and Blackwell.

Blackwell,[33] Helen Blackburn, Garrett Anderson, and other like noble souls, that the social and political prestige of women has advanced so tremendously all over the English-speaking world. It only remains now for a few women, full of enthusiasm of humanity and gifted with the power of public speaking, to gain another and important step for the womanhood of the world in the direction of economic freedom. Before leaving England I was gratified at receiving a cheque from Mrs Westlake, contributed by the English proportionalists, to help me in the cause. This was the second gift of the kind I had received, for my friends in San Francisco had already helped me financially on my way to reform. Socially I liked the atmosphere of America better than that of England, but politically England was infinitely more advanced. Steadily and surely a safer democracy seems to be evolving in the old country than in the Transatlantic Republic. I left England at the end of September 1894.

My intended visit to Paris was cancelled through the death a short time before of the only friend I wished to meet there, the Baroness Blaze-de-Bury,[34] and I went straight through to Bale. I made a detour to Zurich, where I hoped to see people interested in proportional representation who could speak English. An interesting fellow-worker in the cause was Herr Karl Bürkli,[35] to whom I suggested the idea of lecturing with ballots.[36] The oldest advocate of proportional representation on the Continent, M. Ernest Naville,[37] I met at Geneva. In that tiny republic in the heart of Europe, which is the home of experimental legislation, I found effective voting already established in four cantons, and the effect in these cantons had been so good (said Ernest Naville) 'That it is only a matter of time to see all the Swiss cantons and the Swiss Federation adopt it'. In Zurich Herr Bürkli was delighted that they had introduced progressive taxation into the canton, but the effect had been to drive away the wealthy people who came in search of quiet and healthy residence. Progressive taxation has not by any means proved the unmixed blessing which so many of its advocates claim it to be. In New Zealand, we are told, on the best authority, that land monopoly and land jobbery were never so rampant in the Dominion as since the introduction of the progressive land tax. One wondered how the three million Swiss people lived on their little territory, so

33 Elizabeth Blackwell (1821–1910), born in England, became the first woman doctor in the United States of America. She founded the London School of Medicine for Women.
34 Marie Pauline Rose Blaze de Bury, Baroness, (1813–1894), French novelist and writer.
35 Karl Bürkli (1823–1909), Swiss social thinker and journalist.
36 Giving practical demonstrations of the working of proportional representation by conducting mock elections during lectures.
37 Ernest Naville (1816–1909), Swiss writer and lecturer on philosophy, religion, politics, morals and modern physics, advocate of proportional representation.

much occupied by barren mountain, and lakes which supply only a few fish. My Zurich friends told me that it was by their unremitting industry and exceptional thrift, but others said that the foreign visitors who go to the recreation ground of Europe circulate so much money that instead of the prayer 'Give us this day our daily bread' the Swiss people ask, 'Send us this day one foreigner'.

In Italy I saw the most intense culture in the world – no pleasure grounds or deer parks for the wealthy. The whole country looked like a garden with trellised vines and laden trees. Italian wine was grown, principally for home consumption, and that was immense. Prohibitionists would speak to deaf ears there. Wine was not a luxury, but a necessity of life. It made the poor fare of dry bread and polenta (maize porridge) go down more pleasantly. It was the greater abundance of fruit and wine that caused the Italian poorer classes to look healthier than the German. In Germany, which taxed itself to give cheap beet sugar to the British consumer, the people paid 6d. a lb. for the little they could afford to use; and in Italy it was nearly 8d. – a source of revenue to the Governments, but prohibitive to the poor. There were no sweet shops in Italy. England only could afford such luxuries. I visited at Siena, a home for deaf mutes, and found that each child had wine at two of its daily meals – about a pint a day. It was the light-red wine of the country, with little alcohol in it; but those who warn us against looking on the wine when it is red will be shocked to hear of these little ones drinking it like milk. Those, however, who live in Italy say that not once a year do they see any one drunk in the streets.

I reached South Australia on 12 December 1894, after an absence of 20 months. I found the women's suffrage movement wavering in the balance. It had apparently come with a rush – as unexpected as it was welcome to those whose strenuous exertions at last seemed likely to be crowned with success. Though sympathetic to the cause, I had always been regarded as a weak-kneed sister by the real workers. I had failed to see the advantage of having a vote that might leave me after an election a disfranchised voter, instead of an unenfranchised woman. People talk of citizens being disenfranchised for the Legislative Council when they really mean that they are unenfranchised. You can scarcely be disfranchised if you have never been enfranchised; and I have regarded the enfranchisement of the people on the roll as more important for the time being than adding new names to the rolls. This would only tend to increase the disproportion between the representative and the represented. But I rejoiced when the Women's Suffrage Bill was carried,[38] for I believe that women have thought more and accepted the responsibilities of voting to a greater extent than was ever expected of them. During the week I was

---

38 On 18 December 1894, the Constitution Amendment Act was passed, granting women the right to vote and to stand for parliament, two Australian firsts.

Mary Lee, leader of the campaign for votes for women in South Australia, photograph courtesy of the State Library of South Australia

accorded a welcome home in the old Academy of Music, Rundle Street, where I listened with embarrassment to the avalanche of eulogium that overwhelmed me. 'What a good thing it is, Miss Spence, that you have only one idea', a gentleman once said to me on my country tour. He wished thus to express his feeling concerning my singleness of purpose towards effective voting. But at this welcome home I felt that others realised what I had often said myself. It is really because I have so many ideas for making life better, wiser, and pleasanter – all of which effective voting will aid – that I seem so absorbed in the one reform. My opinions on other matters I give for what they are worth – for discussion, for acceptance or rejection. My opinions on equitable representation I hold absolutely, subject to criticism of methods, but impregnable as to principle.

CHAPTER 19

PROGRESS OF EFFECTIVE VOTING

My journalistic work after my return was neither so regular nor so profitable as before I left Adelaide. The bank failures had affected me rather badly, and financially my outlook was anything but rosy in the year 1895. There was, however, plenty of public work open to me, and, in addition to the many lectures I gave in various parts of the State of effective voting, I became a member of the Hospital Commission, appointed that year by the Kingston Government to enquire into the trouble at the Adelaide Hospital.[1] That same year saw a decided step taken in connection with effective voting, and in July a league was formed, which has been in existence ever since. I was appointed the first President, my brother John became secretary pro tem, and Mr A.W. Piper[2] the first treasurer. I felt at last that the reform was taking definite shape, and looked hopefully to its future. The following year was especially interesting to the women of South Australia, and, indeed, to suffragists all over the world, for at the general election of 1896 women, for the first time in Australia, had the right to vote. New Zealand had preceded us with this reform, but the first election in this state found many women voters fairly well equipped to accept their responsibilities as citizens of the state. But in the full realisation by the majority of women of their whole duties of citizenship I have been distinctly disappointed. Not that they have been on the whole less patriotic and less zealous than men voters; but, like their brothers, they have allowed their interest in public affairs to stop short at the act of voting, as if the right to vote were the beginning and the end of political life. There has been too great a

1   A dispute lasting from 1894–1901 which involved the Board of Management, doctors, nurses, politicians and an interested world of journalists and citizens and was not solved by the Royal Commission into the Adelaide Hospital to which Spence was appointed.
2   Arthur William Piper (1865–1936), federationist, barrister 1886, King's Counsel 1911, Judge of the Supreme Court of South Australia 1927.

tendency on the part of women to allow reform work – particularly women's branches of it – to be done by a few disinterested and public-spirited women. Not only is the home the centre of woman's sphere, as it should be, but in too many cases it is permitted to be its limitation. The larger social life has been ignored, and women have consequently failed to have the effect on public life of which their political privilege is capable.

At the close of a second lecturing tour through the State, during which I visited and spoke at most of the village settlements,[3] I received an invitation from the Women's Land Reform League to attend a social gathering at the residence of Miss Sutherland,[4] Clark Street, Norwood. The occasion was my seventy-first birthday, and my friends had chosen that day (October 31, 1896) to mark their appreciation of my public services. There were about 30 of the members present, all interesting by reason of their zealous care for the welfare of the State. Their President (Mrs C. Proud)[5] presented me, on behalf of the members, with a lady's handbag, ornamented with a silver plate, bearing my name, the date of the presentation, and the name of the cause for which I stood. From that day the little bag has been the inseparable companion of all my wanderings, and a constant reminder of the many kind friends who, with me, had realised that 'love of country is one of the loftiest virtues which the Almighty has planted in the human heart'. That association was the first in South Australia to place effective voting on its platform.

My long comradeship with Mrs A.H. Young began before the close of the year. A disfranchised voter at her first election, she was driven farther afield than the present inadequate system of voting to look for a just electoral method. She found it in effective voting, and from that time devoted herself to the cause. Early in 1897 Mrs Young was appointed the first honorary secretary of the league. January of the same year found us stirred to action by the success of Sir Edward Braddon's[6] first Bill for proportional representation in Tasmania. Though limited in its application to the two chief cities of the island State, the experiment was wholly successful. We had our first large public meeting in the Co-operative Hall in January, and carried a resolution protesting against the use of the block vote for the Federal Convention

---

3   The Kingston ministry passed legislation in 1893 to provide for associations of 20 or more settlers to work land as a community. The first settlements were along the River Murray.
4   Miss Caroline Sutherland.
5   Emily Proud, née Good, second wife of Cornelius Proud, shorthand writer and share-broker, advocate of women's rights. The Prouds were the parents of Dorothea Proud, later Pavy, first recipient of the Catherine Helen Spence Scholarship.
6   Sir Edward Nicholas Braddon (1829–1904), business man and politician, Premier of Tasmania 1894–1899.

elections. A deputation to the acting Premier (Mr – afterwards Sir Frederick – Holder[7]) was arranged for the next morning. But we were disappointed in the result of our mission, for Mr Holder pointed out that the Enabling Act distinctly provided for every elector having ten votes, and effective voting meant a single transferable vote. I had written and telegraphed to the Hon. C.C. Kingston[8] when the Enabling Act was being drafted to beg him to consider effective voting as the basis of election; but he did not see it then, nor did he ever see it. In spite, however, of the shortsightedness of party leaders, events began to move quickly.

Our disappointment over the maintenance of the block vote for the election of ten delegates to the Federal Convention[9] led to my brother John's suggestion that I should become a candidate. Startling as the suggestion was, so many of my friends supported it that I agreed to do so. I maintained that the fundamental necessity of a democratic constitution such as we hoped would evolve from the combined efforts of the ablest men in the Australian states was a just system of representation; and it was as the advocate of effective voting that I took my stand. My personal observation in the United States and Canada had impressed me with the dangers inseparable from the election of Federal Legislatures by local majorities – sometimes by minorities – where money and influences could be employed, particularly where a line in a tariff spelt a fortune to a section of the people, in the manipulation of the floating vote. Parties may boast of their voting strength and their compactness, but their voting strength under the present system of voting is only as strong as its weakest link, discordant or discontented minorities, will permit it to be. The stronger a party is in the Legislature the more is expected from it by every little section of voters to whom it owes its victory at the polls. The impelling force of responsibility which makes all Governments 'go slow' creates the greatest discontent among impatient followers of the rank and file, and where a few votes may turn the scale at any general election a Government is often compelled to choose between yielding to the demands of its more clamorous followers at the expense of the general taxpayer or submitting to a ministerial defeat.

7   Sir Frederick William Holder (1850–1909), Mayor of Burra, journalist and politician, Premier of South Australia 1892 and 1899–1901, and enthusiastic supporter of federation. Speaker in the first Federal House of Representatives.
8   Charles Cameron Kingston (1850–1908), barrister, radical and quarrelsome politician, federationist, Premier of South Australia 1893–1899. Minister in the first Federal Parliament.
9   In 1897 the second Convention planning federation was held in Adelaide, with elected representatives from all colonies except Queensland. It drafted a Commonwealth Bill which was then put to the people.

As much as we may talk of democracy in Australia, we are far from realising a truly democratic ideal. A state in a pure democracy draws no nice and invidious distinctions between man and man. She disclaims the right of favouring either property, education, talent, or virtue. She conceives that all alike have an interest in good government, and that all who form the community, of full age and untainted by crime, should have a right to their share in the representation. She allows education to exert its legitimate power through the press; talent in every department of business, property in its social and material advantages; virtue and religion to influence public opinion and the public conscience. But she views all men as politically equal, and rightly so, if the equality is to be as real in operation as in theory. If the equality is actual in the representation of the citizens – truth and virtue, being stronger than error and vice, and wisdom being greater than folly, when a fair field is offered – the higher qualities subdue the lower and make themselves felt in every department of the state. But if the representation from defective machinery is not equal, the balance is overthrown, and neither education, talent, nor virtue can work through public opinion so as to have any beneficial influence on politics. We know that in despotisms and oligarchies, where the majority are unrepresented and the few extinguish the many, independence of thought is crushed down, talent is bribed to do service to tyranny, education is confined to a privileged class and denied to the people, property is sometimes pillaged and sometimes flattered, and even virtue is degraded by lowering its field and making subservience appear to be patience and loyalty, and religion is not unfrequently made the handmaid of oppression. Taxes fall heavily on the poor for the benefit of the rich, and the only check proceeds from the fear of rebellion. When, on the other hand, the majority extinguishes the minority, the evil effects are not so apparent. The body oppressed is smaller and generally wealthier, with many social advantages to draw off attention from the political injustice under which they suffer; but there is the same want of sympathy between class and class, moral courage is rare, talent is perverted, genius is overlooked, education is general, but superficial, and press and pulpit often timid in exposing or denouncing popular errors. An average standard of virtue is all that is aimed at, and when no higher mark is set up there is great fear of falling below the average. Therefore it is incumbent on all states to look well to it that their representative systems really secure the political equality they all profess to give, for until that is done democracy has had no fair trial.

In framing a new constitution the opportunity arose for laying the foundation of just representation, and, had I been elected, my first and last thought would have been given to the claims of the whole people to electoral justice. But the 7,500 votes which I received left me far enough from the lucky ten. Had Mr Kingston not asserted both publicly and privately that, if elected,

I could not constitutionally take my seat, I might have done better. There were rumours even that my nomination paper would be rejected. But to obviate this, Mrs Young, who got it filled in, was careful to see that no name was on it that had no right there, and its presentation was delayed till five minutes before the hour of noon, in order that no time would be left to upset its validity. From a press cutting on the declaration of the poll I cull this item of news: 'Several unexpected candidates were announced, but the only nomination which evoked any expressions of approval was that of Miss Spence'. I was the first woman in Australia to seek election in a political contest. From the two main party lists I was, of course, excluded, but in the list of 'ten best men' selected by a Liberal organisation my name appeared. When the list was taken to the printer – who, I think, happened to be the late Federal member, Mr James Hutchison[10] – he objected to the heading of the 'ten best men', as one of them was a woman. He suggested that my name should be dropped, and a man's put in its place. 'You can't say Miss Spence is one of the "ten best men". Take her name out.' 'Not say she's one of the "ten best men"?' the Liberal organiser objected, 'Why she's the best man of the lot.' I had not expected to be elected, but I did expect that my candidature would help effective voting, and I am sure it did. Later, the league arranged a deputation to Mr Kingston, to beg him to use his influence for the adoption of the principle in time for the first Federal elections. We foresaw, and prophesied what has actually occurred – the monopoly of representation by one party in the Senate, and the consequent disfranchisement of hundreds of thousands of voters throughout the Commonwealth. But, as before, Mr Kingston declined to see the writing on the wall. The Hon. D.M. Charleston[11] was successful in carrying through the Legislative Council a motion in favour of its application to Federal elections, but Mr Glynn[12] in the Lower House had a harder row to hoe, and a division was never taken.

    Mrs Young and I spent a pleasant evening at Government House in July of the same year, as Sir Fowell and Lady Buxton[13] had expressed a desire to

---

10 James Hutchison (1859–1909), printer and politician, supporter of the United Labor Party, member of the State Children's Council, member of Federal House of Representatives 1906–1909.

11 David Morley Charleston (1848–1934), engineer, unionist, politician, State and Federal Parliamentarian, supporter of proportional representation.

12 Patrick McMahon Glynn (1855–1931), lawyer, politician, supporter of female suffrage, South Australian delegate to the Federal Convention and member of the first Federal House of Representatives.

13 Sir Thomas Fowell Buxton (1837–1915), philanthropist and Governor of South Australia. Lady Victoria Buxton, née Noel (1839–1916), first president of Church of England Mothers' Union in Adelaide and founder of several working girls' clubs.

understand the system. In addition to a large house party, several prominent citizens were present, and all were greatly interested. On leaving at 11 o'clock we found the gate closed against us, as the porter was evidently unaware that visitors were being entertained. We were amused at the indignation of the London-bred butler, who, on coming to our rescue, cried with a perfect Cockney accent, 'Gyte, gyte, yer don't lock gytes till visitors is off'. This was a memorable year in the annals of our cause, for on his election to fill an extraordinary vacancy for North Adelaide Mr Glynn promised to introduce effective voting into the House. This he did in July by tabling a motion for the adoption of the principle, and we were pleased to find in Mr Batchelor,[14] now the Minister for External Affairs in the Federal Government, a staunch supporter. Among the many politicians who have blown hot and cold on the reform as occasion arose, Mr Batchelor has steadily and consistently remained a supporter of what he terms 'the only system that makes majority rule possible'.

When Mrs Young and I began our work together the question was frequently asked why women alone were working for effective voting? The answer was simple. There were few men with leisure in South Australia, and, if there were, the leisured man was scarcely likely to take up reform work. When I first seized hold of this reform women as platform speakers were unheard of. Indeed, the prejudice was so strong against women in public life that although I wrote the letters to the *Melbourne Argus* it was my brother John who was nominally the correspondent. So for 30 years I wrote anonymously to the press on this subject. I waited for some man to come forward and do the platform work for me. We women are accused of waiting and waiting for the coming man, but often he doesn't come at all; and oftener still, when he does come, we should be a great deal better without him. In this case he did not come at all, and I started to do the work myself; and, just because I was a woman working single-handed in the cause, Mrs Young joined me in the crusade against inequitable representation. For many years, however, the cause has counted to its credit men speakers and demonstrators of ability and talent all over the state, who are carrying the gospel of representative reform into every camp, both friendly and hostile.

It was said of Gibbon[15] when his autobiography was published that he did not know the difference between himself and the Roman Empire. I have

---

14 Egerton Lee Batchelor (1865–1911), engineer, politician, central figure in South Australian Labor Movement, only South Australian Labor member in the first Federal House of Representatives.

15 Edward Gibbon (1737–1794), English historian, author of *The History of the Decline and Fall of the Roman Empire*, 6 vols, 1776–1788; and Edward Gibbon, *Memoirs of my Life and Writing*, 1796.

sometimes thought that the same charge might be levelled against me with regard to effective voting; but association with a reform for half a century sometimes makes it difficult to separate the interests of the person from the interests of the cause. Following on my return from America effective voting played a larger part than ever in my life. I had come back cheered by the earnestness and enthusiasm of American reformers, and I found the people of my adopted country more than ever prepared to listen to my teaching. Parties had become more clearly defined, and the results of our system of education were beginning to tell, I think, in the increased interest taken by individuals as well as by societies in social and economic questions. I found interesting people everywhere, in every mode of life, and in every class of society. My friends sometimes accused me of judging people's intelligence by the interest they took in effective voting; but, although this may have been true to a certain extent, it was not wholly correct. Certainly I felt more drawn to effective voters, but there are friendships I value highly into which my special reform work never enters. Just as the more recent years of my life have been coloured by the growth of the movement which means more to me than anything else in the world, so must the remaining chapters of this narrative bear the imprint of its influence.

CHAPTER 20

WIDENING INTERESTS

During this period my work on the State Children's Council continued, and I never found time hang heavily on my hands; so that when Mr Kingston met me one day later in the year, and told me he particularly wished me to accept an appointment as a member of the Destitute Board,[1] I hesitated. 'I am too old,' I objected. 'No, no, Miss Spence,' he replied laughingly, 'it is only we who grow old – you have the gift of perpetual youth.' But I was nearly 72, and at any rate I thought I should first consult my friends. I found them all eager that I should accept the position. I had agitated long and often for the appointment of women on all public boards, particularly where both sexes came under treatment, and I accepted the post. Although often I have found the work tiring, I have never regretted the step I took in joining the board. Experience has emphasised my early desire that two women at least should occupy positions on it. I hope that future Governments will rectify the mistake of past years by utilising to a greater extent the valuable aid of capable and sympathetic women in the branch of public work for which they are peculiarly fitted. Early in my career as a member of the board I found grave defects in the daily bill of fare, and set myself to the task of remedying them as far as lay in my power. For 30 years the same kind of soup, day in and day out, followed by the eternal and evergreen cabbage as a vegetable, in season and out of season, found its way to the table. My own tastes and mode of life were simplicity personified, but my stomach revolted against a dietary as unvaried as it was unappetising. An old servant who heard that I attended the Destitute Asylum every week was loud in her lamentations that 'poor dear Miss Spence was so reduced that she had to go to the Destitute every week for rations!' My thankfulness that she had misconceived the position stirred me to leave no stone

---

1   The Destitute Board, to administer the distribution of relief to the destitute in Adelaide, was first formed in 1849.

unturned for the betterment of the destitute bill of fare. I was successful, and the varied diet now enjoyed bears witness to the humanitarian views of all the members of the board, who were as anxious to help in the reform as I was. My heart has always gone out to the poor old folk whose faces bear the impress of long years of strenuous toil, and who at the close of life at least should find a haven of restfulness and peace in the State for whose advancement they have laboured in the past.

She was a witty woman who divided autobiographies into two classes – autobiographies and ought-not-to-biographies – but I am sure she never attempted to write one herself. There is so much in one's life that looms large from a personal point of view about which other people would care little, and the difficulty often arises, not so much about what to put in as what to leave out.

How much my personal interests had widened during my absence from home could be gauged somewhat by the enormous increase in my correspondence after my return. American, Canadian, English, and Continental correspondents have kept me for many years well informed on reform and kindred subjects; and the letters I have received, and the replies they have drawn from me, go far to make me doubt the accuracy of the accepted belief that 'letter writing has become a lost art'. A full mind with a facile pen makes letter writing a joy, and both of these attributes I think I may fairly claim. My correspondence with Alfred Cridge was kept up till his death a few years ago, and his son, following worthily in the footsteps of a noble father, has taken up the broken threads of the lifework of my friend, and is doing his utmost to carry it to a successful issue. My love of reading, which has been a characteristic feature of my life, found full scope for expression in the piles of books which reached us from all parts of the world. It has always been my desire to keep abreast of current literature, and this, by means of my book club and other sources, I was able to do. Sometimes my friends from abroad sent me copies of their own publications, Dr Bayard Holmes invariably forwarding to me a presentation copy of his most valuable treatises on medical subjects.[2] Mrs Stetson's poems and economic writings have always proved a source of inspiration to me, and I have distributed her books wherever I have thought they would be appreciated. Just at this time my financial position became brighter. I was fortunate in being able to dispose of my two properties in East Adelaide, and the purchasing of an annuity freed me entirely from money and domestic worries. Perhaps the greatest joy of all was that I was once more able to follow my charitable inclinations by giving that little mite which, coming

---

2   Dr Bayard Taylor Holmes (1852–1924), published *The Surgery of the Abdomen* and *The Surgery of the Head*, both in 1904.

opportunely, gladdens the heart of the disconsolate widow or smoothes the path of the struggling worker. Giving up my home entirely, I went to live with my dear friend Mrs Baker,[3] at Osmond terrace, where, perhaps, I spent the most restful period of a somewhat eventful life.

The inauguration of a Criminological Society in Adelaide was a welcome sign to me of the growing public interest in methods of prison discipline and treatment. I was one of the foundation members of the society, and attended every meeting during its short existence. My one contribution to the lectures delivered under its auspices was on 'Heredity and Environment'.[4] This was a subject in which I had long been interested, holding the view that environment had more to do with the building up of character than heredity had to do with its decadence. How much or how little truth there is in the cynical observation that the only believers in heredity nowadays are the fathers of very clever sons I am not prepared to say. I do say, however, that with the cruel and hopeless law of heredity as laid down by Zola and Ibsen[5] I have little sympathy. According to these pessimists, who ride heredity to death, we inherit only the vices, the weaknesses, and the diseases of our ancestors. If this, however, were really the case, the world would be growing worse and not better, as it assuredly is, with every succeeding generation. The contrary view taken of the matter by Ibsen's fellow-countryman, Bjørnsen,[6] appears to me to be so much more commonsense and humanising. He holds that if we know that our ancestors drank and gambled to excess, or were violent-tempered or immoral, we can quite easily avoid the pitfall, knowing it to be there. Too readily wrongdoers are prepared to lay their failings at the door of ancestors, society, or some other blamable source, instead of attributing them, as they should do, to their own selfish and weak indulgence and lack of self-control. Heredity, though an enormous factor in our constitution, need not be regarded as an over-mastering fate, for each human being has an almost limitless parentage to draw upon. Each child has both a father and a mother, and two grandparents

---

3 Mrs Baker, formerly Annie Herford, née Macnee (1840–1900), was a Unitarian friend of Spence. She married Arthur John Baker J.P. (1814–1900), 'one of the best known men in Adelaide' with wide interests, in 1892, a second marriage for both. They lived at 106 Osmond Terrace, Norwood.

4 The Criminological Society of South Australia published this lecture as a pamphlet in 1897; Catherine H. Spence, *Heredity and Environment*, (Webb & Son) Adelaide.

5 Emile Zola (1840–1902), French writer of naturalistic fiction, particularly presenting vice and crime. Henrik Ibsen (1828–1906), Norwegian writer of satirical problem plays directed at social reform.

6 Bjørnstjerne Bjørnsen (1832–1910), Norwegian dramatist, novelist and poet. With Ibsen, one of the pioneers of modern drama.

on both sides, increasing as one goes back. But, besides drawing on a much wider ancestry than the immediate parents, we have more than we inherit, or where could the law of progress operate? Each generation, each child who is born, comes into a slightly different world, fed by more experience, blown upon by fresh influences. And each individual comes into the world, not with a body merely, but with a soul; and this soul is susceptible to impressions, not only from the outer material world but from the other souls also impressed by the old and the new, by the material and the ideal.

The History of the Jukes is continually cited as proving the power and force of heredity.[7] Most people who read the book through, however, instead of merely accepting allusions one-sided and defective to it, see clearly that it forms the strongest argument for change of environment that ever was brought forward. The assumed name of Jukes is given to the descendants of a worthless woman who emigrated to America upwards of a century and a half ago, and from whom hundreds of criminals, paupers, and prostitutes have descended. But how were the Jukes' descendants dealt with during this period? No helping hand removed the children from their vicious and criminal surroundings known as one of the crime-cradles of the State of New York. Neither church nor school took them under its protecting care. Born and reared in the haunts of vice and crime, nothing but viciousness and criminality could be expected as a result. Without going so far as a well-known ex-member of our State Legislature, whose antagonism to the humanitarian treatment of prisoners led him to the belief that 'there wasn't nothin' in "erry-ditty," it was all tommy rot', I still hold to the belief that environment plays the larger part in the formation of character. Every phase of criminal reform is, I candidly admit, dealing with effects rather than causes. Effects, however, must be dealt with, and the more humanely they are dealt with the better for society at large. So long as society shuts its eyes to the social conditions under which the masses of the people live, move, and have their being as tending towards lowering rather than uplifting the individual and the community, the supply of cases for criminal treatment will unfortunately show little tendency to decrease. The work before reformers of the world is to prevent the creation of criminals by changing the environment of those with criminal tendencies as well as to seek to alleviate the resulting disease by methods of criminal reform.

Many interesting lectures were given by prominent citizens under the auspices of the society, which did a great deal to awaken the public conscience

---

7 *The Jukes: a study in crime, pauperism, disease and heredity*, 1884, by Richard Louis Dugdale (1841–1883). The history of the Jukes family was being quoted in medical textbooks as an argument for sterilising criminals.

on the important question of criminal reform. The Rev. J. Day Thompson,[8] who was then in the zenith of his intellectual power and a noble supporter of all things that tended to the uplifting of humanity, dealt with the land question in relation to crime. He gave a telling illustration of his point – which I thought equally applicable to the question of environment in relation to prison reform – that no permanent good could result from social legislation until society recognised and dealt with the root of the social evil, the land question. 'In a lunatic asylum,' he said, 'it is the custom to test the sanity of patients by giving them a ladle with which to empty a tub of water standing under a running tap. "How do you decide?" the warder was asked. "Why, them as isn't idiots stops the tap."' It was the Rev. J. Day Thompson who first called me the 'Grand Old Woman' of South Australia. When he left Adelaide for the wider sphere of service open to him in England I felt that we had lost one of the most cultured and able men who had ever come among us, and one whom no community could lose without being distinctly the poorer for his absence.

Just at this time the visit of Dr and Mrs Mills created a little excitement in certain circles. Their lectures on Christian science, both public and private, were wonderfully well attended, and I missed few of them. I have all my life endeavoured to keep an open mind on these questions, and have been prepared to accept new ideas and new modes of thought. But, although I found much that was charming in the lectures that swayed the minds of so many of my friends, I found little to convince me that Christian scientists were right and the rest of the world wrong in their interpretation of the meaning of life. So far as the cultivation of will power, as it is called, is concerned, I have no quarrel with those who maintain that a power of self-control is the basis of human happiness. So far as the will can be trained to obey only those instincts that tend to the growth and maintenance of self-respect – to prevent the subordination of our better feelings to the overpowering effects of passion, greed, or injustice – it must help to the development of one of the primary necessities of a sane existence. When, however, the same agency is brought to bear on the treatment of diseases in any shape or form I find my faith wavering. Though there may be more things in earth and heaven than are dreamed of in my philosophy, I was not prepared to follow the teachings set before us by the interpreters of this belief, whose visit had made an interesting break in the lives of many people. Truth I find everywhere expressed, goodness in all things; but I neither look for nor expect perfection in any one thing the world has ever produced. 'Tell me where God is,' a somewhat cynical sceptic asked of a child. 'Tell me where He is not,' replied the child; and

---

8   J. Day Thompson, Primitive Methodist minister, advanced social, religious and political thinker, conducted services in a church in Wellington Square, North Adelaide.

the same thing applies to goodness. Do not tell me where goodness is, but point out to me, if you can, where it is not. It is for each one to find out for himself where the right path lies, and to follow it with all his strength of mind and of purpose. Pippa's song, 'God's in His heaven – all's right with the world',[9] does not mean that the time has come for us to lay down our arms in the battle of right against wrong. No! no; it is an inspiration for us to gird our loins afresh, to 'right the wrongs that need resistance'; for, God being in His heaven, and the world itself being right, makes it so much easier to correct mistakes that are due to human agencies and shortcomings only.

I found time to spend a pleasant week at Victor Harbour with my friends, Mr and Mrs John Wyles.[10] I remember one day being asked whether I was not sorry I never married. 'No,' I replied, 'for, although I often envy my friends the happiness they find in their children, I have never envied them their husbands.' I think we must have been in a frivolous mood; for a lady visitor, who was present, capped my remark with the statement that she was quite sure Miss Spence was thankful that when she died she would not be described as the 'relic' of any man. It was the same lady who on another occasion, when one of the juvenile members of the party asked whether poets had to pay for poetical licence, wittily replied, 'No, my dear, but their readers do!' Although so much of my time has been spent in public work, I have by no means neglected or despised the social side of life. Visits to my friends have always been delightful to me, and I have felt as much interested in the domestic virtues of my many acquaintances as I have been an admirer of their grasp of literature, politics, or any branch of the arts or sciences in which they have been interested. This seaside visit had been a welcome break in a year that had brought me a new occupation as a member of the Destitute Board, had given me the experience of a political campaign, had witnessed the framing of the Constitution of the Commonwealth 'neath the Southern Cross, and had seen effective voting advance from the academic stage into the realm of practical politics. During the year Mrs Young and I addressed together 26 meetings on this subject. One of the most interesting was at the Blind School, North Adelaide. The keenness with which this audience gripped every detail of the explanation showed us how splendidly they had risen above their affliction. I was reminded of Helen Keller,[11] the American girl, who at the age of 21 months had lost

9   From *Pippa Passes*, 1841, dramatic poem by Robert Browning.
10 John Wyles (1856–1903), land and financial agent, born in Scotland, public figure, councillor and Mayor of St Peters.
11 Helen Keller (1880–1968), American writer and lecturer, was left blind and deaf after an illness before she was two. She developed formidable intellectual powers and became a public campaigner for civil rights, women's suffrage, world peace, and for people with disabilities.

sight and hearing, and whom I had met in Chicago during my American visit, just before she took her degree at Harvard University.

To all peacelovers the years from 1898 to 1901 were shadowed by the South African war. The din of battle was in our ears only to a less degree than in those of our kinsmen in the mother country. War has always been abhorrent to me, and there was the additional objection to my mind in the case of the South African war in that it was altogether unjustified. Froude's chapters on South Africa had impressed me on the publication of his *Oceana*,[12] after his visit here in the seventies. His indictment of England for her treatment of the Boers from the earliest days of her occupation of Cape Colony was too powerful to be ignored. I felt it to be impossible that so great a historian as Froude should make such grave charges on insufficient evidence. The annexation of 1877,[13] so bitterly condemned by him, followed by the treaty of peace of 1881, with its famous 'suzerainty' clause, was, I think, but a stepping stone to the war which was said to have embittered the last years of the life of Queen Victoria. The one voice raised in protest against the annexation of 1877 in the British House of Commons was that of Mr Leonard (now Lord) Courtney.[14] Not afraid to stand alone, though all the world were against him, the war at the close of the century found Leonard Courtney again taking his stand against the majority of his countrymen, and this time it cost him his Parliamentary seat. I have often felt proud that the leadership of proportional representation in England should have fallen into the hands of so morally courageous a man as Leonard Courtney has invariably proved himself to be.

We are apt to pride ourselves on the advance we have made in our civilisation; but our self-glorification received a rude shock at the feelings of intolerance and race hatred that the war brought forth. Freedom of speech became the monopoly of those who supported the war, and the person who dared to express an opinion which differed from that of the majority needed a great deal more than the ordinary allowance of moral courage. Unfortunately the intolerance so characteristic of that period is a feature, to a greater or lesser extent, of every Parliamentary election in the Commonwealth. The clause in the Federal Electoral Act which makes disturbance of a political meeting a penal offence is a curious reflection on a so-called democratic community. But, though its justification can scarcely be denied even by the partisans of the noisier

---

12 James Anthony Froude (1818–1894), English historian. J.A. Froude, *Oceana: England and her Colonies*, (Longmans, Green) London, 1886.
13 The Boer province of Transvaal had been annexed by the British. The Boers fought to regain their independence and succeeded, subject to the suzerainty of the British Government.
14 Leonard Henry Courtney, Baron Courtney (1836–1918), English politician and man of letters, advocate of proportional representation and women's rights.

elements in a political crowd, its existence must be deplored by every right-minded and true-hearted citizen. In Miss Rose Scott[15] I found a sympathiser on this question of the war; and one of the best speeches I ever heard her make was on peace and arbitration. 'Mafeking Day'[16] was celebrated while we were in Sydney, and I remember how we three – Miss Scott, Mrs Young, and I – remained indoors the whole day, at the charming home of our hostess, on Point Piper Road. The black hand of death and desolation was too apparent for us to feel that we could face the almost ribald excesses of that day. I felt the war far less keenly than did my two friends; but it was bad even for me. No one called, and the only companions of our chosen solitude were the books we all loved so much, and

> The secret sympathy,
> The silver link, the silken tie,
> Which heart to heart and mind to mind,
> In body and in soul can bind.[17]

I had hoped that the Women's National Council, a branch of which was formed in Adelaide a few years later,[18] would have made a great deal of the question of peace and arbitration, just as other branches have done all over the world; and when the Peace Society was inaugurated a short time ago I was glad to be able to express my sympathy with the movement by becoming a member. As I was returning from a lecturing tour in the south during this time, an old Scotch farm-wife came into the carriage where I had been knitting in solitude. She was a woman of strong feelings, and was bitterly opposed to the war. We chatted on the subject for a time, getting along famously, until she discovered that I was Miss Spence. 'But you are a Unitarian!' she protested in a shocked tone. I admitted the fact. 'Oh, Miss Spence,' she went on, 'how can you be so wicked as to deny the divinity of Christ?' I explained to her what Unitarianism was, but she held dubiously aloof for a time. Then we talked of other things. She told me of many family affairs, and when she left me at the station she said, 'Ah, well, Miss Spence, I've learned something this morning, and that is that a Unitarian can be just as good and honest as other folk.'

15 Rose Scott (1847–1925), Sydney social reformer and leader of the New South Wales campaign for votes for women. She became one of Spence's friends and allies.
16 The town of Mafeking in Cape Province in South Africa, held by the British, had been besieged for 217 days during the South African War. There was much rejoicing in Britain and the colonies when the town was relieved.
17 Sir Walter Scott, *The Lay of the Last Minstrel*, Canto V, stanza 13.
18 The National Council of Women in South Australia was formed in 1902 with Spence as Vice-President. It did not last. The South Australian Council of Women was formed in 1920.

CHAPTER 21

PROPORTIONAL REPRESENTATION AND FEDERATION

In the debates of the Federal Convention I was naturally much interested. Many times I regretted my failure to win a seat when I saw how, in spite of warnings against, and years of lamentable experience of, a vicious system of voting, the members of the Convention went calmly on their way, accepting as a matter of course the crude and haphazard methods known to them, the unscientific system of voting so dear to the heart of the 'middling' politician and the party intriguer. I believe Mr Glynn[1] alone raised his voice in favour of proportional representation, in the Convention, as he has done consistently in every representative assembly of which he has been a member. Instead of seeing to it that the foundations of the Commonwealth were 'broad based upon the people's will' by the adoption of effective voting, and thus maintaining the necessary connection between the representative and the represented, these thinkers for the people at the very outset of federation sowed the seeds of future discontent and Federal apathy. Faced with disfranchisement for three or six years, possibly for ever – so long as the present system of voting remains – it is unreasonable to expect from the people as a whole that interest in the national well-being which alone can lead to the safety of a progressive nation.

Proportional representation was for long talked of as a device for representing minorities. It is only in recent years that the real scope of the reform has been recognised. By no other means than the adoption of the single transferable vote can the rule of the majority obtain. The fundamental principal of proportional representation is that majorities must rule, but that minorities shall be adequately represented. An intelligent minority of representatives has great

---

1   Patrick McMahon Glynn (1855–1931), Irish barrister, moved to South Australia 1882, editor of *Kapunda Herald*, Parliamentarian, delegate to Federal Convention, member of the first Federal House of Representatives. See also, above, Chapter 19, n. 12.

weight and influence. Its voice can be heard. It can fully and truly express the views of the voters it represents. It can watch the majority and keep it straight. These clear rights of the minority are denied by the use of the multiple vote. It has also been asked – Can a Government be as strong as it needs to be when – besides the organised Ministerial party and the recognised Opposition – there may be a larger number of independent members than at present who may vote either way? It is quite possible for a Government to be too strong, and this is especially dangerous in Australia, where there are so many of what are known as optional functions of government undertaken and administered by the Ministry of the day, resting on a majority in the Legislature. To maintain this ascendancy concessions are made to the personal interests of members or to local or class interests of their constituencies at the cost of the whole country.

When introducing proportional representation into the Belgian Chamber the Prime Minister (M. Beernaert[2]) spoke well and forcibly on the subject of a strong Government: –

> I, who have the honour of speaking to you today in the name of the Government, and who have at my back the strongest majority that was ever known in Belgium, owe it to truth to say that our opinions have not a corresponding preponderance in the country; and I believe that, if that majority were always correctly expressed, we should gain in stability what we might lose in apparent strength. Gentlemen, in the actual state of things, to whom belongs the Government of the country? It belongs to some two or three thousand electors, who assuredly are neither the best nor the most intelligent, who turn the scale at each of our scrutiny de liste elections. I see to the right and to the left two large armies – Catholics and Liberals – of force almost equal, whom nothing would tempt to desert their standard, who serve it with devotion and from conviction. Well, these great armies do not count, or scarcely count. On the day of battle it is as if they do not exist. What counts, what decides, what triumphs, is another body of electors altogether – a floating body too often swayed by their passions, by their prejudices; or, worse still, by their interest. These are our masters, and according as they veer from right to left, or from left to right, the Government of the country changes, and its history takes a new direction. Gentlemen, is it well that it should be so? Is it well that this country should be at the mercy of such contemptible elements as these?

---

2   Auguste Marie François Beernaert (1829–1912), Belgian lawyer, statesman, Prime Minister 1884–1894, winner of Nobel Peace Prize.

How often have I longed to see a Premier in this, my adopted country, rise to such fervid heights of patriotism as this?

M. Beernaert is right. It is the party Government that is essentially the weak Government. It cannot afford to estrange or offend any one who commands votes. It is said that every prominent politician in the British House of Commons is being perpetually tempted and tormented by his friends not to be honest, and perpetually assailed by his enemies in order to be made to appear to be dishonest. The Opposition is prepared to trip up the Ministry at every step. It exaggerates mistakes, misrepresents motives, and combats measures which it believes to be good, if these are brought forward by its opponents. It bullies in public and undermines in secret. It is always ready to step into the shoes of the Ministry, to undergo similar treatment. This is the sort of strength which is supposed to be imperilled if the nation were equitably represented in the Legislature. In the present state of the world, especially in the Australian States, where the functions of government have multiplied and are multiplying, it is of the first importance that the administration should be watched from all sides, and not merely from the point of view of those who wish to sit on the Treasury benches. The right function of the Opposition is to see that the Government does the work of the country well. The actual practice of the Opposition is to try to prevent it from doing the country's work at all. In order that government should be honest, intelligent, and economical, it needs helpful criticism rather than unqualified opposition; and this criticism may be expected from the less compact and more independent ranks in a legislative body which truly represents all the people. Party discipline, which is almost inevitable in the present struggle for ascendancy or defeat, is the most undemocratic agency in the world. It is rather by liberating all votes and allowing them to group themselves according to conviction that a real government of the people by the people can be secured. When I look back on the intention of the framers of the Commonwealth Constitution to create in the Senate a States' rights House I am amazed at the remoteness of the intention from the achievement. The Senate is as much a party House as is the House of Representatives. Nothing, perhaps, describes the position better than the epigrammatic if somewhat triumphant statement of a Labour Senator some time ago. 'The Senate was supposed to be a place where the radical legislation of the Lower Chamber could be cooled off, but they had found that the saucer was hotter than the cup.'

The long illness and death of my ward, Mrs Hood,[3] once more gave to my life a new direction. History was repeating itself. Just as 40 years earlier Mrs Hood and her brothers had been left in my charge on the death of their

3   Rose Hood died on 12 October 1899. Spence became guardian of George 18, Catherine 15 and Charles 13 years of age. They lived with Spence and Ellen Gregory in Clark Street, Norwood.

mother, so once again a dying mother begged me to accept the guardianship of her three orphan children. Verging as they were on the threshold of manhood and womanhood, they scarcely needed the care and attention due to smaller children, but I realised I think to the full, what so many parents have realised – that the responsibilities for the training of children of an older growth are greater and more burdensome than the physical care of the infant. The family belongings were gathered in from the four quarters of the globe to which they had been scattered on my giving up housekeeping, and we again began a family life in Kent Town. Soon after we had settled, the motion in charge of the Hon. D.M. Charleston[4] in favour of the adoption of proportional representation for Federal elections was carried to a successful issue in the Legislative Council. The Hon. A.A. Kirkpatrick[5] suggested the advisableness of preparing a Bill at this stage. A motion simply affirming a principle, he said, was not likely to carry the cause much further, as it left the question of the application of the principle too much an open one. The league, he thought, should have something definite to put before candidates, so that a definite answer could be obtained from them. In New Zealand, Mr O'Regan,[6] a well-known solicitor, had also introduced into the House of Representatives during 1898 a Bill for the adoption of effective voting. Unfortunately members had become wedded to single electorates, and when a change was made it was to second ballots – a system of voting which has for long been discredited on the Continent. In France, it was stated in the debates on electoral reform in 1909, for 20 years, under second ballots, only once had a majority outside been represented by a majority inside the Chamber, and the average representation for the two decades had amounted to only 45 per cent of the voters. Writing to me after the New Zealand elections in 1909, the Hon. George Fowlds (Minister of Education),[7] who has long supported effective voting, said, 'The only result of the second ballot system in New Zealand has been to strengthen the movement in favour of proportional representation.' And Mr Paul,[8] a Labour member in

---

4   David Morley Charleston (1848–1934), engineer, unionist, politician, State and Federal Parliamentarian, supporter of proportional representation. See also, above, Chapter 19.

5   Andrew Alexander Kirkpatrick (1848–1928), South Australian printer, pioneer Labor parliamentarian who served in both houses and helped to form the United Trades and Labor Council.

6   Patrick Joseph O'Regan (1869–1947), New Zealand solicitor, newspaper editor, politician and judge, follower of Henry George and supporter of proportional representation.

7   Sir George Fowlds (1860–1934), New Zealand bookkeeper, business man, parliamentary supporter of single tax and the rights of women.

8   John Thomas Paul (1874–1964), Australian-born New Zealand compositor, editor, journalist, trade unionist, national labour leader and labour politician.

the Dominion, is making every effort to have effective voting included in the platform of the New Zealand Labour Party. Further encouragement to continue our work came when Belgium adopted the principle of proportional representation in 1898.

The closing year of the century found the Effective Voting League in the thick of its first election campaign. There is little doubt that the best time for advancing a political reform is during an election, and it was interesting to note how many candidates came to our support. We had an interesting meeting at Parliament House for members just about that time. An opponent of the reform, who was present, complained that we were late in beginning our meeting. 'We always begin punctually under the present system,' he remarked. 'Yes,' some one replied, 'but we always finish so badly.' 'Oh, I always finish well enough,' was the pert rejoinder; 'I generally come out on top.' 'Ah,' retorted the other, 'I was thinking of the electors.' But the doubter did not come out on top at a subsequent election, and his defeat was probably the means of his discovering defects in the old system that no number of successes would have led him into acknowledging. From the two or three members who had supported Mr Glynn in the previous Parliament we increased our advocates in the Assembly during the campaign to 14. The agitation had been very persistent among the electors, and their approval of the reform was reflected in the minds of their representatives. We inaugurated during that year the series of citizens' meetings convened by the Mayors of the city and suburbs, which has been so successful a feature of our long campaign for electoral justice, and at the present time very few of the mayoral chairs are occupied by men who are not keen supporters of effective voting.

The Hon. Theodore Bruce's[9] connection with the reform dates from that year, when he presided at a meeting in the Adelaide Town Hall during the temporary absence of the Mayor. A consistent supporter of effective voting from that time, it was only natural that when in May 1909 the candidature of Mr Bruce (who was then and is now a vice-president of the league), for a seat in the Legislative Council, gave us an opportunity for working for his return, against a candidate who had stated that he was not satisfied with the working of the system of effective voting, we availed ourselves of it. So much has been written and said about the attitude of the league with regard to parliamentary candidates that, as its President, I feel that I ought to take this opportunity of stating our reasons for that attitude. From its inception the league has declined to recognise parties in a contest at all. Its sole concern has been, and must be, to support effective voters, to whatever party they may belong. To secure the just

---

9   Theodore Bruce (1847–1911), auctioneer, dedicated to civil affairs, Mayor of Goodwood 1897–1898, Mayor of Adelaide 1904–1907, Member of Legislative Council 1909.

representation of the whole electorate of whatever size, is the work of the Effective Voting League, and, whatever the individual opinions of the members may be, as an official body they cannot help any candidate who opposes the reform for which they stand.

I remember meeting at a political meeting during a subsequent general election a lady whom I had known as an almost rabid Kingstonian. But the party had failed to find a position for her son in the Civil Service, although their own sons were in that way satisfactorily provided for. So she had thrown in her lot with the other side, which at the time happened to gain a few seats, and the lady was quite sure that her influence had won the day for her former opponents. Leaning forward to whisper as if her next remark were too delicate for the ears of a gentleman sitting near, she said, 'Do you know, I don't believe the Premier has any backbone!' I laughed, and said that I thought most people held the same belief. To my amusement and astonishment she then asked quite seriously, 'Do you think that is why he stoops so much?' There was no doubt in her mind that the missing backbone had reference to the physical and not to the moral malformation of the gentleman in question.

CHAPTER 22

A VISIT TO NEW SOUTH WALES

Early in the year 1900 the Hon. B.R. Wise,[1] then Attorney-General of New South Wales, suggested a campaign for effective voting in the mother State, with the object of educating the people, so that effective voting might be applied for the first Federal elections. Mrs Young and I left Adelaide on May 10 of that year to inaugurate the movement in New South Wales. During the few hours spent in Melbourne Professor Nanson,[2] the Victorian leader of the reform, with another earnest worker (Mr Bowditch),[3] called on us, and we had a pleasant talk over the proposed campaign. The power of the *Age*[4] had already been felt, when at the convention election, the ten successful candidates were nominees of that paper, and at that time it was a sturdy opponent of proportional representation. The *Argus*, on the other hand, had done yeoman service in the advocacy of the reform from the time that Tasmania had so successfully experimented with the system. As we were going straight through to Sydney, we were able only to suggest arrangements for a possible campaign on our return. Our Sydney visit lasted eight weeks, during which time we addressed between 20 and 30 public meetings. Our welcome to the harbour city was most enthusiastic, and our first meeting, held in the Protestant Hall, on the Wednesday after our arrival, with the Attorney-General in the chair, was packed. The greatest interest was shown in the counting of the 387 votes taken at the meeting. Miss Rose Scott, however, had paved the way for the successful public meeting by a reception at her house on the previous Monday, at

---

1   Bernhard Ringrose Wise (1858–1916), New South Wales barrister, politician and federationist, opponent of women's suffrage and supporter of child welfare reform.
2   Edward John Nanson (1850–1936), Professor of Mathematics at the University of Melbourne 1875, electoral reformer and advocate of proportional representation.
3   William Lamprey Bowditch (c.1850–1917), Victorian clergyman and teacher of mathematics.
4   Melbourne daily newspaper.

which we met Mr Wise, Sir William McMillan,[5] Mr (afterwards Senator) Walker,[6] Mr (now Sir A.J.) Gould,[7] Mr Bruce Smith,[8] Mr W. Holman,[9] and several other prominent citizens. The reform was taken up earnestly by most of these gentlemen. Sir William McMillan was appointed the first President of the league, which was formed before we left Sydney. During the first week of our visit we dined with Dr and Mrs Garran, who, with their son (Mr Robert Garran,[10] C.M.G., afterwards the collaborateur of Sir John Quick[11] in the compilation of the *Annotated Constitution of the Australian Commonwealth*), were keen supporters of effective voting. Among the host of well-known people who came after dinner to meet us was Mr (now Sir) George Reid,[12] with whom we had an interesting talk over the much-discussed 'Yes-No' policy. We had both opposed the Bill on its first appeal to the people, and seized the occasion to thank Mr Reid for his share in delaying the measure. 'You think the Bill as amended an improvement?' he asked. 'Probably,' replied Mrs Young, 'but as I didn't think the improvement great enough I voted against it both times.' But I had not done so, and my vote on the second occasion was in favour of the Bill.

But, as Mr Reid admitted, the dislike of most reformers for federation was natural enough, for it was only to be expected that 'reforms would be difficult to get with such a huge, unwieldy mass' to be moved before they could be won. And experience has proved the correctness of the view expressed. Anything in the nature of a real reform, judging from the experience of the past, will take a long time to bring about. I am convinced that had not South Australia already adopted the principle of the all-round land tax, the progressive form would have been the only one suggested or heard of from either party. Politicians are so apt to take the line of least resistance, and when thousands of votes of small landowners are to be won through the advocacy of an exemption,

---

5 Sir William McMillan (1850–1926), merchant and politician, active member of the Proportional Representation Society of New South Wales.
6 James Thomas Walker (1841–1923), Scottish born bank manager, and Senator for New South Wales 1901–1913.
7 Sir Albert John Gould (1847–1936), New South Wales lawyer and politician, free trader who served in both Houses of Parliament.
8 Arthur Bruce Smith (1851–1937), quixotic New South Wales businessman, barrister and politician, free trader who founded New South Wales Employers' Union.
9 William Arthur Holman (1871–1934), Labor politician and Premier of New South Wales.
10 Robert Randolph Garran (1867–1957), Sydney barrister, active federationist.
11 Sir John Quick (1852–1932), Sydney lawyer and politician, campaigner for Federation.
12 Sir George Houston Reid (1845–1918), barrister, free trader, Premier of New South Wales, Prime Minister of Australia.

exemptions there will be. The whole system of taxation is wrong, it seems to me, and though, as a matter of expediency, sometimes from conviction, many people advocate the opposite course, I have long felt that taxation should not be imposed according to the ability to pay so much as according to benefits received from the State. We are frequently warned against expecting too much from Federation during its earlier stages, but experience teaches us that, as with human beings, so with nations, a wrong or a right beginning is responsible to a great extent for right or wrong development. I have the strongest hopes for the future of Australia, but the people must never be allowed to forget that eternal vigilance, as in the past, must still in the future be the price we must pay for our liberty. Later, Mr Reid presided at our Parliament House meeting, and afterwards entertained us at afternoon tea. But one of our pleasantest memories was of a day spent with the great free-trader and Mrs Reid at their Strathfield home. I was anxious to hear Mr Reid speak, and was glad when the opportunity arose on the occasion of a no-confidence debate. But he was by no means at his best, and it was not until I heard him in his famous freetrade speech on his first visit to Adelaide that I realised how great an orator he was. At the close of the no-confidence debate the triumphant remark of an admirer that 'Adelaide couldn't produce a speaker like that' showed me that a prophet sometimes hath honour, even in his own country.

Mr Wise was a brilliant speaker, and a most cultured man, and a delightful talker. Of Mrs Parkes,[13] then President of the Women's Liberal League, I saw much. She was a fine speaker, and a very clear-headed thinker. Her organising faculty was remarkable, and her death a year or two ago was a distinct loss to her party. Her home life was a standing example of the fallacy of the old idea that a woman who takes up public work must necessarily neglect her family. Mrs Barbara Baynton[14] was a woman of a quite different type, clever and emotional, as one would expect the author of the brilliant but tragic *Bush Studies* to be. She was strongly opposed to Federation, as, indeed, were large numbers of clever people in New South Wales. Frank Fox[15]

13 Hilma Olivia Edla Johanna Parkes, née Ekenberg (1859–1909), political organiser and activist, member of Womanhood Suffrage League of New South Wales and founder of Women's Liberal League 1902.

14 Barbara Baynton née Barbara Janet Ainsleigh Kilpatrick (1857–1929), Australian writer and astute business woman. Her first and most famous book *Bush Studies* ((Duckworth) London) was published in 1902. She married Alexander Frater 1880, Dr Thomas Baynton 1890, Lord Headley 1921.

15 Sir Frank Ignatius Fox (1874–1960), journalist, worked for *Sydney Daily Telegraph*, *Truth* and the *Bulletin*, and became first editor and manager of the *Lone Hand*.

(afterwards connected with *The Lone Hand*), Bertram Stevens[16] (author of *An Anthology of Australian Verse*), Judge Backhouse[17] (who was probably the only Socialist Judge on the Australian Bench), were frequent visitors at Miss Scott's, and were all interesting people. An afternoon meeting on effective voting was arranged at the Sydney University, I think, by Dr Anderson Stuart.[18] We were charmed with the university and its beautiful surroundings. Among the visitors that afternoon was Mrs David, a charming and well-read woman, whose book describing an expedition to Funafuti is delightful. We afterwards dined with her and Professor David, and spent a pleasant hour with them.[19]

I was not neglectful of other reforms while on this campaign, and found time to interest myself in the state children's work with which my friend, Mrs Garran, was so intimately connected. We went to Liverpool one day to visit the benevolent institution for men. There were some hundreds of men there housed in a huge building reminiscent of the early convict days. If not the whole, parts of it had been built by the convicts, and the massive stone staircase suggested to our minds the horrors of convict settlement. I have always resented the injury done to this new country by the foundation of penal settlements, through which Botany Bay lost its natural connotation as a habitat for wonderful flora, and became known only as a place where convicts were sent for three-quarters of a century. Barrington's couplet,[20] written as a prologue at the opening of the Playhouse, Sydney, in 1796, to a play given by convicts –

> True patriots we, for it be understood
> We left our country for our country's good –

---

16 Bertram William Mathyson Francis Stevens (1872–1922), New South Wales editor, literary and art critic. His *Anthology of Australian Verse*, (Angus and Robertson) Sydney, 1906, was the first seriously edited collection of its kind.

17 Alfred Paxton Backhouse (1851–1939), New South Wales Crown Prosecutor and Judge.

18 Sir Thomas Peter Anderson Stuart (1856–1920), medical administrator, Professor of Physiology at Sydney University.

19 Sir Tannatt William Edgeworth David (1858–1934), geologist, Professor of Geology at Sydney University, member of Shackleton's expedition to Antarctic 1907. In 1885 he married Caroline Martha Mallett (1856–1951), who accompanied him on an expedition to Funafuti in the Ellice Islands. Mrs Edgeworth David, *Funafuti, or Three Months on a Coral Island: an unscientific account of a scientific expedition*, (John Murray) London, 1899. Mrs David was the State Commissioner for Girl Guides.

20 George Barrington (1755–1804), pickpocket, convict and later Chief Constable at Parramatta. According to *Australian Dictionary of Biography* he was not the author of the oft-quoted prologue reputedly spoken by him at the opening of the first Australian theatre in 1796.

Catherine Helen Spence in Rose Scott's garden, c.1902,
photograph courtesy of the State Library of South Australia, SLSA: B 6759

was clever, but untrue. All experience proves that while it is a terrible injury to a new country to be settled by convicts, it is a real injury also to the people from whom they are sent, to shovel out of sight all their failures, and neither try to lessen their numbers nor to reclaim them to orderly civil life. It was not till Australia refused any longer to receive convicts, as Virginia had previously done, that serious efforts were made to amend the criminal code of England, or to use reformatory methods first with young and afterwards with older offenders. Another pleasant trip was one we took to Parramatta. The Government launch was courteously placed at our disposal to visit the Parramatta Home for Women, where also we found some comfortable homes for old couples. The separation of old people who would prefer to spend the last years of their life together is, I consider, an outrage on society. One of my chief desires has been to establish such homes for destitute couples in South Australia, and to every woman who may be appointed as a member of the Destitute Board in future I appeal to do her utmost to change our methods of treatment with regard to old couples, so that to the curse of poverty may not be added the cruelty of enforced separation. Women in New South Wales were striving for the franchise at that time, and we had the pleasure of speaking at one of their big meetings. And what fine public meetings they had in Sydney! People there seemed to take a greater interest in politics than here, and crowded attendances were frequent at political meetings, even when there was no election to stir them up. It was a Sydney lady[21] who produced this amusing Limerick in my honour:–

> There was a Grand Dame of Australia,
> Who proved the block system a failure!
> She taught creatures in coats
> What to do with their votes,
> This Effective Grand Dame of Australia!

The third line will perhaps preclude the necessity for pointing out that the author was an ardent suffragist! To an enlightened woman also was probably due the retort to a gentleman's statement that 'Miss Spence was a good man lost,' that, 'On the contrary she thought she was a good woman saved.' 'In what way?' he asked. 'Saved for the benefit of her country, instead of having her energies restricted to the advantages of one home', was the reply. And for this I have sometimes felt very thankful myself that I have been free to devote what gifts I possess to what I consider best for the advantage and the uplifting of humanity. Before leaving Sydney I tried once more to find a publisher for

---

21 Rose Scott.

Gathered In but was assured that the only novels worth publishing in Australia were sporting or political novels.

I was in my seventy-fifth year at the time of this visit; but the joy of being enabled to extend the influence of our reform to other States was so great that the years rolled back and left me as full of life and vigour and zeal as I had ever been. Our work had by no means been confined to the city and suburbs, as we spoke at a few country towns as well. At Albury, where we stopped on our way back to Victoria, we were greeted by a crowded and enthusiastic audience in the fine hall of the Mechanics' Institute. We had passed through a snowstorm just before reaching Albury, and the country was very beautiful in the afternoon, when our friends drove us through the district. The Murray was in flood, and the 'water, water everywhere' sparkling in the winter sunshine, with the snow-capped Australian Alps in the background, made an exquisite picture. Albury was the only town we visited in our travels which still retained the old custom of the town crier. Sitting in the room of the hotel after dinner, we were startled at hearing our names and our mission proclaimed to the world at large, to the accompaniment of a clanging bell and introduced by the old-fashioned formula, 'Oyez! oyez! oyez!' Our work in Victoria was limited, but included a delightful trip to Castlemaine. We were impressed with the fine Mechanics' Hall of that town, in which we spoke to a large audience. But a few years later the splendid building, with many others in the town, was razed to the ground by a disastrous cyclone. Returning from Castlemaine, we had an amusing experience in the train. I had laid aside my knitting, which is the usual companion of my travels, to teach Mrs Young the game of 'patience', but at one of the stations a foreign gentleman entered the carriage, when we immediately put aside the cards. After chatting awhile, he expressed regret that he had been the cause of the banishment of our cards, and 'Would the ladies not kindly tell him his fortune also?' He was as much amused as we were when we explained that we were reformers and not fortune tellers. I have been a great lover of card games all my life; patience in solitude, and cribbage, whist, and bridge have been the almost invariable accompaniments of my evenings spent at home or with my friends. Reading and knitting were often indulged in, but patience was a change and a rest and relief to the mind. I have always had the idea that card games are an excellent incentive to the memory. We had an afternoon meeting in the Melbourne Town Hall to inaugurate a league in Victoria, at which Dr Barrett,[22] the Rev. Dr Bevan,[23] Professor

22 Sir James William Barrett (1862–1945), Victorian ophthalmologist, publicist and worker for social and reformist causes.
23 Llewelyn David Bevan (1842–1918), Congregational minister in Melbourne and Adelaide.

Nanson,[24] and I were the principal speakers. Just recently I wrote to the Victorian Minister who had charge of the Preferential Voting Bill in the Victorian Parliament to ask him to consider the merits of effective voting; but, like most other politicians, the Minister did not find the time opportune for considering the question of electoral justice for all parties. I remained in Victoria to spend a month with my family and friends after Mrs Young returned to Adelaide. The death of my dear brother John, whose sympathy and help had always meant so much to me, shortly after my return, followed by that of my brother William in New Zealand, left me the sole survivor of the generation which had sailed from Scotland in 1839.[25]

24 Edward John Nanson (1850–1936), Professor of Mathematics at Melbourne University 1875, electoral reformer and advocate of proportional representation.
25 John Brodie Spence died in 1902 and William Richard Spence in 1903. See also Appendix A, Family Tree.

CHAPTER 23

MORE PUBLIC WORK

For the cooperative movement[1] I had always felt the keenest sympathy. I saw in it the liberation of the small wage-earner from the toils of the middlemen. I thought moreover that the incentive to thrift so strongly encouraged by cooperative societies would be a tremendous gain to the community as well as to the individual. How many people owe a comfortable old age to the delight of seeing their first small profits in a cooperative concern, or their savings in a building society accumulating steadily and surely, if but slowly? And I have always had a disposition to encourage anything that would tend to lighten the burden of the worker. So that when in 1901 Mrs Agnes Milne[2] placed before me a suggestion for the formation of a woman's cooperative clothing factory, I was glad to do what I could to further an extension in South Australia of the movement, which, from its inception in older countries, had made so strong an appeal to my reason. A band of women workers were prepared to associate for the mutual benefit of the operatives in the shirtmaking and clothing trades. Under the title of the South Australian Co-operative Clothing Company, Limited, they proposed to take over and carry on a small private factory, owned by one of themselves, which had found it difficult to compete against large firms working with the latest machinery. I was sure of finding many sympathisers among my friends, and

---

1   In co-operatives people or a community combined for the purposes of economic production or distribution for the benefit of the whole body of producers or customers, rather than for the profit of an individual capitalist. The movement began in Adelaide in 1868.
2   Agnes Milne (1850–1919), owner of a garment workshop, activist and member of Working Women's Trade Union, and the Women's Christian Temperance Union. She was appointed Inspector of Factories and worked to eliminate sweating in the garment industry. In 1906 she became manager of the South Australian Co-operative Clothing Factory.

was successful in disposing of a fair number of shares. The movement had already gained support from thinking working women, and by the time we were ready to form ourselves into a company we were hopeful of success. I was appointed, and have since remained the first President of the board of directors; and, unless prevented by illness or absence from the state, I have never failed to be present at all meetings. The introduction of Wages Boards[3] added to the keen competition between merchants, had made the task of carrying on successfully most difficult, but we hoped that as the idea gained publicity we should benefit proportionately. It was a great blow to us, when at the close of the first year we were able to declare a dividend of one shilling a share, the merchants closed down upon us and reduced their payments by sixpence or ninepence per dozen. But in spite of drawbacks we have maintained the struggle successfully, though sometimes at disheartening cost to the workers and officials of the society. I feel, however, that the reward of success due to this plucky band of women workers will come in the near future, for at no other time probably has the position looked more hopeful than during the present year.

During this same year the Effective Voting League made a new departure in its propaganda work by inviting Sir Edward Braddon[4] to address a meeting in the Adelaide Town Hall. As Premier of Tasmania, Sir Edward had inaugurated the reform in the gallant little island State, and he was able to speak with authority on the practicability and the justice of effective voting. His visit was followed a year later by one from Senator Keating,[5] another enthusiastic Tasmanian supporter, whose lecture inspired South Australian workers to even greater efforts, and carried conviction to the minds of many waverers. At that meeting we first introduced the successful method of explanation by means of limelight slides.[6] The idea of explaining the whole system by pictures had seemed impossible, but every step of the counting can be shown so simply and clearly by this means as to make an understanding of the system a certainty. To the majority of people an appeal to reason and understanding is made much more easily through the eye than through the ear. The year 1902 saw an advance in the Parliamentary agitation of the reform, when the Hon.

3   Wages Boards were state tribunals introduced to determine minimum wages as an alternative to arbitration. South Australia introduced them in 1900.
4   Sir Edward Nicholas Braddon (1829–1904), business man and politician, Premier of Tasmania 1894–1899.
5   John Henry Keating (1872–1940), Tasmanian lawyer and politician, Government whip in the Senate in the first Barton and Deakin governments.
6   A 'Magic Lantern' used to project hand-coloured slides onto a large canvas screen. An oxy-hydrogen lime light was used.

Joseph (now Senator) Vardon[7] introduced a Bill for the first time into the Legislative Council. The measure had been excellently prepared by Mr J.H. Vaughan, LlB,[8] with the assistance of the members of the executive of the Effective Voting League, among whom were Messrs Crawford Vaughan[9] and E.A. Anstey.[10] The Bill sought to apply effective voting to existing electoral districts, which, though not nearly so satisfactory as larger districts, nevertheless made the application of effective voting possible. With the enlargement of the district on the alteration of the Constitution subsequent to federation becoming an accomplished fact, the league was unanimous in its desire to seek the line of least resistance by avoiding a change in the Constitution that an alteration in electoral boundaries would have necessitated.

To Mr Vardon, when he was a candidate for Legislative honours in 1900 the usual questions were sent from the league; but, as he had not studied the question he declined to pledge himself to support the reform. Realising, however, the necessity of enquiring into all public matters, he decided to study the Hare system, but the league declined to support him without a written pledge. Still he was elected, and immediately afterwards studied effective voting, became convinced of its justice, and has remained a devoted advocate. Our experience with legislators had usually been of the opposite nature. Pledged adherents to effective voting during an election campaign, as members they no longer saw the necessity for a change in a method of voting which had placed them safely in Parliament; but in Mr Vardon we found a man whose conversion to effective voting was a matter of principle, and not a question of gathering votes. That was why the league selected him as its Parliamentary advocate when effective voting first took definite shape in the form of a Bill. When, later, Mr E.H. Coombe, M.P.,[11] took charge of the Bill in the Assembly although the growth in public opinion in favour of effective voting had been surprising, the coalition between the Liberal and Labour parties strengthened their combined position and weakened the allegiance of their elected members to a reform which would probably affect their vested interests in the Legislature. Mr Coombe had not been an easy convert to

---

7   Joseph Vardon (1843–1913), printer and South Australian parliamentarian, later Senator in Federal Parliament, supporter of proportional representation.
8   John Howard Vaughan (1879–1955), South Australian lawyer and Labor politician, supporter of proportional representation.
9   Crawford Vaughan (1874–1947), journalist and Premier of South Australia, supporter of proportional representation, brother of John Howard Vaughan.
10 Edward Alfred Anstey (1858–1952), South Australian builder and Labor politician.
11 Ephraim Henry Coombe (1858–1917), South Australian journalist and politician, editor of *Gawler Bunyip* and Adelaide *Daily Herald*.

proportional representation. He had attended my first lecture at Gawler, but saw difficulties in the way of accepting the Hare system as propounded by me. His experiments were interesting. Assuming a constituency of 100 electors with 10 members, he filled in 60 Conservative and 40 Liberal voting papers. The proportion of members to each party should be six Conservatives and four Liberals, and when he found that by no amount of manipulation could this result be altered he became a convert to effective voting. His able advocacy of the reform is too well known to need further reference; but I should like now to thank those members, including Mr K.W. Duncan,[12] who have in turn led the crusade for righteous representation in both Houses of Parliament, for of them may it truly be said that the interests of the people as a whole were their first consideration. Before I left for America I saw the growing power and strength of the Labour Party. I rejoiced that a new star had arisen in the political firmament. I looked to it as a party that would support every cause that tended towards righteousness. I expected it, as a reform party, to take up effective voting, because effective voting was a reform. I hoped that a party whose motto was 'Trust the people' would have adopted a reform by means of which alone it would be possible for the people to gain control over its Legislature and its Government. Alas! for human hopes that depended on parties for their realisation! As time after time I have seen defections from the ranks of proportionalists, and people have said to me: 'Give it up, Miss Spence. Why trouble longer? Human nature is too bad,' I have answered, 'No; these politicians are but the ephemeral creations of a day or a month, or a year; this reform is for all time, and must prevail, and I will never give it up.'

During my many visits to Melbourne and Sydney I had been much impressed with the influence and the power for good of the local branches of the world-famed National Council of Women. I had long hoped for the establishment of a branch in South Australia, and was delighted to fall in with a suggestion made by the Countess of Aberdeen[13] (Vice-President-at-large of the International Council), through Lady Cockburn,[14] that a council should be formed in South Australia. The inaugural meeting in September 1902 was

12 Kossuth William Duncan (born 1857), prominent citizen of Port Pirie, member of the Legislative Council.
13 Ishbel Maria Marjoribanks (1857–1939), daughter of Lord Tweedmouth, wife of John Campbell Gordon, Earl of Aberdeen, Governor-General of Canada 1893–1898. She was President of the National Council of Women of Canada and longtime President of International Council of Women.
14 Sarah Holdway Cockburn, née Brown (died 1931), wife of Sir John Alexander Cockburn (1850–1929), medical practitioner and Premier of South Australia, Agent-General in London 1898–1901, and resident there afterwards.

splendidly attended, and it was on a resolution moved by me that the council came into existence. Lady Way[15] was the first President, and I was one of the Vice-Presidents. I gave several addresses, and in 1904 contributed a paper on 'Epileptics'. In dealing with this subject I owed much to the splendid help I received from my dear friend Miss Alice Henry,[16] of Victoria, now in Chicago, whose writings on epileptics and weak-minded children have contributed largely to the awakening of the public conscience to a sense of duty towards these social weaklings. In 1905 I contributed a paper to the quinquennial meeting of the International Council of Women, held at Berlin, on the laws relating to women and children in South Australia, and gave an account of the philanthropic institutions of the state, with special reference to the State Children's Council and Juvenile Courts. The work of the National Council in this state was disappointing to many earnest women, who had hoped to find in it a means for the social, political, and philanthropic education of the women of South Australia. Had the council been formed before we had obtained the vote there would probably have been more cohesion and a greater sustained effort to make it a useful body. But as it was there was so apparent a disinclination to touch 'live' subjects that interest in the meetings dwindled, and in 1906 I resigned my position on the executive in order to have more time to spare for other public work.

A problem which was occasioning the State Children's Council much anxious thought was how to deal effectively with the ever-increasing number of the 'children of the streets'. Boys and girls alike, who should either be at school or engaged at some useful occupation, were roaming the streets and parks, uncontrolled and sometimes uncontrollable. We recognised that their condition was one of moral peril, and graduation to criminality from these nurseries of crime so frequently occurred that State interference seemed absolutely imperative to save the neglected unfortunates for a worthier citizenship. It is much easier and far more economical to save the child than to punish the criminal. One of the most effective means of clearing the streets would be to raise the compulsory age for school attendance up to the time of procuring employment. That truancy was to a great extent responsible for these juvenile delinquents was proved by the fact that more than one-half of the lads sent to Magill had committed the crimes for which they were first convicted while truanting. Moreover, an improvement was noticed immediately

15 Katharine Gollan Way, formerly Blue, née Gordon (1854–1914), wife of Sir Samuel Way.
16 Alice Henry (1857–1943), Victorian journalist, lecturer on female suffrage, women's rights advocate. In the United States of America she became secretary of the National Women's Trade Union League of America. Miss Henry was a close friend and correspondent of Spence in her last years.

on the amendment of the compulsory attendance clauses in the Education Act. Truancy – the wicket gate of the road to ruin in youth – should be barred as effectively as possible, and the best way to bar it is to make every day a compulsory school day, unless the excuse for absence be abundantly sufficient. Another aspect of the neglected children problem, which Federal action alone will solve, is in dealing with cases of neglect by desertion. At present each State is put to great trouble and expense through defaulting parents. Federal legislation would render it possible to have an order for payment made in one State collected and remitted by an officer in another State. By this means thousands of pounds a year could be saved to the various States, and many a child prevented from becoming a burden to the people at large. These are some of the problems awaiting solution and the women of South Australia will do well to make the salvation of these neglected waifs a personal care and responsibility. Perhaps no other work of the State Children's Council has more practically shown their appreciation of the capabilities of the children under their care than the establishment of the State children's advancement fund. This is to enable State children who show any aptitude, to pursue their education through the continuation schools to the University. To private subscriptions for this purpose the Government have added a subsidy of £50, and already some children are availing themselves of this splendid opportunity to rise in the world. The longer I live the prouder I feel that I have been enabled to assist in this splendid work for the benefit of humanity.

The years as they passed left me with wider interest in, deeper sympathies with, and greater knowledge of the world and its people. Each year found 'one thing worth beginning, one thread of life worth spinning'. The pleasure I derived from the more extended intellectual activity of my later years was due largely to my association with a band of cultured and earnest women interested in social, political, and other public questions – women who, seeing 'the tides of things' – ,desired so to direct them that each wave of progress should carry the people to a higher place on the sands of life. To the outside world little is known of the beginnings and endings of social movements, which, taken separately, perhaps appear of small consequence, but which in the aggregate count for a great deal in what is popularly known as the forward movement. To such as these belonged an interesting association of women, which, meeting at first informally, grew eventually into a useful organisation for the intellectual and moral development of those who were fortunate enough to be associated with it. This was the 'Social Students' Society', of which Miss A.L. Tomkinson[17] was

---

17 Amy Louisa Tomkinson was born in Adelaide in 1856, spent 13 years in Europe and returned to Adelaide in 1900 at the death of her father. Her interest in social issues led her to work with Spence in many areas.

the secretary and I the first President. One of the addresses I gave was on 'Education', and among others whose addresses helped us considerably was the Director of Education (Mr A. Williams).[18] Speakers from all parties addressed the association, and while the society existed a good deal of educational work was done. Much interest was taken in the question of public playgrounds for children, and we succeeded in interesting the City Council in the movement: but, owing to lack of funds, the scheme for the time being was left in abeyance.

In the agitation for the public ownership of the tramways, I was glad to take a share. The private ownership of monopolies is indefensible, and my American experiences of the injustice of the system strengthened my resolve to do my utmost to prevent the growth of the evil in South Australia. My attitude on the question alienated a number of friends, both from me personally and from effective voting, so intolerant had people become of any opposition to their own opinions. The result of the referendum was disappointing, and, I shall always consider, a grave reflection on a democratic community which permits a referendum to be taken under a system of plural voting which makes the whole proceeding a farce. But the citizens of Adelaide have need to be grateful to the patriotic zeal of those who, led by the late Cornelius Proud,[19] fought for the public ownership of the tramways.

These years of activity were crossed by sickness and sorrow. For the first time in a long life, which had already extended almost a decade beyond the allotted span, I became seriously ill. To be thus laid low by sickness was a deep affliction to one of my active temperament; but, if sickness brings trouble, it often brings joy in the tender care and appreciation of hosts of friends, and this joy I realised to the fullest extent. The following year (1904) was darkened by the tragic death of my ward,[20] and once more my home was broken up, and with Miss Gregory I went to live with my good friends Mr and Mrs Quilty,[21] in North Norwood. From then on my life has flowed easily and pleasantly, marred only by the sadness of farewells of many old friends and comrades on my life's journey, who one by one have passed 'through Nature to eternity'.

18 Alfred Williams (1863–1913), dynamic educationist, follower of J.A. Hartley, strong advocate of child-centred learning, Director of Education in South Australia 1905–1913.
19 Cornelius Proud (1854–1905), shorthand writer, sharebroker and literary man, helped establish the Adelaide Stock Exchange and presented to the House of Assembly the petition carrying 11,000 signatures supporting women's suffrage.
20 Catherine, sometimes spelled Katherine, Helen Hood committed suicide in June 1904, after a period of depression.
21 Kate Quilty, née Breen, and her husband John Quilty, a builder. Kate Breen and her sister Maggie had been maids in the Spence's house when Mrs Spence was alive. Spence moved with the Quiltys to Queen Street, Norwood, in the last year of her life.

Much as I have written during the past 40 years, it was reserved for my old age to discover within me the power of poetical expression. I had rhymed in my youth and translated French verse, but until I wrote my one sonnet, poetry had been an untried field. The one-sided pessimistic pictures that Australian poets and writers present are false in the impression they make on the outside world and on ourselves. They lead us to forget the beauty and the brightness of the world we live in. What we need is, as Matthew Arnold says of life, 'to see Australia steadily and see it whole'.[22] It is not wise to allow the 'deadbeat' – the remittance man, the gaunt shepherd with his starving flocks and herds, the free selector on an arid patch, the drink shanty where the rouseabouts and shearers knock down their cheques, the race meeting where high and low, rich and poor, are filled with the gambler's ill luck – fill the foreground of the picture of Australian life. These reflections led me to a protest, in the form of a sonnet published in the *Register* some years ago:[23] –

> When will some new Australian poet rise
> To all the height and glory of his theme?
> Nor on the sombre side for ever dream –
> Our bare, baked plains, our pitiless blue skies,
> 'Neath which the haggard bushman strains his eyes
> To find some waterhole or hidden stream
> To save himself and flocks in want extreme!
> This is not all Australia! Let us prize
> Our grand inheritance! Had sunny Greece
> More light, more glow, more freedom, or more mirth?
> Ours are wide vistas bathed in purest air –
> Youth's outdoor pleasures, Age's indoor peace –
> Where could we find a fairer home on earth
> Which we ourselves are free to make more fair?

Just as years before my interest had been kindled in the establishment of our system of state education, and later in the university and higher education, so more recently has the inauguration of the Froebel system of kindergarten training appealed most strongly to my reason and judgment. There was a time in the history of education, long after the necessity for expert teaching in primary and secondary schools had been recognised, when the training of the

---

22 The quotation from 'To a Friend' by Matthew Arnold (1822–1888) should read 'who saw life steadily, and saw it whole'.
23 Spence's sonnet was published in the *Register*, 8 January 1903, in 'Notes and Queries,' and in *Woman's Sphere*, vol. IV, no. 51, November 1904.

infant mind was left to the least skilled assistant on the staff of a school. With the late Mr J.A. Hartley, whose theory was that the earliest beginnings of education needed even greater skill in the teacher than the higher branches, I had long regarded the policy as mistaken; but modern educationists have changed all that, and the training of tiny mites of two or three summers and upwards is regarded as of equal importance with that of children of a larger growth. South Australia owes its free kindergarten to the personal initiative and private munificence of the Rev. Bertram Hawker, youngest son of the late Hon. G.C. Hawker.[24] I had already met, and admired the kindergarten work of, Miss Newton[25] when in Sydney, and was delighted when she accepted Mr Hawker's invitation to inaugurate the system in Adelaide. Indeed, the time of her stay here during September 1905 might well have been regarded as a special invitation of educational experts, for, in addition to Miss Newton, the directors of education from New South Wales and Victoria (Messrs G.H. Knibbs[26] and F. Tate[27]) took part in the celebrations. Many interesting meetings led up to the formation of the Kindergarten Union.[28] My niece, Mrs J.P. Morice,[29] was appointed honorary secretary, and I became one of the vice-presidents. On joining the union I was proud of the fact that I was the first member to pay a subscription. The free kindergarten has come to South Australia to stay, and is fast growing into an integral part of our system of education. I have rejoiced in the progress of the movement, and feel that the future will witness the realisation of my ideal of a ladder that will reach from the kindergarten to the university, as outlined in articles[30] I wrote for the *Register* at that time.

---

24 Bertram Hawker (1868–1952), Anglican clergyman, educationist and benefactor, youngest son of George Charles Hawker (1818–1895), South Australian grazier and politician.
25 Frances Newton, principal of Sydney Kindergarten Training College.
26 Sir George Handley Knibbs (1858–1927), New South Wales educationist and first Commonwealth statistician.
27 Frank Tate (1864–1939), Victorian reformist educationist.
28 The Kindergarten Union of South Australia was formed in September 1905 through the efforts of Rev. Bertram Hawker and other concerned citizens.
29 Louise (Lucy) Morice, née Spence (1859–1951), daughter of Spence's beloved brother John, kindergarten teacher, social reformer and close ally of Spence.
30 The articles appeared in the *Register*, 30 and 31 October, and 4 November 1905 and were published as a pamphlet *From Kindergarten to University* in 1905.

Chapter 24

The Eightieth Milestone and the End

On 31 October 1905, I celebrated my eightieth birthday. Twelve months earlier, writing to a friend, I said: 'I entered my eightieth year on Monday, and I enjoy life as much as I did at eighteen; indeed, in many respects I enjoy it more.' The birthday gathering took place in the schoolroom of the Unitarian Church, the church to which I had owed so much happiness through the lifting of the dark shadows of my earlier religious beliefs. Surrounded by friends who had taken their share in the development of my beloved State, I realised one of the happiest times of my life. I had hoped that the celebration would have helped the cause of effective voting, which had been predominant in my mind since 1859. By my interests and work in so many other directions in literature, journalism, education, philanthropy, and religion – which had been testified to by so many notable people on that occasion, I hoped to prove that I was not a mere faddist, who could be led away by a chimerical fantasy. I wanted the world to understand that I was a clear-brained, commonsense woman of the world, whose views of effective voting and other political questions were as worthy of credence as her work in other directions had been worthy of acceptance. The greetings of my many friends from all parts of the Commonwealth on that day brought so much joy to me that there was little wonder I was able to conclude my birthday poem 'Australian spring'[1] with the lines:

> With eighty winters o'er my head,
> Within my heart there's Spring.

Full as my life was with its immediate interests, the growth and development of the outside world claimed a good share of my attention. The heated

---

1 'Australian Spring' appeared in the *Register*, 31 October 1905, and was issued with the paper as a single leaflet on 1 November 1905.

Catherine Helen Spence,
photograph courtesy of the State Library of South Australia

controversies in the motherland over the preachings and teaching of the Rev. R.J. Campbell[2] found their echo here, and I was glad to be able to support in pulpit and newspaper the stand made by the courageous London preacher of modern thought. How changed the outlook of the world from my childhood's days, when Sunday was a day of strict theological habit, from which no departure could be permitted! The laxity of modern life, by comparison is, I think, somewhat appalling. We have made the mistake of breaking away from old beliefs and convictions without replacing them with something better. We do not make as much, or as good, use of our Sundays as we might do. There is a medium between the rigid Sabbatarianism of our ancestors and the absolute waste of the day of rest in mere pleasure and frivolity. All the world is deploring the secularising of Sunday. Not only is churchgoing perfunctory or absent, but in all ranks of life there is a disposition to make it a day of rest and amusement – sometimes the amusement rather than the rest. Sunday, the Sabbath, as Alex McLaren[3] pointed out to me, is not a day taken from us, but a day given to us. 'Behold, I have given you the Sabbath!' For what? For rest for man and beast, but also to be a milestone in our upward and onward progress – a day for not only wearing best clothes, but for reading our best books and thinking our best thoughts. I have often grieved at the small congregations in other churches no less than in my own, and the grief was aggravated by the knowledge that those who were absent from church were not necessarily otherwise well employed. I derived so much pleasure from the excellent and cultured sermons of my friend the Rev. John Reid[4] during his term of office here that I regretted the fact that others who might gain equally from them were not there to hear them. I would like to see among the young people a finer conception of the duties of citizenship, which, if not finding expression in church attendance, may develop in some way that will be noble and useful to society.

In the meantime the work of the Effective Voting League had been rather at a standstill. Mrs Young's illness had caused her resignation, and until she again took up the work nothing further was done to help Mr Coombe in his Parliamentary agitation. In 1908, however, we began a vigorous campaign, and towards the close of the year the propaganda work was being carried into all parts of the State. Although I was then 83, I travelled to Petersburg[5] to lecture

---

2   Reginald John Campbell (1867–1956), writer, preacher, pastor of the City Temple, London, and controversial theologian. *The New Theology*, (George Bell & Sons) London, 1907, created much discussion.
3   Alexander McLaren (1826–1910), outstanding Baptist minister in Manchester.
4   Rev. John Reid M.A., minister of the Unitarian Christian Church in Adelaide.
5   Now Peterborough.

to a good audience. On the same night Mrs Young addressed a fine gathering at Mount Gambier, and from that time the work has gone on unceasingly. The last great effort was made through the newspaper ballot of September, 1909, when a public count of about 10,000 was completed with all explanations during the evening. The difficulties that were supposed to stand in the way of a general acceptance of effective voting have been entirely swept away. Tasmania and South Africa have successfully demonstrated the practicability, no less than the justice of the system. Now we get to the bedrock of the objections raised to its adoption, and we find that they exist only in the minds of the politicians themselves; but the people have faith in effective voting, and I believe the time to be near when they will demand equitable representation in every Legislature in the world. The movement has gone too far to be checked, and the electoral unrest which is so common all over the world will eventually find expression in the best of all electoral systems, which I claim to be effective voting.

Among the many friends I had made in the other states there was none I admired more for her public spiritedness than Miss Vida Goldstein.[6] I have been associated with her on many platforms and in many branches of work. Her versatility is great, but there is little doubt that her chief work lies in helping women and children. Her life is practically spent in battling for her sex. Although I was the first woman in Australia to become a parliamentary candidate, Miss Goldstein has since exceeded my achievements by a second candidature for the Senate. It was during her visit here last May–June as a delegate to the State Children's Congress that she inaugurated the Women's Non-party Political Association, which is apparently a growing force. In a general way the aims of the society bear a strong resemblance to those of the social students' society, many of its members having also belonged to the earlier association. It was a hopeful sign to me that it included among its members people of all political views working chiefly in the interests of women and children. Of this society also I became the first president, and the fact that on its platform was included proportional representation was an incentive for me to work for it. The education of women on public and social questions, so that they will be able to work side by side with the opposite sex for the public good, will, I think, help in the solution of social problems that are now obstacles in the path of progress. In addition to other literary work for the year 1909 I was asked by Miss Alice Henry to revise my book on state children in order to make it acceptable and applicable to American conditions. It was a big

---

6   Vida Jane Mary Goldstein (1869–1949), Victorian feminist, fighter for women's suffrage, leader in the 1914–18 anti-war movement, the first British Empire woman to nominate for a national parliament. She stood unsuccessfully for election to the Senate in 1903, 1910, 1913, 1914 and 1917.

undertaking, but I think successful. The book as originally written had already done good work in Western Australia, where the conditions of infant mortality were extremely alarming, and in England also; and there is ample scope for such a work in America, which is still far behind even the most backward Australian state in its care for dependent children.

As a president of three societies, a vice-president of two others, a member of two of the most important boards in the state for the care of the destitute, the deserted, and the dependent, with a correspondence that touches on many parts of the Empire, and two continents besides, with my faculty for the appreciation of good literature still unimpaired, with my domestic interests so dear to me, and my constant knitting for the infants under the care of the State Inspector – I find my life as an octogenarian more varied in its occupations and interests than ever before. Looking back from the progressive heights of 1910 through the long vista of years, numbering upwards of four-fifths of a century, I rejoice at the progress the world has made. Side by side with the development of my state my life has slowly unfolded itself. My connection with many of the reforms to which is due this development has been intimate, and (I think I am justified in saying) oftentimes helpful. While other states of the Commonwealth and the Dominion of New Zealand have made remarkable progress, none has eclipsed the rapid growth of the state to which the steps of my family were directed in 1839. Its growth has been more remarkable, because it has been primarily due to its initiation of many social and political reforms which have since been adopted by other and older countries. 'Australia, lead us further' is the cry of reformers in America. We have led in so many things, and though America may claim the honour of being the birthplace of the more modern theory of land values taxation, I rejoice that South Australia was the first country in the world with the courage and the foresight to adopt the tax on land values without exemption. That she is still lagging behind Tasmania and South Africa in the adoption of effective voting, as the only scientific system of electoral reform, is the sorrow of my old age. The fact that South Australia has been the happy hunting ground of the faddist has frequently been urged as a reproach against this state. Its more patriotic citizens will rejoice in the truth of the statement, and their prayer will probably be that no fewer but more advanced thinkers will arise to carry this glorious inheritance beneath the Southern Cross to higher and nobler heights of physical and human development than civilisation has yet dreamed of or achieved. The Utopia of yesterday is the possession of today, and opens the way to the Utopia of tomorrow. The haunting horror of older civilisations – divorcing the people from their natural inheritance in the soil, and filling the towns with myriads of human souls dragged down by poverty, misery, and crime – is already casting its shadow over the future of Australia; but there is hope in the fact that a new generation has arisen untrammelled by tradition, which, having the experience of older countries before it, and benefiting from the advantages of the freer life and the greater opportunities afforded by a new country, gives promise of ultimately finding the solution of the hitherto unsolved problem of making country life as attractive to the masses as that of the towns and cities. As time goes on the effect of education must tell, and the generations that are to come will be more enlightened and more altruistic, and the tendency of the world will be more and more, even as it is now, towards higher and nobler conceptions of human happiness. I have lived through a glorious age of progress. Born in 'the wonderful century', I have watched the growth of the movement for the uplifting of the masses, from the Reform Bill of 1832 to the demands for adult suffrage. As a member of a church which allows women to speak in the pulpit, a citizen of a state which gives womanhood a vote for the Assembly, a citizen of a Commonwealth which fully enfranchises me for both Senate and Representatives, and a member of a community which was foremost in conferring university degrees on women, I have benefited from the advancement of the educational and political status of women for which the Victorian era will probably stand unrivalled in the annals of the world's history. I have lived through the period of repressed childhood, and witnessed the dawn of a new era which has made the dwellers in youth's 'golden age' the most important factor in human development. I have watched the growth of Adelaide from the condition of a scattered hamlet to that of one of the finest cities in the southern hemisphere; I have seen the evolution of South Australia from a province to an important state in a great Commonwealth. All through my life I have tried to live up to the best that was in me, and I should like to be remembered as one who never swerved in her efforts to do her duty alike to herself and her fellow-citizens. Mistakes I have made, as all are liable to do, but I have done my best. And when life has closed for me, let those who knew me best speak and think of me as

> One who never turned her back, but marched breast forward,
>   Never doubted clouds would break,
> Never dreamed, though right were worsted, wrong would triumph,
>   Held we fall to rise, are baffled to fight better,
>   Sleep to wake.[7]

No nobler epitaph would I desire.

---

[7] From the Epilogue to *Asolando: Fancies and Facts* by Robert Browning, 1889. Young has substituted 'her' for Browning's 'his' in the first line.

Catherine Helen Spence's grave, St Jude's Church, Brighton. Note the irony of the grave having a cross on it, despite its occupant being a Unitarian, photograph by Barbara Wall.

Catherine Helen Spence's Diary: 1894

A Preface

The story of Catherine Spence's diaries is a sad one.

Jeanne Young refers to Catherine Spence's entries in her diary for the years when she was between the ages of, approximately, fifteen and twenty-five. These entries were, notes Young, a 'poignant self-communing and self-revelation'. 'C ... and A ... contend that if I do really not wish for marriage', Catherine Spence admonishes herself, then 'I should talk much less about it, for my talking gives to people an entirely wrong impression'. To this she adds the resolution:

> Let your ideas never dare to fancy what may happen in case of marriage; that is the forbidden subject. Place the garret steadily before you and endeavour to train your mind so as to be a useful and amiable member of society, but no one's wife and no one's mother.

After this period of her life, Jeanne Young notes, Catherine Spence's diaries 'turned in a different direction'. We learn nothing more about Catherine Spence's diaries from Jeanne Young, either in her role as ventriloquist for the final section of Spence's autobiography, or in her own book, *Catherine Helen Spence: A Study and an Appreciation* (1937) where these 'self-communings' are published.

Yet it is clear that Catherine Spence kept a diary every year of her life, from her later twenties onwards. When she died, her niece Eleanor Wren gave 'Diaries & papers' to Jeanne Young to enable her to complete the autobiography. Eleanor Wren did not think the diaries had much value; she said they were 'really only letter books noting the correspondence received &c', Lucy Morice reported. However, Jeanne Young kept them, and must still have had them when she wrote her study of Catherine Spence, since she quoted from them. But when 'Mr Pitt of the Archives' in Adelaide endeavoured to persuade

Mrs Young of the desirability of handing on the diaries to a proper repository, she refused to give them up. Her view – contrasting with Eleanor Wren's – was that 'the diaries were too private for any eyes but hers'.

Her comment provokes the thought that they contained secrets about Catherine Spence's loves. I suspect that, on the contrary, what was 'too private' in the diaries was Catherine Spence's view of Jeanne Young's husband, Alfred Howard Young. Her letters to Alice Henry written in the first decade of the twentieth century – the last decade of her life – contain an outburst that is, uncharacteristically, almost incoherent with indignation.

> Mrs Young's baby [two month-old Courtney Spence Young] thrives and is promising, but she herself has a life of such slavery unappreciated by her husband – His monstrous egotism is comic, if it was not so tragic – I hope her children will repay her, for he never will – It would make it worse for her if I quarrelled with him – and there are sides of his character – intellectual – that appeal to me – But his sublime unconsciousness of the daily hourly labour of his wife – His idea that all she knows and all she is able for is due to his teaching – and that it is a privilege for her to exist as <u>his</u> wife and the mother of <u>his</u> children – his requiring her to help him with his newspaper work the lowest dept [sic] of it – as well as do everything for the household would be called untrue and overdrawn if it were made into fiction. Like Dickens he is all nerves – and like Dickens he has no patience with the nerves of his wife – [C.H. Spence to Alice Henry, 22 November [1907?]]

If comments of this order – in letters well away from the object of their outrage – also appeared in Catherine Spence's diaries, then it is not so surprising – though it is still a great pity – that Jeanne Young refused to hand them over to the South Australian Archives. She also refused to hand them over to Lucy Morice who sent some of Catherine Spence's papers to Miles Franklin to be deposited in the Mitchell Library at around the same time, as Helen Jones' meticulous research has established.

When I was first carrying out research for a life of Catherine Spence in the late 1960s, I pursued the possible existence of her diaries endlessly. I was working in Canberra when, finally, my mother in Adelaide contacted Courtney Young, Jeanne Young's son. It was Courtney Young's wife who told my mother, airily, that she was pretty sure that diaries had gone out with the newspapers, once Jeanne Young's book was finished. A frustrating dead end.

More than twenty years later, though, and quite by chance, a new acquaintance told me that she knew that one of Catherine Spence's diaries still existed. It does. It was, then, and still is as far as I know, in private hands in Brisbane. Unfortunately, my own efforts to persuade its owners that it should be in an archive were no more successful than were Lucy Morice's with Jeanne Young. And its present owners wish not to be known themselves, so I am not in a position to enable someone more persuasive to contact them. However, this sad and frustrating tale does have one good element in it.

In 1989, I was allowed to borrow the diary – and it is incontrovertibly Catherine Spence's diary, for 1894 – for a week, and to make notes from it. The notes are patchy because Catherine Spence's handwriting is so difficult to read and my time was limited. Nevertheless, these are Catherine Spence's own words, a rich and detailed record of her days, her work, her feelings, her conversations and the people she met and spent time with. We can only marvel at the quantity of writing that she produced – writing long-hand with a steel pen and ink – while travelling, visiting and lecturing. With the explanatory notes that I have interpolated into the text, this is a wonderful moment of both social history and intimate biography, an important supplement to *An Autobiography*. This is material that has not been available to the reading public before.

A Note on the Text

When I made notes from the Diary, I copied as much as I could read, and had time to transcribe by hand. Where there were gaps, I have indicated them with ellipses, like this … Where I have guessed at a word I could not be sure of having read accurately, I have added a question mark in square brackets after the word. Towards the end of the diary, when I was running out of time, there are a few places where I summarised what I had read, instead of copying it; I have indicated this by surrounding those passages with curly brackets.

The transcript of my notes was made by the incomparable Maryan Beams. I have added to them, where possible, explanations of who Catherine Spence was talking to, or what was the publication or event that she referred to. These explanations are interpolated in the text of the Diary, in square brackets. Some of the notes reproduce information that Barbara Wall provided for the notes on *An Autobiography*. Some owe a debt to my colleague, Margaret Allen. If I have not explained something or someone, it is because I have not been able to find out anything about them. Sources in the Introduction are also given in square brackets, as are some of the words that Catherine Spence abbreviates.

This was a diary kept by an extremely busy jobbing journalist. There are inconsistencies in spelling, punctuation and abbreviation, and in people's names. Mrs Bramlick appears also as Brannlick and as Branlich – all three on Sunday 15 March 1894 – just for instance. I did not want to interrupt the text further than I have already by adding '[sic]' each time some inconsistency occurred. Instead, Wakefield Press and I have edited it to make it easier to read. We have not signalled where we have done this. Readers can be sure, though, that our work is entirely consonant with the original; and scholars might like to check the transcripts in the State Library of South Australia.

I add here a list of the abbreviations that Catherine Spence used most consistently. Most will be readily intelligible, but a list might be helpful.

Aust	Australian
Pro rep	proportional representation
Mg	morning
Whch	which
Evg	evening
Feby	February
W.S.	Women's Suffrage
Appt	appointment
MLH	Margaret Louisa Home
No	number
Ass	association
Novr	November
Refm	Reform
Aft	afternoon
PC	postcards
Sept	September
Octr	October
Xtian	Christian
Phila	Philadelphia

An Introduction

Catherine Helen Spence left Adelaide on 4 April 1893, stopped in Melbourne – where she spent time with her niece, Eleanor Wren, and left her purse behind her – and took ship in Sydney on 17 April 1893, followed by 'my purse and a sermon' from Eleanor [C.H. Spence to Family, 17–20 April 1893]. She was bound for the United States of America as government commissioner and delegate to the Great World Fair and Congresses to be held in Chicago that year. She was to represent the South Australian State Children's Council at the International Congress of Charities, Correction and Philanthropy. She carried a letter of introduction to Henry George, United States politician, a radical free-trader, author of *Progress and Poverty* in which he argued that taxes should be confined to economic rent derived from land, a single tax, which would eliminate all other government levies and thus enable the unimpeded and benevolent operation of the economy; his gospel of 'the single tax' became central to the English socialist movement. She was to report to the South Australian Single Tax League on similar efforts to combat poverty in North America. She was to learn about education in the United States and report to J.A. Hartley, Director of Education in South Australia. She was to make contact with North American activists in the cause of female suffrage and tell them about the highly promising campaign under way at home. She carried a letter of introduction to revered anti-slavery campaigner, William Lloyd Garrison. She was charged to report on the Silver Conference and current concerns about the standard for a currency to the progressive South Australian bimetallists; bimetallism was a popular issue in the United States at this time probably because the gold reserve on which the United States' currency was based was in such decline as to precipitate a stock market crash in June 1893, followed by a four-year depression. She would, of course, be in touch with co-religionists in the Unitarian Church.

    She was to write letters that would be published in the press, in South

Australia, to help pay her way on her travels, as would, she hoped, some of her lectures. She took with her one titled 'A Democratic Ideal'; another which she had first presented to Adelaide University's Shakespeare Society in 1892 [*Adelaide Observer*, 10 November 1894], on the controversy current over rival claims by readers of William Shakespeare and Francis Bacon to authorship of the works of Shakespeare; yet another on the works of novelist George Eliot [*Adelaide Observer*, 16 June 1894]; and of course her well-practised exposition of the principles and practice of proportional representation. For, above all, she would carry on her own campaign for the introduction of 'effective voting' – proportional representation – into the electoral processes of the largest democracy in the world. She had been invited to the United States by Alfred Cridge, a San Francisco journalist who was also an enthusiastic proponent of proportional representation. She arrived in San Francisco on 12 May 1893, an ominous moment in time for that was the month when the price of stocks on the New York Stock Exchange began falling.

Her letters home report that the 'Single Taxers are dead against silver and this prevents them co-operating with the Populists and probably with the Socialists. The same letter instructs Lucy to write: 'We want to know about New Australia and the Fabians' [C.H. Spence to J.B. Spence, ?August/September 1894]. She investigates the price of bread [letter without address or date]. She considers Chicago 'the most crowded and bustling and noisy city in the world' [*Adelaide Observer*, 5 August 1893], but the World Fair is huge and beautiful. She visits the Women's Building where, she reports, it is difficult for a speaker to be heard.

> There is constant going and coming, and the sound of feet and voices all around. Many ladies fail to make themselves audible beyond a foot or two in front, as the hall is badly built for acoustic purposes, but everyone complimented me on making myself heard all over the hall. [*Adelaide Observer*, 26 August 1893]

A South Australian had described her voice, with its distinctive Scottish burr, as 'rather carrying', a quality that clearly came to her aid in Chicago. She finds that 'People generally are more interested in ... the children of the State than in my account of the work done by the South Australian Destitute Board in keeping families together by judicious outdoor relief, and in providing for the protection of infant life in the Lying-in Home and through supervision of licensed foster mothers ' [*Adelaide Observer*, 26 August 1893].

In Chicago, she meets Melusine Fay Peirce, who picks her up in 'a carriage with liveried servants', and makes her promise to visit 'this fall' in New York where she lives [letter without address or date]. Mrs Peirce 'is poor herself, but she is keeping house for a rich brother; or a brother apparently rich, who has a complete establishment' [letter without address or date; see also below entry for 11 January 1894]. She meets Susan B. Anthony 'a Veteran Woman's Suffragist' who was, at the time, president of the National American Women's Suffrage Association. Spence believes that she has converted Anthony to proportional representation and reports that Anthony also wants her to visit New York state, where she lives in Rochester [another letter without address or date, also *Adelaide Observer*, 21 October 1893 and 4 November 1893]. Miss Anthony persuades Miss Spence to attend the National Women's Suffrage Convention in Washington in February the next year [*Adelaide Observer*, 3 March 1894]. She meets other suffragists, too – she listens to a paper by Henry Blackwell, husband of Lucy Stone; Stone and Anthony were at that time two of America's most famous suffragists. She encounters Margaret Windeyer, a suffragist from Sydney where her mother was president of the Womanhood Suffrage League of New South Wales [*Adelaide Observer*, 30 September 1893].

On 4 July she visits the Woman's Temple, 'the great pile of building erected by the W.C.T.U. [Women's Christian Temperance Union] in the centre of the business part of the City of Chicago'. It is, she reports

> twelve stories high, and is supplied with elevators. On the ground floor is the Willard Hall [named after Frances Willard, north American leader of the World Women's Christian Temperance Union 1839–1898] for large meetings, religious and prohibitionist, and the premises of the great Banks. On the eleventh floor is the printing and publishing establishment for the *Union Signal* and other prohibitionist literature. The rest of the vast building is let, for offices so as to provide income beyond interest on money borrowed of about $50,000 a year for extinction of the debt. This property is entirely managed by women. [*Adelaide Observer*, 30 September 1893]

Unfortunately, by 1897 it would have become a financial quagmire. Catherine Spence speaks there, but she is by no means a supporter of prohibition. 'From my personal intercourse with Americans', she notes, 'I should say that they are the most temperate race of people in the world, and wonder at the zeal and the indignation of the Prohibitionists'. [*Adelaide Observer*, 4 November 1893]

She visits Hull House, the settlement that Jane Addams and Ellen Starr founded in Chicago in 1889 on the model of Toynbee Hall in the east end of London – an endeavour combining welfare work and teaching by resident female college graduates among the poor and labouring classes who attend meals and classes [letter without address or date].

She is present at what must have been an exhilarating exchange.

A Professor from the South explained to us the five methods by which the negro was cheated out of his vote, and justified them by the necessity of securing dominancy to the white race, whereupon the aged, white-haired Frederic Douglas [sic] rose in his might and turned the argument inside out [Frederick Douglass was a former slave and a great orator]. I never heard more eloquence, more sarcasm, or more humour than he compressed into his twenty minutes' speech. There was also a coloured woman, a Mrs. Harper, well to do, who also showed all the powers of the orator. [Frances Ellen Watkins Harper was the only African American on the executive of the American Women's Christian Temperance Union's executive committee.] [*Adelaide Observer*, 21 October 1893]

She also goes with Alfred Cridge to a 'real unemployed meeting at the Carpenters' Council-room in Washington-street' [*Adelaide Observer*, 4 November 1893]. Chicago, she relates, 'is somewhat like a slumbering volcano and although it is necessary to preserve law and order, some citizens have been clubbed by policemen in plain clothes and attempts are made to prevent free speech in public places – Chicago is very foreign – but not as Irish as New York'. [letter without address or date]

In Chicago, she takes pride in her 'social qualities'. 'Every day I meet here people worth talking to. My insatiable curiosity finds food, and my solitude is cheered by human companionship ... But I must take into consideration that here I am talking to strangers, perhaps as hungry for companionship as myself, and not afraid of committing themselves.' [*Adelaide Observer*, 26 August 1893] She takes pride in her public addresses, too. For one, she reports, 'I had a most attentive hearing, and was frequently interrupted by applause, which is not such a common thing in America as it is in Australia'. This is a lecture on schooling, and her hearers afterwards petition her for copies of her book, *The Laws We Live Under*, the first economics text written for Australian secondary schools, published in 1880 but out of print by the time she leaves for the United States in 1893. [*Adelaide Observer*, 14 October 1893]

Her letters also show her proud of herself over her arrival in New York city, where she goes to stay with Margaret Sanger – who can't have been the Margaret Sanger who would become so famous in the second decade of the twentieth century for her campaign for birth control – because that Margaret Sanger was only fifteen years old in 1893.

> I landed in N. York in the dark – I went to the baggage room to recheck my big trunk – I was directed to a street car which took me straight to Long Island Station. I sat there ... for an hour and a half and I reached Rockville Centre at 11 o'clock and the station was closed – there I was with my

Gladstone and my tin hatbox both heavy with a handbag, an umbrella and a parasol – Nobody who came out of the train knew anything about Mrs Sanger and I felt a somewhat forlorn if not despairing little woman – But out of the darkness came a young man – and more of that invaluable family of Smith to whom is owe [sic] so much – He said he knew Mrs Sanger and he was going that way – He took my Gladstone and my umbrellas and led the way. Mrs Sanger had been three times to the depot to meet me and had gone to bed. But she knew who it was when the knock came and hastened down to admit me and her welcome was as warm as you could imagine – Now do not you think that – idiot as I am ab[ou]t localities – I managed the trials through arrivals in such cities as Chicago and New York wondrous well.

Catherine Spence is especially pleased at having arrived at Mrs Sanger's 'charming cottage' with 'such an atmosphere of repose in it' when she finds that Mrs Sanger 'likes whist and cribbage' – 'I have pined for a game of cards for months'. [letter without address or date]

She receives letters. The Reverend Anna Garlin Spencer, President of the Children's Section of the Charities and Correction Congress in Chicago [*Adelaide Observer*, 13 January 1894], and a pastor in the Unitarian Church in Rhode Island, writes to ask her to give a lecture [letter without address or date], and she has 'a splendid time' there, earning money: 'I got $35 for the Winter lecture – the Democratic Ideal $10 for the Normal School and $2.50 from the Brown University in aid of travelling expenses' [C.H. Spence to 'dear John and Family, from 12 Chestnut Street, Boston, home of the Rev. C.J. Ames, 28 November 1893, also *Adelaide Observer*, 13 January 1894]. She had 'the friendliest letter from W. Lloyd Garrison, son of the great Abolitionist – who is a strong Single Taxer and also firm for Proportional Representation'. [C.H. Spence to My dear John, Rockville Centre, 31 October 1893, 'my birthday']

Her very good friend, Australian novelist Catherine Martin, is still in touch with her: 'Katie Martin writes alarmed lest I should be ill – one of my letters is lost or delayed – for I have been most regular – She is in Vienna and reports the weather cold' [letter without address or date; Catherine Edith Macauley Mackay was born on the Isle of Skye in 1847, migrated to South Australia with her family in 1855, lived first in Mt. Gambier, then in Adelaide where she worked for the Education Department from 1877 until 1885, and wrote contributions for the local newspapers. She met Catherine Spence at the inauguration of the University of Adelaide in 1876. She married Frederick Martin in 1882 and they travelled in Europe in 1888–90 and again in 1891–95. Her most famous novel, *An Australian Girl* was published in 1890. *The Silent Sea* was published in 1892. She finished 'The Born Egoist' while she was in Siena in October 1894, but her English publisher rejected it. Her other novels are *The Old Roof-Tree: The Letters of Ishbel to her Half-Brother, Mark Latimer* (1906), and the remarkable work, *The Incredible Journey* (1923). Her husband died in 1909. Martin died in 1937.].

Spence reports on letters that she has had from home. 'C.W. Wren says that New Castle [sic] is suffering because Victorian railroads are using Victorian black coal.' [C.H. Spence to My dear Family, Roxbury, Boston, 2 December 1893]. 'The accounts of poverty are very depressing – everywhere – Miss Clark said the Coltons had lost very much.' [portion of letter headed 'c/o "Sentinel", Indianopolis', nd] Caroline Emily Clark must have been writing about the impact of the drastic economic depression in Australia, and their friends Mary and John Colton. Mary Colton was president of the Young Women's Christian Association in South Australia from 1884 until her death in 1898, and an activist in the South Australian Woman Suffrage League.

By November she is in Boston, staying at the home of the Unitarian Reverend C. Ames

> I wrote to Miss Clark a few days ago from the house of her cousin Mrs Ashley (at Birkbeck Hill) whose husband is professor of Historical Economics at Harvard Cambridge near Boston – I have had some new experiences having endured <u>three</u> receptions ... I not only was offered the church for Thursday, but the hospitality of this house from Saturday and I am most kindly entertained – This is a luxurious house for a Unitarian Minister ... But Mrs Ames is not an idle woman. She is the chief inspector of factories and workshops for women and children, and the law is so good and the inspection so thorough that there are but 300 or fewer children employed in the whole state of Massachusetts – which is a hive of industry ... [C.H. Spence to My dear John and Family, 12 Chestnut St., Boston, 28 November 1893]

She is still in Boston at the beginning of December, now staying at the house of Mr Frank Garrison, son of William Lloyd Garrison.

> This house is where [W.L.] Garrison lived for the last fifteen years of his life – It is an old house full of relics of the campaign, from the bound copies of the Liberation from its first issue in 1831 to its concluding number in 1865 when the battle was over – to portraits of all the noted men and women in England and America who worked for the slave – Out of the window where I sit, I see a great dry stone dyke 250 years old, which encloses the gardens. Except for a few fir and pine trees the trees are leafless – I can guess what beauty must be in the spreading elm in summer. O[liver] W[endell] Holmes [Professor of Anatomy and Physiology at Harvard

University from 1847 to 1882; essayist, poet, humourist, scientist, teacher, strenuous opponent of Calvinism, author of *The Autocrat of the Breakfast Table* (1858)] whom I am going to see, wrote of the Boston & Cambridge elms coeval with the settlement of the Commonwealth of Massachusetts with such enthusiasm that I am sorry to miss their full beauty. [*Adelaide Observer*, 31 March 1894]

She describes Holmes as 'a plain looking New England man', but, she notes, 'his talk is good still though I think there are some directions in which his memory is treacherous'. He is, she continues:

> The last of the great race of Americans of whom Boston and Massachusetts are justly proud – He lives very carefully and probably will reach extreme old age – He sat in his library – surrounded by gifts from many hands and many lands. [letter without address or date]

At that time, Holmes was eighty-four years old, with only a year more to live. Catherine Spence is escorted on this visit by Frank Garrison who is 'an important person in the house of Houghton Mifflin & Co who publish the *Atlantic Monthly* and who publish Oliver Wendell Holmes'. [letter without address or date] She has tried to persuade the *Atlantic Monthly* to publish two of her articles, one of 3,000 words and another 'long' one. This effort has not succeeded, but she has gained some financial support from the Garrisons and the Unitarian Ames family. They do not pay her for the sermon they asked her to preach for them, but following the sermon, the attendance at her lecture – for which her friends had hired a hall, advertised and printed blank ballot papers for her to demonstrate how effective voting worked – was great enough for Charles Ames to 'put into my hands a check for $50' and 'both the Garrisons & the Ameses say the written lecture was the finest political address given in Boston for ten years'. [letter without address or date]

She meets two heroines of the struggle against slavery. One is Elizabeth Chace, 'one of the active agents in slavery days for the escape of runaway slaves to Canada. She is eighty-six', writes Miss Spence, 'full of memories for the past and hopes for the future'. [*Adelaide Observer*, 31 March 1894] The other is Harriet Tubman 'an old coloured woman' who

> in the old slavery days made 19 journeys South to assist Negro slaves to escape and in all helped 300 to safety – She rescued her three brothers and her old father and mother – She acted as a scout during the [civil] war and as hospital nurse to wounded and sick soldiers for four years – but while tens of thousands of people ... get pensions they do not deserve this old woman

has not a cent. She took care of her parents till their death and now her poor cottage is the refuge for poor sick or blind colored people – She never could read or write but she is a marvellously sagacious old woman – She thinks she is 76 but may be older. [letter without address, dated 21st [?December 1893]]

In New York, she stays at the Margaret Louisa Home, run in connection with the Young Women's Christian Association. It

is a very beautiful Ladies Hotel built by Mrs Sheppard daughter of Vanderbilt for a temporary home for self-supporting women. The accommodation is excellent for half a dollar a day – and the breakfast & lunches at 20c – and the good evening dinner at 30c – are such as appears worth double the money – No one is allowed to stay more than a month in one year. [C.H. Spence to My dear John, Auburn, New York State, 20 December 1893]

It does have one disadvantage, though: its lights are extinguished at 10.30pm [C.H. Spence to My dear Family, Brookline, Boston, 25 January 1894], a time considered appropriate for all residents to be in bed. On 11 January 1894, she has scarcely had time to undress before being plunged into darkness. Baths do not cost anything extra – Catherine Spence likes to take a cold bath daily – 'and the bathrooms are beautiful – glazed tiles and marble all round and beautiful baths with hot and cold water.' [C.H. Spence to My dear Family, Brookline, Boston, 25 January 1894] Here she reports that she has letters from Ellen Gregory and 'the first I have ever had from Lucy Morice since I returned to New York'. [letter without address or date]

Here, too, she encounters the world whose decline is depicted by Edith Wharton in *The Age of Innocence* (1920).

I went out accompanied by Mr & Mrs Mills to midday dinner at Mrs Bagg's ... and we went out to evg dinner at the house of an American millionaire a Major Davis whose wife was a May a cousin of Louisa Alcotts [Louisa May Alcott, 1832–88, novelist, author of the lastingly popular *Little Women* (1868–9)] – Everything was very grand and very English – wine & champagne – and evening dress. Mrs Davis a large good looking lady in expensive corded white silk with no end of glistening spangles on it. Two grown up girls good looking and intelligent but all the family spend half their lives in Europe – They are going to take possession of a palace in Naples that is being fitted up with American comfort ...

The wealth is inherited the chief source of income is from the ownership of all the street cars in Louisville Kentucky a city of 220,000 inhabitants which the old man acquired and bequeathed to his only son – The May family is not rich – None of the family were at church so I did not feel at all uncomfortable with regard to my presentation of the Democratic Ideal – two men servants waited at table – the dinner was good but not extravagant – not quite equal to a Chicago dinner I had for four ladies. [letter without address or date]

From such people, and the Osbornes – Mrs Osborne is sister to Mrs William Lloyd Garrison – she learns more about the state of the economy. And politics.

The Osbornes are working but most of the people in Auburn (30,000 inhabitants) have shut down their mills and factories – At Syracuse the chief industry was salt and potteryworks, but salt is procured more cheaply from Warsaw, and though the Republicans blame the threatened Democratic Tariff for the collapse, well-informed persons tell me it had to come and that the extravagance of the Rep[ublican] party with regard to pensions and buying silver to coin at face value are greatly to blame for the state of things – the times are bad and will be worse so – bankers say – the winter will be one of the worst ever known – It snows every day – and the poor out-of-work must feel the cold – Fuel is dear: the coal-barons control the output, that it may not fall below the prices that suit them. [letter without address or date]

Throughout these travels, she promotes the fiction of her Australian novelist friend Catherine Martin.

Mrs. Martin's friends and admirers will be interested to hear that "An Australian Girl" would have been brought out by Harpers in America if it had not been published in England before the new Copyright Bill was passed I sent it to Harper, and the opinion given was of the highest description. [*Adelaide Observer*, 13 January 1894]

International copyright means, she explains, that 'an American publisher can protect himself from pirated cheap editions by paying the English author for the exclusive right for a time'. But there is an awkward result. 'If an English friend sends an English book to an American the receiver must pay duty at the rate of 40 percent.' [*Adelaide Observer*, 10 February 1894]

A month later, she complains:

I do not know why Mr. Bentley has not long ere this brought out a cheaper edition of "The Silent Sea". Harpers, who read every new book that comes from any publisher of note, wrote for a right to republish this before it was well launched in England, and American readers have a well-printed though paper-covered half-dollar edition. I was much pleased by learning from J. Henry Harper, the literary head of the house, that he has the highest opinion of the book, and is eagerly looking out for a successor, for if the author can produce another book as good she ought to take the first rank as a writer of fiction.

The 'many friends of Mrs. F. Martin must feel pleased', she comments, 'that her work has met with so much appreciation in such influential quarters as Franklin-square, New York City'. [*Adelaide Observer*, 10 February 1894] But that still does not make up for the lack of a cheaper edition by Bentley. By the time that Miss Spence is preparing to depart from New York, she has bought fourteen copies of the cheaper Harper edition of *An Australian Girl*, given eight away among friends in America, and packed six to give to friends in England.

She has also encountered enquiries about two other novels of the late nineteenth century by Australian writers: Ada Cambridge's *The Three Miss Kings* and *Uncle Piper of Piper's Hill* by 'Tasma', pen-name of Jessie Couvreur [*Adelaide Observer*, 16 June 1894]. And she is taking with her to England a book of satirical verses by north American Charlotte Perkins Gilman, *In This Our World*, first published in Oakland, California, to seek for it an English publisher, thus laying the foundation for Gilman's transatlantic reputation.

Among so much serious thinking, writing, speaking and getting about, Catherine Spence's humour still ripples. 'A lady from Ohio, whom I met at the World's Fair, was surprised how well I spoke the language, as I had not been then three months in America' she tells us. 'She evidently thought I should speak the language of the Australian natives, though she did not talk that of the Red Indians...' [*Adelaide Observer*, 10 February 1894]. She is interested in differences in language. 'I met with many "lovely" people, to use their own phrase, in Syracuse. We apply the term lovely to youth and beauty; Americans apply it to worth and lovableness, not exactly amicability, for that seems to imply lack of strength of character. It is', she continues – and one can hear the smile in her tone – 'the first time in my long life in which I have been characterised as "one of the loveliest of women".' [*Adelaide Observer*, 13 January 1894]

The Diary

Monday 1 January 1894

Shakespear[e] Discussion

I began the new year of 1894 in Orange New Jersey ['a fashionable district of Jersey City', C.H. Spence to my dear John, 20 December 1894] having preached The Democratic Ideal the Sunday before the 31st. Although my voice rather suffered I had agreed to read the Shakespeare Bacon lecture to Mrs Perkins; she had met Mr Laurence in London and heard about the matter – Mrs Chubb Mr and Mrs Taylor Mrs Brown and Miss Swan were of the party. Mr Taylor is a lawyer and a great Shakespeare reader. I think I shook him a good deal. Anyhow they all thought it a most interesting lecture and worthy of being given to lay audiences – Mr Swan said he would ask the Orange S[hakespeare] Society which he did but they think they are equal to their needs and object to paying ...

    Mr Marsh came in mg to ask if I would give a lecture on Saturday evg to the Orange NE Club 10 dollars. I answered with alacrity Yes.

Tuesday 2 January 1894

I begged Mr Hale for paper and began my press letters in earnest – first the *Register*. There were also various private letters to answer but this continuous bud opening takes a good deal out of me.

    Mrs Perkins copied out part of my lecture for her husband –

Wednesday 3 January 1894

Worked on at my press letters till both were three quarters done ...

Thursday 4 January 1894

<u>Womans Suffrage</u> 15 minutes

Now I must return to the Margaret Louisa House – I left my Jamsera silk ...

my birthday book and voting papers and took as much as I could carry ... I got home a little tired but after dinner and prayers I started off for a Womans Suffrage meeting and heard Mrs Chapman [Carrie Chapman, later leading suffragist and peace activist Carrie Chapman Catt, 1859–1947] tell of the victory in Colorado which she attributed to the proximity of Wyoming [and] to the Australian ballot and to other conspiring causes [voters in Colorado approved female suffrage on 7 November 1893. Carrie Chapman held that the success owed something to the precedent set in the nearby Territory of Wyoming which, together with Mormon Utah, legislated in favour of Womanhood Suffrage as early as 1870. There were also, in Colorado, strong mining unions with a history of belief in equal rights for women.] ... I spoke ten or 15 minutes with good effect ...

Friday 5 January 1894
Mrs Davison is very charming – all the more because she was charmed with me. She asked two important gentlemen by special messenger to dine both engaged. She expected Mr Seward he did not come but I had her husband and Mr Flick and as one runs a magazine Godeys [*Godey's Lady's Book*, a monthly magazine founded by Louis A. Godey in 1830, sold in 1877, passing through several hands, ultimately ceasing publication in 1898] and the other a Pennsylvania paper at Wickes-Barre; they were quite congenial. Pro rep was new to both but I sold them two pamphlets and I think interested them both.

Saturday 6 January 1894
Orange New England Club ...
It seems as if I was always ... a tremendous scrimmage when I go anywhere – I wrote before breakfast to Katie Martin and had it in my own room. Spoke to Mr and Mrs Davison ... any opening in Godeys Mag for pro rep. He said yes –
 Home by 9.45 and worked desperately hard to finish my press letters ...
 Before lecture Mrs Cutts talked about Bacon and is most anxious I should give that lecture somewhere in Orange. The audience was not half what I expected but it was most appreciative – not so much as a joke was lost on them – I sold 19 copies of Cridge's pamphlet for him ... – I had half a glass of sherry and then crackers for supper – ...

Sunday 7 January 1894
This was a quiet day but contained a quite new experience. I went to church in mg and stayed over Sunday School – a grown up class in Church History ... the Protestant Episcopal Church whch ... to be known as the American Catholic ...
 Mr Hale [probably a member of the Hale family, prominent in New

England social reform and intellectual circles; Edward Everett Hale of Boston was an uncle of Charlotte Perkins Stetson/Gilman] a good deal struck with the power of my personality ... visionary – His mg reunion was a retrospect of the year – This evg sermon was a good exposition on the idolatry of beauty ... and of so called liberalism a rebound from the mistaken ideas of our ancestors.

Monday 8 January 1894
Had breakfast and returned New York by 9.39 train. Found all right. Got a no of Godey which seems to have a whole novel or novelette in each issue. I wrote letters till I was thoroughly tired out to Eleanor the longest...

Tuesday 9 January 1894
Political Study 15 minutes women
... Wrote for a very long time – the short article for Sol Schlinders – letter to Cridges with $5 and Divers shorter letters and postals despatched. From Godmother to Katie Hood and began letter to Katie Martin – In after[noon] went to meeting – a 'social' for political study and was taken far past Lexington Ave 4 – so only heard lag end of Mrs Loziers [Dr Jennie M. Lozier was president of Sorosis, a famous New York Club formed to promote exchanges among women with literary and artistic interests. See also Melusine Fay Peirce in 11 January below] ... – I spoke next for 15 minutes – then Mrs Blake [probably Lillie Devereux Blake, prominent New York women's suffragist] last Mrs Clymer – A good many ladies came to talk to me, but I am disappointed as the Feby W.S. Meeting is filled up – I went specially in the hope of making an appt – Home very tired, borrowed a darning needle and mended pair of stockings pretty bad – Made an attempt to go to service of song but was turned back for a bonnet [?] and stays [?] ... I bought for 1.10 equal to 4/7-

Is this a change? – Yes – Is it a holiday? No – this is precious hard work every day and all day long.

Wednesday 10 January 1894
Rain + snow all day stayed indoors and first finished my letter to K ... Then wrote 7 pages for Mr Flicks['] Wickes Barre paper subject the militant versus the Cooperative in Election of representatives.

Received letter ... saying his wife was too busy to acknowledge *Silent Sea* [novel by Catherine Martin] which she liked much – so that is put straight – Had a talk with ... a magazine writer. She says $10 per 1000 words is about the rate for a known writer – I wish I could get it – I think Flick's article is that length but I shall get nothing for it – I mended some stockings read Steiners book – and cleared out a lot of old letters and papers.

Thursday 11 January 1894

Mrs Fay Peirce called on me to ask me to dine ... [Melusine Fay Peirce (1836–1923) was an early feminist and founder of the Cooperative Housekeeping Association, a body concerned to experiment in cooperative living. Her articles began appearing in 1868, and were collected and published as a book, *Cooperative Housekeeping: Romance in Domestic Economy*, in 1870. She was also involved in the 1869 Woman's Parliament in New York with journalist Jane Cunningham Croly, founder of Sorosis, see also above, 9 January 1894, and below, 22 March 1894 and 1 July 1894.]

Weather not much better overhead and probably worse underfoot but after writing no end of letters I sallied forth – ... I struggled to get to the Georges but thought it was 23rd street and not so ... [ended up] trailing through no end of wet streets. H[enry] George at Washington ... I stayed as long as I could, and did without my lunch and scarcely missed it. In the mg I got to my bank and bestowed there many of the books so that I might take with me the tin box, with some valuable space. I was copying out the Adelaide scrutiny [an assessment of the votes cast in an election conducted by proportional representation, which Catherine Spence used in lectures about effective voting] when Mrs Peirce interrupted me – I changed my dress had half an hour rest and went forth for Washington Sq. A pleasant dinner and talk with the ladies and a gentleman originally from Nova Scotia. In evg Mrs Peirce read me her Anti Irish anti Catholic anti Tammany letter. I read her my paper – She read me the topical chapters of a novel [this may have been a novel that Peirce was writing in which she planned to expound her ideas about government including a council of women] ... and I laid open for her the Shakespeare Bacon controversy. Could not get the stage so walked home and was scarcely undressed when the electric light went out. Feel satisfied I saw Mr Remsen [Daniel S. Remsen, a Wall Street counselor at law, author of a book on primary elections.]. He says he is right glad I came.

Friday 12 January 1894

A pretty busy day packing up and destroying letters – ... I found I had to pay 1.35 for <u>letter rates</u> on [a MS novel] and ... more for registration. John's Almanac only cost 9c for postage – Still it is off my mind – only I am so much the poorer – It is terrible work getting so much into these two receptacles – ...

I made about £10 out of the Syracuse and Sherwood trip beyond experience and $20 out of Orange $5 from Cabt [Cabot?] Shaw.

When I thought I had cleared up everything at 8 pm I got a letter from Mrs Fay Peirce proposing a course of lectures or matinees in March – I feel disposed to them they would do good and give a tentative reply.

Saturday 13 January 1894

Made a start in right enough time but found I had to leave a lot of things in Mrs Ames bag and bandbox – left Cridges pamphlets by mistake – Left at 10.5 and arrived at Providence 3.15 took cab to 61 Congdon St then washed and dressed. Mrs Spencer [Anna Garlin Spencer, see above *Adelaide Observer*, 13 January 1894] and Lucy arrived – She stayed till 8 and we had talk about Charitable work the state and the individual and the difference between East & West. In the West the Universities are State organisations and linked to the common schools through the High schools. In the West a little township becomes a city and this is more direct and less contrary than the NE Town – The little city is pure and may remain pure – When a town grows large in the E it fears like Brookline [Massachusetts] to become a city for the wealth tempts the politicians and the Ward system allows them to exercise baleful power. Mrs S agrees with me as to the value of State action but under present circumstances it is dangerous. The purification of politics is the one thing needful for social reforms. She says that since the war the national spirit has strengthened but state patriotism is less. They think of the U.S. and of their city or their country but not of their state (except perhaps Massachusetts) – Mr and Mrs Ballon [Mr Ballon was a jeweler with a large business in Providence, Rhode Island] are most kind. I had a comfortable bedroom and a good rest.

Sunday 14 January 1894

In course of talk with Mr Ballon read him the Berk[e]ley Electric lighting article which pleased him so much that he gave me 5 dollars for 20 copies for a year which he will circulate. I think he is clear for pro rep – and his son of 24 and his daughter of 17 made each a copy of the Adelaide scrutiny of 3824 votes – Interesting discussion from Miss Alice Fletcher on the Indian with whom she has lived for years and who divides the land allotted indirectly to the Omaha tribe – She thinks it absolutely necessary the young Indians should be separated from their parents and taught the English language [ethnologist and archaeologist, and head of a commission of women to find 'solutions' to 'the Indian Question', Alice Fletcher lived among the Plains Indians for many years and adopted a young Omaha, Francis La Flesche, as her son. She was instrumental in securing the allotment of land in severalty for the Indians, and acted as a special – President-appointed – agent to carry out the allotment work among the Omaha, the Winnebago and the Nez-Perce Indians. At the time when Catherine Spence heard her, she had recently presented a pioneering paper on American Indian music to the 1893 meeting of the Anthropological Congress in Chicago. From 1886 she worked with the Peabody Museum of American Archaeology and Ethnology at Harvard, and in 1896 she was made vice-president of the American Association for the

Advancement of Science.] ... I prepared what was to follow the rejected article (3 times) to make my lecture long enough for the Boston women –

Monday 15 January 1894
New England Womens Club
I prepared some ballots for the Boston NE [New England] Womens Club...

I made out a scrap of a letter to Cridge to accompany the belated $5 [throughout her time in the USA, Catherine Spence sent sums of money to Alfred Cridge to support his publication, titled *Hope and Home*. It can be surmised that this was a means of advocating proportional representation. Spence thought the title should be *The Key*. She also sent sums of money to Cooley, 'our secretary', who seems to have been the publisher of the *Proportional Representation Review*, see above letters to the family no address or date; C.H. Spence to My dear Family, 27 March 1894; letter without address or date from Chicago] and was interrupted by Mr Spencer who wanted to hear about Shakespeare & Bacon. I read the lecture to him and to Mrs Ballon and he said he should like to study it carefully; there were too many points to be taken up on a sudden – I recommended him to Donnelly [Ignatius Donnelly (1831–1901) American congressman noted primarily for his work *Atlantis, Myths of the Antediluvian World*, 1882, which claimed that Atlantis lay at the bottom of the Atlantic Ocean]. Left the kind Ballons upset, but they think I will return. Boston district then Providence tonight Mrs Hooper in the Clubroom. She had been to the Garrisons on Saturday to see me – W.L. Garrison was there and says I kept all the women awake which is hard to do – Unfortunately the ballot as constructed does not fit the women –

I had to stay for the tea or supper for there was turkey and cranberry sauce – but left after that was over and did not stay like long performances – I talked a good deal with Mrs Dietrick [Ellen Batelle Dietrick, a Massachusetts female suffragist] whom I met at Mrs Garrisons and who is staunch for Bacon and pro rep –

I was guided to a Reserved Car and arrived at 7 Richter Terrace a little after 8 – Mr and Mrs Halliwell of W[est] Medford cousin of Mrs G[arrison] her daughter and niece [Richard Halliwell, a strong republican, and a Quaker who left the Society of Friends in support of the abolition of slavery. 'Everywhere I am among abolitionists who left their churches because those churches were the bulwarks of slavery', Miss Spence wrote in a letter without address, 29 January 1894] ... they left ... and then Mr and Mrs Ames and her mother Mrs Donaldson an old Virginian arrived and we had two capital Rubbers of whist.

A pile of letters awaited me many needing immediate reply – And a hearty welcome from my friends – ...

Mr Ames and I had a <u>slam</u> against Mr Samson.

Tuesday 16 January 1894

Had these letters on my mind to disturb my slumber – breakfast and then correspondence – Did not answer them all but answered what was peremptory ...

Afternoon ... had a nap on the bed ...

In even[in]g Mr Garrison read Tom L. Johnsons Free Trade speech reproaching the Democratic party with halfhearted views + pusillanimity. He is an iron man who manufactures steel rails – not one of the Carnegie ring [Tom Loftin Johnson (1854–1911) was a member of Congress for the Democrats 1890–1894, influenced by Henry George, and an advocate of free trade, single tax and street railroads. During the 1890s, Andrew Carnegie – second in wealth in the US only to the oil baron Rockefellers – was acquiring a virtual monopoly of steel production. The 'ring' was the term used for those within his sphere of influence]. I read Mr Garrison my latest *Register* editorial on Commercial Telephones.

We played whist though Mrs Garrison would rather read *An Australian Girl* with which she is enchanted. I played two games of cribbage with Charlie Garrison bald like his father but of course comparatively young. I gave him some Aust stamps – On the whole this was an easy day.

Letter in evg from Womens Club Council enclosed in one from Mr Ames.

Wednesday 17 January 1894

Chester [Boston] Nationalist Club ...

Had two rooms to address at once – My skeleton [for a mock election to illustrate proportional representation] seemed satisfactory and I think I did well on the whole 130 votes taken – ... Showed it on the black board [sic] but John Pickering Putnam [a nationalist architect; he had organized the occasion] was a little impatient at the end so it was not quite complete.

I could not sell but 3 pamphlets I gave away a good many H[ope] & H[ome] – but the rules of the ass. or the Hotel or something prevented offering for sale. Mrs Putnam and her daughter gave me $25 for the lecture – to which friends were admitted by ticket ... – I was kept at work till past ten ...

Thursday 18 January 1894

Wrote Walter Boone and Gove [W.H. Gove had framed the Gove system of proportional representation which would do away with the need to transfer all the ballot papers to a central office to be counted, something that Americans were suspicious of, fearing that they would be tampered with] and then started for the W.S. deputation ... Many speakers of 10 minutes each and I as a foreigner took 5 or so – Home to find seven letters 3 from Aust – and cheque for $5 from New Eng Woman's Club and the most interesting letter from a Mrs Dunham not the lady I meant to address.

I make something out of my mistakes – I went with Agnes to Pro[fessor] Wilson's lecture [Thomas Woodrow Wilson, Professor of Jurisprudence and Political Eonomy at Princeton University 1890–1902, later President of the United States of America.] ... which was not particularly interesting except the recapitulation of the previous one but Mrs Twichell was there and she spoke to someone who's in communication with Labour organisations about me and I may get an opening no pay –

My people had not got my Philadelphia letter written on 11 Novr.

Friday 19 January 1894

Mr. Samson pointed out to me a leader on Miss Spences Crusade in yesterdays *Boston Transcript* [written by Edward Henry Clement, editor-in-chief of the *Boston Transcript*, 1881–1906, anti-imperialist, anti-vivisectionist and in favour of improving the conditions of the Boston work-houses.] – ordered 2 doz copies for friends and newspapers.

Took fish chowder for lunch and after writing till 3 o'clock went for walk with Mrs Garrison but got home to be pretty sick – They sent away Mrs Smith [probably Harriette Knight Smith, contributor of character sketches to the *Boston Transcript*] of the *Transcript* but I made them keep Mr Bliss – born Constantinople son of a missionary (long) married to a Greek now with Anglicans and a Xtian Socialist – interesting – Lost a child – mother has gone to Europe with the surviving child and he is alone – The good Garrisons asked him to stay to tea + we had talk and whist – then he went away at 8.30 we then went to the Ames's and played more whist and I had a glass of lager which did me good – Others had chocolate which would not have done me good.

Saturday 20 January 1894

Did not seem to do much except a few letters and finishing up the new copy of my 3 times rejected article ...

Sunday 21 January 1894

To church in mg; fell in with my dear Mrs Ames and walked a bit with her. An admirable sermon: 'I have seen an end of all perfection thy commandment is exceeding broad' – Found Mrs Osborne's two daughters and sons in law here for a little. Mr and Mrs Frank Garrison came to dinner I got a hint from him about my article – Several neighbours and friends called ... Mrs Dietrick and Mr and Mrs Twichell came for tea and we had good talk – I read Mr Garrisons papers on the Chinese – and a little of Peter Ibbetson. [*Peter Ibbetson*, title of a novel, a fantastic romance about dreams, which first appeared in *Harper's Magazine*, then as a book in 1892, by George DuMaurier, a French-born son of a naturalised Englishman, who moved to England where he became a permanent member of staff at *Punch*, to which he contributed illustrations and satirical drawings.]

Monday 22 January 1894
Made a new end to my paper ... Whither shall it go? Lunch at Mrs Ashley who wanted me to go to stay with her when her husband was away. I must then be in New York – Family thriving now – Home by daylight ...

Tuesday 23 January 1894
Albany [?] Church of Disciples/Industrial and Educational Union afternoon.

Went early to the Church of the Disciples. Mrs Garrison's offer to get some sewing done was taken advantage of and I had the skirt of my serge repaired both upper and lower skirt where they were frayed – Three papers read on the spiritual and moral education of Children – all very good but not on the same lines ... – I had a short speech about teaching duties of citizenship –

Went to Boyston St In[dustrial] and Ed[ucational Union] – had about a hundred for an audience scarcely so enthusiastic as at Park St perhaps I was not as effective only 60 votes and many candidates very neglected. Home in same car as Mr[s?] Garrison who gave me her [his?] hat – ...

Wednesday 24 January 1894
Wrote to Katie Martin and seven other letters. Went to take lunch at the *Xtian Register* Office. Met Mrs Whiting of Springfield and Alice Blackwell [Alice Stone Blackwell, daughter of Lucy Stone one of the leaders of the campaign for female suffrage, and her husband Henry Blackwell. See below] – Home earlier than Mrs Garrison who had [been] shopping for dressmaker ...

In evg Mr Clement and Miss Smith Mr Blackwell [Henry Blackwell, husband of Lucy Stone who insisted on keeping the name Lucy Stone when she married. Stone was a leading abolitionist as well as being a women's rights advocate. She and Henry Blackwell, prominent activists in abolition movement, broke away from the American Equal Rights Association in 1867, when it divided over priority for black male suffrage or female suffrage; Stone and Blackwell threw their weight behind the campaign for black male suffrage first. They founded the American Woman Suffrage Association in 1869] and his daughter Mr and Mrs Bowditch came and we had good talk but I think Mrs Garrison did too much.

I hope Clement may help me substantially through the *Transcript*. I think I impressed them with the crusade – and its importance.

THURSDAY 25 JANUARY 1894

Did not seem to do very much – though I really began *Register* letter and family letter well ahead – Mrs Garrison had headache so went alone to Mrs McCrackens ... – Evg ... went to Pro[fessor] Wilson's lecture and were disappointed – I played cribbage with Mrs Garrison and she read me some of Sir Charles Danvers [Sir Charles Danvers (1568–1601), an intimate of Henry Wriothesley, third earl of Southampton, took part in the rebellion of the Earl of Essex against Queen Elizabeth I. It failed and he was beheaded on 18 March 1601. Perhaps this was a new book about these events] – I was not disappointed – Only letter today with check from Ind. and Ed. Union.

FRIDAY 26 JANUARY 1894

Pretty busy mg with correspondence and preparing for two meetings Saturday and Sunday – Letter from John via Frisco also from Whiting [John B. Whiting, first Secretary of the South Australian State Children's Department] re new State Childrens Bill slaughtered after passing through Commons by Parliament proroguing before it c[oul]d pass assembly order 4 copies S.S. Rested in afternoon and read Sir Charles Danvers. Called on Mrs Barrett Wendell [Barrett Wendell was an assistant professor at Harvard; Oliver Wendell Holmes had given Miss Spence an introduction to them] and saw her and the professor – Met the Garrisons in Park St went with them to the Halliwells in West Medford – Mrs Davis daughter of Lucretia Mott mother of Mrs R.P. Halliwell, Mrs Garrisons cousin ...

I had a drawing room explanation of pro rep stopped because we had to catch the train.

R.P.H[alliwell] a red hot republican who thinks the extinguished negro vote prevented Harrison from being president and he wants that set right before pro rep – but intelligent so far. Family charming.

SATURDAY 27 JANUARY 1894

Snow storm.
Concord.
Good speech in Philadelphia by Samuel B. Capen on pro rep as the only cure for Municipal bad govt ordered 6 copies of paper – [for] J.B. Spence Cridge Tyson Miss Astor Cooley ...

Went to Concord for lunch at Mrs Jacksons ... She is bright ... Chaplain at the Concord Refm person came to see me and talked all the time between lunch and lecture – 30 votes more present. Old Mr Holland – his son my correspondent has studied pro rep for 20 years but prefers the Swiss free list to the Hare method – I asked for tea and bread and butter and had it from Mrs Wortal whose house this meeting took place got 50 dollars and very small expenses and on the whole was glad I went – thankful for small mercies. The weather was such I could not have visited the famous place in Concord so it was less matter that I had not time – heavy snow – Home in exactly two hours from Concord depot –

Sunday 28 January 1894 ... Equity

A pretty full day. Went to the Church of the Disciples and had a splendid sermon from Mr Ames stayed half an hour or more for Sunday school and heard Mrs Bentley teach the story of Moses and the burning bush and prepare for the Exodus ... I got home at 11 o'clock or later a pretty tired woman.

Monday 29 January 1894

Salem

A very busy morning till I could get away ... – Wine at table – like England – spent much voice in explaining and elucidating E.V. and then gentlemen took a cab did not [go] ... to depot straight to Salem – Mr Gove met me – snow again. We talked hard till lecture time. Boston lecture fell rather flat on Salem folk. They were grave but Gove thought they understood 58 medical men less than 50 voters but four regulars and one homeopath returned – which was the right proportion ... I met a Mr Latimer Cong. [regationalist] minister whom I had met at Hull House [in Chicago, see above] who had joined in the election for poets but he is not at all sound ... I think we must trust to education ... pretty tired glad to go to bed. Mr Gove has Willie Lydia and little Mary 14 months old – not a rich man – no money for lectures for him or for me. [Catherine Spence wrote to her family on this date: 'I have not made as much out of Boston in the way of money this time but I am satisfied with the prominence given to the subject I advocate. Don't think I am going to be a bloated plutocrat. I am about £20 richer than when I began to speak, and I have <u>lived</u>. I wanted to earn what it has cost me to travel through and live in America but I do not think I shall do as much as that'.]

Tuesday 30 January 1894

Hearing State House

Weather bad – Mr Gove and I started for the 9.20 train I had to lend him four dollars rather than have him go to the bank. We were early at the State House and met there McCracken. TC Brophy to whom I introduced myself, Mrs Avery the socialist who spoke about pro rep at the Womans Suffrage Petition ... that was quashed yesterday. Gove asked me to speak first then McCracken, Mr Brophy, then Mrs Avery and he summed up himself ... Got home at 2 pm had little rest and a lot of work – Mr and Mrs Ames came in for a farewell rubber and Mr Ames and I again had a slam or what they call whitewashing here.

Wednesday 31 January 1894
Springfield Mass

Up betimes and finished packing. Wrote Rachel Avery accepting all sessions [Rachel Foster Avery of Philadelphia was the corresponding secretary of the National Council of Women in the United States, and an advocate of rational dress for women. See also above 30 January]. Said goodbye to the good Garrisons with real grief as probably we shall not meet again. WLG himself took me to depot + in steam train 2½ hours journey $2.33 fare – No one to meet me paid 40c for cab – Arrived at Mrs Wessons for lunch – No one asked to meet me. Had to scramble my papers together and fill up skeleton ... 88 or so there. On the whole satisfactory – Had nearly an hours rest then got up for 7 o'clock dinner ... I was asked about Shakespear[e] and thought it easier to read my lecture than to answer miscellaneous questions and I think I answered them all – pretty tired and glad to get to bed at 10.20.

Thursday 1 February 1894

This was comparatively a leisure day but I devoted it chiefly to my press letters and when I had finished them all at 3.30 was too tired to go out to see Springfield especially as it was cold and snowing ... Mrs Wesson is a widow whose husband was killed in a terrible railroad accident ... We had Mrs Burmaid here in evg and I read nearly all the Shakespeare article to her as she had missed it.

Friday 2 February 1894
Hartford

I went early to Hartford as I wanted to get acquainted with Mrs Collins but as it turned out she could not entertain me at all as she had unexpected visitors a Mrs Brown met me and took me to see the old lady of 80 handsome and vigorous living with her son Dr Pettier so she must have been twice married – We had a poorly cooked lunch – I had a little rest reading a strange story – Mrs B. is a mind cure doctor her husband ... connected with music or instrument trade. Library full of the occult ...

We had to be at hall by 5 and I had to shake hands and talk to more than a hundred people before 8 when the performance began – ... a ... lecturer on suffrage began – spoke well – I gave the required article on that when a reporter had settled to quote from the *Springfield Republican* he was rather out of it for that was the Boston lecture + I was kept late and was very very tired, but I heard that the ... people ... who were there in considerable force thought they ought to have had me there ten dollars notwithstanding ...

SATURDAY 3 FEBRUARY 1894

Had a terrible rush to finish my Australian letters ... Got $13 which helps expenses. Had Charles Dudley Warner [essayist, novelist, and editor of the highly respected *Hartford Courant*, Hartford, Connecticut, where he and his wife were neighbours of Samuel Clemens – alias Mark Twain – and his wife, the former Olivia Langdon; women's rights activist Isabella Beecher Stowe and her husband John; and Isabella's half-sister, Harriet Beecher Stowe, author of, among other things, the international best seller *Uncle Tom's Cabin* (1851–2) and her husband, Calvin. Warner was also a contributing editor of *Harper's New Monthly Magazine*, and vice-president of the National Prison Association] as travelling companion and we talked hard for three hours. He is great on prison reform. Went to MLH and got my bandbox with oddments and ... my trunks at station – Found there was no room vacant at the [indecipherable] but I could sleep in the boy's room ... I was really very tired but had a little rest. Mrs Peirce very busy with invitations and replies. [Catherine Spence wrote to her family: 'After I return from Washington, Mrs Fay Peirce is going to try to introduce me to New York circles by giving me a tea when I may read one of my lectures. She says that I am full of beautiful thoughts and valuable suggestions, and that my dumbness in New York City is a misfortune to it'.]

Miss Amy Fay came in afternoon I saw again the people I had met here before when invited to dinner by Mrs F.P. Very glad to get to bed and slept well.

SUNDAY 4 FEBRUARY 1894

... Had false pleurisy and Mrs Peirce gave me .?.. Read some of *Uncle Tom's Cabin* [see above, 3 February 1894] and loafed all day thinking rather drearily of what was before me if I should be ill. The .?.. did me good.

MONDAY 5 FEBRUARY 1894

Worked over voting papers and other things till time to set out for Plainfield [Massachusetts]. Went to wrong station and had to go another mile. Missed train waited over an hour for the next – bought Lotis *Child's Romance* to read 35c too late for Miss Kemp's lunch but had it in bedroom – A real good meeting crowds interested – 12 orders for pamphlets and sold all my newspapers. Was asked if I could come back Thursday evg and speak to men and women in ... Church lecture room – said yes – got $12 –

Accepted Miss Kenyon's offer of a bed and kept pretty hard talking all the evg ...

I went to bed soon after 9 and fell asleep soundly was roused by a loud bell which misreading my watch I thought was rising as I heard breakfast was to be at 7 – When half dressed I looked again and found it was a little after 11 so went to bed till 6.30 –

Tuesday 6 February 1894

Early breakfast after church ...

Wrote Cridge and sent him addresses and $2 and wrote new beginning to George Eliot lecture ...

Home a little tired for latish dinner. Got possession of a room of my own – brought into it most of my possessions – Recd letter from Ellen Gregory from Hawker – She feels the neglect of the Wrens a good deal – and now she is out of the way of my letters [on 10 March, Catherine Spence wrote to Charles Wren with some anxiety about her financial responsibilities: 'Dear Charlie ... I wonder if Cousin can live about among her friends till I return say in Sept or Octr – I was in hope that Nell [Eleanor Wren] might ask her over for a visit – especially now that my stay abroad has been prolonged – There was a talk of a seaside house for the Gregory connection in February and March which Cousin was to help run but it had not taken shape when she wrote last on 14th Janry.] – Must write to her – After a rest of 15 minutes started off with Mrs Peirce ... – 2½ miles off and had a chance to speak at the fag end of the meeting ...

Wednesday 7 February 1894

... Went after lunch to the M.L.H. but without my key ...

Home to read over a large packet of letters received at ML Home – newspapers I cannot find here to read.

Thursday 8 February 1894

Plainfield Mass Lecture Hall 93 votes.
Went shopping with my friend Mrs Pum and spent about twenty dollars for bonnet, shoes, gloves and caps + fichu and lace for cuffs.

Home for dinner did a little work correspondence Ellen Gregory, Katie Martin and went wandering in the wrong direction to get to Liberty St Ferry and miles to walk but arrived before Miss Kenyon herself sat down to dinner – Had a blessed half hours rest and then sallied forth with Miss Arnott – The Boston lecture did not fall flat – ...

Friday 9 February 1894

Miss Kenyon's school

Slept till near eight had breakfast ... – Spoke an hour to Miss Kenyon's school after nearly an hour's delightful talk about books and religion with herself in her den up stairs.

Weather wet and dirty so took cab home – Found Remsen's book [on proportional representation, see below] here skimmed it – Mrs Peirce full of work for me and others. We played cards in evg after we had talked our ...

out. I feel much pleasure with my Plainfield work – Promised *Agnostics Progress* [her own work, a religious allegory, published in London, 1884] to Miss Kenyon.

SATURDAY 10 FEBRUARY 1894
Made engagement for the evg of March 6th workingmen's club through Mr Reynolds friend Mr Poldy. Wrote Cooley with $2. Went to see my printer Gregg [?] Brothers and arranged for 2000 ballots to cost 4.55 on cardboard – I hope they are not too small [These would be used in her lectures on proportional representation in the conduct of mock elections.]

Letter from Remsen hoping I pay sufficient attention to his ideas about Primaries. I wish I could thoroughly understand them.

After printer tried to get to Harlem but stopped half an hour in Broadway thinking it was 6th Ave – Too late for lunch, but the family had not left the table – Mrs Sanger had intended to go to teach poor girls sewing, but stayed with me instead and we chatted and had three games of cribbage ... I had ... 24 hands. Home a little after [?by the] elevated railroad. Mrs Peirce thinks we should strike while iron is hot and take the Pol [itical] Stud[ies] Hall at $10 for Wednesday – I wish the friends of Monday to bring each a friend & pay 10c which could clear Hall rent – for Proportional Representation and a Womans ...

SUNDAY 11 FEBRUARY 1894
I put on my new shoes which are wide enough – last down for breakfast. Mrs Peirce made me write that I should not be at Washington till Thursday after – as she is set on Wednesday. I read all my lecture to her and she thinks I should not abridge it. She likes it extremely, much better than I expected.

In evg went to the Judson Memorial Church and followed out for ... Service of Song – Women of Samaria the subject ... was the sermon so simple as the preacher asserted – Interesting to see what efforts are made by this and other churches to reach the people and how many[?] escape from them all – Ah! this is a complex world –

Cannot read at all at night, could write letter on acct of the ... gas – but too tired to write. To bed and churn all sorts of things in my head wrote to Riggs [House] to Mrs Rachel Avery [see above 31 January 1894]. In afternoon sewed ... and mended 3 prs of stockings ... Mrs Pierce's work bag.

MONDAY 12 FEBRUARY 1894
Corrected my proofs of ballots which were correct – Wrote some letters – recd from Cridge and Mrs Howland [wife of either Oliver Aiken Howland (1847–1905), barrister, Mayor of Toronto, one of the founders of the union of

Canadian Municipalities, author of *The New Empire* (1891), and advocate of proportional representation, or Sir William Holmes Howland (1844–1893), Canadian businessman, politician, social reformer and philanthropist] letters but surely some are missing.

Our George Eliot aft. was injured by a snow storm but nearly 50 people turned up and were most appreciative. The Judsons were there and Canon Knowley and Mr Gates – Mrs Remsen turned up but none of the personal friends. I feel this tries Mrs Peirce heavily. She cannot well afford – but she feels as if we might start a course that would pay. I spoke about the beautiful family life I had seen in America in an extempore sentence ... thrown in – Miss Lillie Blake [who had addressed the Women's Congress in Chicago on 'Our Forgotten Mothers'] advised me to communicate with a Miss Spence, a teacher of a fashionable school [Clara B. Spence, a graduate of Boston University who carried out postgraduate studies in London; principal of the Spence School for Girls] – We announced we [would?] speak at 125 East 23 for pro rep.

We stayed [for] dinner and went home in a cab – another expense for Mrs Peirce.

Tuesday 13 February 1894

I spent most of the morning in with letters and postals for tomorrows meeting ...

In after[noon] I read George Eliot and Mrs Browning to Miss Elliott and Miss Warren – I read over my Browning lecture and think it needs some pains taken with it. Mrs Peirce very busy on my behalf.

Wednesday 14 February 1894

Again the evening snow spoiled the attendance at the meeting Mrs Peirce had taken so much trouble with.

I spoke to Dr Judson the day before re Baptist ministers. He referred me to Rev Leighton Williams.

Mr Remsen came late. Miss Spence sent her teacher of English & Rhetoric – There were some important people but only 30 in all Mrs Kay and Jenny ... I don't think I was quite so happy as I am generally – We stayed to dinner and went home in a cab after an expense to Mrs Peirce but the snow was bad and wind blew it about.

Thursday 15 February 1894

... to Phila[delphia] with Dr and Mrs Flagg ... they live at Swarthmore near Phila. Mrs Barnes is Dean of that Quaker college – I arrived on time had coffee while waiting for luggage and went to Riggs which is too expensive 3.50

a day – Saw Miss Howland [possibly a daughter of one of the Canadian Howlands, see above, 12 February] and found I could get with her cheaper quarters.

Alice Atkinson and her grandmother called while I was at dinner with Miss Clapp of Morton [Montague?] and another older lady.

Friday 16 February 1894

[Washington, DC] A long day of congresses. I saw a good many people who recognised me of old – left Riggs House at 2.30 and moved to Wimodaughsis [a national women's club] 13–28 I St at night. Slept there in a [shared?] room but slept well and I hope disturbed no one . . .

Miss Anthony introduced me personally to the Convention and I spoke a few sentences – The evening session I got very tired of . . .

. . . Mrs Henry of Kentucky [Josephine K. Henry, Kentucky suffragist] is too empassioned [sic] and flowery – She has however a splendid voice and delivery – Miss Clay [Laura Clay, Kentucky suffragist] is quieter – Miss Blackwell [see above, 24 January 1894] elaborated the distinction between W.S. in the South and in the North.

Saturday 17 February 1894

I did not go in the mg – as there was merely delegation work – Made a skeleton wrote pr notes.

In aft found I was to have only one hour for my whole exposition and had to cut down my skeleton. Am not sure that I was complete enough. Some people understood it, but many did not. I sold some pamphlets 28 or 29 – Very bright evening session.

Sunday 18 February 1894

Miss Howland went to Riggs House for business, I read letters for Mrs Fay Peirce – Evenings cannot be carried out – Very disturbing and yet I might have known how risky it was [this may well refer to Catherine Spence's disappointment at having so abbreviated a period of time in which to present her arguments for, and illustrations of, effective voting.] Miss Isabel and I went to Dr Kent's Church (Peoples) and heard Carrie Lane Chapman [see above 4 January 1894] and the pastor gave out the Arena Program – . . .

Felt too disturbed about failure in programme to sleep, heard #2 3 4 5 strike.

Monday 19 February 1894
Convention again.
Report of Worlds Fair Committee.
Kansas campaigners with council appeal for funds which brought promises of over $2000 – $10,000 is said to be needed –
Electoral officers.
Evg short addresses from state delegates bright and telling.

Tuesday 20 February 1894
During mg session on Resolutions, I went to talk in Convention room to Mr Digger and had him pretty thoroughly <u>enthused</u> in P.R. and the Queensland system for absolute majority – Took lunch with Mrs Kendrick of Hartford and Sara W[inthrop] Smith Seymour ... – Walked back between the War Office and the White House to Wimodaughsis – Closing session of the Convention – Ida Hultin the finest speaker [Unitarian minister, suffragist from Iowa] – Miss Windeyer [Australian suffragist from Sydney, in the United States to study librarianship; she would establish the National Council of Women in New South Wales when she returned in 1896. See also above, Introduction, and below, especially 8 July 1894] had three minutes – There were some men from the West. I was introduced to Jerry Simpson [populist Kansas congressman]. Thanks to the *Star* I had heard of him.

Wednesday 21 February 1894
Had porridge and a little roll at Log Cabin at 9.20 and hurried to Capitol. There we went to the ... room of the Senate House, perhaps the handsomest room anywhere – ... Mrs Ann Shea and Miss Ida Hultin spoke at both[,] Mr Digger ... read his speech as others did. It answers the women and does not trick the hearers. So long as neither party can see any advantage from the women's vote so long will they organise against it as a party though individuals may see the equity of the demand –

    12.20 ... I met Mrs Tipton – who never asked if I was hungry. I went with her to the House – heard Judge Maginammus to his name and called him out for a short talk but he is very lukewarm about PR compared with SF.

    Heard delegate in Senate Poor [?] Laws + others on the Tariff – Then to the Nat Museum and home – A scrap tea <u>so</u> good – Digger called Miss H had Miss Humm and Mr and Mrs Rice Young – coloured people though she is quite fair. He is super[intendent] of coloured schools in Washington. I promised to stay till Monday and see the schools open for work. Went through heavy snow to Reception. Was introduced to a great many Washington people. Mrs Dolittle interested in Children. she will send for the State Agent to me 10 am Saturday to talk about Australian B[oarding].O[ut].

Thursday 22 February 1894
Washington's birthday public holiday.
Isabel Howland left after a hurried breakfast at the Log Cabin. Snow and slush – Miss Howland went to a meeting of the Management Board for Ind schools for Colored children ...

Miss Howland went to visit friends and I made my way to Dr Kent's 930 O St. He was 12 years pastor of a Universalist Church but outgrew his congregation and now has a Liberal Society meeting at the ... Hall opposite the Patent Office – He is a nationalist and has great affinities with Mr Digger ... I offered to preach for Dr Kent but he declined for the mg but will give me the after[noon] – at which time he thought I might have a better congregation – I explained the scrutiny – and I think he understood it though perhaps not as well as Mr Digger.

Miss Windeyer had called just after I had left and wanted me to dine with her at Riggs house.

Miss Anthony came here on business on her way to train looking very tired – I said goodbye to her and I don't expect to see her again – My mind misgives me about the subsidy for travelling expenses for Suffragists.

Friday 23 February 1894
I wrote letters in mg after Bohemian breakfast. Lunched at Wilson Cafe ... When I was out for a dinner with Mr and Mrs Montgomery the latter told me that Mattier Lawrence the Jubilee Singer who went to Australia was a schoolfellow and great friend of hers – that she had married an Englishman and lived near the Crystal palace. Saw the English legation and some very handsome residences ...

Rested a while – Miss Windeyer called while Miss Howland was out –

My mind misgives me about John Glenn and Baltimore – and indeed about most things – Even the Canadian institute prize is a mere dream [Catherine Spence seems to have entered an article on effective voting for an essay competition with a lucrative prize being run by the Canadian Institute which published a book of the essays submitted; there is no evidence of her hearing any more about it after she had received a copy of the book containing the submitted pieces.] – A solitary tea and reading Mrs Stetson's book the only good opportunity I have had – very good indeed.

Gave out a week's work and got it back 40c.

Saturday 24 February /1894
Letter in mg fr John Glenn time too short need a week. Wrote I could give him a week and marked it at once –

Spent the day in writing as far as I could an article for Pro Rep Rev[iew?]

and felt pretty well worked out when done [Cathrine [sic] Helen Spence, 'The transferable vote', *Proportional Representation Review*, vol.1, no.4, Chicago, June 1894, pp. 108–15] – Also wrote a biographical sketch of myself for the publisher of addresses in Women's Building [Directory?] – according to Miss Windeyer's advice.

SUNDAY 25 FEBRUARY 1894
I started off without overshoes or umbrella as Miss Howland said it was not going to snow – but before I got to the Peoples Church it came on – I went with Mr Digger to Mrs Londall's ever so far out beyond the Bridge and after waiting long had a curry lunch or dinner baked beans and Boston ... – Coffee and raspberrie ale.

... I thought there not be a dozen people there but there were about 40. When I had finished a collection defrayed the rent of the Hall – and Dr Kent said if he had known what sort of a lecture The Democratic Ideal was he would have given me his pulpit in the morning but he had never heard me – We had voting and all seemed interested except Mr Tipton and his son who reminded me of Mrs Allard and her sister ... They said no word good or bad on the matter – Oh I hatless and footsore but glad to get home under Con's escort and Mrs Tipton's overshoes after a good supper and a warm at the *Register*. Such driving snow we went through and stood 15 minutes in a shelter [though] not much of one – Glad to reach home and go to bed – but it broke down and I had to go into Miss Howland's who did not come home that night.

MONDAY 26 FEBRUARY 1894
Breakfast at Franklin spoke to some Southern ladies who do not believe in negro women voting at all. Miss Howland came home early and we sallied forth for the coloured school cnr of 17th St the Summer School. The streets were dirty and wet beyond description so the attendance was meagre – but so far as I can judge the pupils are quite on a level with children the same age in white schools. The reading especially was good – agreeable and intelligent – the singing sweeter than I ever heard ...

[The children were] Of all shades from the deepest black to quite white with fair hair or tawny yellow – Children of mostly poor parents who make sacrifices to keep them there ... I spoke to them on the duties of a citizen in a free country ... [the] children give a cent a week to buy books. Very ... and obedient – More girls than boys + at the High School nearly 3 to one but the no. of boys in increasing – Salaries the same – but all teachers are coloured ...

Miss Windeyer came about 4 – ... Miss H[owland] sent out for food for our supper. Mrs Dolittle and Mrs Adelie Gates came about 9 and stayed an hour and half – Both are friends of Mr Cridge ...

Tuesday 27 February 1894

Last day at Washington. Wrote to Cridge at length – also made addendum to Pro Rep Rev.

Miss Howland had a cab and I had the good of it but we were put into separate cars.

Just missed K.J.M. also had been at theatre and enjoying it but I left station ere she came up. Kind welcome from the Mussons – go into the nook room – and sleep in a folding bed which is not to be folded for me – ... Glad to see copy of Sydney *Telegraph* ... my press letter of 11 Nov published Dec 27.

Wednesday 28 February 1894

... I sat down to write first to Mr Glenn offering to go to Baltimore for $20 and expenses after 20th March – then to Mrs Birks [Rose Birks, honorary treasurer of the Women's Suffrage League of South Australia, see below 14 December 1894] next to Family and Pro Rep Rev ...

Thursday 1 March 1894

Finished and despatched the article for Pro Rep Review and wrote a lot of letters – Went afterwards with K Musson to town where she had her hair manipulated by an expert – she did not go to U.S.A. Club but to Mrs Brooke whom she considers one of the brightest women.

Friday 2 March 1894

Worked hard all mg over my press letters ... She took me in afternoon to hear Mrs Jeness Miller at the Academy of Music but we were obliged to get a smaller place and we had to go to the gallery of the Gods.

... Keep healthy and beautiful may be right but they need so much time and attention that one could do nothing else – porridge steamed six hours etc and fiddling with skin and hair and clothes are all too exacting.

This life is more the heart and the soul ... than the body.

Saturday 3 March 1894

Received a great batch of letters ... In evg after my letters were despatched recd one from Ellen Gregory from Petersburg [Peterborough in northern South Australia] –

... He said we had just elected a president in Australia and stuck to it – He meant Brazil! ...

Read some stories by Olive Schreiner – very sad [probably Olive Schreiner, *Three Dreams in a Desert*, 1887. These works were immensely influential among suffragists, in Britain and Australia, and among suffragettes in Britain;

in Holloway prison in London in 1909, suffragette leader Emmeline Pethick-Lawrence recited the second of the three to cheer the departing Women's Freedom League prisoners].

[William] Gladstone has resigned [as Prime Minister of Britain] and Roseberry [the fifth earl of Rosebery] succeeds...

Sunday 4 March 1894

... Went to Ethical Society in mg and heard Mr Blankenburg [Rudolph Blankenburg, Philadelphia social reformer] and Mr Salter [William Mackintire Salter, Lecturer in Ethical Culture, philosopher and author] on Pawnbroking – very effective...

Monday 5 March 1894

I left very sad to part from K.J. Musson for ever. Her life is a sad one – although able to do more ... [than some] years ago she seems to suffer as much pain. Washing day but still managed to [come?] and see me off – Goodby Katharine Goodby – The hottest closed railway carriage – I got to M.L.H. at two o'clock, 3 hours from departure. Had my tea and a wash and went to see Mrs Sanger. She was on the lookout for me ... I waited for her an hour and half. Miss Tyler [told me about?] Mrs Sanger's husband and two sons and the cruel anxiety of her life for thirty years and more – Courtship was done by correspondence. He did not drink daily [?] but went off for a fortnight for a bender [?] and had to be hunted up and all sorts of work to retain him in his practice and his positions. Mrs Sanger and Miss Jewitt [?] came at last...

Found another batch of letters from Australia via England – a long one from Eleanor enclosing one from Nene Murray [a nephew. See Appendix A, Family Tree] –

Singularly tired – sent to bed at 8.

Tuesday 6 March 1894

... Did not feel bright all day but wrote a good many letters and made a beginning of an article on An Australian's Impressions [published in *Harper's Monthly*, no. 89, July 1894, pp. 244–51] of America rather heavier than it should be I fear. Took warm (it should have been hot) milk for supper and went to the meeting – a small poor and insignificant one. Mr Ashworth not there at all so introduced by Mr Polding who knew as little about this gathering of the 5th Ave Baptist Church as I did – I had a bad interruption in the course of my lecture but got back to it. No, New York is not to be touched or reached by me –

...

Wednesday 7 March 1894

Had rather a disturbed night not quite settled. Had a nice letter from Mrs Ames about *An Aust Girl* which I enclosed to K. Martin as also a few lines from Miss Windeyer – I wrote to Magdelene [or Madeleine, see below 14 April 1894] Bell and hope she will reply ere I leave.

Mrs Peirce called after lunch and I lent *Rectification of Parliament* and read her several poems of Mrs Stetsons. She will order the book – I am discouraged by hearing nothing about Connecticut or New Jersey – not to speak of Baltimore.

Thursday 8 March 1894

Had a note from Dr May H... advising me to go to a Friends School to hear Carrie Lane Chapman speak as Mr Powell was to be in the chair. I went early with Miss George and had a pleasant day – saw little of the Prophet [Henry George, 'prophet' of the single tax] as he was very busy but yours faithfully.

In evg Mrs George + sister in law went with me to the meeting. Except the introduction about the Friends I think, I had heard all Mrs Chapman Catt's speech – Rather a phlegmatic audience but of course all answered. I was called out to speak – and did. I asked at the end if there would be any opportunity for me to speak in that School. Very doubtful I think – but I must not leave a stone unturned – They took me right home – Felt the better for my day out –

Friday 9 March 1894

... Made a new diagram for my scrutiny of 3826 votes, finished my letter to Eleanor and wrestled with my Impressions of America...

One suspects people who crack themselves up too much...

Got address of London office for David Murray [a nephew. See Appendix A, Family Tree].

Saturday 10 March 1894

A sudden inspiration impelled me to try my hand at an article on Dependent Children in Australia – especially as the other is so refractory and will not write itself – so I spent most of the day over it – Not a letter yesterday or today – I am not umbrageous but I feel a little put out by neglect.

I went to Mr Judson's to dine and have a good talk and a game of cards with Mrs Peirce – but I did not get my belongings – They must be fetched on Monday.

Sunday 11 March 1894

Went to Church in forenoon not very exciting – Spent the afternoon and evg in writing. It rained and prevented me from going to the ... meeting ... to hear a Mr Sherman.

Monday 12 March 1894

Letters from Cridge, Garran and Egremont all interesting but none from those I want to organise meetings for me. Egremont is too exalted in his expectations. As I was going with the express bag Mr Remsen came in to ask the names of Boston men likely to want pro rep in the primaries. I gave him some work but not enough ... I went straight for my things and then came home to go into my Saratoga [trunk] ...

Tuesday 13 March 1894

Political Study
Received a letter forwarded by Miss Fay from Miss C[lara] Spence the teacher about tickets for literary lectures; wrote her that I would give a Geo lesson for ten dollars to her school.

In afternoon went to Pol Study Club and Mrs Peirce thinks I did more good than at the snowy day. She counted the ballots with Mrs Neiman – I had an hour but always expected to be stopped and was less felicitous than usual –

Mrs Peirce came home with me but we could not summon resolution to go to Charity Hall in evg, she was tired and I had muscular rheumatism.

Mrs Peirce had her own ballots for current New Yorkers.

Wednesday 14 March 1894

Wrote Cridge with two dollars which is more than I think I have got ...

I worked at my Impressions but felt the rheumatism a good deal and I feel every day the chance less and less of making a cent from this center. Of course if I get paid for my writing it is more profitable but experience is against me in these United States.

Thursday 15 March 1894

A long solid day's work over the Impressions fair copy which was completed at supper time all but the last, the 22nd page. Muscular rheumatism not so bad as the previous days –

Had a letter from Mr McDougal saying the awards were delayed further, Dr Sandford Fleming having put additional names on the list in his travels. 100 experts have to read the essays and pronounce on them!!! [This is the Canadian Institute competition. Catherine Spence seems to hope that the prize would help with her expenses, see above 23 February, and below 19 March 1894]. This at first discouraged me profoundly but it was indispensable that I should complete my literary work and I lost myself in the Impressions – I wrote to John as he always thinks I have failed when the awards are delayed but I gave him all my depressions and disappointments which was a pity as they brightened out considerably when I had to take the bull by the horns with regard to my literary work.

Friday 16 March 1894
Concluded my Impressions with a fresh conclusion to Effective Voting, and sallied out to Harpers – Was misdirected to 6th Ave Elevated [Railroad] and had a long dirty walk into crowded crossing. Mr J Henry Harper [son of James Harper, founder of *Harper's New Monthly Magazine*] introduced me to Mr Alden editor – and he introduced me again to Mrs Sangster. I left the Impressions with Alden and the Dependent Children with the *Bazaar*. I hope I may have some luck I got my best ticket No 10 – ...

Wrote to Mrs Hale offering to call on him on Monday also to K Musson saying my day of departure was fixed – ... [Wrote?] to Mrs Peirce told her I had used two of her ideas and acknowledged one of them – She thought I should have acknowledged both and she is right but the reader gets impatient with so much quotation and interruption of the current of thought. Still the Women's Council is perhaps the more original of the two.

Saturday 17 March 1894
An important day I wrote to Mrs Spencer Stetson + to Cridge about delay. Went to the Charities and discovered that no children are Boarded out in N.Y. State. Only Institutions and Free Homes, the last generally out of the state in ... Michigan etc. – After lunch I thought I should strengthen up but Dr Lessen called and while he was here Mr Remsen came and brought me the Essays [the essays submitted for the Canadian Institute prize, it would seem.] terribly closely printed – My 90 pages go into 30, Cridges takes 20 ... Well, if clearness of style and vigor of thought should carry the day Cridge and I stand well ...

Short type written letter from Mr Alden which accepted if he may prune it to 5000 words – prize $75. Good news. Went ... to Miss Stillman [possibly daughter of Dr William Olin Stillman, philanthropist physician, worker for humane societies] who is making an article about the Children of the State – too much excited to sleep till almost 3 o'clock.

Sunday 18 March 1894
Went to church with Miss Stillman to Dr Ramsforth's Episcopal – earnest but not very logical – less congregation not High Church. Miss Julia Ward Howe sat in front of me – so I could say goodbye to her – In after[noon] went to Bible class and heard a fluent woman expound 'And they shall be mine on the day when I make up my jewels' to a great hall full of women.

In evg went to hear Dr McGlynn very good but lengthy – sat by the

Misses George older and younger – It was settled who should take me to the two meetings.

Read the Essays with more and more satisfaction with my own and Cridges and Cooleys which is brief. Bought H. George letters to the Pope [*An Open Letter to the Pope*, 1891] ... for 20c wonder if I can have him to read it. I do not get on fast with [Mark Twain's] *God's Fool* perhaps because it is sad and cynical – But the Essays ought to be read and returned.

Monday 19 March 1894
Letter from Mrs Rachel Foster Avery with check for $20 for Washington expenses – this is a satisfaction. I wish I had not written yesterday – Wrote Cridge, Mrs Peirce, McDougal and a letter to Egremont to accompany $10 but as it was wet did not go round to 13th St but went straight to ... Orange and had lunch and a delightful afternoon with Mr and Mrs Hale.

Home for dinner letter from John saying Handyside [Andrew Dods Handyside, husband of Catherine Spence's niece, Mary Anne Murray, see Appendix A, Family Tree] has paid in £50.12.2 I wonder if that is all for the year. Anyhow it reduces my debt to Charles [Wren] to £100 and I have in hand at present about £80 and have a chance of £100 for prize essay.

Things do not look so blue after all.

Tuesday 20 March 1894
Offer of $20 for Effective Voting for *Arena* [on *Arena*, see below 29 March 1894.] and accepted it so I have in hand at present £40 in drafts and with *Harper's* and *Arena* $200 or £40 after sending Egremont his $10 – the *Bazaar* is all that is uncertain. Idea of writing a story somewhat like Hester's Xmas gift [a short story of seven chapters which Catherine Spence contributed to the *Sydney Mail* in 1878]. Mrs Peirce called at home bringing a rather heavy Canadian Appeal ... and a long letter in which she speaks strongly and justly of her right to acknowledgement of her idea in the matter of the Second *Harper* that of a Council of Women.

I sat down and wrote a draft of letter to Alden re acknowledgement and was interrupted by lunch and then by Miss Windeyer who lives near. She sat over ... and then we went together to the Pol Study Club and heard a most tedious paper about the Italian Republics of the Renaissance – which must have cost a great deal of labour to the writer – The discussion which followed was lively – I spoke a while and so did Miss Windeyer – She leaves a week or two after me for Liverpool. I sent to Egremont $10 – may send as much for some months yet but promise nothing. I mailed the Essays to Mr Remsen so that I cannot waste any more time over them. Bought a strong letter box for $4.50 and think one at $14 will serve my turn.

Wednesday 21 March 1894

After breakfast went to my Saratoga [trunk] and brought up there [three?] full Gladstones [Gladstone bags] which did not quite fill the strong ... trunk. Enclosed some slips for Mrs Musson and began letter to K Martin – Unearthed Hawker estimate of expenses & income. He did not reckon I should earn a penny but I have kept afloat with no earning. If I could leave Am[erica] with £40 – I landed with £60, so as to have spent only £20 in ten months it would be a triumph, but I scarcely think so as I must help Cridge and Cooley.

I got my cheque from *Harper's* for $75 – this makes three cheques in hand; my dollar bills are melting away.

Thursday 22 March 1894

Manhatten [sic] Single Tax Club 137 E26 left

I worked pretty hard and finished the draft of peradventure article for *Xtian Advocate*. Read Mrs Peirce's book which is excellent [probably a version of her Parliament of Women. In 1869, Peirce spoke at a meeting called by journalist Jane Cunningham Croly – (1829–1901), editor of *The Home* – to form a Women's Parliament, and when it was formed, she presided over it. See above 11 January 1894. As appears below, Catherine Spence was impressed with the notion of a Council of Women and included a reference to it in the article that she wrote for *Harper's New Monthly Magazine*, vol. lxxxix, no. dxxx, 1894, p. 250 where she wrote:

> All over the world Upper Houses are on trial. How far and how long should a hereditary House of Lords in the United Kingdom, and a curiously anomalous representation of States of the most various weight and population in the American Senate, obstruct the will of the people expressed directly at the polls?
>
> I may be looking a long way ahead, but perhaps in the future the two Houses may be a Parliament of men elected by men and a council of women chosen by women. There is nothing which the classes can contribute to the masses so valuable as the best thought of woman to aid the best thought of man.

This does not, unfortunately for Melusine Fay Peirce's protest and Catherine Spence's effort to gain recognition of her idea for her, have anything crediting the idea as Peirce's. Is it a coincidence that, in Australia, a decade after Miss Spence had spent so much time with Mrs Peirce, the Women's Political Association in Melbourne established a Mock Parliament under the leadership of Vida Goldstein?]

– After my 10c lunch went to Mr Rothwell who has a sprained arm from a fall off a cycle – He says the campaign is to be carried on in England ...

Rain – Found two reporters from the *Recorder* man and woman wanting to hear the subject of my lecture to the S[ingle] T[ax] Club – picking my brains to the extent of 1½ columns and a photo but I think I [convinced?] him about pro rep and dep[endent] children. Dr L ... came for me before I was ready. I took no *H[ope] & H[ome]* but sold 10 pamphlets ... – small attendance and no women. Long interesting letter from Cridge just glanced through ere I went to work. I think though Lever [letter?] was impatient and almost rude about the introduction to the Boston lecture as not being pro rep – the audience considered it quite pertinent and interesting.

Home through the wet but he paid my fares. No news from Mrs Sangster re Dependent Children – I paid for my room till I leave $5 – only food after this and car fares 2c –

Friday 23 March 1894
Webster Hall 320 Ave 140 St
I seem to work in the midst of confusion – I packed together what I want for evg – skeleton – *H[ope]&H[ome]* – pamphlets – Ballots etc. Wrote receipt to *Harper's* enquiring re *Bazaar* wrote to Cooley with $10 which will rejoice his heart – Wet dark mg but did not light the electric [fire?] ...

Miss Crane from Canada was too tired to accompany me and her friend departed on her but Miss Stillman came up to the scratch nobly ... A Socialist cabinet meeting Cranks mostly but I spoke very well.

Had a disappointment before I left Mrs Sangster returned the MS with a polite note she liked it much personally but did not think it suited the *Bazaar*. Only a week to place it elsewhere.

Saturday 24 March 1894
Went early to see the flower market Union Square – Easter decorations. Then went to Charities and talked to Miss Mason ... then to Mr Folkes following her advice took MS to Forum office did not see the Editor but left a note – not at all sanguine.

Then to Dr Buckley. He too was out of town but interviewed ? ... re article and representation story – He wants a paragraph from me about what I have done and what I mean to do. Then home [for] lunch [and] a little rest disturbed by Miss Windeyer who repaid 10c.

Went in evg to Mrs Peirce – Mrs Eliot came in and sat a long time we played some games at gravouche – I left a sheaf of my literary articles I had meant to read two. I feel sad at leaving her – She is intellectually isolated and feels neglected – She certainly has great ability I wonder if her novel will hit or miss she seems unlucky ...

I did a good afternoon's work to my story.

Sunday 25 March 1894
Easter Sunday. It flashed on me in the mg that my story should be syndicated.

Mr Rothwell called at 10.15 and I agreed to go in evg.

Wrote up and finished tentative article for *Xtian Advocate* very good I think ...

Went to Uni church in mg ...

As article was finished went out for evg with easy mind – Had a French dinner at Hotel Martin with Mr Rothwell and Mrs Brannlich. [Dr Rothwell was the Editor of a journal with a title that Catherine Spence's handwriting makes impossible to determine. Mrs. Brannlick was his 'right hand woman', and, incidentally, a member of the English Engineering Society.] His daughter lives with friends in Harlem and does not keep house for him. Wet unpleasant evg – He left us at Mrs Croly's door – She does not impress me much. She is a society journalist a lionhunter – has had very hard times and an indifferent husband but this is not a journalist as I understand the term. When I spoke of the story I am writing she shook her head. If it had a purpose the syndicate would not take it. I appointed to go with Mrs Brannlich on Tuesday to the American Press Convention to see what could be done –

Wrote to Mrs Sanger to prevent her from coming tomorrow after[noon] – asking her to come for lunch but did not <u>mail</u> the letter.

Monday 26 March 1894
... Worked at my story which will be different from first intention. Went after lunch to Dr Buckley ... – He took my article when I told him its drift – I did not need to speak of the literary workmanship for my articles had satisfied him that that was admirable. He said he could give $20 for it and I took it. It is cheap but no time for haggling. Mrs Peirce is pleased. I have brought forward her ideas at greater length than in *Harper's* and fully acknowledged my obligations.

A short rest – and I dressed to go to Mrs George's – There was a great gathering of men and women – Single Taxers – 60 votes. I met Mr Graham but do not know if I [like?] him ... I read 'The Eagle and the Hen' [by Charlotte Perkins Gilman subsequently published in *Suffrage Songs and Verses* (The Charlton Company) New York, 1911] to start with and I think I spoke fairly well – This will be my last utterance ...

Tuesday 27 March 1894

Wrote ... at story till I went to Park place. Mrs Brannlich took me to 45 and introduced me to Mrs Connor – whom I impressed and she introduced me to Mr Hill whom I also impressed – but both threw cold water on the prospects of the story for syndicate – Love stories, not stories with a purpose, suit the people. But he said he might serve [my purpose?] by giving publication to say six articles of a thousand words – did not tell the terms – So that is what I am to work for – I went upstairs and had a pencil likeness taken for the syndicate and left my *Register* reprint and wrote up my American career and my proposed plans to make up an article to accompany this plain likeness ...

Went to dinner at Judson's felt my mouth very sore my plate wants attending to ... tea in bedroom and a lot of belladonna which relieved me ...

I feel as if I had a terrible lot to do – It keeps me from sleeping as much as I should – K Musson sends me NSW Electoral Act and cuttings from *Telegraph*, my Brothers letter of Dec 6.

Wednesday 28 March 1894

Miss Leven 10 East 33rd 4.30

Wrote to JB Spence and the family after sending rec[eip]t to FC [?] and order to *Harper's* and made up diary to date while waiting for Mrs Sanger.

She did not come as she was unwell so I wrote article on God Save the Queen set to American ears with

Confound their politics

Frustrate their knavish tricks

applied to the machine and the boss, a very good strong article.

Mrs Peirce came about 2.30 ... We went to the dentist ... and I had to leave my plate for repairs in his hands and return at 11 on the morrow – Meeting at Miss Levens[,] Mrs McBride and child there – It was interesting. I think Mrs Peirce will take it up. Home to Margaret Louisa.

Thursday 29 March 1894

Wrote article on Dependent Children Home v. Institution ... before I went out. Went to Bank and found I must go again for the Ten sovereigns and the £20 m[oney] order I was to get for my $147 – Forget the name and number of the street of the dentist – back to the Judson just caught Mrs Peirce who gave me them and went our ways –

Found my plate splendidly welded and paid $13 more than I expected – and I hoped for something for articles to make up $30 for Cridge.

After dentist went to Mrs Sanger, Mrs Hubbard not there at lunch or after. We talked and played cribbage but she felt sadder than she let me see – Home found article on God Save the Queen returned able and forceful but not for a syndicate. Wrote to editor saying I hoped Dep[endent] Ch[ildre]n would not be rejected. *Forum* sent back my long article. Sent it to Ed of *Arena* with note to Flower [Benjamin Flower, Editor of *Arena*, characterised as an audacious and outspoken journal; Australian Maybanke Wolstenholme daringly reproduced an article of his titled 'A Vital Question', concerning 'the problem of prostitution within the marriage relation' in her monthly journal, *Woman's Voice*, September 1895] to send it to Mrs Ames if he could not use it.

Friday 30 March 1894

Sent God Save the Queen to Clement *Boston Transcript* ...

Acknowledged 11th received in Educ.

Worked like a steam engine over my press letters finished *Telegraph* and had *Register* underweigh [sic] before lunch time. Went in after[noon] to say goodby to the Georges. Wrote in evg odds and ends heard by second telegram that Furness would not sail till Tuesday at 4 pm. Felt relieved from the terrible rush and strain yet sorry that I am 3 days later in beginning my English campaign.

Wrote Mrs Peirce that I would be with her Sat[urda]y evg.

Homes v. Institutions sent back with a printed circular notice. Even that is too revolutionary for a syndicate I suppose.

I got my money in forenoon at the Knickerbocker Fruit Bank.

Saturday 31 March 1894

Mr Remsen came to say goodby ... I finished and despatched my two press letters and one to the family. Meant to go to Mrs Peirce but had postal saying she was engaged with Mrs Thomas and her paper for Pol Study Club so went after dinner to Mrs Georges instead and did not have cards but talk.

Was asked the following day for dinner and accepted.

Had talk with Mrs Eadnay and her daughter Miss Eddy at M.L.H. dinner and lent my Shakespeare lecture to the young women ...

Sunday 1 April 1894

By no means a demon [?] for work whatever may be the pay [?] – Wrote article on 'Snobs and Social Ambition' before going to church. Hope it is not too revolutionary ...

Wrote a second article on 'English Speaking Woman' and a letter to A.A. Hill – Wrote also to Mary Hussey ... Just got through in time to go off to Henry Georges – I took with me *The Silent Sea* [by Catherine Martin] one of my six copies to give to Mrs George – Dinner there Mrs George still reclining [?]. Evg went to Chickening Hall to hear Dr Kramer on Single Tax.

pretty tired

Monday 2 April 1894

I washed my hair and comb and brush in the bath room – Mrs Sterling came for voting papers and a talk and Miss Eddy returned me the Shakespeare-Bacon lecture with thanks and a determination to study the subject further –

Find that I have written in the month 230 sheets or pages larger or smaller besides articles and the draft of story and 100 letters.

Spent the last evg with Mrs Peirce somewhat sad. Said goodbye to Miss Eliot and the others at the dinner table. I read 'Talking Shop' she took a different view of the French salon from some. She read me her paper for tomorrow very good I think. We played three games of Gravouche and won the last – I am sure she will miss me. She has done more for me than many and for the sake of the cause.

I began letters to John and to Mr Cridge Also wrote Mrs Ames and Mr Garrison ...

Tuesday 3 April 1894

Finished and despatched my letters to John and Cridge – sent S 5 [sic] and £5 [sic] to Cridge for the cause – Farewell to America !! [On 31 March 1894, Catherine Spence wrote: 'Now as I am on the point of sailing from America to Glasgow ... I feel many regrets on parting with friends, comrades, sympathisers and fellow-workers. When I think that I only knew two human beings in America in the flesh, and only two more souls through correspondence, and look back now on the hundreds of people who have personally interested me, it seems as if there was some animal magnetism in the world and that affinities are drawn together as if by magic', *Observer*, 16 June 1894. On 2 April 1894, she wrote to her brother John: 'I am satisfied with my public success. It was more than I could have expected or hoped for. But I am amazed at my social success.

The farewell letters that are poured in upon me, the affectionate and (I feel this) quite sincere expressions of friendship and appreciation of myself and my work are quite beyond what I fancy I deserved']

Packed my belongings as well as I could – by no means perfectly was late about experience and went to give my own order and bought what I have washed for months: 3 washrags

Mr George called and said he would come for me with a carriage and his sister which he did before Mrs Peirce came –

My cabin is good and I have it to myself.

Mrs Peirce hurried back to her Pol Study Club H George and his sister saw me all right and went away and about 4.45 we set sail. I recognised Mrs Trueman ... I made a good dinner too.

WEDNESDAY 4 APRIL 1894
I slept very well on the whole and kept about all day.

I talked where I could find people to talk to especially to Mr Anderson. Suggested whist – was not going to miss it as I did on the Morrowan [?Monopea, the ship on which Catherine Spence journeyed from Sydney to San Francisco] and Mr and Mrs Bakewell and a Miss Robertson were willing to play without money on the game …

I made Mrs Anderson's acquaintance in her cabin.

THURSDAY 5 APRIL 1894
It was rough but I got up to breakfast and then was sick and lay down and then undressed and had my meals brought in for me – shameful laziness – all the other ladies got up and walked about.

I made some pencil headings for peradventure lecture on America but could not write any verses on the Syndicate of Six Hundred.

FRIDAY 6 APRIL 1894
Thought I must pull myself together and do some work but could not do it. Could do some knitting but no head or brainwork even with pencil.

SATURDAY 7 APRIL 1894
… I read some of Mrs Stetson's poems 'Wedded Bliss' 'Similar Cases' … Went in the gangway in the mg. Lazed in afternoon. Whist in evg.

James Bakewell a far away cousin of the Bakewells [mentioned in *An Autobiography*: James Bakewell (1817–1870), solicitor, member of parliament, Crown Solicitor, was the friend who found a publisher for Catherine Spence's first novel in England, and wrote an introduction for it. He married Jane Warren and they had five children between 1845 and 1854. Presumably, the Jack and John mentioned here are two of those children.] Knows about Jack and about the John Bakewell godfather of Jack Howitt a more distant relation Quaker family originally like the Howitts.

SUNDAY 8 APRIL 1894
… Recited part of 'Tale of a Trumpet' in evg ['Tale of a Trumpet', a comic poem by Thomas Hood (1799–1845), English poet, humourist and journalist, most famous for his bitter protest against sweated labour, *The Song of the Shirt* (1843) published in *Punch*].

MONDAY 9 APRIL 1894

Very heavy sea. Kept in berth all day reading *Martin Chuzzlewit* [Charles Dickens, *The Life and Adventures of Martin Chuzzlewit*, 1843–4, written after his visit to north America in 1842] which I got out of Library after finishing masterpieces of George Eliot. Was pretty happy in my book.

TUESDAY 10 APRIL 1894

Weather better though very cold. Read the *Review of Reviews* [a comprehensive digest of the most important English periodicals, established in 1890 by controversial journalist, W.T. Stead] and finished *Martin Chuzzlewit*. A wide difference between the America he painted and what I saw – but I was among the best people, Martin and Martha among the worst. Dollars are still pretty predominant, newspapers too personal and lurid – politics still a profession. But the war has done some good and the real greatness of the country has made the brag less absurd and the patriotic braggard less sensitive.

WEDNESDAY 11 APRIL 18

Finished *Martin Chuzzlewit* and read some of Leverson's pamphlets [Dr Leverson was an advocate of proportional representation].

THURSDAY 12 APRIL 1894

Morning at breakfast Anderson talked about railroads. Indian R[ail] Rd under government management. The greatest abuse is giving free + luxurious carriages to bosses and big men ... What can you expect from a man who says Australia is nearly as big as England and has only 4 000 000 of inhabitants yet!!! Another gem for my constellations. Such is the homage done to the Southern Cross ...

FRIDAY 13 APRIL 1894

—

SATURDAY 14 APRIL 1894

... On the Brownlow Wharf at 9 – got away after ... waiting about 11 ... Queen Street Station – got away 2.30.

    ... young Madeleine Bell there to meet me. We walked home [and] two boys brought my luggage. A most kind welcome from Mrs Bell and a pleasant after[noon] and evg. I landed with £25.0.0. and $40.40 of American money. The first day cost me over 16/-.

Sunday 15 April 1894
Had a splendid nights rest and rose for 9 o'clock breakfast and made a good one.

Twelve o'clock church mg service in the church for the combined parishes of Prestwick and Moncton ... Wrote letter to Katie Martin in after[noon] ... Went through my Birthday book and read a great many of Mrs Stetsons poems in evg. Must leave one copy here the other free one in the box –

[These dates re-ordered. Mon 16/4 is crossed out and renamed Wednesday 18th and vice versa]

Monday 16 April 1894
Up for 8 o'clock breakfast and off by 8.45 to Glasgow. Bought stamps and cards and posted K Martin's letter, took boat for Lutham ...

Tuesday 17 April 1894
Quiet day resting after the fatigues of Monday. Did not get on with letters because of conversation ... and then I go to Edin[burgh] on Saturday.

Wednesday 18 April 1894
A quiet day writing letters ... Telegram from W. Murray that his wife and son had returned on Friday and that he had recd my letter.

Madeleine sallied forth to invite guests for Thursday to meet me and play whist but every one desirable was engaged.

Thursday 19 April 1894
I went in mg to Prestwick school introduced by Miss Bell + the second master. Children look poorer than I have seen elsewhere many with bare feet + legs and the school looks bare and not attractive ...

Friday 20 April 1894
<u>Glasgow</u> met Mr Bent after some delay ... Mr Nicol H ... Chamberlain gave me a book he had compiled of the progress of Glasgow from 1885 to 1891 which would answer most of my questions ...

Saturday 21 April 1894
... Mr Hugh Reid telegraphed to James Brodie that I would arrive 7.15 as thus I could see Lord Wolsely review the Boys Brigade ... [in Glasgow] Came on to Edin 3rd class for 2/6 but gave porter 1/- and cab 2/-.

James Brodie looks very well and was most kind in his welcome. If he had his teeth he would look young but he says they hurt him –

Norah was frightened of me but soon recovered from that – ... talk and toddy at night – A comfortable bed and a good sleep.

Sunday 22 April 1894

A quiet day.

Went to church at 11 to St Bernards where AHKB [sic] preached in 1865 and heard Dr ___ [sic] the blind poet preacher. One of his elders read the lesson from Johns Gospel for him. He has great action and a good deal of declamation – perhaps [too much?] for his congregation – but very impressive. The subject was the second coming as distinguished from the first and the last.

Cold dinner to let both girls go to church – they are from Dunbar – Norah teaches Sunday school in afternoon 4 to 5 ...

Monday 23 April 1894

Went ... with Miss Church to do some shopping ... I went to McLarens in High Street and bought stuff for dress black – mantle, stays, skirt, stockings, frilling, cap and shoes 6/9 at the store in St Andrews Square.

Afternoon James took me to Spottiswood St where I found Kate Melville much changed ...

Tuesday 24 April 1894

Wrote some letters – got one from J.B. Spence ...

Nora went with me to have my dress fitted on old stays as they had been missent and then on to see Mr Grey who kept us waiting half an hour [as he had] to see a man who had a grievance.

He has only 220 children boarded out doing well, the others he has not a chance of –

... I went to Fourteen Bridge 128 ... Dickenson stationer + newsagent Sec. Fabian Society elected by the cumulative vote of Socialists one of 15 for School Board – I talked to him for an hour and half or 2 hours – He earns his bread by journalism, the shop pays the rent and the message girl – it is a centre for what he calls the true labour movement (not Threlfalls) in the Fork rds of the town – He is a free church man – a Xtian Socialist. I bought stationery and Flurscheims book [Michael Flurscheim, *Rent, Interest and Wages, or, the Real Bearings of the Land Question. Private Rent the Mother of Interest, the Cause of Commercial Depressions and Social Misery* (William Reeves), London, nd, c.1893.]

Weather wet rather.

Whist in evg James + Helen agst me and Ethel Berawood.

Wednesday 25 April 1894

Had letters from E[llen]G[regory], Mrs Clayton [daughter of Thomas Hare whom Catherine Spence had met when she was in England in 1865–6, married Lewis Clayton (c.1838–1917), Canon, suffragan Bishop of Peterborough and later Bishop of Leicester] and K Martin ...

I wrote to Mrs Howard Blyth if she knew anything about Miss Gossip's school – Went to St Bernards Board School ... all the teachers of a lower stamp than American I think than Australian.

... Intelligent reading all through – but no questions as to meaning given in my presence – Kindergarten twice a week – class dull very good and action songs – Many barefooted and ragged children but none that I thought looked starved ... More male teachers than in Australia ... 3 hours sewing for girls weekly cookery.

[In the] afternoon James took me to Duncan Church at Newington. His wife ... more interesting than D.C. but a life which is dull stagnation. Mrs McLaren, John Bright's sister [Priscilla Bright McLaren, a veteran leader of the women's suffrage movement; John Bright (1811–89), English nonconformist politician and statesman, renowned for his oratory] lives near. She is rather depressed at the slow and impeded progress of W[omen's] S[uffrage]. I think I impressed her a little by my earnestness and energy – She says nobody understands pro. rep. I dont think she quite does herself Edinburgh is no good – nor Glasgow. She thinks I may do something in London.

Thursday 26 April 1894

Spent a very long morning and part of afternoon over letters [to] John, Ellen Gregory, Sir John Lubbock [first Baron Avebury (1834–1913), banker, natural historian, parliamentarian, advocate of proportional representation, and participant in the meeting organised around Catherine Spence's visit to London, in Chelsea on 10 July, see below], Mr Courtney [Leonard Henry Courtney, Baron Courtney (1836–1918), English politician and man of letters. Advocate of proportional representation and of women's rights] – Miss Gossip ... Went to No 6 and found Mr Muller packing to go to ... Perthshire. Had a good long talk with him and got papers relating to the Central African settlement on Dr Hertskas principles Freeland – but the documents are two years old nearly. He is well and very pleased to see me next day Mrs Grant told me that he had offered to buy the Socialist or Independent Labour Party [ILP] a Hall ... but his name was to be kept out of it ... [story indecipherable] He withdrew and would have nothing to do with it much to the grief of the ILP.

Friday 27 April 1894

Wrote asking Dickenson for figure[s] of School Board election [see below, 9 May 1894]. Letter[s] from Mrs Maxwell – Mrs Blyth and Miss Gossip.

Mr Brodie took me to see the Forth Bridge which is quite as grand as I expected. We went through beautiful country – part an estate to be fenced up which a branch railroad runs 2½ miles ... – Home for late Lunch. Afternoon Mrs Duncan Church – and John Crabbie came – Such a hearty laugher, he is a Liberal humanist ...

Mrs Grant ... called wanted me to speak somewhere I thought it impossible – She is a Theosophist like Annie Besant [Annie Besant (1847–1933), abandoned her marriage to the Reverend Frank Besant, became a secularist, and, with Charles Bradlaugh, a vociferous advocate of birth control. In the 1880s she took up socialism, joining the Fabian Society, working as an organiser for the first match-girls' strike in London in 1888, and in the same year joining the Marxist Social Democratic Federation. In 1889, though, she turned to theosophy, becoming the second president of the Theosophical Society in 1907, and in 1913 she embarked on a campaign for home rule for India, in combination with theosophy. A speaker of immense power.]

The more I read of Flurscheim's book the more impressed I am with it. But I should fear they would have to pay far too much for the land if they bought it – as Wallace [Alfred Russell Wallace] and Flurscheim propose. The interest question too is sticken in my mind.

Saturday 28 April 1894

Norah went with me to Maclarens to have my dress finally tried as I bought a cap, a pr of gloves and – ... cotton.

Mrs Handyside [see Appendix A, Family Tree] came when I was writing to Helen Murray about my boxes and my reception. She is well, but just a little overpowering ...

Kate Maule and Maude were very pleased to see me ... After tea we went to Mrs Gover and had a great set to. She is a Theosophist, a womans righter and stronger about reduction of population than I ever heard –

The daughter was busy preparing her course of lectures – a delicate girl – Another daughter has disappointed her mother by marrying a well to do man but not her superior nor her equal –

Sunday 29 April 1894

Went to the Church of the Sacred Heart with Kate Maule her boys went to All Saints and her girl stayed at home ... Indeed the failures in marriage I have heard of in the course of talk are terrible ...

Monday 30 April 1894
I said goodby to the Maules and gave Kate £2 to help her moving –

... In evg Mrs Grant called for me to go to the Fabian meeting. Most [of] the business was about a function on the Queens birthday but a manifesto of Dickens was read and criticised. I thought with the Rev Mr Sloane that he was too hard on the Liberal party to which we owe much though they may not be equal to the present exigencies –

Tuesday 1 May 1894
Wrote Mr Maclaren and Flurscheim.

John writes me the tender for Colliness is £20.13.0 – £5 may be taken off if the drawing room does not need such strong girders. I feared a larger sum [to do with repairs to one of the houses that she owned in Adelaide] ... Disappointed no letters have been put in [to the Australian press] in a week ...

Wednesday 2 May 1894
Miss Murray writes saying she leaves London 5th June which is disconcerting for John Lubbock and Mr Courtney reply courteously ...

Evg at John Crabbies only Mrs Otto and her son Alex[ander] a pleasant family party and a good rubber of whist to wind up – I think James enjoyed it much though the champagne does not suit him.

Thursday 3 May 1894
... Also letters of old date from Mrs Hartley [wife of J.A. Hartley, Inspector-General of Education in South Australia 1878–95] and Edith Hübbe [formerly Edith Cook, under-aged but educationally distinguished when she was appointed headmistress of the South Australian Advanced School for Girls in 1880, a post she held until 1885; she was also a Unitarian] with a lot of interesting news.

Friday 4 May 1894
[Letters] ... and one to Helen Murray asking where Barrs was, how I was to get to it and if she would be contented with a week ...

In evg Mrs Mackellar for Womanhood and her niece Miss Pennycruik came to tea and were impounded for whist ...

Saturday 5 May 1894
Finished my letter to Katie Martin and closed it before James Brodie and Norah arrived bringing *Register* of 27 March enclosing cut out letters from Boston + New York.

SUNDAY 6 MAY 1894
Prayers morning and evg with the maids present – Presbyterian church in the mg ...

MONDAY 7 MAY 1894
No letters from anybody – till later when I had a note of invitation from Louisa Murray and one of welcome from Dr Mackintosh.

TUESDAY 8 MAY 1894
Womens Suffrage Edinburgh
I received a great packet of letters. Johns enclosing one from Nene about Co[usin] Handyside. [Michael] Flurscheim, Miss [Caroline Emily] Clark ... Queen St Hall – ... was crowded and I had difficulty in getting a seat on the platform and behind Miss Stevenson and next Mrs Maclaren [see 25 April 1894] – I had a good 5 minutes and Mrs Church said I made the best of it and was the most audible of all the speakers – ... The speakers were much such as I have heard often except a lady from Leeds ...

WEDNESDAY 9 MAY 1894
After breakfast went to Advocates Library, as recommended by Mr Courtney [see 16 April 1894] and spent 2 and $^{1}/_{2}$ hours over the Report of elect [sic] Committee on School Board elections – not of much value after all but sent if off at once to Mr Cridge ...

THURSDAY 10 MAY 1894
I finished my letter to Jessie Handyside and wrote a long one to John also to W. Murray saying I would go to Barrs.

FRIDAY 11 MAY 1894
Wrote regretfully to Flurscheim that I could not go to Lugarno in June ...

SATURDAY 12 MAY 1894
Agnes and Eric came by 11 train for the day – which was a fine one – and went home by 8.30 train – Eric had a great day – I had my first lesson probably also my last – at golf – on the lawn –

SUNDAY 13 MAY 1894
Saw Sunday School teaching at Fenton very different from Board school instruction – It is lessons to learn and to say – little explanation – perhaps none – I said a few words to the 21 children ...

Monday 14 May 1894
Finished my letter to Mrs Peirce wrote to Kate Maule and to Mr Westlake [John Westlake, MP, husband of another daughter of Thomas Hare, sister of Katie Clayton ...

Tuesday 15 May 1894
... Received ... four letters – JBS, Charles, Ellen Gregory and Katie Martin in reply to mine of the 5th – ...

Wednesday 16 May 1894
...

Thursday 17 May 1894
Louisa Myles [daughter of Alexander Brodie and his second wife Jourdiana Gray, see Appendix A, Family Tree] JB Spence letters to them. Wrote up my Australian letters and others ... When out in mg I bought elastic sided walking boots for 12/6 –

... After I had written to John that I had been balked – I got telegrams from Miss [Jane Hume] Clapperton [Scottish-born woman living in England, member of the exclusive Men and Women's Club, and of the Malthusian League, author of *Scientific Meliorism and the Evolution of Happiness*, 1885, the work which Catherine Spence drew on very extensively in her last work of fiction, 'A Week in the Future', published in the *Centennial Magazine*, 1888–89; see also below 29 June–2 July 1894] asking if I would speak to Fabians on Monday or Wednesday. I replied by telegram Wednesday 8 pm.

Friday 18 May 1894
Wrote a long letter to K.J. Musson ...

In evg we went to the Competition for photos at Mr ... school which collapsed for want of pay and must be repeated – In going out Agnes introduced me to Mrs Ralston who is a sister of Mrs Tom Barr Smith [Thomas Elder Barr Smith (1863–1941), a son of Catherine Spence's friends Robert and Joanna Barr Smith; his bequest to the University of Adelaide enabled the construction of the Barr Smith Library named after his father] and a handsome and young looking woman – We spent the evening after that over backgammon and I got beaten as usual I am the inferior player no doubt of it.

Saturday 19 May 1894
It never rains but it pours. Just after it is fixed that I am to speak to the Fabians in the Oddfellows Hall Forest Road on Wednesday evg – I have a letter from Mrs Maclaren asking if I will go to a Drawing room meeting at Mrs Muir

Dowie's [mother of Ménie Muriel Dowie, author of *A Girl in the Karpathians*], daughter of Robert Chambers [Robert Chambers, 1802–71, founded the Scottish publishing house, W. and R. Chambers, with his brother, William], on Wednesday after[noon] at 3 pm. I reply by telegram – yes –

Sunday 20 May 1894
I read *Binghams Idea* by Miss Plubank ... I read a good deal of Cardinal Manning and some of Dr Mackintosh which is much more sane theological theory ...

Monday 21 May 1894
... Took train to Melrose and such a crowd of excitement returning to Blackburn and Bolton found one man in the area who knew who Fabians were and a lady who had read Charles Booth's book [*Poverty*, which forms the First Series (4 vols.) of his *Life and Labour of the People of London* (collected edition, 1904)] – and apparently were members of Mr Downer's Church at G. Cross – Knew about the crofters and others Beatrice Potter and Sydney Webb [Beatrice Potter married Sidney Webb and together they became prominent founders of the Fabian Society, the principal organisation of English socialism in the late nineteenth century] ... Rev W + Louisa Murray met me and we walked home [to] an early and abundant meal and then a walk to call on the 2 Mrs .?s at the Homeopathic on the Denuck road ...

Tuesday 22 May 1894
Miss Murray took me after breakfast to the Abbey where we had a guide who knew something about it – We wandered through the church but I could find no newer gravestone than that of Janet Park my grandmother and her three children who all died when my father was in Jamaica [See Catherine Helen Spence, *Tenacious of the Past: The Recollections of Helen Brodie*, ed. Judy King and Graham Tulloch (Centre for Research in the New Literatures in English & Libraries Board of South Australia), Adelaide, 1994] ...

Then to Mrs Davidson's – the house is so changed – ... James old room is added to by throwing in my little room or most of it ... The Bank office is Mr Davidson's he is an auctioneer sells stock at St Bowells and elsewhere. The dining room was the same and the kitchen and I think my mothers bedroom. The attics were the same, but everything looked rather small – The garden was less changed and the stable –

Wednesday 23 May 1894
Mr Murray read us snatches of his wife's poems in mg after I had written most of letter to John and looked over my skeletons – I got to train in time and took my luggage ... and reached Dean Terrace for lunch ... We had only 24 votes –

but I think the effort was not wasted – ... I got an envelope with £1 note from Mrs Maclaren who was not able to come. Miss Burton of the School Board was most interested in the lecture and the voting – She thinks cumulative voting is absurdly wasteful. She and another lady wanted the ... Hare system one constituency for the whole country or at least Scotland. Miss Louise Stevenson took exceptions – and another lady thought things worked <u>very</u> well at present and there was no necessity for disturbing them. [at Oddfellows Hall Forestload:] I think it was the better lecture of the two but Norah expressed no opinion at all – She tells me her cousin Frank Deers is an intimate friend of Edward Carpenter's [a socialist and homosexual who lived with a succession of lovers in a cottage near Sheffield, where he grew his own vegetables and made sandals which he gave to his friends; his major works *Love's Coming of Age: Papers on the Sexes*, London, 1896, and *The Intermediate Sex: Study of Transitional Types of Men and Women*, London, 1912 were still to be published, but he had made his views about sex clear in his Walt Whitmanesque cycle of poems *Towards Democracy*] and brought him to ... [meet?] her ... mother and aunt.

Thursday 24 May 1894

Wrote David Murray at Australia.

Queen's Birthday and great procession in Edin[burgh] in connection with General Assembly but I could not stay. James Brodie walked with me to Caledonian Station and got excursion ticket for 4/- only available one day for Dumfries. Met a gentleman who knew about Fabians and ILP who got out at Abington – ... Train late W. Maxwell and May met me ... I had the warmest welcome here and two good rubbers of whist at night – I was taken rather hard and slept well.

Friday 25 May 1894

... Mr Watson of the Liberal paper came in evg – As a Gladstonian [follower of William Gladstone (1809–98), four times Prime Minister of England, a Liberal] he sees no saviour in pro rep but W. Maxwell said it was a revelation to him to hear what I said in finance and economics. Lent him the interview of Adelaide.

Saturday 26 May 1894

...

Sunday 27 May 1894

...

Monday 28 May 1894

Wrote a long letter to Mr Cridge and made up my diary to date – Have a little cold … In afternoon May Maxwell took me to Mrs Hutchins at Lichanbriggs where there are great stone quarries of red free stone – The men earn 30/- a week and a boy of fourteen from school can get 9/- a week carrying water to the engines – There are thousands of workmen – Miss H. speaks of a syndicate who have 6 or 7 quarries and want to take this one from the lady who works it now and in case she is ousted she is looking out for some other quarries on which to employ her energies. Miss H. was one of a committee for armaments during the winter at Lochenbriggs …

Tuesday 29 May 1894

Wrote to Kate Martin and to Michael Flurscheim enclosing cutting of fifth letter from Chicago. Mary and I went in afternoon to see the Boys' Industrial school which is only for destitute and neglected boys. The govt grant is 5/- for big and 3/- for small boys – the Co. of Dumfries get £30 and Galway less – there are private benefactors and the boys earning – Only 3 hours school daily – only the elements of education 3 hours work at netting, wood cutting, wood turning, tailoring, shoemaking – The only school holidays they have are when farmers need them for weeding etc at 1/- a day for big boys and food but no wages for little ones. Some one gave a steam engine and some one a wood splitting machine. A kind lady provides the kilts etc for 17 of the boys who are the band – and play the drum and bagpipes. These boys generally go into the army and do well. At 16 the boys go into the world and generally are apprenticed, some in the town such as two at Mr Maxwell's. Their wages are paid into the institution and they are fed and clothed and have a little pocket money … Mr Pilgrim a director – says their greatest trouble was with the children of worthless parents – tramps – for at the age of 16 control ceases and they know the day and the place of release – Boys are required so [?] to report themselves once a year for three years as the Dept wants to hear of their after career but it is only optional.

Wednesday 30 May 1894

A long quiet day at home – I wrote to Eleanor on W.M[urray]'s typewriter.

Thursday 31 May 1894

We had a long day at the Crichton … {refs to buildings, endowments, pauper patients, doctors}

Friday 1 June 1894

Got a letter from Mrs Murray saying she could not leave till the night of the 12th – and proposing I should join her at Stirling – I made up my mind to stay another day at Dumfries and Willie sent a carriage to take me and Mary and Lizzie to Sweetheart Abbey ...

I had a letter from K. Martin about the death of Mrs Day [wife of John Medway Day, a Baptist minister in Adelaide, and leader of what was called 'the Forward Movement' in the early 1890s in Adelaide. The Forward Movement was a collectivity of radical utopian socialist reforming groups which, in Adelaide, included a considerable number of dissenting church-congregations and their ministers] on the 14 April. It had opened a great many old wounds – the wreck of the Gothenburg and the cruel wound of fate, and the indifference of nature [this refers to the wreck of the vessel on which Catherine Martin's brother, Alick, was travelling, and his death by drowning]. I wrote to her in reply at once and both telegraphed and wrote to Mrs Maule.

Saturday 2 June 1894

Felt war [sad] to leave the Maxwells ... Very nearly missed my train had to run for it – because May and I were talking in the waiting room [back to Edinburgh].

Sunday 3 June 1894

A quiet day at home ... I wish I could get rid of my cough.

Monday 4 June 1894

Wrote a lot of letters and notes and made up my diary.

Weather too cold to tempt any one out.

Tuesday 5 June 1894

Wet day at home till evg – I hemmed 6 table napkins and one table cloth while Janet read me her novel – weak in plot – and in character but not without some merits in description and in style – But every criticism I make meets with opposition – so it cannot be mended ... Letter from JB Spence F[lorence] D[avenport] Hill, Mrs Beveridge

Wednesday 6 June 1894

Letters from CW Wren ... [after this Catherine Spence has put in 'Thursday 7th'] ... Was too late almost for my boxes but managed to get them out and took books ... and put Saratoga into the left luggage office.

THURSDAY 7 JUNE 1894
['Thursday' crossed out and 'Wednesday written at head of entry]
... Asked Mary for some lunch and a needle and thread, and impressed her with my cough ... Mrs Dowie [mother of Ménie Muriel Dowie, writer, of the Sex and the New Woman school of fiction, see also above 19 May 1894] wants me to go to the British Association meeting in Oxford in September. She tells me Mrs Maclaren considers I have the finest political mind of any woman she ever met – Her daughter Minnie Muriel is married to Norman, chief editor of *London Morning Chronicle*, the so-called Labour organ – Philip Mennell [Fellow of the Royal Geographical Society, author of *Mennell's Dictionary of Australasian Biography*, London, 1892] travelled reporting for that paper ...

[young lady:] ... Her girls were at school with the Barr Smiths and Minnie had had an Australian Birthday book that her mother had retained – I had mine and we exchanged signatures –

FRIDAY 8 JUNE 1894
Had to get into my book box in the mg.

Wrote to W Maxwell with [CP Gilman's poems] *In this our World* and had only a penny to pay for his and for a copy for Mrs Martin in Italy the same cost – Found that 5d would send *The Silent Sea* to May Maxwell and went on to Mrs Beyer just as dinner was being set on table ...

SATURDAY 9 JUNE 1894
Mrs Beyer went with me to a shop to buy materials for caps for Maud Gaulle to make up after midday dinner ... read more of her book and Maud made up one cap and I hemmed a tablecloth ... The novel was finished and the winding up was weaker than the rest. Half of the characters died in a simultaneous epidemic of yellow fever and cholera complicated by delerium tremens in the case of some of the characters ... Oh it is hopeless and all the more hopeless because she cannot see any fault in her [ie a character].

SUNDAY 10 JUNE 1894
... Kate made me up another cap and I read and Mrs Maule began *The Silent Sea* – ... Maud said it was rather nice Janet liked some parts of Mrs Lindsay's letter [Mrs Lindsay was a Scottish character in Catherine Spence's novel, *The Author's Daughter* (R. Bentley), London, 1868] – .

Of course I have praised the one and criticised the other [i.e. Katie v. Janet] – though nothing like so hardly as it required.

Monday 11 June 1894

Made rather a fiasco of the Australian visit, as Mrs David Murray and Mrs Pitterdriech had obeyed a summons for David to go with him to see a fishing lodge somewhere near Barrs – I had telegraphed too late for they had gone and Mr P telegraphed to D Murray to meet me at station and prevent me but that he did not receive till too late. So I had a tête-a-tête with the Rev Mr P for near four hours and we both survived it. Caught with difficulty the 6-16 train to Joppe.

Tuesday 12 June 1894

Letters from John and *Advertiser* with his letter. I wrote to John as I feared it would be too late at Barrs ... [talking with Frank Deas:] He says Edward Carpenter lives near Sheffield and makes his livelihood by literature. F. Deas says Socialism has made some way at least quite as much in Britain as in America –

Wednesday 13 June 1894

A glorious morning for my northwesterly journey ... Met Mrs Murray and Charlotte at Stirling and W Murray met us all there. We had a beautiful view all along ... I was much the better for Helen Murray to point out the features as we passed. We reached Ach-na-cloich by 12 o'clock and then took the steamer which WM had chartered for us and our belongings, an hour's sail down Loch Eline [?].

Thursday 14 June 1894

A dull rainy day. Helen sat with me when she was not engaged over settling all her household affairs, which are many – I read *The Firm of Girdlestone* [*The Firm of Girdlestone: A Romance of the Unromantic* (Chatto and Windus), London, 1890] by Conan Doyle [Sir Arthur Conan Doyle, 1859–1930, novelist and controversialist, inventor of Sherlock Holmes and his side-kick Dr Watson] – and re-read *Some Emotions an[d] a Moral* [*Some Emotions and a Moral* (T. Fisher Unwin), London, 1891, by Mrs Pearl Mary Teresa Craigie (1867–1906). She wrote using the pseudonym 'John Oliver Hobbes'].

Friday 15 June 1894

... {raining, letters}

Saturday 16 June 1894

I read half my prize essay [see above, 23 February, 15 March and 19 March 1894] to Helen Murray and read through all the others pretty nearly and am quite convinced mine is the best and Cridge's next best ... [Letters from Cridge + Mrs Peirce]

Sunday 17 June 1894

... Wm Murray read an excellent sermon by Charles Kingsley [(1819–75) clergyman, novelist, historian and miscellaneous writer, a Christian socialist, possibly most famous for his novel about chimney-sweeps, *The Water Babies*, 1863] ... I finished my prize essay to Mrs Murray who of course thinks it should get the prize.

Monday 18 June 1894

I began the business week by writing to Cridge and to Katie Martin ...

Tuesday 19 June 1894

... I wrote to E. Gregory to Rose Hood as well as to the family – ...

In evg after tea I read to W & H my Shakespeare lecture and both liked it though W says he does not recollect travelling with Ignatius Donelly which H has an impression he had told her he did after his return from America with Willie.

After that I coughed a good deal but Mrs Maule had sent me a little bottle of Powell's Balsam of Anniseed [sic] and I took a dose which kept me quiet at night – ...

Wednesday 20 June 1894

This was my day of goodbye to Barrs and it was a fine day so that things smiled on me – [stayed at Station Hotel in Oban].

Thursday 21 June 1894

A very long day of sunshine and wind ...

{Boat. Complained of cost of B&B – 8/9}

It was a beautiful sail – Arran the last land we saw in 1839 in the distance while we hugged the coast of Britain ... [in a steamer, 8 locks up + down – 4 each way] ...

Talked to a lady perhaps not quite a lady who put me in mind of Lydia Warren – We had to stop at Greenock ... and my black box was left behind and it had not been addressed beyond Greenock. At Glasgow we stopped about three quarters of an hour – reached Edin. 7.30 and then I found my box was left – Went straight to Dean Terrace rather late for dining but it was good and I enjoyed it ... had a lot of letters – Wrote Mrs Murray and Miss Clapperton P[ost]C[ards] ...

Friday 22 June 1894

... James Brodie himself took me to the station – To my joy and surprise the black tin trunk was at the left luggage office ... started for Peterborough ... Had a peep at the Durham Cathedral and York Minster – Glad to travel by daylight – four times I went through this journey by night express on my previous visit left the train at Grantham and got into another that had come direct from Bradford – No one met me at station but I got into an omnibus and my luggage and that of other two passengers was put on top – Precincts lovely and this is the oldest of houses – Katie Clayton [one of the daughters of Thomas Hare whom Catherine Spence met with their father on her visit to Britain in 1865–6, now married to Canon Clayton, sister of Mrs. Westlake] looks young and well and so does her husband though there are two sons at Cambridge. He and she were 13 years at Leicester in a parish with 13,000 poor people in it – They have been six years in the Canonry here ...

Saturday 23 June 1894

... Over 500 Girls Friendly Society from Leicester came in afternoon most factory hands and warehouse girls to attend 3 pm service in the Cathedral and to be shown round in two detachments ... I glanced through *The Yellow Aster* [Kathleen Mannington Caffyn, *The Yellow Aster* (Hutchinson), London, 1894, so this copy must have been hot off the press; considered one of the 'sex' novels, calling into question the double standard of morality, of the 1880s and 1890s] and think it unnatural.

Sunday 24 June 1894

Mrs Clayton was four times at Cathedral ... except myself who only went at 11 – + 7 – A beautiful building for very poor sermons – I am told both preachers were good men and the evg one a splendid pastor – but such twaddle as he talked with endless repetitions – Athanaeum Creed chanted in mg. Litany in evg – music fine and the intonation most musical but what a sense of unreality about it all – ... Alas to me God is indeed a God far off – but I do not care to have such a God too near me – All Katie Martin's passionate rebellion at the blank of a question and Helen Murray's more prosaic lamentation does not make me desire a stronger faith for with the faith comes the fear – If this God could save us and does not he is not good – If he saves me and does not save others he is not just. So my aloofness has its compensations ...

Monday 25 June 1894

I read Mrs Clayton a great part of *The Laws We Live Under* [Catherine Spence's social studies text book for schools] and she liked it very much, though what may come of it I cannot guess ...

TUESDAY 26 JUNE 1894

Great telegraph from Jack Bakewell offering to take me to Col[onial] Conv[ention] – and from Mr Petherick – The Bakewells are 3 miles from Stenford [Stamford?] and 15 miles from Peterboro [sic] – I determined to go to them and go home with Pethericks [Edward Augustus Petherick (1847–1917), worked in Melbourne for George Robertson's bookselling and publishing business and became the firm's representative in London, where, eventually, he set up business in 1887 as the Colonial Booksellers' Agency at 33 Paternoster Row with a capital of £800, the backing of a number of publishers and the assistance of Australian banks as distributing branches in Sydney, Melbourne and Adelaide. This enabled him to exert considerable influence over the content of reading about Australia. However, in 1894 Petherick went bankrupt; his book stocks were sold to E.W. Cole of Melbourne and his Collection of Favourite and Approved Authors was taken over by George Bell & Sons. But he had married in 1892 in Dorset, a widow named Mary Agatha Skeats, born Annear, and the help of his wife and some friends enabled him to meet his difficulties so that they were able to save his own collection of Australiana. In 1908, he and his wife brought the collection to Australia and negotiated with the Federal Parliament, with the result that the Commonwealth Library acquired it and provided Petherick with an annuity of £500 a year to tend it. An agreement to this effect was signed on 4 November 1909, and Catherine Spence travelled from Adelaide to Melbourne to be a witness to it. This magnificent collection would eventually become a foundation part of the National Library of Australia] to sleep as there is no room at Langton … It is settled that I am to speak on the 4th to the Guild of Cooperative Women –

WEDNESDAY 27 JUNE 1894

… Was met at Stamford [Stenford?] by Mrs J.W. Bakewell and – John Saville who is settled in this hunting country as a dealer in horses – {Life of leisure: hunting, mixing only with county, reading etc. daughter has French governess} …

Helen Hankey has been keeping her spare room for me for months – but her husband has become such a hypochondriac that I fear he will irritate me beyond – This is rather too much luxury and stall [presumably food] for me.

THURSDAY 28 JUNE 1894

After lunch we three set off for London – and reached the Langton in time to dress before dinner. I dined in haste in Jack's room – Mrs J.W. [John Westlake, MP; his wife is another daughter of Thomas Hare, inventor of Proportional Representation] dressed at leisure in her own – She has taken some four or five boxes with her to stay over Sunday possibly. She looked gorgeous but she told me it was a dyed dress. I was disappointed with the Colonial Convention. All I saw who I knew were Miss Nichibic [?] and E.P. Nesbitt and Mrs OHalloran – I was introduced to a Geo Tomkinson and Mr and Mrs Brodrib – and that was all. I sat more than an hour and a half before Mr Petherick recognised me. It was a pretty bad time towards the close. I looked for a gentleman with his wife – He has not [heard] much about me – He must have passed me three times –

There was only time to get slight refreshment, to say goodby to Mr Bakewell and to take the Underground and surface railway to 30 Buxton Hill – Mrs Petherick was in bed with a bad cold but I saw her cousins. His financial position is bad, because the Federal Bank is in liquidation and drains him of his receipts so that other creditors are pressing him hard – A sadly different outlook from what he had on April 4th 1893 when we talked in the train at Murray Bridge [eventually the Petherick Collection, which survived this financial crisis, was presented to the National Library of Australia in 1909; it comprised 16,500 titles] –

Friday 29 June 1894
I found Mrs Petherick very pleasant and intelligent emancipated woman. It [This?] is his second marriage[,] from supposition she has an income [?] from Australia reduced lately by £300 a year – I wrote to D. Murray on that subject of Petherick, and finished my family letter – and talked to the cousins ... Too late for train, telegraphed to Mrs Rotherham and took the next – Was met at Coventry by Miss Clapperton who is not so like me after all: 7 yrs younger. Mrs Rotherham is a widow whose daughter has married ...

Saturday 30 June 1894
{Explored with Miss Clapperton}
Miss C. says has grant to have Socialist lectures and fraternal concerts in these old buildings. After dinner drove to Mrs Poysers farm [in George Eliot's novel, *Adam Bede*, 1859] which looks like an old hall – no griffins at each side of the gate {Admiring countryside – trees etc}

Sunday 1 July 1894
Received my rings and a letter from Mr Petherick and a dressmaker's crate as likely to need clothes – *Harper's* leaves out acknowledgement to Mrs Peirce, wrote to her expressing my sorrow.

Opened the Baconian controversy with Miss Clapperton to whom it is quite new but she was open to ... Hurried away refusing tea in the garden to Mrs Cash [Mary Cash, née Sibree (1824–95), met and admired George Eliot when she was only sixteen, a friendship that extended into Eliot's last years] ...

to have some George Eliot talk. A very pretty tall old lady with a delicate pink and white complexion. She lives on the site of the Bray mansion and the old fashioned garden is as it was when the gate was as the Gate of Paradise to the intellectually starved Mary Ann Evans [George Eliot's real name] – and Mr and Mrs Bray, Charles and Sara S. Hennell [(1812–99), she and Caroline Bray, her sister (1814–1905) were longstanding friends and correspondents of George Eliot], opened to her intellectual and moral and social companionship. She told me Geo Eliot could not live alone – She depended on Lewes and afterwards Mr Cross for help and care. She was the breadwinner for Lewes who was a badly paid man of letters. There is no truth in the slander that Lewes was unfaithful to her and that she discovered it after his death … Miss Clapperton introduced me well and we saw some … a water color picture done by Mrs Bray of Maryann Evans at 24 … After supper we had Mrs Stetson and all was well.

Monday 2 July 1894

… In afternoon said goodby to Coventry. Miss Clapperton gave me the black lace mantle she lent me on Sunday for the heat, which is rather too handsome a gift. She took me to the station and Annie Fridlander came there with four exquisite roses – … At Rugby had a distant peep at Dr Arnolds [school] [Rugby, one of the original 'public' schools for the education of the male children of the upper classes, presided over by Thomas Arnold (1795–1842) as headmaster (1828–42).]

{Back to Claytons} …

Mrs Clayton says I have missed or lost a letter of Mrs Westlake's saying that Arthur Balfour, Sir John Lubbock and Mr L Courtney are to be at the meeting on the 10th –

My trouble is rather about clothes.

Tuesday 3 July 1894

I feel strangely stupid – I read some *Arena* and *Star* and *Hope and Home* but cannot evolve rightly my first address – read a little of Mrs Bray's moral education [see above, 1 July 1894] –

Wednesday 4 July 1894

… Afternoon rested and in evg had my meeting and my address was exceedingly well received. One man, Mr Kerry, a Scotchman and the lamplighter … and about 60 women – Mrs Clayton very pleased that I have given this public utterance in Peterboro – I did not keep Effective Voting quite out of it after all –

THURSDAY 5 JULY 1894

Received letter from Mrs Frances E. Russell, Minneapolis St Paul wanting article for *Arena* to be in by 15 July for Woman's Symposium so I set about it and sent it to B.O. Flower [for *Arena* and B.O. Flower, see above, 29 March 1894; C.H. Spence, 'Effective voting – the only effective moralizer of politics', *Arena*, vol.10, no.xl, Boston, November 1894] direct and wrote to her – Had my packing to do – Was charged for excess luggage 4/8 which Mrs Clayton paid as I was short of change.

Oh! it is a plunge – I arrived – and was bothered about luggage –

Mrs Westlake looks well and young – This is a beautiful home for two very busy people –

There are five women servants, the man was got rid of after 30 years service as he bossed the house and was not replaced –

FRIDAY 6 JULY 1894

Worked at letter writing for Australian and for London friends. In mg Mrs Westlake took me to Leonard Courtney and I carried my point about a 5 member ballot – instead of 3 – In afternoon went with him to Suffrage meeting [Westminster Town Hall] at which he took the chair. Sir George Grey [(1812–98), governor of South Australia 1841–5, of New Zealand 1845–53, and of Cape Colony 1854–9; worked in England in favour of state-aided emigration 1868–70; returned to New Zealand in 1871 and became Prime Minister of that country, 1877–9; he returned to England in 1894] was the great guest but he was rather tautological about the desire of women for the ballot in order to do good to their fellow creatures. I spoke after Mr Cohen and was told I was best heard of all. In evg Mrs W. was at an election meeting for School board and was kept till half past eleven – Mr Westlake read pro rep rev – He thinks the Droop quota [devised by H.R. Droop, and adopted also by Sir John Lubbock who was a leading member of the British Proportional Representation Society, this quota was calculated by dividing the total formal votes cast by the number of seats to be filled plus one, and adding one to the quotient. This was supposed to prevent parties achieving majority returns, whereas the Hare quota only hampered such a result. Spence believed that the Droop quota left more of the votes un-used.] the just one and will not allow that there is [sic] any waste votes –

SATURDAY 7 JULY 1894

In the mg I wrote a good many letters. In the afternoon I went with Mrs Westlake as far as Lambeth palace and left her there for a garden party, she went to another afterwards. In evg with Mrs Kydmann and Miss Miller sister of Mrs Alfred Hare of New Zealand to Madame S ... G ... very sorry I could follow this dialogue not a little bit – Very good acting indeed. Saw the Baroness Burdett Coutts [Angela Burdett Coutts (1814–1906) a rich philanthropist whose chosen work was the 'redemption' of prostitutes] and her young husband – the Duchess of St Albans and her daughter[,] Ellen Terry and her daughter – the first most youthful got up for 55 [there seems to be some confusion here: the Duchess of St Albans had been Harriot Mellon, an actress, and mistress of the elderly, wealthy banker, Mr. Coutts, until his wife died. By this time, Coutts was eighty-five years old. He and Mellon had always been accepted into Regency society in Brighton, as Coutts had obliged the Prince Regent with loans, when he needed them. When Coutts died in 1822, Harriot became fabulously wealthy. She was also considered eccentric. She married the Duke of St. Albans who was twenty years younger than she was. Even when she had become the Duchess of St. Albans, Queen Victoria would not receive her. She died in 1837 and her fortune went to Coutts's grand-daughter, Angela Burdett-Coutts, who was enobled in her own right. Ellen Terry (1848–1928) was Britain's 'Queen of the Stage', and her daughter, Edy, was also an actress] – Mrs Randolph Caldicott [he was a prominent artist] and other notabilities.

Sunday 8 July 1894

Read *Esther Waters* in mg [a novel published in 1894 by Anglo-Irish novelist George Moore (1852–1933)].

{Visitors at lunch – English – French – and more after} My own were Mr and Mrs Archie Stirling[,] Miss Windeyer [see above An Introduction] – Miss Helen Blackburn [(1821–1903), Irish social reformer, early leader of the struggle for women's emancipation in Britain, Secretary of the National Society for Women's Suffrage, 1874–95], Canon Blackley – Mrs Alfred Hunt and her daughter ... and her niece. Lord Monkswell of the County Council, two artists – Miss Windeyer was rather loud – it is unfortunate she has such an aggressive tone –

Mr Westlake took course with Mr Blackley on the Old Age endowments – He is an individualist of the old school –

The fall in interest to 3 per cent must however affect Mr Blackley's calculations and if Flurscheim is right it will lower and lower till it is extinguished.

Monday 9 July 1894

I think I get low spirited in this great London. I wrote a lot of letters to hunt up my friends but I feel as if there were few indeed that could be depended on.

Mrs Kydmann went away, Mrs Westlake took me to call on Mr and Mrs Corbet, married artists, and then to the Royal Academy. I am disposed to admire what is not really admirable. Mrs Westlake is an impressionist.

Tuesday 10 July 1894
Lydia Clayton too ill to receive me on Thursday as we had intended.

I was pretty nervous – I could do nothing to help and every one was looking about my meeting. I was introduced first to Mr Balfour and told him my mother was born at Writlingbone Maris [?] – Sir John Lubbock looks younger than I expected and so does Balfour – A good room full and many important people – as per list Lord Rothschild [(1840–1915) previously Sir Nathaniel Rothschild, created Baron in 1885, the first Jewish peer in England; a major philanthropist] away. I did not use nearly all my notes – but think I spoke pretty well though without the humour that lighted up my Am[erican] address. How could one be funny with these people – Neither *Register* nor *Telegraph* represented. Did not give enough explanation of method and as the votes were counted in the MS room the audience could not hear the altercation. Out of 81 first votes – Balfour had 52!!! 14 was the Droop quota which was not the quota I spoke of – Mr Hare 16 – Balfour complimented me but said that good men are not kept out of Par[liament] as was the case in America – Sir John Lubbock showed that faddists had much pressure and might be stronger there than if they had direct representation. Courtney said [J.S.] Mill, Charles Bradlaugh – W.E. Gladstone, a young Gladstone[,] would have no chance in the unusual electorate of today – Both spoke very well as did also Mr Westlake – Sir John Hall [(1824–1907), Premier of New Zealand 1879–82, retired from the Assembly in 1897. He was considered New Zealand's most significant democratic reformer; his ministry enfranchised – white – men in 1879, and he was a leader in the campaign which won the vote for – white – women in New Zealand in 1893] explained why the Bill of 1887–8 was tort [wrong]. He said the districts were too large – Now that did not strike me as a feature of the bill. The other reason however was sufficient – that it was introduced by a weak ministry near the time of a dissolution ... I cleared up for Mr Westlake the question of initiation of quota rep in Adelaide – He thought it was the Upper House which was a *scrutin de liste* – and that Frederick Hill brought that claim forward from his brother – whereas it was the Municipal Act in which quota rep was actually carried out [see *An Autobiography*, p. 40].
I spoke to Mrs Chas Booth [see above 21 May 1894] to Miss Shrew, Lady Stanley of Alderley [Henrietta Maria, daughter of the thirteenth Viscount Dillon, married Edward John, Lord Stanley of Alderley in 1826. He was the Chief Whip and later Postmaster General in the government of Viscount Palmerston; as his wife she had influence and used it to campaign for the development of women's education: she was among the founders of the Girls' Public Day School Trust and of Girton College, Cambridge. Despite this, she was also one of the 104 signatories to the famous – or infamous – article titled 'A Plea Against Female Suffrage' published in *The Nineteenth Century* in

May 1889] and others. Had tea and was glad it was over – As the Westlakes were going to a big city dinner Mrs Courtney kindly asked me to a small family dinner at 8 – me (and Mr Hobhouse MP, Mrs Richardson and another lady). It was very pleasant and refreshed me. There were reporters. One from the *Critical [?] Press* verbatim of which copies can be had but I afterwards heard such copies are very expensive – Sir John Hall would like copy.

Wednesday 11 July 1894
I seem to have no end of letters to receive and to write.

In afternoon Mrs Courtney called and took me to the Liberal Woman Suffrage league meeting at the Water Color Exhibition rooms. She introduced me to Mrs Phillips, a Jewess, the president and her sec took down my name and address in case there was any opportunity to speak though the season's late. I found a Mrs Becan [?] for a pilot when Mrs Courtney had to go – I met again Miss Windeyer who wanted me to meet her at the special Institute on Friday evg at 9 but I saw it was impracticable – Mrs Sheppard from New Zealand [Kate Wilson Sheppard (1848–1934), another Scottish-born emigrant, but in this case to New Zealand where she became the chief figure in the Women's Christian Temperance Union's campaign for votes for women in New Zealand, the first country in the world to grant – white – women the right to vote] spoke well on the campaign there. Mrs Ashton Dilke [a leading suffragist, attended the first meeting of the International Council of Women in Washington in 1888] … Mrs Cook was in the Chair, Mrs Maclaren on the platform, her daughter was not well enough to come so Mrs Phillips orated – I was amused at what she said about choosing a nursery governess for her children – Mrs W[estlake] says she neglects her children + family for suffrage but then Mrs W. is from the other wing of the army – I walked home from Sloane Square and only went wrong once.

Thursday 12 July 1894
Fair report of meeting in *Times*.

Mrs Westlake took me to Marlboro [sic] H Board School and I went through the Infant and Girls dept … In after[noon] Mrs Westlake took me to a concert at Surrey House (Lord Battersea Flower he married a Rothschild) for Children's Holiday friend got up by Miss Brooke – Rajah Brooke's daughter or granddaughter [Charles Brooke (1868–1917) the white rajah of Sarawak] a very good concert indeed …

We went next to a reception at Mrs Joyce's where I was introduced to Miss Garrett Anderson [Elizabeth Anderson, née Garrett (1836–1917), first woman medical doctor in England, sister of Dame Millicent Fawcett, leader of the campaign for women's suffrage, and for higher education and independent employment for women]. She asked after Dr Stewart but meant Stirling [Edward Charles Stirling (1848–1919), son of the Stirling who was Catherine Spence's friend – see *An Autobiography* chapter 6. He was a surgeon and first professor of physiology at Adelaide University, and, as a member of the House of Assembly in the South Australian parliament, he introduced the first motion, and then the first Bill, to enfranchise women, in 1885 and 1886. These did not succeed and he lost his seat, but he continued to campaign with the Woman Suffrage League] who has been ill – typhoid, knew when she was at Cambridge. She is not so charming as Mrs Fawcett. We had next a drive in Hyde Park … When I reached home I found a letter … from Cooper of the *Register* … [His request illegible] I referred him to the *Times* report and supplemented it – Mr and Mrs Westlake went to an evg party at 10.15. I read a little and went to bed tired and rather lonely though this has been a pretty lively day.

Friday 13 July 1894

Mrs Westlake up and away before I came to breakfast – A long quiet day's letter writing in my own room. After all letters despatched got one from F[lorence] D[avenport] Hill enclosing one from Miss [Caroline Emily] Clark with particulars of Mr Mark's death. He had failed much mentally for some months. Her letter is sad all though Mrs Watts with her – she too weaker – … Mr + Mrs Westlake very tired came home for dinner and almost immediately thereafter went to a School Board meeting about 300 present to elect or rather nominate for election the two candidates the Progressive Party think they can carry for Chelsea out of five members. The Labour party hope to secure one, the Clerical party will run three – … I feel pretty solitary[,] vexed to hear verbat[im] copy of [report of the proportional representation] meeting so expensive.

Saturday 14 July 1894

… After lunch Mrs Westlake took me to the new Hospital for Women entirely attended by women physicians and surgeons who perform the most critical operations. It is large bright and airy looking, all dine upstairs four meals a day 6.30 – 9.30 – 3. – 7.30 … about 500 women benefit yearly. Next we went to the New Gallery stands for the Grosvenor and admired a great many of the pictures. He is not so exclusively impressionist as his wife – Mrs W. said I may leave my boxes so I had to make a hasty transfer of a very few things, so little time for it. Cab to Buxton Hill – A Most kind welcome – in time for dinner – … but both Mr and Mrs Petherick seem to think I am no intruder.

SUNDAY 15 JULY 1894

These are indeed good people and good friends with whom I am now – and the undeceived trouble they are in makes them the more interesting – It is a splendid library especially the Geographical and Australasian parts of it – I read Mme Potts Poems – but the day was mostly spent in conversation. I walked in the garden with Mr P. for an hour or more and heard all his history.

Ah me! I am powerless to help.

Mrs sang – She has a splendid voice of two octaves compass – She is a good sympathetic wife.

MONDAY 16 JULY 1894

Mrs Petherick kindly took me to he [?] Bar Mersche's and I chose the same good Sarah [Susah? Serge?] – for a dress and for a blouse – I am told I shall have to pay £7.11 for both – I went in aft with Miss Loan to have it tried on – I bought lace and frilling etc. It is a good shop and I come on a half yearly sale.

I had a letter from Mrs Courtney saying the *Manchester Guardian* Gladstonian whose editor … is a believer in pro rep, wants me to be interviewed on Wednesday at 12 on pro rep – of course accept with alacrity and write Mary Ingram that I must go to her after lunch …

TUESDAY 17 JULY 1894

…

WEDNESDAY 18 JULY 1894

A big day. Finished and despatched to *Times* letter which I enclosed to Miss Shaw. Started for Chelsea and had a long walk to 15 Cheyne Walk. Mrs Fawcett … Mr Courtney helped me well but his illustration was rather for 3 member const[ituency?] than for 5 or 6. After lunch talked to Mrs C. She took me to the Carlyles' statue and drove me to 65 Cromwell Rd …

Sir Wm came in before I left and I had my name and Mr Courtney in my book two MPs. Mary I think begins to take in that I am somebody. We had a good talk all round. Herbert saw me to the Gloucester Rd underground and I went to Gower St but had a long walk for about 300 to 6. Found the Bakewells not in the lap of luxury – business he says is so bad he thinks of going out to Bangalore where his brother-in-law is professor …

The Bakewells drew me out though tired … – He took me to the bus that took me to … station and thence straight to Brixton a little before 11. Letters of course. Pretty tired.

THURSDAY 19 JULY 1894
... Went to have my dress and blouse fitted, think they will do ...

Evening Mr Petherick was late – the climax has come – A friend came to talk business with him and his wife ...

Miss Shaw [Flora L. Shaw, later Lady Lugard (1851–1929) worked with W.T. Stead on the *Pall Mall Gazette* and later, also with him, on *The Times* where she became head of the colonial department] cannot be rushed; my letter can go in in time the coed[itors]s of the *Times* are so ...

FRIDAY 20 JULY 1894
... Mrs Petherick had to go to the city on anxious business and I wrote my letters to Adelaide and to K Martin. Had scarcely finished when had to prepare for Beehive meeting on behalf of museum of the Jews! ...

Mr Petherick much depressed after lot examination. We cannot get him to rally – When playing cribbage a letter came asking if I would prepare and deliver a paper for the Royal Col[onial] Inst – I shall but scarce can think of a subject ... F[lorence Davenport] Hill fears I cannot speak on Monday

SATURDAY 21 JULY 1894
Slept fairly well in spite of thinking about subject for R Col Inst lecture ... Beautiful drive in afternoon round by Tooting Common, Streatham, Dulwich park and gallery.

SUNDAY 22 JULY 1894
No one went to church – Mr Petherick had said the same thing about Aust furnishing the necessary luck as I had done in my Boston lectures – ... Prof Edwin Johnson [author of *Antiqua Mater: A Study of Christian Origins*, London 1887] and his wife. He is a resourced [?] man says he shd have written and thanked me for my book which he and his wife had read with pleasure ... Bonwick is a Baconian and a free thinker. We were all pretty advanced. I think there is more in Johnson's contention than I saw at first but it is a very large order yet.

MONDAY 23 JULY 1894
After a little note writing I made a beginning to my paper for the Colonial Institute and I think it will go well enough.

After early lunch Mrs P[etherick] and I went to the meeting of the Local Govt Board to petition Mr Shaw Lefevre [President of the Local Government Board] to recommend a public enquiry into the whole subject of Reformatory[?] schools – I wrote my name as one but there was too full a program for me to speak ...

I met Miss F.D. Hill, Miss Dorling and Miss Ida Baker – was introduced to the Rev Sam Barnett [English clergyman and social reformer (1877–1914), instituted university settlements like Toynbee Hall to bring university graduates into contact with poorer people in the cities. He became warden of Toynbee Hall. He married Henrietta Octavia Rowland, philanthropist and charity worker]. It was a large and most influential deputation – and friends of B[oarding] O[ut] hope for much from it. We next went to R Col Inst and … showed me round – I have to speak in the Library which holds 200 – Afterwards we went to M … Exchange and had tea – … Mrs P. left her purse her husband went back for it took train and got to Brixton before us.

Tuesday 24 July 1894
Did something to my paper for Col Institute and packed up to go to Brighton left Mrs Petherick with regret but promise to return.

Had early lunch found 7/6 would get return ticket but it will cost a great deal more for cabs.

Thought Helen [Hankey] much changed at first but in ten minutes saw she was her old self. Mr Hankey has his meals separately from the family and I shall see little of him … An aunt, Mrs Jameson Hankey, went with the girls to Chevaliers costermonger singing and left Helen and myself to a quiet evg.

Wednesday 25 July 1894
Helen took me [for] a drive and we got permission to see a school on the morrow.

Thursday 26 July 1894
This is the day the schools close for the summer vacation so Mrs Hankey and I went to one and found it rather disorganised on account of sports and prizes – 12 o'clock was the end of school.

Friday 27 July 1894
Spent the day till about half past three in writing – notes + family letter and finishing paper for Royal Inst and making abstract.

Saturday 28 July 1894
Hilda finished her copying of the River House proceedings [ie the meeting on 10 July 1894 about Proportional Representation] and I made a good start with mine …

Sunday 29 July 1894
Went to church service pretty high but not so high as North Berwick. Sermon weak – attributed Aust. larrikinism and dishonesty to secular schools and leaving out the ten commandments…

Monday 30 July 1894
My last day. I have got very fond of the girls…

Tuesday 31 July 1894
A day of trial – Helen H took me to the station. I thought I would save a cab and took train at Victoria for Brixton. Between Clapham & Brixton I lost or was robbed of my purse with £6 in money and stamps and two money orders –

Quite gone – so had to go to the R[oyal] Col[onial] Inst[itute] to give my address which was very well received indeed. Sir F. Young wants it printed in a Review by 19th Century.

Wednesday 1 August 1894
… Mr Petherick fears Knowles will not publish what has been spoken.

Thursday 2 August 1894
Went to the city with Mr Pond [and] was introduced by him to Mr Marston both about 19th Century and about *Gathered In* [Catherine Spence's fifth novel, serialised in the *Adelaide Observer* from September 1881 to March 1882. Caroline Emily Clark had taken it on a fruitless search for an English publisher in 1878. But it was not published as a book until 1977. She seems, here, to be hoping for a publisher both for her novel, and for an article previously published in the South Australian *Register*, in *The Nineteenth Century*, a monthly periodical. See also below, 8 August 1894 and 12 September 1894]. What will be my luck – Was in Bankruptcy court waited for him – At Juan Stanislas he waited for me – No good for poor Mrs Maule as I feared – Mrs Petherick had her own friends in aft and Miss Goodbar came and she kept her till I returned. I had to write once again first and last page of Col Inst address to make it more acceptable to Knowles –

Went to Miss Davenport Hill 15 Hinton Road rather a round about way but arrived – Miss Ellen Hill was there for dinner.

Friday 3 August 1894
Miss F. Hill and I wrote letters I had a pleasant drive round Hampstead with Miss Hill who has a maid and a secretary and is generally well taken care of – She had three or four or five operations Cataract … of part of the eyelids which were too heavy to uplift…

Saturday 4 August 1894
{Still with F.D.H.}

Sunday 5 August 1894
{still with FDH – visitors, and from USA for CHS}
... F.D. Hill is set on printing the River House proceedings whereat I rejoice –

Monday 6 August 1894
Nasty wet dismal day Miss F. Hill did not take me to station but the sec.[retary] did. Very restive horse – ... {mostly about Bacon-Shakespeare}

Tuesday 7 August 1894
... Mr P[etherick] hopes little from 19th Century – I think he is more cheerful about his own affairs but his wife is less so about hers as she fears ... reductions in Melbourne income.

Wednesday 8 August 1894
Wrote an addendum to the River House proceedings and went through the MS and despatched the packet at night.

Also some other letters that wanted doing. Felt excited to think that *Gathered In* and *The Social and Intellectual Aspects* [of Australian Life: abstract of paper read at the Royal Colonial Institute, London, 31 July 1894] were on approval and the proceedings at River House sent to printer and could not sleep till daylight.

Thursday 9 August 1894
Mr Petherick made me write an account of myself for Washington Moon's *Men and Women of the Time* and also stirred me up to do the same for Mrs F. Martin.

I despatched my letter to her in the course of the day and started my other letters –

Friday 10 August 1894
Letters from Norah Church Cridge and M. Macfie.

Had my accident

... have a long talk at the breakfast table with Mr and Mrs Petherick re leaving house and going into apartments –

... Wet – home by train changed at Victoria – In trying to escape being run over by hansom cab and other traps missed my footing fell and dislocated my right shoulder – Home in a cab, Dr Andrews had three wrenches at it but did not get it in place –

Pretty bad night!!! ...

Saturday 11 August 1894
Miss Osborne came to interview me for *Washington Gazette* but met the doctor on the stairs and had to go away.

    I was put under chloroform and the arm was satisfactorily set and I felt greatly relieved – Still strapped round the body and kept in bed but Mr and Mrs Petherick adjoin to my room and I am not lonely. It is difficult to hold a book up so as to be able to read it and the light is very bad in my room.

Sunday 12 August 1894
… Mr J.A. Cooper of the *Register* came in afternoon and interviewed me in bed. It was a break in the day –

    I did not think the wretch would telegraph my accident!!! ['Miss Spence. A nasty accident', *Register*, 15 August 1894]

Monday 13 August 1894
Miss Osborne came in afternoon and I had an hour and a half with her … She is a Newnham [Cambridge] girl, interesting – …

Tuesday 14 August 1894
Another day in bed – My mind much exercised about the Petherick affairs.

Wednesday 15 August 1894
Got out of bed and some clothes on and my arm in a sling – not a very tight one. Wrote a pencil note to Mrs Hankey – Wonder if I can manage to go to Tunbridge Wells – It is well I had some letters written at Hampstead –

Thursday 16 August 1894
{Mr Cowan visited. Finding the day monotonous.}

Friday 17 August 1894
– I enclosed to John the Con Inst [?Colonial Institute] letter having first had it copied by Mrs Petherick –

    Miss Bulow came in afternoon and wrote for me to Mrs F. Martin (answered on 26th). We asked her back on Sunday and told her to bring her songs and her essay 'Revolt of One of the Daughters'.

Saturday 18 August 1894
Began reading *Gathered In* to Mrs Petherick who had read the first two chapters. She is interested so is Mr P when he comes home. But it will take several days … I told the doctor I do not need him every day.

Sunday 19 August 1894

I read a good bit of my novel ... Miss Bulow came in at 3 ... She ... read us the beginning of the 'Revolt of a daughter'. I think she goes too far, it is too risky.

Monday 20 August 1894

... Percy Russell came in afternoon he wants me to write something ...

In evg Mr + Mrs Matras interrupted our cribbage and Mrs Petherick made me read George Oswald at home [a chapter in *Gathered In*, in which George Oswald speaks with a pronounced Scottish accent, so Catherine Spence's reading would have given it an added piquancy for non-Scottish listeners] to them ...

Tuesday 21 August 1894

Still going on with my reading aloud – There was no slackening of interest on the part of either Mr or Mrs P.

Wednesday 22 August 1894

Went on with my reading aloud when I could but Mrs P. had to go to the West end for final trying on of her new dress.

However I finished it and Mr P. read between when he was not present and both husband and wife are much pleased and he is surprised at the critics ...

Thursday 23 August 1894

... I read part of the *Stickel Minister* which I think is good. Mrs Petherick had packed my belongings for me before the weather was so bad.

The Valuator Hodgson and a clerk were here from 10 to 5 valuing the books – A bitter experience for Mr Petherick.

After they had gone he showed me his old books of travel, his maps and charts and his grounds for the theory that the Portuguese were the first discovers of the great South land.

Friday 24 August 1894

Mr Petherick took *Gathered In* to town – Mrs Petherick accompanied me to Streatham Station ... Mrs Griffin met me on a platform and I got home early for lunch – ... {with Mrs Griffin Mr Cowan}

Saturday 25 August 1894

... Had a rest in after read *If Christ Came to Chicago* [by William T. Stead, journalist and editor, a work about Hull House in Chicago and the Maxwell Street Market nearby; its subtitle is 'A Plea for the Union of All Who Love in the Service of All Who Suffer', published in 1893]. Mr Cowan came home early as it is Saturday and Mrs Griffin had invited Mr and Mrs Ningan ...

Sunday 26 August 1894
... This mg was occupied by a drive ... all round this part of Surry [sic].

Monday 27 August 1894
Wrote some post cards and Mrs Tom Griffin wrote for me to Katie Martin. We went to the village of Sutton for a walk and I ordered silk gloves short –

In aft we had a call from Mr James Martin of D & W Murray. I spoke of drawing more money and about my boxes at the River House [where the meeting about proportional representation had been held on 10 July 1894] – In evg I had my Aust letters, Handyside had paid £20.14.6 to my credit. Coz [Ellen Gregory] wrote me that Lucy Holmes was drawing out £10 which she thinks is all her balance but by my book it looks as if there were £18 and some interest so she is not quite at the end of her resources – Coz has drawn all or more of her allowance for her Melbourne trip on the mourn [?] by Cooks excur[sion?].

Tuesday 28 August 1894
I get Mrs T Griffin to write for me to Mr Cridge and write a P.C. to Mrs Stetson [CP Gilman] myself – I also enclosed Rutherford's letter to K Martin ... In finished *The Raiders* and *If Christ Came to Chicago*.

Wednesday 29 August 1894
... Went to the village as they call it, and got the gloves I ordered and ribbon for my slippers ... I began *The Woodlanders* [novel by Thomas Hardy, published 1887].

Thursday 30 August 1894
Corrected and despatched the pamphlet [on the proportional representation meeting on 10 July 1894]. At night had memo fr[om] F.D. Hill suggesting corrections which I made in the preface but she is pleased with it.

Friday 31 August 1894
... In afternoon went to Mrs Magnus for tea and dinner ... Mr and Mrs Parkes came to dinner ... A good deal of music and singing but some good talk ... I got on my Edinburgh dress and kept it on all day – Read some stories of Mary Wilkins.

Saturday 1 September 1894
... I began to be rather despairing about my novel and my article. It is not in the Sept *19th Century* ...

Sunday 2 September 1894
At last! arrives the *Xtian Advocate* with my article in it ['Notes political and social of ten months in America', *The Christian Advocate*, New York, 23 August 1894]. I hope it will please Mrs Fay Peirce ... {sightseeing} ...

I like Mr Morgan very much. He went with me to meet Miss Bulow. She smoked a cigarette while she read my two articles in the drawing room – Mr Cowan enjoyed the drive with the Ningans and on the whole is better –

Miss Bulow says she sent her 'Revolt of one of the daughters' to [W.T.] Stead.

Monday 3 September 1894
Packet of PR Reviews from Cooley to be distributed with my new pamphlet and letter from Mrs Petherick – article and *Gathered in* shllg [?] contingencies. Wrote to Leydell in her name.

I read part of *A Son of Belial* ... Recd at night letters from John Chamber with K. Hood's report enclosed W.L. Garran and F.D. Hill.

Tuesday 4 September 1894
Wrote Mrs Peirce with 3/-.

Mr Westlake sent me back Cooley's documents with a letter which I enclosed to Miss Hill adding something. Wrote Cridge to enclose ... P.O.O. [Post Office Order] for 6/4 – (which curiously got exchanged for Mrs Fay Peirce's for 3/-).

Wednesday 5 September 1894
I wrote 68 addresses ... for the pamphlets and there are not nearly enough.

Thursday 6 September 1894
{with Mrs Griffin to visit Mrs Christen} ... She said I spoke so Scotch ... But she thinks my novels *Mr H[ogarth]'s Will* and *Tender & true* much better than Mrs Martins – these were dull ...

Friday 7 September 1894
... I read to Mrs Griffin and Miss Emmie Lilley my Bacon Shakespeare lecture and they said it was very interesting. Miss Lilley copied out mottoes from Birthday book till last moment. Went off by 4.50 train and had to walk along

platform and over bridge with working box, cloak, handbag and umbrella – Mr + Mrs Petherick very pleased to see me – He has had a nasty accident falling down a sort of well 4½ feet deep in a house and had Dr Andrews. Mrs P. has got a new German maid who needs much teaching – Cook still here. Mrs P went out to see houses and 85 not to compare with this, looked at another £350 asked if there were no stables!!! –

Saturday 8 September 1894
Spent forenoon in wrapping up pamphlets ... Mr Petherick helped me in aftn and posted 2 great lots also got me 60 more wrappers. Mrs Petherick is instructing her German maid and finds it demands much running about –

Sunday 9 September 1894
Went to church with Mr Petherick. Unitarian. Saw David Martineau [presumably a relation of James Martineau, the most influential of Unitarian religious leaders of the nineteenth century in England] not particularly cordial. Read Shakespeare Bacon literature and used up all my wrappers and almost all my Reports –

Monday 10 September 1894
Letter from Mrs Hankey. Telegraphed I should go to Tunbridge Wells today.
    Mrs Hankey met me at station and I was persuaded to stay all night to meet Cousin [?] Rose and over lunch time to meet Helena [?] who is at St Leonards. Telegraphed to Mrs Petherick.
    ... Talked too much and brought back my cough.

Tuesday 11 September 1894
Read a little of Baring Gould's stories *Joel + Jacquette* [Sabine Baring-Gould (1834–1924), rector of Lew Trenchard in Devon, wrote novels, books for children, historical works, and several theological works. His most famous hymn is 'Onward Christian Soldiers'] ... Reached Brixton a little after 4 ...

Wednesday 12 September 1894
... Mr Petherick was out in the evg at Mr Silwer's, but he was home for dinner and he brought me a great disappointment. Martins seems professional advisor says *Gathered In* will not interest Eng readers so that unless I am prepared to pay for the publication – he will not [handle/publish?] it – I wish I had not mentioned it to my friends –

Thursday 13 September 1894
... Dr Andrews says I am quite fit to travel by the 24th.

Friday 14 September 1894

Went in aft to Moorgate St with Mrs Petherick to see her lawyer and afterwards on to Prof Edwin Johnson's for tea and supper – Their eldest girl, a Girton graduate made the acquaintance of a Brahman girl who introduced her to her brother, high caste Brahmans educated entirely in England from three years old – They fell in love and married last Nov. She has been most cordially recd by her husband's people and all the ceremonies gone through on their arrival to feast for 700 people. She and her husband learned the Hindoo language together – She is asked to take an active part in furthering the education of men + women – They appear to be most happy. Mr Johnson's family are very interesting … The mother is a good and sensible woman – They must be living on her money.

Saturday 15 September 1894

Information received from Lizzie [about] Miss Gregory['s] – father married again when Amy was 5 years old – she went then to stay with Lolly [?] – who had 11 children – 7 survived her – others died in infancy – She herself died 8 years ago. Last Sept the oldest son died 19 yrs old – Eldest girl Florence is at business. Lizzie keeps house for Mr Souther [?] Walter lives with Minnie Mrs Rothy who has a bad husband and 3 children. Walter works for Mr Souther [?] – who makes bitters and essences for … Emma stays half with Mr Scrutton and half with her stepmother. Amy lives with Mrs Gregory – dress and mantle makers – very busy in the season. Mrs G is very fond of her and kind to her from the first. Eldest uncle Gregory who went to America was never heard of since. Doesn't know about his family Adany [?] died about 5 years ago. Mrs Sumner has been dead 3 yrs. Mr Sumner died just before George Gregory. The Scruttons live in Putney and Mrs Roth lives near – Nelly Scrutton was learning millinery but her sight got so bad that she had to give it up. She wears glasses – Roth is a lawyer's clerk – the 3 children nice – Only 3 children in ten years. Mr Scrutton keeps his old father.

Sunday 16 September 1894

Ada and Beatrice Loan arrived Saty evg. Mrs Petherick done up, the cook ill, the German maid … I was busy I scarce know how all morning writing to Cridge, Dr Holmes only a post card and finishing up Percy Russell and notes … for Mrs Barnett – The letters I had on Saturday night show that the *Register* telegraphed about my arm and John says it would have been better to telegraph about my work – They don't know where I am and how kindly I have been cared for.

In aft Mr Petherick read a fine passage of Von Ranke's on the death of Cromwell and his services to England and the world [Leopold von Ranke

(1795–1886), generally recognised as the father of 'the modern objective' historical school, otherwise described as 'historicist' and 'empiricist', wrote *inter alia* a six-volume *History of England*, 1875] – I got him to read the pamphlet about Bacon Orville Owens he found three of his points wrong – ... *The Anatomy of Melancholy* was not published when Burton [Robert Burton (1577–1640) produced in 1621 his great compendium, *The Anatomy of Melancholy*] was 10 yrs old but a book on melancholy by Timothy Bright – ...

Monday 17 September 1894

I wrote in all fourteen letters and post cards – which worked me out. In evg got letters from Flurscheim saying he could not stay longer at Florence also from K. Martin saying she would like to stay longer at Siena.

Tuesday 18 September 1894

I wrote to K. Martin to telegraph if she could wait for me to read her book in proof and to Flurscheim to communicate with the Martins – I heard from Dobbs, Playford, Hergub, Siegfried and my Doctor's bill £6-7 very moderate –

Mrs Griffin came early and I think enjoyed her day – When I was occupied with Mrs G Miss Duerdin also came by 3 pm Mrs Petherick played cribbage with her – We had them all at tea and afterwards in the drawing room when the Misses Loan and Mrs Petherick played and sang. Mrs P. has miserable rheumatism in her left hand – but it swelled toward evg and that relieved it – We are a sorry lot.

Wednesday 19 September 1894

Made an effort and nearly finished a letter for *Register* as well as some other work which took me till near lunch time. Read the *Arena* which I think I shall send to J.B.S.

Mrs Petherick going all over the place looking for a gardener

... Mr Petherick very depressed and weary –

Beatrice out all day not successful but had lunch and tea with a friend Ada ...

Thursday 20 September 1894

Was surprised and pleased by receiving a letter from Wesllesb[y?] enclosing cheque for 18/3 – from Mr W[estlake] per John Hubbard – Mr Morrison and Miss Davenport Hill – This makes me easier with regard to money.

In evg had letter from Lizzie [G]regory asking help for her mother to pay her taxes to save seizure of furniture ... Fare to Florence will be £20/11 via Zurich 7/0/9.

FRIDAY 21 SEPTEMBER 1894

A hard day's writing yet did not accomplish letter for *Telegraph*. Telegram from Katie Martin. Won't keep manuscript – satisfactory –

Mrs James Martin called in afternoon – very pleasant –

Miss Bulow came in time for dinner – We were in the midst of a musical evg – when David Murray and James Martin came to see me – The latter greatly admired the ... and singing and fraternised with these ... Cornish ladies. Mr Petherick showed D. Murray his books in hopes he might help or stir up someone else to help to keep them together.

SATURDAY 22 SEPTEMBER 1894

Wrote to Zurich and to L[izzie] Gregory. Mrs P. procured the postal notes for me – Ada Loan went with me to River House and as we could not get a cab at the station we had a long tramp partially lightened by a girl and a lad. My Saratoga trunk could have held all the books and was heavy enough but I could not sacrifice my book box.

SUNDAY 23 SEPTEMBER 1894

No church for anyone. Mrs Petherick fears Kunze [the German maid] has spent my 5/- [tip] in paste ear rings which she forbade her wearing in house as she had forbidden coral earrings before[.] Kunze's Sunday out results in her giving notice to leave at end of month.

I read great part of Mr Petherick's account of *Navigators* written for *Melb[ourne] Review* and he read nearly all that was not published when the *Review* ceased to exist.

The household is rather sad especially as there is a difference of opinion between Mr and Mrs Petherick as to the possibility of saving the books. She thinks they must go and that he is no more unfortunate than other men who lose all by bankruptcy. He feels the books a sort of public trust and that their being dispersed by forced sale would be a public misfortune.

MONDAY 24 SEPTEMBER 1894

Mrs Petherick not well enough to go to West End about her dress very much disquieted about the manner her husband is set on keeping his books. His co-executor trustee will not advance a penny on them – I got through a great deal of correspondence in the way of farewells – ... I wrote letter to Smith Elder & Co to go with *Gathered In*, but had little or no hope – Also got a paragraph composed to go with my press letters about ... [? Mr. Petherick and] how helping him to keep on with his [collection] ... of books to Australia. He himself is leaving no stone unturned to save his books writing to all friends.

Kunze gave notice she wants to go home to Germany – Beatrice and Ada put some braid on my Edin dress.

Tuesday 25 September 1894
Farewell to England and my friends.

Mrs Petherick was so good as to accompany me to Dover and see me on board the boat. A heavy sky dull and gloomy. I talked with a French governess telegraphed for to Geneva on acct of her father's dangerous illness but as she went via Paris we separated at Calais – No Cook's agent visible. I was put into a ladies carriage which I had to myself all the way to Bâle. Rain and clouds the scenery not to compare with that in England flat and not so fertile – but I must recollect that the day was gloomy – I ate my provisions and knitted a little – I had nothing to read – Night closed early and I could see no moon. Memories of friends and anxieties about them especially the Pethericks filled my mind.

Wednesday 26 September 1894
Amused at an old lady at Bâle who said she had been 44 yrs in America and felt strange with her mother tongue who nevertheless would talk to me only in voluble German – No Cooks appear to live at Bâle or anywhere else.

Daylight stole in among the Swiss lakes and mountains and a glowing sunshine delighted my eye – At Bâle had to wait and having got coffee and rolls telegraphed to Burkli [Karl Bürkli (1823–1909), Swiss social thinker and journalist] got into carriage with four Germans arrived at 10.10. Burkli met me, took me to Lummalhoff and talked for two hours leaving me some pamphlets – I dined at Table d'hôte – at 3 Burkli came again I had got my book with questions. He could not answer all – {What follows, here, is a short-hand account of different systems of proportional representation} He is agst Swiss List and against Hagerlach Bischoff's cumulation and against d Honde [?] and in favour of the saigh trans role of Hacs [?]. But he has an exaggerated idea of the value of the Ins. and Ref. even if pro rep had its best expression. He would reduce the rep. body to insignificance – He took me to Arbett riding [?]. Grenlech and I shall go tomorrow to the bureau and talk to him and Mlichli – he has been in America and speaks English well {then repeats story in first sentence of this entry} Got chambermaid to do my hair – I walked by the Lakes with Burkli and F Wihlle [?] 83 – who translated [J.S.] Mills Rep. Govt [*Considerations on Representative Government*, 1860] into German in the sixties – but too old to do much now though this earliest adv. of Hare system – he is rich, a conservative.

Thursday 27 September 1894
Tyrroll

I went to the Arbeiten Halle with my questions and Muggli answered some but after all was done he recommended me to see a pamphlet on the In. and Rel. bringing the matter down to end of 1893 – which Cridge can get a friend to translate – I felt the day rather long after this morning talk – Went to seek the public lib[rar]y but could not find it – so sat at home in my room with the big french book of pro rep of 1888 – in which I learn something but not down to date – not what Cridge wants to know – Zurich is a manufacturing and commercial town of 130,000 ... Chief industry silk and cotton not watches ... [then something about taxation being so high it drives away wealthy residents].

Friday 28 September 1894
My bill at the Lummalhoff for the two days was only F13 little over 10/- but it cost something for luggage ... porter and straps which tore on the way. A beautiful journey, deal of it tunnel but when out of tunnels what magnificent prospects – I noted about 170 houses along the line marked telephone – these are homes of the line keepers – There is much spent in Europe for the sanctity of human life which is saved by the conferences in Chicago – After ... the greatest tunnel ... I noticed the enormous number of chalets which did not seem fit for human habitation on the sides of the hills. And besides how could these bare hills support so many. I was told by Mr F. that these chalets are filled with hay for winter stock ... The cheese making is cooperative, each cows milked [sic] is weighed and credited – this is the most important domestic industry of Switzerland – I had to wait over two hours at Lugarno station for the Flurscheims and was glad to meet Madame's father who could speak a little English – Mrs Flurscheim was taken ill in the train and was suffering much – no carriage at the station went on ... to hotel and got carriage there. She was carried by her husband and maid downstairs to her room to bed.

Saturday 29 September 1894
Lugarno

Never was such a quaint old villa. My room belongs to another house and M[ichael] F[lurscheim] must go through it to his study to which I was introduced at once – Wrote to John and to Katie Martin. Walked to Lugarno with Herr M.F. and back and felt very tired – Mrs Flurscheim invisible must lay up completely. I was told what was the matter and fear her condition is very critical – the loss of her oldest daughter 3½ years ago has never been overgot [sic] and though her husband takes comfort in spiritism she won't believe it –

Both are Jews by birth and breeding but are more like Unitarians – What M.F. says about the pharisaism of the orthodox Jews the immense majority is most surprising. This he says drives young men to Atheism.

Sunday 30 September 1894
A quiet day. I wrote a long letter to Cridge and sent him the two German pamphlets ... I fear much he will be dissatisfied with what I can say about all these things ... In evg M.F. began reading me from his own book the chapter on the Currency question with his ideas as to a merchand [?] bank – Mrs Flurscheim had her doctor and a visit from her mother today so she could not have the excitement of seeing me added but delayed till tomorrow.

Monday 1 October 1894
I made a good beginning to a letter to the Sydney *Telegraph* dating the first part London next Zurich then Lugarno. Must wait letter from Katie Martin before I decided on anything.

Tuesday 2 October 1894
I finished so far my letter to the *Telegraph* and wrote to Mrs Petherick ... I was twice for a considerable time in Mrs Flurscheims room and introduced her to Mrs Stetson's poems. She asked her husband to translate 'A Hope' and 'A Conservative'. He did the first but was not quite pleased with it and thought the other too difficult ... After supper I read to M.F. my Shakespeare Bacon lecture which I had mentioned in the course of the day – and it made a great impression on him. He was particularly struck with the repetition of the incorrect quotation from ... Young men do not like to learn moral philosophy – for Young men will not study political philsophy.

Wednesday 3 October 1894
Got a postal from K. Martin which I answered – I have made up my mind to stay here till Mr Flurscheim goes which will be Tuesday or Wednesday. I grudge staying longer from her, but I think Lugarno and M.F. can teach me much.

Mrs F. up on the sofa a frail delicate creature – little taller than myself, but very much thinner.

I had two runs to Lugarno one in mg – and one in afternoon to pay a call on Madame Gesthel but we missed the cable car and it was a great climb to the hotel she has chosen. Found the old lady playing patience on her lap – Felt tired and my cold was worse and I could not hook my skirt that I had done three weeks ago so was depressed. Fell asleep for the first time over the Chapter on Socialism.

THURSDAY 4 OCTOBER 1894

Eighteen months today since I left Adelaide and it will be two more months ere I return – I wrote to Mrs Henry George and Mr Flurscheim added a short letter to her husband – but I made a poor day's work of it – took a little walk from the town with M.F. and had more talk about rent and interest. Mrs Geotlich and maid came in afternoon. To me her life is sad – for she cannot rest, read or work, and her maid is her companion. Mrs Flurscheim was carried down stairs and lay on a lounge in the garden for hours. She sat up for dinner. Finished my ball of cotton and Fiorine held the skeins for me to wind in Madame's room. We finished the chapter on Socialism and it concluded with an excellent application of Beatrice Potter Webb's conclusions at … the Cooperative movement that it was not to the transcendent genius of a few but to the general fair intelligence of the many that the success of the movement is due. Given hope for the future.

FRIDAY 5 OCTOBER 1894

I had discovered that there was a bath in the house so I had a delicious cold bath in the mg – which did me good. Had slept badly but I think that was because I had taken no Balsam of Aniseed – as I coughed little – M.F. is disposed to go with proportional representation and translated Hegenbach's pamphlet and part of Burkli's to me which shows that H-B has changed from the cumulated 22 votes to one vote for one man transferable only within the list showing no preference –

I sat too long listening and felt sickish when I went to bed – Slept little. Had two attacks of sickness 11 – and 5 – and then diarrhoea.

SATURDAY 6 OCTOBER 1894

Half dressed and had my hair done – but did not go down stairs till dinner time, when I asked for brandy and water – No I had it earlier – All the blame was put on the cold bath and not to eating too much duck – I had a letter from Ernest Naville so far satisfactory.

Dies non for work [no work done today].

SUNDAY 7 OCTOBER 1894

I made a good day's work writing to Cridge on M.F.'s typewriter which is pleasant but weak in the e's –

We went over what M.F. had written in English of his introductory chapter in the afternoon … In evg tell it not in Gath ['Tell it not in Gath, publish it not in the streets of Askelos, lest the daughters of the Philistines rejoice, lest the daughters of the uncircumcised triumph', Second Book of Samuel, ch.1, verse 20, King James' *Bible*] I played Bezique with Madame F.

who was able to sit up till 8.30 M.F. read in German the mother in law by George Sims Dagonet [George Robert Sims, *Dagonet Ballads*] – and laughed considerably –

I see in the little front garden two loquat trees coming into flower and the Mexican agare or aloe ... He calls the loquat some unknown name japonica as coming from Japan.

Monday 8 October 1894

I need not speak about a cold bath now. It was a gloriously fine day. I wrote to Katie fixing Thursday up for meeting. Wrote to Burkli and to Cooley ... I regret to say I put Flurscheim's typewriter out of gear working it when it should have been turned – At one o clock a carriage came for Mrs Flurscheim to take her to Lugarno and she was so much the better for her bath with salt from Salsa Maggiore, yellow with iodine, in it that she enjoyed the drive and the shopping ... but shopping takes a long time in Lugarno. We had a good tea at the bakers and we got some biscuits for me to carry – M.F. sends $10 to Cridge for the Cause –

Tuesday 9 October 1894

I began a letter to Ellen Gregory to be finished at Siena also one for the *Register* – Little we know what is before us or that nearly a fortnight will elapse before I saw them [the letters] again – ...

Wednesday 10 October 1894

... Mr and Mrs Flurscheim took me in the boat to Lugarno and said goodbye. It was perfect weather
{boat, the narrow gauge train to Bellagio ...} ... bought a N[ew] Y[ork] Herald with O.W. Holmes ... {along Lake Como, took omnibus to station} ... got all my luggage in carriage to Milan – Had three hours there from 5.20 to 8.40 – took train, went to Duomo, walked three times round it in the evening light its vastness and its elaborate ornamentation as well as its noble proportions strikes one with wonder and awe – but yet to me it seems as if the great wealth of the middle ages was poured out like water in building fanes [flags or weather-cocks] of fruitless prayers ... Could not get my blk [black] box in carriage with me booked it ... Before I reached Milan I found I had lost my purse and as I had fallen asleep I could not tell how it had gone but thought one of the three who departed had taken it. Getting out ... I told my keeper that I had lost my purse. He lighted a match and looked for it.

Thursday 11 October 1894

{Disaster about lost purse because had in it ticket for black box. Chef de gare at Pisa could do nothing. Made to change trains, + shut in, in night.}
Glad to see Fred M[artin] at station and he and I gave information but a mistake was made in saying I had come from Lugarno – ...

But after this exciting night I was glad to reach 12 Passeggio dAfla Lizza [?] and have a civilised breakfast – ...

Katie looks more lined in the face and she has been far from well but it is a delight to see her again.

We started with the book *A Born Egotist* [see above An Introduction, and below 12 October 1894] and between us we managed to get through nearly half of it. I do not think it has so attractive a beginning as either of her others but Fred thinks it is the best work she has ever done. Never before has he entered into her work – He has copied so much of it. When I reached them I found that they had received many letters for me – J.B.S. [John Brodie Spence] C.W.W. [Charles Wren] E.B.W. [Eleanor Wren] E.L.G. [Ellen Gregory] Miss [Caroline Emily] Clark Mrs [Edith] Hubbe

Friday 12 October 1894

I found I had to write any letters for Australia this day because Siena is off the direct route. I wrote a PC to Flurscheim telling of safe arrival of self, but nothing about box. I did mention that a box had been left in my letter to John in case it was really gone + prepare them for it.

We had dinner this day and yesterday sent in – cheap enough but not very hot. I am to pay 5 lire a week for room and sitting room – 3/9 – high bed and hard pillows but a large airy sitting room with hard couch, three chairs, chest of drawers stand for hanging clothes – They gave me the use of their sitting room for nothing – I could not be more cheerfully served –

After reading aloud part of *The Born Egotist* I seized the MS for myself and read it by myself – The end is very strong and there is some prospect of happiness for Margaret at the last though it is but a distant glimpse – The whole plot turns on a spiteful lie which is rather a pity told by a country town gossip – But the plot is new of the ... of bigamy – on the part of the innocent bigamist.

I do not find it as interesting as either of the other two but then I was tired and agitated and perhaps did not do it justice [this novel, also referred to as *The Born Optimist* was rejected by Bentley: it was not published as a book; if it was serialised, the serial has not been found; and the manuscript has been lost].

Saturday 13 October 1894

I had promised to write to Mrs Ames and I did so keeping out King Charles Head [a subject which occurs in every utterance because the speaker is obsessed about it] which at present is not pro rep but my missing box.

We went to a trattoria in town and had soup good with a sort of macaroni stuffed slightly with sausage looking a little too like oysters – veal and potatoes with a goblet of wine plenty of bread for one lire each –

Fred was making the corrections and finishing touches to *A Born Optimist* it was to be sent off tomorrow Sunday.

Sunday 14 October 1894

Katie went to service at the little church leaving me and Fred writing letters.

I wrote to Mrs Sanger the first decent letter I sent her since I left America.

We played whist in the evg. I am getting painfully anxious about my box ...

Monday 15 October 1894

After waiting four days we heard that an answer had come that the box had been asked for in the usual way and I gave up in despair – and wrote a letter to Flurscheim on the subject.

But afterwards Fred ... noticed that the enquiry had been sent to Lugarno so we again put in an enquiry about a black japanned box with two leather straps and such and such contents which had been booked from Milan to Siena so as there was still a gleam of hope. I retained the letter to F – ...

Tuesday 16 October 1894

In the morning Katie took me to see the Franciscan church the Cathedral being closed for repairs and in the afternoon as we could not get an omnibus – we had a drive of an hour for two lire to see the country. as I am showing myself a very poor walker. I watch the close cultivation coming up to the very walls of the town which cannot expand – It had been more populous when ... fought with Florence, the gate towards Florence being far stronger and more fortified than over that towards Rome ... There are however new houses being built outside of the walls ...

Wednesday 17 October 1894

I paid my board which with rent £5 l[ire]17.65 very little indeed.

We went to the church of the Franceci ...

THURSDAY 18 OCTOBER 1894
I began a letter for the *Register* but did not please myself much.

We got into the Cathedral at three oclock and I was amazed at the enormous expenditure of labour, money, and invention and ingenuity on this lofty vast structure. I think the repairs going on show how very light the walls are ... – the pillars of – [sic] are the most massive I ever saw [presumably the duomo in Siena. This is one of Italy's great Gothic churches with a façade of white, green and red polychrome marble]...

FRIDAY 19 OCTOBER 1894
As nothing has been heard from police after 4 more days felt I must make a clean breast about the lost box and wrote to John and also finished letter to Flurscheim. Fred told me at breakfast time that he has made up his mind to go by the first German boat to leave Genoa on 5th Novr and I settled to go with him. Katie cannot hear from Bentley for nearly a month as to terms and then the proofs may take months more – besides she may want to visit her brothers in West Australia so she is to be left behind in Florence. She thinks it best. It is not at all on my account though it suits me to have him to take care of me – Passage money only £30 expenses at ports may be 40 l or £5 – I shall draw £35 and only spend what I have in hand ere I go. The very worst part of the loss of my box was that I had to write about it and after all the next day brought tidings.

SATURDAY 20 OCTOBER 1894
Fred was surprised to receive a note from the chief of police ... after our dinner at the trattoria Katie went home. Fred went to fetch Signora Quasine to act as interpreter and we three went to the officer –

And joyful to tell the box had been heard of ... We identified the box sufficiently for the police to order it to be forwarded to Siena.

SUNDAY 21 OCTOBER 1894
Joy – I got my box all right at 11.15 – and charges were moderate – Katie rejoiced with me on the value of the recovered property – We had a drive for the afternoon out of the San Marco gate and back by the Porta Cannolio ... Siena is wonderfully rich in its ... of Sacred Art and though I don't like such a surfeit of it, it is interesting to trace its development –

MONDAY 22 OCTOBER 1894
A beautiful drive in the afternoon to a plain barn-like church, but full of wonderful ... frescoes ... and Luca De Robbias [Luca della Robbia (1400–1482) sculptor of Firenze] ...

Katie took me to the picture gallery and showed me the history of art as shown in the gradual rise from barbarian Byzantium with no anatomy with a wooden Madonna and a mature looking infant to the lovely skill of ... {indecipherable description of paintings}.

TUESDAY 23 OCTOBER 1894

We left F.M. writing and went to the Town Hall which has all the more importance because Siena was an independent republic and the walled city was a political centre [the Palazzo Pubblico, also known as the Palazzo Comunale, has a graceful bell tower 102 metres high and a characteristic Sienese-Gothic arcade housing the Museo Civico, based on a series of rooms with frescoes by artists of the Sienese school]. There are many fine frescoes – and a chapel with beautiful iron work and pictures by Godoma [?] – ... One room interested me as it was modern history dating from the freeing of Italy ... won by Victor Emanuel at the victory of San Martini ...

In afternoon K. + F. packed up putting books in my tin box and my dresses etc in their dress hamper. F. took the heavy goods to the station but could not get them despatched that night.

WEDNESDAY 24 OCTOBER 1894

A day's journey. Fred went to get the heavy goods booked for Firenze before breakfast and we were rather rushed at the last – A lovely day and I tried to understand how agricultural Tuscany maintained 273 to square mile ... {about Tuscan economy. Have to import coal. No trees.}

THURSDAY 25 OCTOBER 1894

Florence – We liked our rooms very much. We went to Post Office. F.M. got his money from London and from the Dresden bank so he sent the passage money for both of us to Antwerp – K. and I went to the Uffizi gallery [Galleria degli Uffizi houses what was the Medici family's fabulous art collection, bequeathed to the city of Florence by the last of the Medicis, Anna Maria Ludovica, in 1737, on condition that it never leave the city] and stayed from 11 to 2 – leaving F. to write an article.

FRIDAY 26 OCTOBER 1894

All three of us hard at work with our correspondence ... We went to the Cloisters of Sante Croce where [there] are some very beautiful tombs but could not get inside it.

After drive at the Grotto we studied the sculptures Loggia de Lanzi – Fred had telegram from Antwerp re our passages to reply to and as we could not find the omnibus or train, Kate and I took a cab for 10 80 to the

San Miniato [al Monte] where there is such a lovely view of Florence mentioned in the prologue to Romola [George Eliot, *Romola*, 1863] – In the centre is a bronze of David taken from Michelangelo's original with figures round the base also copied from his works. I bought a pretty little watch ... We walked home from San Miniato.

SATURDAY 27 OCTOBER 1894
... We went to Fiesole per electric train winding round the foot of the hills growing beautiful vines – ... We had an hour and half to give to the Cathedral which is ancient and most interesting ... The Crypt is a remarkable feature in this Cathedral – and the marble reredos by Feruccia is a fine work of art ...

K and I went to the church of S Marco in mg church plain. It is the cloisters that are remarkable for Fra Angelico's work –

SUNDAY 28 OCTOBER 1894
I began tentative letter for *Telegraph* while Katie went to do a little shopping. We went to the Pitti palace [a palace built for the wealthy merchant Pitti family, rivals of the Medici, but acquired by the Medici in the sixteenth century and expanded. It houses four museums and its collection includes works by the artists Raphael, Fillippo Lippi, Tintoretto, Veronese and Rubens] to look through the galleries – ...

Portraits of contemporaries are to me more interesting than the endless sacred subjects ...

MONDAY 29 OCTOBER 1894
F.M. went in mg and afternoon after the heavy luggage without any success. K.M. and I wrote to Miss Bulow in mg and I scribbled some more ... venture pages for *Telegraph*.

We met Fred at the Porta Romano and took steam train to Certosa very slow such long stoppages – A wonderful old monastery on top of a hill Carthusians ...

Fountain or well by Michelangelo

Sculptures by Donatello ...

TUESDAY 30 OCTOBER 1894
Joy – Fred found the boxes had been three days at the station but on a train that had never been unloaded ... – Katie had a relapse, perhaps did too much yesterday at Certora, and was sick and her head and back ached badly – She however could do a little in separating goods and chattels – We gave out our washing in faith –

I wrote a little for *Telegraph* – and felt very heartless over it as Katie felt so ill – Fred and I went alone to Grotto and indulged in a sumptuous meal not knowing we were to have a set dinner with courses at Mr Lontessa's. We looked in at the Duomo. I bought gloves a ... and a purse and Fred saved me about 5 lire. I felt a little mean over the chaffering [bargaining].

Katie was better, but thought we should be all the better for a cup of tea which was nice. A pleasant evg with Italians. La contessa is the daughter of a conti and the widow of a conti who was syndico of Pracenza [?] ... Fred had three games of chess with the Contessa and won two – one of them was scholar's mate which was new to him ...

Wednesday 31 October 1894
My 69th birthday.

Went to Santo Maria Novello and saw the Cloisters and the Spanish chapel which Ruskin considers the finest thing of the kind in the world ...

Thursday 1 November 1894
Wrote hard in the mg at the beginning of a letter for America ... Went to the Camp Santi by steam train at San Minati and as it is All Saints day All Hallows – there were hundreds of people carrying wreaths to place on graves –

... Worship was going on in one church which K. and I went into before San Croce – She said it would have done her good if I had not been with her, for my critical temper spoils it even if I did not say a word – I got my Adelaide letters and two newspapers and a lot of pro rep *Revs* – with articles by Naville [Ernest Naville (1816–1909), Swiss writer and lecturer on philosophy, religion, politics, morals and modern physics; advocate of proportional representation] and Cridge – Slept very badly, feel anxious about accomplishing all that lies before me – Changed my watch probably it was because I could not wind it up properly but the pretty little one stopped. Can do nothing about another.

Friday 2 November 1894
San Croce

Finished my peradventure letter for America and got all my letters despatched. Fortunately I could acknowledge receipt of the last mail from Australia ...

Tried to play whist but late and tired – Katie would not promise to go to Pisa with us, Fred secured our two tickets.

Saturday 3 November 1894
Katie made up her mind to go with us to Pisa, the Contessa and her daughter saw us off at the hour to say goodbye – We walked to the Piazza del Duomo, did not go up the leaning tower but marvelled at the Baptistry so high so large with such magnificent carved pillars ...

SUNDAY 4 NOVEMBER 1894

... Went to San Lorenzo. High mass going on – ...

Home very tired but not too tired to sleep ... I wrote three pages to Katie before I succumbed to fatigue.

MONDAY 5 NOVEMBER 1894

Fred was told the ship wd sail at 3 and that we must be on board by 2 ...

{sightseeing} ... I find I have a lady with a cough ... a London board school head teacher going out to New Zealand for 18 months and a medical missionary lady from Utica, New York in my cabin – No idea of giving up berth to me – Cabin very crowded. I cannot get in a box. There are second class 36 at the table. Weather fine. Five lady missionaries from England ... Fred and I write [sic] to Katie. He posted a Baedekker to her. Genoa looks beautiful from the ship all lighted up the Samarenla [?] setting sun on the hills.

TUESDAY 6 NOVEMBER 1894

Was not conscious of sleeping at all but must have slept some. Miss Cuthbert coughed for hours. We seem to be sailing between Elba and Italy and could see the north shore of Corsica behind the little island on which the master of Europe was first confined – too near land and too near France for security. St Helena which I saw Jany 1855 [sic] was really remote and inaccessible for his friends –

I made acquaintance with Miss Benham of Kapunda who has had two years in Europe chiefly with an aunt in Germany whose husband is chaplain to the English legation in Vienna ... She came to perfect herself in the French and German languages and on the way to French Switzerland with a cousin, she stopped at Karlsruhe and the Egremonts entertained both for a week ... she gives a more cheerful acct of the Egremonts than their letters. I said I feared they had not enough to eat – She said at present that seemed to be sufficient – but Mrs E. said often there had been worse times –

I write [sic] a postcard to Mrs Sanger – and also made this ... the chief part of my letter to Katie – Fred covered 8 pages. His heart is pretty sore over this parting – ...

WEDNESDAY 7 NOVEMBER 1894

Naples Pompeii – We landed and went first to see the churches, names unknown ... We took train to Pompeii but by mistake one station short and had a long hot dirty walk after our 2½ mile tramp through Naples in mg – ... The size of the city is greater than I expected and at this distance from Rome how Roman it all is! – Pagan Rome – temples open to the light of day not with the dim religious light of the Cathedrals, where they teach light to counterfeit a gloom – The open air theatres for comedy and tragedy the latter far the larger – the marble fountains worn by the hand of the holders of the jars and the faces worn by the mouth of those who came to drink without any vessel ... But it was not the details that struck me so much it was the maimed but yet real reproduction of a city of the past with its life, its labour and its engagements, its superstitions and its worship. The slaves who did the drudgery did the [crying?] ... How much and how little did they venerate the gods who were the subjects of this art most frequently the least godlike of the epistle? ... {more questions}

Oh for a cyclopedia to answer questions about dates!

Thursday 8 November 1894

Quiet day – cannot do more than copy over more pencilled diary a great deception for it takes more time to decipher the faint and rubbed marks than to write afresh ... [this refers to the portion of the diary immediately after Catherine Spence's accident in London, when she wrote in pencil.]

Friday 9 November 1894

Friday was really a very lazy day. I cannot record anything happening at all.

Saturday 10 November 1894

The sea rougher than before. Fred Martin was sick and I was a little afraid of myself – However I ate little and kept on deck and knitted a square and a half. I read a little of *Middlemarch* [George Eliot, *Middlemarch*, 1871–2] when Miss Benham felt too unwell to read it. F.M. and she got better in evg and we began whist after 8. F. + I got beaten but not desperately. Mr McMartin will introduce me to my cousin William Brodie of Colombo whom he knows well.

Sunday 11 November 1894

Began the day with *The Raiders* the first volume of which Mr McMartin had finished ... {wrote to Katie ...}

... Expected to reach Port Said by 6.30, dinner to be hurried –

I did not land chiefly because Fred did not care to do so ...

Monday 12 November 1894

In the Suez canal – Although one of the greatest works of modern engineering it is not an imposing sight – low land banks and an arid plain and here and there a station and a little greenery round it.

Arabs seem to keep up with the ship for the sake of pennies thrown by the passengers for which they dive when the water not too deep ...

I think I finished *The Raiders* this day. I liked it better than on first reading...

Tuesday 13 November 1894
...I knitted a square. I read some of *The Raiders* and some of *Suspected* which is trash –...

Wednesday 14 November 1894
Head wind and cross sea and very hot – Fred had his second and worse attack of sea sickness...

Thursday 15 November 1894
Poor Fred is still pretty bad...

Friday 16 November 1894
A tremendous sea came in at 6.30. I got least of it being high – our deck washed over by cross seas and great waves very frequently –

Terribly hot...

I wrote a short letter to Katie to add to Fred's – presumably written some days ago as he had collapsed, though he picked up today and spoke of landing at Aden if there was time – We had a bottle of beer together in evg over cribbage –... I read the *Marriage of Figaro* in French and 30 close pages of preface and postscript very interesting when we consider it was brought out on the eve of the French Revolution [*Le marriage de Figaro*, 1778, by Pierre-Augustin Caron de Beaumarchais (1732–99), dramatist and publicist; the libretto for Mozart's comic opera, *The Marriage of Figaro*, first performed in Italian in Vienna in 1786 is by L. da Ponte based on Beaumarchais's work.]

Saturday 17 November 1894
Cold wine soup for lunch –

We reached Aden before ten and were said to sail at one – not time to go either to the town 5 miles off or to the tanks a little further but I wanted in a faint degree to see the port so I got down the ladder but felt nervous when I saw the boat rocking and returned and read *Maum Dadche* [?] instead...

Sunday 18 November 1894
Read an Adelaide *Chronicle* of 29th Sept lent me by Miss Benham – Gave Mr McMartin my River House Report to read and return –

Fred is well today...

I borrowed *Middlemarch* which Miss Benham has done with. It is good to read over and over again.

MONDAY 19 NOVEMBER 1894
I read a very good French drama by Jean Richelieu *Pas la Glace* [?] in heroic verse – ... I also knitted – ...

TUESDAY 20 NOVEMBER 1894
[no entry]

WEDNESDAY 21 NOVEMBER 1894
[no entry]

THURSDAY 22 NOVEMBER 1894
...

FRIDAY 23 NOVEMBER 1894
...

SATURDAY 24 NOVEMBER 1894
We were due at Colombo today but owing to adverse weather we are a day behind – I got out my box and took out of it my lace cloak and from Fred's box my <u>walking silk skirt</u> for Candy ...

SUNDAY 25 NOVEMBER 1894
We had a favourable day for Colombo ...
　　{Went & had tea – went shopping}
　　... I bought 10 of tussore silk for two blouses for 8/- to give away. {Fred in search of two deck chairs. On advice went to shop at some distance ...}
　　... F. left me at the landing for an hour and I watched the tide of people with interest – It is evident this is the land of black and brown folks – Not one white person in thirty passed to and fro – I was asked to buy many things from postage stamps to a monkey – but I was satisfied with spending two sovereigns exchange R17.75 for all my experience at Colombo – Fred returned in triumph with two chairs, one for me and one to go into the hold – We got on board by 4 ...

MONDAY 26 NOVEMBER 1894
A thoroughly wretched day – hot steamy – with very heavy rain ... and the sea washing over the decks, port holes shut.

TUESDAY 27 NOVEMBER 1894
Quite a tolerable day ... Two Indian jugglers gave an exhibition of their skills ... on one deck but 1st & 3rd class looked on across the rails ... Mr Perrell took out and unpacked a new typewriter which he and his [wife? sister?] wants [sic] to learn on board. F.M. and I dissuaded him as it might hurt the instrument which is a Remington with latest improvements but he thought it would save duty if it was in use ere it was landed.

WEDNESDAY 28 NOVEMBER 1894
Miserable day hot and rolling with very heavy rains at short intervals – Ports closed close and muggy –
 I discovered that my new chair is a lounge and that knitting in it makes my arm ache as it has not done for many weeks – I finished *Middlemarch* and regret that it is done –

THURSDAY 29 NOVEMBER 1894
Pretty rough all day ... Fred and Miss Benham sick. Fred not even able to play whist in evg.

FRIDAY 30 NOVEMBER 1894
[no entry]

SATURDAY 1 DECEMBER 1894
[no entry]

SUNDAY 2 DECEMBER 1894
I thought *Sartor Resartus* [Thomas Carlyle (1795–1881) philosopher, critic and historian. *Sartor Resartus (The Life and Opinions of Herr Teufelsdröckh)*, 1836] was good Sunday reading – ...

MONDAY 3 DECEMBER 1894
Read Investors Review Sept – A I Wilson ... {about her reading}

TUESDAY 4 DECEMBER 894
Nobody had been able to sleep with the rolling and pitching ... F. Martin pretty sick – and Miss Benham ...

WEDNESDAY 5 DECEMBER 1894
After a night of tremendous seas dashing over the ship it calmed so that the deck was pretty dry. I felt a little cold so Fred brought me my large cloak – I finished Florence Marryatt's book a *Crown of Shame* [Florence Marryat,

later Church, later Lean (1837–1899), English sensation novelist, editor of the magazine *London Society*, author of 57 novels including *The Crown of Shame* (F.V. White & Co.), London, 1888. She was the youngest of the eleven children of Frederick Marryat, author of *Children of the New Forest*, 1847; married in 1854, divorced in 1878, remarried in 1879, and mother of eight] before lunch and did a little knitting; F.M. busy with his anarchists – He was sick in mg and so was his chum Johannes only 222 miles gone in 24 hours –

Thursday 6 December 1894
rough.

This stormy weather is rather trying –

Finished my book and read 1st vol. of Herr Paulus also Mazzini on the minor works of Dante considered biographically [Guiseppe Mazzini (1805–72), Italian nationalist and patriot, one of the patron saints of the Italian *Risorgimento*; his *Works* were published in English, six volumes, in 1890–1] – I <u>ought</u> to make a study of Dante – when I can find the time.

{whist}

Friday 7 December 1894
rough.

F.M. poorly in morning but pulled himself together barely to grapple with the anarchists [Fred Martin wrote a number of studies of anarchists in Europe] –...

Saturday 8 December 1894
... Anniversary of my mother's death 1877 [sic]

We passed Cape Lewin [sic] at 4 this mg and made 276 miles in 24 hours. We saw the low shores of Western Australia on the left – F. M. worked up Mr Boëttchers [?] information to his satisfaction and is promised a pair of old ruined [rimmed?] spectacles for his trouble ... The rumour goes that Miss Schrusrsden [?] is engaged to a young spectacled German called Kirklisch and a great deal of chaff has been flying around on that head – There was an afternoon tea and he slipped hold of the teapot. I got a cup of tea and all the leaves in my lap and the pot was broken ...

Sunday 9 December 1894
... Finished *The Manxman* [Sir Thomas Henry Hall Caine (1853–1931), author of *The Manxman* (Heinemann), London, 1894] which is really a strong book and the conclusion is beautiful.

Monday 10 December 1894
This was the evg fixed for our concert ...

Tuesday 11 December 1894
For the first and only time in this long voyage I was seasick over packing my boxes just after lunch with a heavy sea on – It was hot and oppressive and when we landed we heard of the extraordinary heat of later Novr and Decr –

This broke a splendid record – all the passengers on the qui vive about landing, which alas none could do but the Adelaide folks and the Pursells who went to visit friends at the Semaphore –

Wednesday 12 December 1894
Land – Kangaroo Island – visible when we got up – Hopes of landing at 7 pm but the capt will not stay long enough to make it worth while for the other passengers to land –

A restless day –

John missed the first boat which brought the health officer – but Mr Botten [?] was greeted and embraced by many middle-aged and elderly Germans and I was accosted by an interviewer from *Register*, with whom I was engaged when John arrived –

I had scarce finished with him when an Aberdeen man came up but I could not stay on the ship for him – Said goodby with regret to fellow passengers. Got my goods passed by the customs and we went together by second boat had to wait a while at Largs: found Mrs Hood and three children had been waiting at Adelaide station from 7 o clock could not stay to speak but hoped to catch 10.30 train. Roland Kelsey jumped into our cab in hopes of our missing the Bay train which we did so he interviewed me for *Advertiser* at station. Found ... and Lucie [Morice] at station. Warm welcome –

Thursday 13 December 1894
As my house has been let for three more months at £5 a month I must stay at Glenelg [in her brother's houshold] for three weeks and Miss Gregory, who arrived here today and who came down in the evg to bring me the latest news of the Wrens is going to stay at the Williams's till we can take possession of Eildon. I heard a worse piece of news and that is that Moncrieff has bought a new house in Marlboro St and has given his three months notice – pays rent up to 1 Feby but will leave before Xmas –

I have now to confront the financial situation.

Mean time it is pleasant enough to be here and feel that for the present I am spending little or nothing – Mrs Watson gave Coz [Ellen Gregory] nothing for her services –

Lucy [Morice] here with her boy who is a beautiful and charming child.

There was not only the ? col of interview by *Register* but my last letter from Siena which however had appeared in the *Observer* of the 1 Dec – so John was authorised to get 2 doz and send to friends.

Friday 14 December 1894
Very hot.

Jessie [Spence, wife of John Brodie Spence, see Appendix A, Family Tree] had a woman in who washed all my clothes – I borrowed some from her to wear.

Florence Kay and Maggie [members of the Unitarian Christian Church of Adelaide] came down to call in spite of the heat. I am sure they are glad to see me back but they are curiously unsympathetic about my work –

The Mouldens came later to see me ... – I went to call on Mrs Martin [Fred Martin's mother] and found her looking well but very deaf. Mrs Birks [Rose Birks, née Thomas, daughter of William Kyffin Thomas, granddaughter of Robert Thomas founder of the first newspaper in the colony, married Charles Birks when his first wife, her older sister, died, leaving six children. She and Charles Birks must have been among the early beneficiaries of South Australian legislation eliminating the prohibition on marriage between a widower and his deceased wife's sister. Rose Birks joined the ladies' division of the Society for the Promotion of Social Purity when it was formed in 1882, a group which continued to meet even after the goal of the society had been achieved. This group became the core of the Woman Suffrage League in South Australia when it was formed in 1888, and Rose Birks was immediately made its honorary treasurer, a position that she held for the following six years. She was also a member of the Young Women's Christian Association and became its president] came to my brothers to see me and followed me to the Martin's – She wanted me to do what I could to aid the passage of the Womans Suffrage Bill especially to interview Mr Hawker [either Edward or George Hawker. George Hawker (1818–95), land-owner and member of the House of Assembly in the South Australian parliament 1858–65, and 1875–95; he served as treasurer, chief secretary, commissioner of public works, and was speaker from 1860; on 23 August 1894, while the third reading of the Women's Suffrage Bill was under way in the Legislative Council, George Hawker presented to the House of Assembly a petition in favour of votes for women carrying more than 11,000 signatures. His son, Edward, however, was also a member of parliament, was more conservative and always voted against policies proposed by the Premier, Charles Cameron Kingston], Mr Castine [Major Castine, who paired for the vote on the second reading, meaning that his vote didn't count], Mr Ash [George Ash, who also paired for the second reading vote in the House of Assembly] and Mr Howe [the Hon. James H. Howe, a conservative country member of parliament, but a supporter of women's suffrage].

She proposed there should be a welcoming meeting for me on Monday at which I should speak in order to show we are in concert about the reform. I said I should be there and promised I would help as far as possible. So she telephoned to Mr [Cornelius] Proud [a sharebroker, but also a strong supporter of the United Labor Party in South Australia, and of women's suffrage] who advertised the meeting but left the place for Monday's papers – Mrs Birks thinks I have come back in the nick of time.

Saturday 15 December 1894
I said there was a Vancouver Island post and I had addressed papers to K. Musson and Mr Cridge when William Beare came in before he caught his train – I believe it was really the S[an] F[rancisco] mail but I could not see it in the paper at all but there is none recd [?] till the 17th Jany.

I find the promises I made rather onerous about the M.Ps.

Sunday 16 December 1894
I wrote a letter to Mr Brient of the *Telegraph* [L.J. Brient, editor of the Sydney *Daily Telegraph* who was also a member of the Womanhood Suffrage League of New South Wales] announcing my return and asking for payment. Also requesting some opening on the paper for social and literary papers –

Monday 17 December 1894
A pretty big day. First I went to the B[oarding] O[ut] Committee meeting and met all. Mrs [Julia] Farr Miss Honart, Miss Baker, Mrs Furley and Miss [Caroline Emily] Clark – grand question whether Xmas cards should be accepted for … their funds with. Their label on the back of it – That was negatived – … Went to talk to Mrs Hood, met Dr Cockburn [Minister of Education and Agriculture] in street who asked me to go to the House at 2 – Had lunch at Beach's with John. To House. John introduced me to Mr Hawker and I had a few words with him – I then went to Ladies Gallery and sat by Mrs Birks. Mr Caldwell [Robert Caldwell (1843–1909), member of the House of Assembly 1893–1902], Howe, Foster [Richard Witty Foster (1856–1932), member of the House of Assembly 1893–1902], Castine, Sir John Downer [(1843–1915), member of the House of Assembly 1878–1901, and Premier and Treasurer until swept from power by the 1893 elections], Jenkins [John Greeley Jenkins (1851–1923), member of the House of Assembly 1887–1902, 1902–5, Commissioner of Public Works 1894–9, subsequently Premier and Chief Secretary 1901–5], McPherson [John Abel McPherson

Mary Lee as seen by Quiz in 1895

(1860–1897), member of the House of Assembly 1892–7], Kingston [Charles Cameron Kingston (1850–1908) was a member of the House of Assembly 1881–1900, and Premier and Attorney General 1893–99], Charleston [D.M. Charleston, a labour supporter and strong supporter of Catherine Spence's campaign for effective voting was not in this parliament], Aspenal, Archibald [William Oliver Archibald (1850–1926) member of the House of Assembly 1893–1910], Giles [Clement Giles (1844–1926) member of the House of Assembly 1887–1902] and perhaps more spoke to me – Mrs Birks and Mrs [Elizabeth Webb] Nichols [President of the suffrage division of the Women's Christian Temperance Union] and Miss [Mary] George [salaried Corresponding Secretary of the Women's Christian Temperance Union, 1891–1903] and I went to Com meeting of W[oman] S[uffrage] L[eague] at 4. Mrs Mary Lee in great dudgeon because my welcome had been arranged outside of her – and she was not adv [advertised] as speaker because she had said she could not or would not go – Mrs Matters had been primed by her. I soothed her down and she consented to be present after all – We then

Elizabeth Webb Nicholls of the suffrage department of the Women's Christian Temperance Union of South Australia, photograph courtesy of the State Library of South Australia

returned to the house and heard a great deal of washy speaking against the bill – We had to go to Mrs Thomas's to snatch a meal and I had ten minutes to collect my thoughts and we went to the welcoming meeting which was well attended and most enthusiastic – It was not long and we adjourned to the House but I did not stay till the end especially as I was not very visible where I sat but returned to Mrs Thomas's to sleep. Mrs Birks stayed till three of our supporters went out and then Kingston [no, it was T.H. Brooker (1850–1927), member of the House of Assembly for West Torrens 1890–1902 and for Port Adelaide 1902–5, Minister for Education and Minister for Industry 1901–2] moved an adjournment which was carried to the disgust of the opponents until 10.30 next day. The arguments were of the old stock order – educated and refined women would not vote and did not want it – It might rain on polling day women don't like their age known – It would strengthen the city and suburbs as against the country. It would lead to dispeace [sic] in families. I[t] was a grave constitutional question and must not be passed without the referendum – Women were not always in health to vote, ... [?, the amendment was supported by Caldwell and Downer] + Downer amendment passed that 3 miles distance or a declaration as to the state of her health would entitle a woman to vote through the P.O. But she must go ... to the P.O. herself – that property was not woman's best qualification – that women generally did not want the vote and would not use it –

Tuesday 18 December 1894

It was well that I had begun my letters to K. Martin and to Mrs Petherick before I went to town on Monday – I went to Miss [Annie Montgomerie] Martin's breaking up [Miss Martin ran a school famed for being progressive] at 10 and was put in the class and made speech and gave the prizes and by passes and very many and valuable A.M.M. gives 5/- for each subject passed and the recipient chooses her own books so they made a goodly curry ... We stayed to hear the 'Ode on the death of the Duke of Wellington' very finely rendered and just missed the final debate & division [in the parliament]. Mrs Lee and Mrs Makolt [?] told of the victory 31 to 14 afterwards said to be 31 to 17. Mrs Birks stayed and saw the Bill through the Upper House and Miss Clark and I went to Glenelg by 12 tram – We had about half an hour to give to the Martins before we came home for lunch.

A very pleasant afternoon – Miss Clark is always delightful – She is however much disappointed that our Bill cannot be pushed through –

Still it can be taken up where it is left and will probably be carried early in the session –

Mrs Birks sent me a note with the final stage of the W.S. Bill.

I finished my letters and had them posted.

Wednesday 19 December 1894
hot and sultry

I wrote an article of 10 pages for Sydney *Telegraph* and hope it may suit and be paid for – The carrying of the Suffrage Bill seemed a topic likely to interest his readers –

Then went to town – saw Mrs Hood bought 12 papers, talked half an hour to Welsh. Out to Mrs Hartley's had lunch after her. She was off to the University celebration. Into Trinity St met Coz [Ellen Gregory] and Miss Bertie [?] returned from Eva's [?] marriage to Mr Darenburg – and saw the traps arriving for some man's wedding on the lawn. Also the drays taking away Mr Moncrieff's furniture to Marlborough St. An eventful day I just had 10 minutes or a q[uarte]r hour at Mrs Wyatts. Mary not back or likely to arrive back soon – things looking woefully dry. We asked Mr Moncrieff's permission to go and look at the marriage – Awfully hot for us and the guests no marquee or sheds – After it was over we went to Miss Williams's for tea which was good. Mrs Haren [?] arrived hot and dusty for celebration. I went to *Register* office but Mr Furlan [?] was at chair meeting [?] – so I told Mr Thomas half of what I felt. He thinks I shd have arranged with Am[erican] papers. They were not so amenable as he fancies – Looked in at Bottans [?] met Mrs Wright told her she should vote – to … house with Mrs Hood and had evg meal fruit and bread – they have all gone off meat. A friend made at Edward St whom they call Uncle Frank is good to the boys and Katie. He came later – I think the boys are a little too troublesome but Rose … [a] pretty good girl for 4 and though 13/- rent leaves little margin she grubs along – If Fernie [?] were to die she would get promotion. Children all well dressed and shod – …

Thursday 20 December 1894
Began article for *Arena* as suggested by Mr. Thomas –

Wrote letters and projected letters for the press.

Hot day – Louisa and Mary Myers came for dinner, Louisa looking well in a well fitting pretty salea [?] a present from Lille [?] who is earning some thing – Mary is changed for the better by new teeth, but for the worse by her draperies which I did not know of –

I heard a poor account of Laura Symon – perhaps a little exaggerated but she is evidently pretty selfish and ungrateful – Louisa corroborates what Nora Church told me of Fred Brothe getting money out of his mother when she was a poor speechless invalid – The egg money her poor eyes gloated over found its way into his pocket and many a fiver besides – I don't know how the Myles's live – It has been long a puzzle to many.

Friday 21 December 1894

It occurred to me that the W.S. business was an opening for America and England and I wrote to Mrs Birks for information –

Made a start with press work and took part of the *Arena* article for one of the tentative articles –

Mrs William Kay called on me alone – apologises for the girls Kate and Milly – Miss Martin called later looking well –

I had written to Mrs Birks to come but she had an engagement and sent for me in evg, and I went over and had a big talk about our educational propaganda. Mr Birks thinks Effective Voting is of far more value than Woman suffrage – I suggested that I should stir up the country again and he thought it might be carried on – I recited three of Mrs Stetsons poems and got an order for two copies – but it appears that Louie Galloway wants to catch the PM of Glenelg ... and I am going to ask for a P[ost] O[ffice] O[rder] when he has closed his books for the month.

Saturday 22 December 1894

Wrote another article longer, meant for America ...

Sunday 23 December 1894

Heavy rains. I address myself to press work in hopes of doing good and getting some payment.

I finished *The Heavenly Twins* [Sarah Grand, *The Heavenly Twins*, 1893, concerned with the socially evil effects of the double standard of sexual morality, including men's pre-marital sexual encounters, and of the repression of political awareness in a married woman] and on the whole like it, but I do not wonder at many disliking it: the subject is unpleasant –

Monday 24 December 1894

I wrote hard all day, at least the working day finishing up other things and writing a long letter for *Woman's Signal* – quite two columns I think – It was not finished when Louie took the packets [of] newspapers and letters to the post.

Harriet Cook and Mrs Hübbe came about 3 just before Mrs Spence went to town – They had called on the Martins and had previously left the children on the beach – I gave Harriet the little parcel for Eleanor – I heard a good deal of news from them –

John and Lucy left alone played a little cribbage – I longed for a little relief from the tension. Jessie came by a latish tram and the young folks later –

TUESDAY 25 DECEMBER 1894

Christmas day [as a Unitarian, Catherine Spence would not have paid any special attention to this Christian festival] – I wrote hard till about three o'clock to K. Musson, to Tyson and to Cridge. This makes in all 8 press letters despatched...

John took up my letters to town. Jessie went with him. The young folks walked home with Mr [husband of Lucy Spence Morice, niece of Catherine Spence] Morice and I read 'Ships that pass in the night' [a poem by Paul Laurence Dubar (1872–1906) a son of former slaves in the United States of America].

WEDNESDAY 26 DECEMBER 1894

Most disagreeable day oppressively hot and heavy rains – Wrote to Charlie [Wren] in answer to a letter recd in mg – also to Nina who lay heavy on my conscience – Did not write to W.R. Still too late for posting... Heavy rain all mg till near 3 but started for the 3 train to confront Mr Furlan [?] – Heard from the Martins he had gone off to Port Lincoln for a month so made my visit then and returned. F.M. says he hopes for ten days work for B.B.A. and means to knock off something for the *Age* – and if possible the *Telegraph* for submit – Letters from W.L. Garrison and A. Cook...

I went up with John to the B... lecture which I liked very much. Frewn was clear and pretty topical – Holder – Downer and CHS moved a vote of thanks – Miss Blanch [?] Wright, Mrs and Miss Duffield were the only ladies – Coz [Ellen Gregory] came down at 7 to ask if I would take the Williamses if they let their house furnished and I said I would – Letter from Katie [Martin] not satisfied with Bentley's terms.

THURSDAY 27 DECEMBER 1894

Sat down to write to Edyvean and Coz and to address some papers and next to tackle three weeks' diary.

I took a letter to Brient for F. Martin to... with his Anarchist article and asked Miss Martin to come for afternoon tea – There was the yearly picnic for the Incurables on the beach and Lucy, Elsie, Louie and Pat went down in hopes of seeing a friend of Jim's a man named Kelly...

Miss Martin and Jessie and I talked chiefly about *The Heavenly Twins* –

I read the *Decay of Lying* and another essay of Oscar Wilde's [Oscar Wilde (1854–1900), dramatist, essayist, poet, and wit]. Played cribbage with John –

Friday 28 December 1894
South Australia 58 years old. Finished up my diary, which is brought down to date – ...

Saturday 29 December 1894
Had a letter from Mrs Hartley asking me to dine there on Monday – also a letter from Eleanor [Wren] telling me of her day at Brighton Beach with Marjorie and Mrs Davies on Boxing Day – Meant to go to see Mrs Birks, but thought the house would be shut up –

Sunday 30 December 1894
Went to town for church and found locked doors for a short time – Small congregation on acct of holidays, but the average now is 100. Spoke to a few friends – No Hoods as there is no Sunday School for two Sundays ...

Monday 31 December 1894
... Went to call on Coz [Ellen Gregory][,] *Register* office Thomas told me they were sending me a cheque amount unknown – Had a talk with Mr Holden ... – then to College town. Coz going to the Bay with Bertie got from her the lists ... – Met Mrs Hood and Lewis Duval in Freds last – ...

Pleasant evg with Mrs Hartley and her husband – He has made a new edition of the primer with many pictures and more reading – ...

1 At Miss Williams to talk over things
2 Miss Clark went to Edy[vean's?]. Party at night
3 Storm stayed at Hazelwood – 4 town Bank cheques £125

Catherine Helen Spence's Letters

An Introduction

Two of Catherine Spence's many correspondents kept the letters that she had written to them, or at least some of them. Her letters to Alice Henry are held with the rest of Catherine Spence's papers in the South Australian Archives in Adelaide, and those to Rose Scott are in the Scott Papers in the Mitchell Library in Sydney. Since all of these letters were written during the first decade of the twentieth century – after her own section of *An Autobiography* ceases – they enlarge our understanding of the Grand Old Woman of Australasia, and our knowledge of her final ten years.

Catherine Spence encountered Alice Henry in 1893, when she was on her way through Melbourne to Sydney to embark for the United States of America. Australian-born of Scots parentage, a member of the Reverend Charles Strong's Australian Church formed as a breakaway from the Presbyterian Church of Melbourne, and – above all – an enthusiast for proportional representation, Miss Henry sought an introduction to Australia's chief advocate of effective voting, Miss Spence. In her turn, Catherine Spence took to this tall, handsome, white-haired woman, with brilliant eyes and a beautiful, firm, mellow speaking voice, a sister-journalist, thirty-two years her junior. The two had a great deal in common, as Alice Henry's biographer, Diane Kirkby, has pointed out.

> Neither was married; they shared a Scots ancestry; and each pursued a public writing and reforming career, occasionally publishing under her brother's name. Most importantly they saw their reform activities as work, not the benevolence of charity appropriate to ladies confined to the private sphere.

Moreover, among the feminists who formed a crucial element in their friendship networks, they shared a view that female sexual pleasure was an important aspect of the emancipation of women, a view that marked their feminist politics off from those of others such as Rose Scott, who regarded heterosexual intercourse as something to be avoided altogether. Both Miss Spence and Miss Henry joined Miss Scott, though, in their wholehearted antipathy to war in general, and the war between the Boers and the British in South Africa in particular.

Catherine Spence met Rose Scott in 1900 when she and Jeanne Young spent two months in Sydney campaigning for effective voting. It was the Attorney-General of New South Wales, Bernhard Ringrose Wise – considered the intellectual giant of Australian liberalism – who suggested the visit, so they were treated as honoured guests of the government. The premier, George Reid, presided over a meeting at Parliament House at which they explained proportional representation, and afterwards took them to tea. They were taken to visit the Parramatta Home for Women by government launch. They spoke at a public meeting urging women's suffrage, too, even though this was a cause that B.R. Wise opposed. As Jeanne Young reports in the twenty-second chapter of *An Autobiography*, they addressed between twenty and thirty public gatherings during those eight weeks. Rose Scott gave material assistance to their whole campaign by holding a reception for them at her house at exclusive Point Piper at the beginning of their stay, and inviting to it a number of influential public identities. Catherine Spence and Jeanne Young visited Rose Scott on other occasions, as well, forming a very specific bond – at least between Miss Spence and Miss Scott – around their horror of war. '"Mafeking Day" was celebrated while we were in Sydney, and I remember how we three – Miss Scott, Mrs Young and I – remained indoors the whole day, at the charming home of our hostess, on Point Piper road', Jeanne Young would write, in the voice of Catherine Spence.

Catherine Spence and Alice Henry forged a strong bond around a sense of kinship, occupational and political solidarity, and mutual affection, sustained through seven years of correspondence, five of them international. Alice Henry's health was suffering from restlessness and frustration at the editorial constraints on what she could write for the *Australasian*, the weekly newspaper of the conservative daily, the Melbourne *Argus*. Her friends in Melbourne came to the rescue. In 1905, the Charity Organisation Society sponsored her to represent them at an international congress on children's welfare in Berlin, and to attend a conference on their behalf in England. Other friends – as we shall see – contributed to her travel-fund. She sailed away for England in March 1905, went on to the United States, where she had introductions furnished by Catherine Spence, arriving in New York in 1906, and eventually settling in

Chicago where she worked for the recently-formed Women's Trade Union League for the ensuing twenty years, a job which included editing the League's paper, *Life & Labor*, with young Australian novelist, Stella Miles Franklin, as her assistant from 1908 until 1915. Alice Henry did not return to Australia to live until 1933, almost a quarter of a century after her friend and mentor, Catherine Spence, had died.

Catherine Spence and Rose Scott developed an affinity based in their shared commitment to improving the conditions of life for women, and their shared status among first-wave feminists in Australia as elders of the Woman Movement: leaders, sources of inspiration for other, younger women. By the time they met, Australian-born Rose Scott – younger that Catherine Spence by more than twenty years, and a woman who prided herself on her fair curly hair and pink cheeks – was, nevertheless, already fifty-three, a woman of substantial independent means, and an established identity in Sydney's social and political scene, leader of the campaign for votes for women which finally succeeded in 1902. They would both be invited to speak on the same platforms in favour of women's emancipation. Like Spence, Scott initiated or participated in the formation of several post-suffrage women's organisations, notably local branches of the National Council of Women and of the Women's Non-Party Political Association. Scott continued to work for such bodies, and for the Peace Society until 1920, when she announced her retirement from public life. She died five years later, fifteen years after Catherine Spence.

The letters that Catherine Spence wrote to Rose Scott and to Alice Henry deserve a study of their own. From them, we learn about moments in Australian and South Australian politics and about the progress of Miss Spence's own campaigns for proportional representation. We learn about developments in Chicago that Alice Henry had reported in letters that have long disappeared, so their remains are limited to those passages that Catherine Spence copied into her own letters to Rose Scott to let Scott know how Alice Henry was faring. Rose Scott cared for such news especially because Alice Henry was rooming with Stella Miles Franklin, the young novelist whom Scott regarded as her own protégée. In Catherine Spence's letters we learn about how she wrote and distributed her book, *State Children in Australia: a history of boarding out and its developments*, Adelaide (Vardon & Sons, Printers) 1907, and how she coped with difficulties over it created by her old friend and collaborator, Caroline Emily Clark. We learn, too, about the history of the Unitarian churches of Adelaide and Melbourne, about the travels in Europe of novelist Catherine Martin and her husband Fred, about the work that Spence's niece, Lucy Morice, did for the foundation of free kindergartens in Adelaide. We see Miss Spence ordering books to send to Alice Henry, and to Catherine Martin, too, and sending copies of her own political pamphlets to all and sundry. We watch her receiving visitors and letters from various parts of the world, and various parts of Australia, including Perth, where her correspondent was Edith Cowan, later to be the first woman elected to a parliament in Australia. We see her travelling to Melbourne and Sydney, to address meetings, to conduct political campaigns, to spend time with friends and family. We watch this fiercely energetic old woman managing the heat of the Adelaide summers, and her wide range of public commitments. 'Oh! What a lot needs to be done', she exclaims at the end of a letter to Alice Henry from 28 August [1907?]. These letters are a daunting testimony to her determination to make a difference to her world, and they make immensely engaging reading.

This is not the study that these letters warrant. Instead, we present here only a very brief selection of the letters, and a recommendation that any reader wishing to know more about these two of Catherine Spence's correspondents read two excellent biographies: Diane Kirkby, *Alice Henry: The Power of Pen and Voice. The Life of an Australian-American Labor Reformer* (Cambridge University Press), Cambridge, 1991 and Judith A. Allen, *Rose Scott: Vision and Revision* (Oxford University Press), Melbourne, 1994.

To Alice Henry

North Norwood
9 Dec [1903?]

My dear Miss Henry

...

you take my breath pleasantly away by saying the desire of your heart was going to be granted, and your friends were making it possible for you to go to England and America – I know you had saved some money but not half enough and this recent accident must have depleted your finances – You will let me help to the extent of £5. I have just got £4 for the two articles one on the Drink Question, and one on the Dominion and the Commonwealth which is about 15/- more than I expected. So I can spare you £5 and you cannot say I am not interested in you and your purposes in travel –

I can give you letters to people in America ...

Oh my dear friend I shall go with you in spirit in this interesting itinerary. I wish we could meet to talk it over. You are so much more likeminded with me than Vida Goldstein or any others to whom I have bidden God Speed that your pilgrimage will [does not continue – page missing?]

North Norwood
3rd Janry [1904?]

My very dear Miss Henry

I had a nice long letter from Mrs Watson Lister [President of the National Council of Women in Victoria] in acknowledgement of my contribution to the fund and she says you hope to get away in April and think it would be best to go to England first – I had thought of America first so that you could see the Children's Courts in full swing there and if possible test the value of the probation officers, the paid and the unpaid, but as Mrs WL puts it perhaps the

Alice Henry

European visit should come first – Is there any prospect of employment on any Australian journal as correspondent – I had a letter every four weeks for the *Register* and another which I risked at first for the *Sydney Telegraph* – which together brought me £25 and £33 but I did not get the money till I returned – I earned £70 for article in *Harper's* and about as much for four newspaper articles and one in *Arena* – I must have earned by lectures between £30 and £40 – This enabled me to spend nearly a year in America. Of course there is included in the £250 that it cost me for the twenty months I was absent and I had a great deal of hospitality – I think I had 3000 miles of travelling or more ... what my through ticket covered which took me from San Francisco to New York – And my friends advised me of the cheapest place to live in Chicago during the Exhibition time – of course also highly respectable fifteen shillings a week for room and meals separate. At New York I was at the Margaret Louisa place 16th St in connection with the Y.W.C.A. where I had a much better room and a free bath for the same money and cheaper and better meals. Out of the 10 months that I had in the States I had private hospitality for half the time and I sometimes wondered how I spent so much money – I gave about £20 of it away to a friend in distress – Well I hope we may have an opportunity of talking things over with you – If you go to England first you might come here first unless you take the White [?] Star line which does not call here –

North Norwood May 18th
[1906]

My dear Miss Henry
...

I am a good deal troubled about our Co-operative Clothing Factory. The big houses want to crush us out and make us see that the minimum wage may be death to all small concerns – The big houses make large profit on the material and can afford to give more wages – We who only live by the piece of work cannot get the girls to earn their allotted pay – when the price of the work has not been raised but if anything lowered –

...

North Norwood
10 Sept 1905

My dear Miss Henry

...

Miss [Lilian] Locke is to be here on the 18th to try to organise the women workers... – I hope to see something of her – My factory manager Miss McGregor is wondering what will be the effect of the Wages Bonus when the regulations are enforced. It is coming very near –

My last letter to you enclosed one I had from Mrs Anna Garlin Spencer to whom I wrote fully about you. She may be able to help you a good deal –

North Norwood
19th Decr 1905

My dear Miss Henry

...

Today I got a *Boston Woman's Journal* with an account of the late Mrs [Carrie Chapman] Catt and a paragraph marked that you were expected a good while before you could arrive –

I am very glad you had four days with Miss F[lorence] D[avenport] Hill. I shall probably hear her account of your visit tomorrow when I am going to [her cousin] Miss Clark's – I am also glad that you are having opportunities of seeing Epileptic homes and schools for the feeble minded in England before you go across the Atlantic.

...

I hope you have received all the packets of booklets I have addressed to you – I am going to venture a few more for my American friends. Miss Scott sent introductions for some delightful Americans from San Antonio Texas. Eleanor [Wren] who is spending three or four weeks here with me and fifty other friends met them at Miss Scott's – They were only here a few days but they came out to call on Sunday and I was at Glenelg.

They hit on my very busy week. Three days at the Destitute, a Council meeting, a Students meeting and a Clothing factory meeting but I managed to put in four visits to introduce them to Mrs Gray and to arrange that they should see a treat in the Children's Court. Also to show how we deal with adult poverty through the Destitute Board – The previous week I was not so occupied but I was not so well – They are going through India and will not be at home till May. The old maiden lady Miss Brackenridge was amazed to think I had gone through America lecturing at her age by myself. Brother George not only came with her but she had a neice, a secretary and a clever middle-aged journalist with her – also a retired colonel and his wife of the name of Varney [?] from Indianapolis had attached themselves to the party for a long time.

They had given much time to New Zealand and to Sydney and very little to Melbourne and Adelaide. But all were deeply interested in a White Australia and Brother George, though a very large landed proprietor, was a Single Taxer – It will please Mrs Young to hear that though the liberals are much divided they are mostly keen on Taxation of land value.

Mrs Young's daughter Freda 14½ has won the Junior Tennyson medal and passed in her six subjects – Lindsay has not passed his Senior and Mrs Young is starting a poultry farm for him. He has always wanted to go on the land and they cannot afford to do it in a larger way – So it happens that I have seen little of her lately. They have 8½ acres three or four miles from town with a cottage and two cows and some poultry – I hope it may be successful. Lin has great liking for all living creatures.

My neice Madge Murray has given up the post & telegraph and gone to Yarragon to start a poultry farm on a scientific principle. Their neighbours, the Barrows, two middleaged single women, say they clear 60/ a week with it – Madge may do only half but that is worth doing. There have been two little rooms added to the house – The old creamery is transformed into a cooperative creamery and butter factory and George Murray is to have 21/ a week as secretary –

The Americans saw and were charmed with Vida Goldstein – ... I had a bit snipped of my uvula early in the month with excellent results – but it was a most skittish operation. I have lost that irritated and irritating cough – I think I must now stop. Eleanor and Ellen Gregory join in love –

Yours ever CH Spence

North Norwood
8th Novr [1906]

My dear Miss Henry

I think I gave you Mrs F Martin's permanent address c/o Bank of Adelaide, 11 Leaden Hall St, London E6 before but have got to make sure – I may send you a *Register* with an account of my 80th birthday celebrations, a sudden inspiration that I might turn it into account of Effective Voting at a cost of £10 – An Effective League meeting would cost me £5 and the League something and not do as much good – But the 60 members of Parliament and their 60 wives did not come at least, only 10 or 12 of the MPs and when I spoke I said I must have it printed that those who did not hear might read – I had written out carefully all I thought I had time to say 30 minutes but the three speakers exceeded the 15 minutes limit especially the Chief Justice who wanted to cover all the ground and though I had taken very careful headings I missed some the vital points though I made some entertaining jokes – So the MS is now in the printer's hands – with my own photo and my mother's to begin with and 'Australian Spring' to wind up with and it may make a pretty little booklet or a souvenir for my friends and as campaign literature for the fight that is yet to be carried on – for I fear we shall not get the Proportional Representation Bill even into Committee this session. But even into the Social Column, Ariel says that though King Charles's Head could not be kept out of the birthday rejoicing, she gathered this much that under Miss Spence's system the Electoral district of Torrens would have got in two Liberal members and the Socialists only two – I recorded the guests and the most of them would not have looked near an Effective Voting gathering – Miss Locke was there to hear the speeches about me but had to go away before I opened my mouth. However she will hear it all. She is staying in SA much longer than she intended. I have seen too little of her but Lucy Morice has seen a lot – Did I tell you I was writing an article divided into three sections. From 'Kindergarten to University' – I want the Kindergarten Union to have that also as a leaflet ... – I shall speak to Lucy about it this afternoon. She is the Secretary – We hope to establish one K[inder]G[arten] in the poorest part of Adelaide – I moved a formal resolution that it should be free.

Since I wrote to you last we have had the jubilee of our church in which I took some part – ...

When I compare what I do – that I have to do at 80 to what I did when I was 30, 40 or 50 – it is amusing – I feel as busy nearly as when I was in America – Of course I have no housekeeping and no financial worry. Mrs Spence's £50 a year in addition to the £100 annually leaves me a margin of nearly as much for church – charity – causes – and fads –

Now my good friend you note that I tell you all I do and much that I propose to do – but your letters, though always interesting, are not enlightening – ... On what terms or for what purpose you went to Brussels to Glasgow and purposed to go to Greenock I don't know – I am glad you spend a week with Miss [Jane Hume] Clapperton and agreed with her on most points – I am getting a little tired of the sex question – Rosamund Benham and her husband are publishing a serial (monthly) which seems to speak of nothing else. [Rosamond Benham, a qualified medical practitioner, and her husband Thomas Taylor, established a journal called *Free Speech*. Benham published *Sense About Sex by a Woman Doctor* in Adelaide in 1905; Taylor was secretary of the South Australian Free Speech and Social Liberty League.] – And here each day I am challenged in the *Register* by a correspondent to say if the middle class women who will not follow Roosevelt's advice and have children galore should not be deprived of the franchise – I think the men are as unwilling to have large families as the women – the cost of bringing them up is so great in this age of hard and cruel competition.

...

    Yours ever, CH Spence

North Norwood
2nd August 1907

My dear Miss Henry

...

    Your last two letters – one received the day after I wrote you a month ago and one a fortnight after – are sad reading for all who are interested in ~~the~~ reform and purification of Chicago; – and the want of courage on the part of Miss Jane Addams was most disappointing – You had previously told me that you especially pitied Miss Addams for she had none of the joy of combat which you and I feel in the face of the evil that is in the world – ... The way in which Americans consent to be plundered, because active protest will cost more time and money than <u>the individual</u> loses, has been long to me a matter of the deepest regret – I believe that in America, reform must begin <u>through</u> the cities, by the creation of a civic spirit – and if you had proportional representation with districts returning six or seven men, instead of single wards engineered and financed by political parties often, perhaps always, in the pay of the corporations all American cities would be moralised and the citizens would no longer be plundered – Do agitate for that – it is the means by which the voice of the wisest and best must be heard and can't be silenced.

    Lord Courtney, known to me as Leonard Courtney, brought forward in the House of Lords a Bill for optional use of the Hare system in Municipal elections, and I have heard it passed its second reading – I had a copy of his speech introducing it – very good it was –

    Here, until we get the Franchise Bill lowering the qualification for the Upper House, we can get no forward legislation – The Leg Council has not yielded – but yet it does not want a double dissolution – ... – Prosperity rules in Australia – every treasury except W[estern] A[ustralia] has large surpluses, but they are wisely almost all employed to pay off debt – amt of 300,000 has nearly all gone in that way. Never were prospects better. Since the beginning of August these last three days an inch and a half of rain has fallen at Broken Hill which previously had been like Gideons father [?], left out – so there is no dread of a water famine. There are now 40,000 population all dependent on the mines – and the mines greatly dependent on the water supply – The Broken Hill traffic is a very large factor in our railway revenue – The pastoralists never had such a lambing all over Australia nor such abundant feed nor such heavy fleeces nor such good prices all together –

...

Lucy Morice lent me a Fabian tract by Sydney [sic] Webb on the Decline of the Birthrate showing that it is universal – most marked in industrial centres where married women work even more marked in members of Friendly Societies not confined to cities but as great in the rural districts. Do you recollect Dr Norris saying we should endow motherhood, and respect maternity however it came about – Sydney Webb says the same – "Infant mortality which kills a third of the population is a quite needless thing. We ought to remember that 1/3 of our paupers are children, and that it is of far more consequence to the community that this quarter of a million over whom it has complete control should be brought up to be respectable and industrious, than the exact degree of hardness with which it may choose to treat the adults. Instead of turning out the children to tramp with the father or beg with the mother, whenever they choose to take their discharge from the workhouse, which is the invariable practice today in England, we should rather jump at the chance of 'adopting' these unfortunate beings in order to make worthy citizens of them."

In Australia we don't allow children to tramp or to beg though we do not get hold of all we ought to have.

...

Miss Scott's cousin David Scott Mitchell died lately, and left no less than £70,000 to build a Library worthy of the great gift of books bestowed eight or nine years ago – I wrote to Miss Scott this week. I hope the cousin left her something – She was almost the only person the invalid and recluse came to see; she spent all her Sunday afternoons with him –

...

The Fred Martins write from Bremen and will be back in S.A. in summer. Fred says that half the time since he left S.A. he has had breakfast in bed – First the lungs – and the last six months chronic diarrhoea had compelled precaution – I half fear that the diarrhoea is another form of tuberculosis –

This is not a short letter but it is not so personal as it might have been – you know however how interested I am in your career – I should think Miles Franklin is too pessimistic to be a cheerful mate – *My Brilliant Career* though very clever was depressing – and I thought crude – so she may mellow with life's experiences ... Lucy Morice quite well but she would like to see the Nat[ional] C[ouncil] of W[omen] die out and leave us to concentrate on our own line of work – Eleanor went back to Sydney after a month but Marjorie stays longer and is getting painting lessons from Hans Heysen, a very clever painter and good teacher. She enjoys the lessons very much –

Always yours affectionately
C H Spence

North Norwood
24th Octr 1907

My dear Miss Henry

...

... But the paper on Homeless Men in that invaluable pamphlet you sent me by Raymond Robbins has also deeply sunk into my mind. Under what circumstances and in what capacity did he become personally acquainted with 33,670 homeless men of whom 4875 were suffering from venereal disease –

I have done a good deal with this pamphlet. First I sent it to Lucy and Jim Morice – next to Mr Gray and Miss Tomkinson read it at their house – Then I took it to Mr Atkinson Churchman [?] and ... Superintendent of D[estitute] Asylum and they passed it on to Dr Morris who is not only doctor for the Destitute but for the jail and the Stockade and yesterday I had half an hour's serious talk with him. He read every word of it and says it gives subject for thought ... – We agreed that it should be sent to Crawford Vaughan [MP] who is moving for reform of the jails – The women drunks who are sent to jail for a week or a fortnight are frequently prostitutes as well and as we have no Magdalene Ward in our hospitals they cannot be sent there to be cured which they would willing do – This very year quite lately such a woman suffering from a bad form of syphilis sentence expired, just on the eve of the September Agricultural and horticultural show when there are thousands of visitors to the metropolis – in a few weeks she was taken up for drunkenness and sent to jail again – She told Dr Morris that she had had connexion with seventy men. The thing is appalling – I shall write to Crawford Vaughan asking him to press for a Magdalene Ward. You cannot and ought not to send such cases to the gynaecological ward where other women are treated. We have not a Lock ward for men either – so that as Dr Morris says while scarlet fever which is a clean disease is strictly isolated, this far worse disease is allowed to spread its poison unchecked ...

Miss Scott tells me Miles Franklin writes gratefully about you but I don't know if you are really still living together – ... – She has had three attacks of influenza one after another and is rather run down – ...

We are to have a conference of Visitors for State children on 19th November – all invited with great concessions from Railway Dept – Lunch

Rundle Street, Adelaide, c.1908,
photograph courtesy of the State Library of South Australia, SLSA: B 45688

and tea provided cooked and served by State Children. Lunch 12.30 at 2 pm meeting. University buildings kindly lent for the occasion. President Mr Rhodes to deliver inaugural address – followed by Miss Spence – on the Work of Committees and visitors C.H. Goode – Our work compared with that elsewhere secretary Mr Gray – Some misconceptions. Two hours will be devoted to open discussion, in which members of the Council will take part – The Council hopes that every one present will freely state their questions, difficulties & suggestions – Tea at 5.30 – Meeting again at 7.30 The Governor will preside – The Premier Thomas Price – Professor Jethro Brown and others will address the meeting –

We think this will be a good thing for both the visitors and the council – but I expect to be a very tired woman at the end of it – for I dare say I will do a good deal of talking besides giving the most important of the addresses –

There is still no word of a minister for our church – I have had help for five services – but tomorrow I take two which makes thirteen in the two months for which I get £13.13 I don't always give them two new sermons – but touch up old ones for our service. I seem pretty full of ideas – but it takes time to write sermons for a very critical and very small congregation ...
...

Mrs Young had a little boy name Courtney Spence – four weeks ago at a private hospital which gave her a chance. He is a fine boy and she is doing much better than last time but that husband of hers is in every way so difficult and so exacting that she always has far too much to do – He thinks house work is nothing and does not think he can afford her a servant. Not only that he expects her to help him with his newspaper work and to read books for his reviews he has to do every Saturday. Bonython (Haydon) [?] gets the most amazing lot of work from his staff for wretched pay – I don't think Mr Young gets much more than £5 a week – He is a hard worker and a quick worker – Mrs Robertson wife of the chief of staff tells me she thinks Mr Young does more than anyone in the office – but I don't see why his wife should be so ... for the blooming *Advertiser* ...

Believe me always yours C H Spence ...

North Norwood
11th March 1908

My dear Miss Henry
...

Is Stella Franklin earning a livelihood with her pen in Chicago or only looking round for materials for future work? Do you find it a saving to live together? I think Chicago a most costly place for clothes on account of the dirt but I did not find clothes so much dearer than in Australia as I had expected –

I am still on the war path in a quiet way for a Magdalene Ward but Rev. J. C. Kirby enquired about the treatment of venereal disease from the Hospital authorities and was told that all could get free outdoor treatment and if a medical man certified to their having complications the woman could be taken inside – I asked Dr Morris if prostitutes were treated in the gynecological ward – he said no but in a little room off it – by the same nurses but it could only hold one or two – it was a matter of favour – and as far as he knew the women were there for a short time – He does not advocate compulsory detention but that every effort should be made to induce the women to stay till the cure is complete – The Authorities wrote to Mr Kirby that the woman was kept till the doctor said she would do with outdoor advice and could attend to herself – But how is she to live? Only in one way – Dr Morris says he believes the women really want to be cured but as you know it is a long process often lasting two or even three years – And no ordinary hospital likes such long periods of treatment – I am writing to Mr Kirby to send the Chicago pamphlet to Mr Young who now is head of the editorial staff for six months while Mr Robertson has his holiday.

Courtney Spence is a dear little fellow – weight 16lb and has cut two teeth – very intelligent – five months old – I made some larger singlets for him as he had grown out of those I gave him and also took two petticoats...

Mrs Martin brought her husband to Adelaide before Mount Gambier got too cold for him but I fear he is not long for this world. Yesterday Lucy and I met him and her in Rundle St. They had been consulting Dr Joseph Vercoe our best diagnoser – I did not have courage to ask the verdict before him but the Mt Gambier Dr had said there was no hope – And as Katie said to me on Monday last they had been such comrades all the 26 years of their married life – She is breaking her heart at the thought of losing him – I said "My dear you have made him very happy all these years – but for you he never would have had all these years of foreign travel – four years when he was quite well – three years more when you had to nurse and care for him – and the 19 years in his Australian home".

Lucy had in her hand yesterday *The Convert* [novel published in 1907 by Elizabeth Robins, United States-born feminist, actor and author, who joined the militant wing of the women's suffrage campaign in England] which I had just returned to her – She handed it to Katie Martin saying she was sure she would enjoy reading it – So will Fred who can read four or five hours day without his eyes getting tired – He has completely lost his voice – and the chronic diarrhoea keeps the same as it has been for 15 or 18 months – the wonder to me is that he is alive – Evg. Here I was interrupted by Mrs Martin herself who stayed several hours – She is very sad – but Dr Vercoe is to see Fred again in a week –

I shall try to do some at least of the things you want when I go to Melbourne – but I am sure I can't do them all – ... you must bear in mind that I am going for a <u>rest</u>.

Always yours affectionately C.H.Spence

> North Norwood
> 10th April 1908

My dear Miss Henry

I am on the wing for Melbourne and Sydney, going tomorrow Saturday the 11th making a saving of 30/- for Easter trip, which allows you to stop off – and lasts three months – I hope to be back within eight weeks. You are the person I miss most now when I go to Melbourne ...

...

– With much love

> Yours ever
> C H Spence

> Edgecliff Rd Sydney [staying with Rose Scott]
> 11th May [1908]

My dear Miss Henry

...

Miss Scott is very anxious about Stella Franklin and her mother does not think she hears sufficient particulars of her health – Is she trying to earn her living by her pen in Chicago? Miss Scott has at present as her guest Mrs Barbara Baynton – who finds London the best place to live in – People admire her work there. She can publish her books there – She and Miss Scott are the antipodes in many ways but they are both most bitter agst federation and hate and fear everything the Commonwealth does or proposes to do – Mrs Baynton leaves for London next week –

...

Miss McDonell [?] whom I met at V. Goldsteins thinks you are likely to stay in America – but I should like you here not perhaps as a journalist but at the head of the Infant Protection or of the probation officers – When I see that the weakness of the departments both in Vic and in NSW is that they have not secured the best officials – anyone who could train them would be invaluable – ...

Stella Miles Franklin,
published with permission, Mitchell Library, State Library of New South Wales

I know and feel that Australia has a great pull on you – but you are doing great and good work where you are ... Eleanor unites with me in love – She has been appointed on the School board for the borough and much to my joy is going into the work con amore – I hear far too little of what goes on in Adelaide. Martina Kramers of *Jus Suffragii* [Martina Kramers of Rotterdam, editor of *Jus Suffragii*, a monthly paper in English, published by the International Woman Suffrage Association] wrote for a copy of my book for the W[oman] S[uffrage] library and it has been sent –

I only write to you once a month but I put a good deal in my letters. Remember me to my Chicago friends. Ever yours in love
Catherine H Spence ...

North Norwood
20th Nov 1908

My dear Miss Henry

I had only a short letter from you by Vancouver mail saying you had been rather done up by work on a congress – and that you were greatly enjoying Mrs Martin's *Old Roof Tree*.
...

Of course long ere this you have had our great news the advent of a new Federal Labour ministry and the passage of State Suffrage in Victoria – I think that one great reason why the [Legislative] Council was nearly unanimous is that experience here has shown that the woman's vote has greatly strengthened the Upper House, for ... votes for property tell largely for conservative candidates – With an enormous majority in the Assembly the Labour Liberal ministry has only four supporters in the Council – and measures are negatived which the people as a whole really demand –

Apparently the Deakinites are disposed to support Mr Fisher's ministry rather than ally with the Reid Forrest Quick lot –

We are engaged in the hottest campaign for Effective Voting that I have experienced. I forget where we were when I wrote last – but since the Deputation to the Premier on 26th Sept we have had meetings with ballots –

Oct 23   Hamley Bridge Mrs Young
            Terowie Crawford Vaughan
    24   Petersburg Miss Spence
            Mount Gambier Mrs Young
    25   Port Adelaide Miss Spence & Howard Vaughan
          counting
    31   Public Meeting St Andrews Hall Adelaide

    Nov 2   <u>Port Wakefield</u> Mrs Young
         3   <u>Saddleworth</u> K. Duncan & Mrs Young counting vote
         7   <u>Riverton</u> Mrs Young
         8   <u>Adelaide</u> Democratic Club Miss Spence & C. Vaughan
      10   <u>Semaphore</u> Pt Adelaide Miss Spence & Mrs Young
      16   <u>Magill</u> Democratic Club Miss Spence & Miss Hawkins

Our Annual meeting of the League is to be held on the 30th – with a special Demonstration.

…

    Freda Young has left school and she runs the home and minds the baby when her mother is absent and Mr Young is so much impressed with the importance of this crisis that he does not murmur…

    Lucy Morice has gone to Sydney for a few weeks rest – <u>nerves</u> – and just as she was arranging to go Dr Helen Mayo says that Miss de Lissa, Director of the Kindergarten and trainer of the students, needs months of complete rest – Lucy will try to get a locum tenens and the wonderful Barr Smiths will pay for Miss de Lissa at a rest home till she is fit to resume work.

    You may think I am well when I went by cocky train to Petersburg 150 miles north to lecture, got up next day at 4 am to catch the Broken Hill express arriving at 11, going home for a rest, and going to Pt Adelaide to lecture and getting back at 12 midnight. On the same day Mrs Young travelled 305 miles – 13 hours to lecture at Mount Gambier to a more sympathetic audience than mine – had to stay over Tuesday and get home Wednesday night. The Mt. Gambier people invited her and paid her fare – but where we offer lectures we may get something but are always much out of pocket – The public meeting of which I send report was held on my 83rd birthday –

    Mrs Martin is showing signs of the three and a half years of constant anxiety about her husband's health – She looks about as ill as he does, but he is drawing near death and I hope she has years of useful work before her – You have never said a word about my suggestion to prepare an abridgement of *State Children in Australia* for publication in America – It is partly done but awaits your approbation …

                                  Ever yours
                                  C H Spence

North Norwood
5th August [?1909]

My dear Miss Henry

I write to tell you that after five days in bed, I got up yesterday and felt all right.

...

I think I will go to Melbourne for a short visit soon. Mr Petherick & his wife are making a deed of gift to the Australasian Library which has been the work of his lifetime and they want me to witness her signature – the sudden death of the Speaker Sir Frederick Holder causes some delay but I think things are sufficiently in train – Mr Petherick gets the Federal Librarianship at £500 a year which was the condition of the gift – I know the library and I know how Mrs Petherick saved it in 1894 by giving up her furniture and living in lodgings for years. This is why he makes it a joint gift.

It was a great subject of discussion when I was their guest in 1894 –

I think Mr Petherick has all my books in the library – and he says he has all I have written but when I see the volumes of press cuttings I have I know that a great deal of my very best work was given to the daily press – that ephemeral channel.

...

Lucy Morice has been to see me every other day. Barr Smith has given a block of land with £1000 for a kindergarten school and training college. Peter Waite a rich pastoralist will give £1000 for building and if it is not enough Barr Smith will supplement it – Lucy is in high spirits about it – Barr Smith will give nothing now for Effective Voting. He says we have worked hard and have effected nothing – We think we have effected a good deal.

...

Always yours C H Spence

E & S Bank
Collins Street
[August 1909? or September]

My dear Miss Henry

I have come to Melbourne earlier than I intended ...

...Vida Goldstein came in the evening ... – She has engaged me to explain to her Assn on Monday 6th Sept how to make the Preferential Vote and Effective Vote. She has since sent me a German Professor of Phil. and Jur. Alfred Mann [?] who will be in Adelaide when I am here who wants information about Dependent Children and Labour conditions and who also is interested in PR but approves of the Belgian conditions of 1 ballot for an adult man 2 for a married man older [?] 3 for education or property – Still he sees the advantage of PR.

...

 I must have told you that Mr Quilty is building a new house in Queen St, Norwood – The moving will be over before I return – I had to clear out two clothes baskets full of letters, papers, pamphlets &c which I thought need not be taken over – in many cases with some regret – I have been five years with the Quiltys and shall probably die in their hands.

 I arrived in time to see Miss Rose Scott who had been in Melbourne for a month on a visit to her nephew Helenus, otherwise Nene Wallace who is with a company here. She looks very well ... – Miss Annie Miller from Lincoln Nebraska delivered a letter of introduction here and we had a talk about you and other interesting topics – but I shall see her in Adelaide.

...

 I say nothing about my book – It is in your hands when you can find time to give to it – I hope you got my P.O.O. for $8
How is Stella Franklin?
Ever yours affectionately
C.H. Spence

Queen St Norwood
18th Dec 1909

My dear Miss Henry

...

 ... I also enclose you ... the first part of an article on Public Speaking for Women which has appeared in the *Register*. I thought the second part would have been in today's paper but it is delayed. This was written by request and will be paid for at the rate of 21/ a column – and is I suppose the last of the series. I sent a proof to Vida Goldstein – she asked me for a telegram to help her in her defence of the Suffragettes which I wired at once and afterwards wrote somewhat more guardedly – for I cannot say I like all the things they do – But their treatment as criminals under the most degrading conditions when as British citizens they only wanted consideration of their claims justified the extreme measures they took – that was my wire –

...

Believe me always
Yours affectionately
CH Spence

Queen St Norwood
28th Jany 1910

My dear Miss Henry

...

I have not yet seen *Some everyday people and Dawn* [*Some Everyday Folk and Dawn* was the second of Miles Franklin's novels to be published] I am afraid to read it for fear I should not like it –

I thought *My Brilliant Career* clever but unpleasant and the notices I have seen are very half hearted – of this new book I mean – I was disappointed with Evelyn Vaughans book – there were no bones in it – nothing to take hold of – I am reading Mrs Oliphant's Autobiography – profoundly sad – She did not think well enough of her own work. I know my novels are not to be compared with hers, but I am always satisfied with my lectures and my journalistic work –

But it has had this effect – I have yesterday began an autobiographic sketch of my own life – I still have my memory – I cannot tell how long I shall have it, and I hope I may keep at this till I bring it down to date.

...

I think of you ... enlarging your scope by leaving the Melbourne *Argus* for the Chicago *Labour Advocate* – If there was anything that could have tempted me to leave Australia it was America – Issues there seemed so vast – and needs so great –

...

Perhaps you are right and that I have been exceptionally fortunate in finding work that I could do and meeting with little opposition to the course I saw before me. My brother John always encouraged and helped me – and as I repeat I did not suffer from diffidence or shyness ...

... I wonder if Vida Goldstein will get in for the Senate. That will be a good record –

    Believe me
     always yours affectionately
      C.H.Spence

Queen St Norwood
12th March 1910

My dear Miss Henry

I find there is a mail going today and have no time to write.

I have been so exceedingly busy over my Autobiography that I seem to forget everything else – I have got about half through with it according to the editors supposition of 100,000 words and that is not bad for six weeks' work –

...

I have Mrs F. Martin with me for a time before she goes to Europe. She has had a short story, the only thing she has written since her husband's death, accepted by the *Leader* and a commission to go to Oberammergau this year and to contribute articles with illustrations. I had the pleasure of giving her a camera and she is getting on with the use of it.

…

Going back over my literary life I see that I had a good many rebuffs about *Mr Hogarth's Will* –

I find the A.B. very interesting – I hope I am not overloading it – Mrs Martin takes a keen interest in its progress – and reminds me of good stories to put into it, but she does not know the earlier part of my life.

…

I am at present in the 80s. My mother still alive in her 90s and myself in full work on the *Register* – I see I was 14 years a regular outside contributor.

…

I enquired at Coles for <u>some Everyday people & Dawn</u> yesterday. They said it had not come yet but that must be nonsense

Yours in haste
C.H.Spence

To Rose Scott

C.H. Spence to 'My dear Miss Scott', College Road, Kent Town, 20 Sept 1902

Just a line of congratulations on the telegraphic news received that the W.S. Bill passed its second reading in the Leg. Council of N.S.W. Now half the women in Australia are enfranchised and more than half in Australasia.

Have you had the copy of a letter from Mrs Carrie Chapman Catt about delegates from Suffrage Associations for Washington Conference of Women Suffragists. The original was sent to Miss Goldstein and copied for my advice as to the practicability of sending one or more delegates with a request that I should lay the matter before the association most fitted to deal with it. The Victorian people would like to send Miss Goldstein so Miss Henry writes to me and wanted my opinion as to what it would cost and what likelihood there was of lectures paying much of the travelling expenses.

I have given my experience in 1893 when I had to wait six months for the lecturing season and had 14 paid lectures chiefly from Women's Clubs – equal suffrage mostly – I also made something on the press – but the twenty months all round the world cost me £200 more than I earned –

It would be an education for Miss Goldstein to be three months in the States and I think it would cost nothing more than she earned –

I consulted the president ... of the W.C.T.U. about the matter and they suggested that Mrs C.E. Clark, press superintendent of the W.C.T.U., who worked hard to win the suffrage in West Australia and who is probably working now ... in Sydney, a good speaker and writer – I missed seeing her when she was here but Mrs Young saw her and was most favourably impressed with her as earnest and capable and broader than most of the W.C.T.U. – She may be able to go at her own charges – Miss Goldstein cannot – and you know how hard it is to raise as much money as will pay return fare to Washington – Miss Goldstein could represent the struggle in Victoria but she

Rose Scott,
published with permission, Mitchell Library, State Library of New South Wales

has not been in S.A. or in W.A. or in N.Z. and could not speak of the marvellous transformation wrought by W.S. I hope delegates are invited from N.Z. Indeed I am rather surprised that I was not communicated with directly – for S.A.

But it has just occurred to me this morning that now the victory is won, you should go yourself to represent the enfranchised women of N.S.W. – No one has worked harder than you for the cause – What charming people I could send you to see – It would be almost like seeing them myself to hear what you thought of them.

Think it over, don't say it can't be done – You would come back ten years younger – as I did I verily believe –

I think Mrs Clark would be an excellent person to go but I should like someone to go also that was not a member of the W.C.T.U. to represent the justice of political equality without having the prohibition axe to grind –
...

Yours etc much love

C.H. Spence to 'My dear Miss Scott', North Norwood, 8 May 1906

You write enquiring about Miss Henry. She will stay in America over next winter when she hopes to have some lecturing engagements – She arrived too late in the season to do much – but my friends have been very kind to her – She is enjoying her travels much and meeting many interesting people – but I do not think she met Susan Anthony – and now she is to be seen no more on this side of time. She says that the Americans have much to learn yet in the way of Juvenile Courts. Instead [of] a private hearing in a quiet room she found the New York Court held in public – at the street corner of an Elevated Railroad where the noise was deafening. It was not so noisy at Philadelphia but it was public and she thinks it is so generally in America – What she saw in Manchester was much better than these two courts –...

...

Miss Henry says the longer she is away from Australia the more she values the broad democratic basis on which the Commonwealth stands.

...

I love Miss Henry she is such a real democrat.

...

Remember me to your Political Education Leagues. I have the leaders framed hanging up before me –

Ever yours

C.H. Spence to 'My dear Miss Scott', North Norwood 29 January 1907

I think you will be pleased to hear that Miss Henry is doing excellent work in America. She has had two lecturing engagements of a fortnight each in Chicago one to speak on Women's Suffrage in Oct, another round in Novr on the Municipal Campaign – which is a vital matter. She went to Pittsburgh for ten days and earned $30 and had hospitality. She had an excellent article on Industrial Democracy in the *Outlook*, a very excellent American weekly, and got $40 or £8 for it before it was published on 3rd Nov – Her last letter to me tells me she has had an article on Woman's Suffrage in Australia accepted by the *North American Review* and that is like the blue ribbon of journalism. Counting that in she tells me she has earned $250 – £50 in three months with her voice and her pen. Of course it was the height of the lecturing season. I think you will be interested in most of her letter of 30th Novr received only yesterday – She writes when she can find time for she does not know of the mails.

...

I enclose you a review of a book written by my dearest friend Mrs F. Martin which is published anonymously and which Longmans stupidly sent neither to the Australian press nor to the Australian booksellers – I want all my friends to enquire for it at the shops so that a book so Australian in sentiment and written by an Australian who came to S.A. at two years old should be purchaseable. I think the <u>style</u> is most distinguished and the subjects treated interesting.

...

Always yours faithfully

C.H. Spence to 'My dear Miss Scott', 18 November 1904

I had a visit from your Russian journalist and liked him very much. He sat an hour or more with me on Tuesday. I don't know if I could give him much information but I gave him the original draft of the paper I wrote for the Quinquennial which was abridged and typed but was not written. I also gave him two pamphlets, mine and Mrs Young's, on Effective Voting.

C.H. Spence to 'My dear Miss Scott',
North Norwood, 25 Sept

Your last letter has been lying heavy on my conscience I did not want to write till I had really seen and rightly talked to [Nene? Rose Scott's actor nephew] and after I did so I have been so overwhelmed with work that I could not breathe. This week is not so bad for I have only one day at the Destitute instead of three and there is no W.C.T.U. Convention – and there is only one Kindergarten engagement – so I take up my pen. In the first place I was very glad indeed to have a talk with your nephew and to see that he likes the life he has engaged in and that he acts his part well. We all think he has a good future before him ...

...

Miss Locke is here from Melbourne trying to organise the women workers – I have devoted two evenings and an afternoon to her in the midst of other things.

It is so hard to get women to join a trades union – and without it they are sadly sweated. She stayed the first week with Mrs [Tom] Price, wife of the premier. This week she is with Lucy Morice, my niece – A third week she will go to Port Pirie the biggest centre out of the metropolitan area – She is liked, and is a good speaker though her voice is not strong. She is a great friend of our friend Miss Alice Henry – from whom I have not heard since she was in Belgium. Mrs Morice has joined the National Council of Women, and she got Miss Locke to speak before the executive on social needs and aims. Lucy tells me the executive were much impressed but the two most conservative members were unavoidably absent – I am out of it –

Well I have given you some news – I may hope to visit Sydney some time next year – but I do not think it will be early –

Remember me to the many friends in your circle and believe me

Always yours affectionately

C.H. Spence to 'My dear Miss Scott',
No Address, Tuesday 14 September

Just a few lines to tell you what a grand meeting we had and how your absence was regretted – The audience had to make the most of me as you were not there to divide the honours – I was glad to be able to speak for you and the W.S.L. of N.S.W. as I had just come from the ... meeting of Wednesday last week ... The speeches were all good, the *Age* gives the better report but the *Argus* does me more justice – It takes my anecdote of Jennie Mason a free born citizen of the US whom I met in the Rocky Mountains in the train. She came from Wyoming the only place … years ago where women had equal rights – What a progress since. I am off to Yarragon, Gippsland care of Miss Murray this mg – and will return to Melbourne on Monday week …

Yours in desperate haste

P.S. All the speakers were happy and the ladies spoke with perfect good taste.

C.H. Spence to 'My dear Miss Scott',
New Address Queen Street Norwood, Easter Monday

The enclosed cutting will let you know what I am doing and I find it a pretty long and difficult thing to know what to put in and what to keep out of my Autobiography.

It is about half done and I think so far it is interesting – The *Register* asked the Melbourne *Argus* and the Sydney *Herald* if they would syndicate the work but they declined.

…

We are working hard for Effective Voting which was again talked out – but I cannot depend on my health as I used to do – The last eight months I have had little recurrent attacks proceeding from the internal growth which was discovered in 1903 – which force me to lie in bed for two, three, four or five days – and I am just up from one now. Not that it is malignant in any way – but it shows its presence by something like a bilious attack – not severe – only that I must keep recumbent –

So I have to save myself all I can for the completion of this autobiography.

After it has been through the *Register* I think it should be published as a book in Australia for the public of Australia and New Zealand – It would be useless to offer my life to an English publisher. It is purely local interest that I can trust to, but there is a public of over five million in Australasia.

I feel sad to think I shall never see Sydney again – I am doubtful if I shall see Melbourne – I had a long visit of four months from Eleanor Wren – She came to Adelaide with me when I returned after you saw me in Collins Street.

I hope you are well and busy. Remember me to my many good friends and believe me always

Yours affectionately

Appendices

Appendix A

Family Tree

We would like to thank the *Australian Dictionary of Biography* and Suzanne Maiden for their energy and hard work in putting this together.

1. Alexander BRODIE

Spouse:	Margaret FERNIE
Birth Date:	1736
Death Date:	1817
Children:	John

1.1 John BRODIE

Birth Date:	1758
Death Date:	1835
Spouse:	Nancy (Agnes)
Marriage Date:	1784
Children:	Betsy
	Margaret
	Alexander
	Helen
	Mary
	Jessie
	William
	Jane
	John

1.1.1 Betsy BRODIE

Birth Date:	1783
Death Date:	1852

1.1.2 MARGARET BRODIE
Birth Date:	1787
Death Date:	1866

1.1.3A ALEXANDER BRODIE*
Birth Date:	1788
Death Date:	1869

Spouse:	Helen CUTHBERTSON
Birth Date:	1793
Death Date:	1817

Marriage Date:	1814
Marriage Place:	Marriage One

Children:	Jane Cuthbertson
	John

Other Spouses	Jourdiana GRAY

1.1.3A.1 JANE CUTHBERTSON BRODIE
Birth Date:	1815

1.1.3A.2 JOHN BRODIE
Birth Date:	1816

1.1.3B ALEXANDER BRODIE*
(See above)

Spouse:	Jourdiana GRAY
Birth Date:	1794
Death Date:	1883

Marriage Date:	1828
Marriage Place:	Marriage Two

Children:	Henry Louis Gray
	Alexander
	Louisa Harriet
	Mary Jourdiana

Other Spouses	Helen CUTHBERTSON

1.1.3B.1 Henry Louis Gray BRODIE
Birth Date:	1829
Death Date:	1854

1.1.3B.2 Alexander BRODIE
Birth Date:	1831
Death Date:	1907
Spouse:	Emma Edmonds GOLDSMITH
Marriage Date:	1883

1.1.3B.3 Louisa Harriet BRODIE
Birth Date:	1833
Death Date:	1930
Spouse:	Charles Hegan MYLES
Death Date:	1903

1.1.3B.4 Mary Jourdiana BRODIE
Birth Date:	1836
Death Date:	1865
Spouse:	Jefferson Packham STOW
Marriage Date:	1855

1.1.4 Helen BRODIE
Birth Date:	1791
Birth Place:	Melrose ROX Scotland
Death Date:	1887
Spouse:	David SPENCE
Birth Date:	1789
Birth Place:	Scotland
Death Date:	29 May 1846
Death Place:	Adelaide South Australia
Burial Place:	West Terrace Cemetery
Spouse Father:	William SPENCE
Spouse Mother:	Janet PARK (–1800)
Marriage Date:	1815
Marriage Place:	Scotland

Children: Agnes
                  Jessie
                  William Richard
                  John Brodie
                  Catherine Helen
                  David Wauchope
                  Mary Brodie
                  Eliza Brodie

1.1.4.1 AGNES SPENCE
Birth Date: 1818
Death Date: 1835

1.1.4.2 JESSIE SPENCE
Birth Date: 1821
Death Date: 1888

Spouse: Andrew MURRAY
Birth Date: 1813
Death Date: 1880

Marriage Date: 1841

Children: Helen
                  Mary Anne
                  Eliza
                  William
                  John David
                  Catherine Helen
                  George Houston
                  Edward Stirling
                  Margaret Brodie
                  Agnes Andalusia

1.1.4.2.1 HELEN MURRAY
Birth Date: 19 Oct 1842
Birth Place: Adelaide South Australia
Death Date: 1846

1.1.4.2.2 Mary Anne MURRAY
Birth Date:	15 Jul 1844
Birth Place:	Adelaide South Australia
Death Date:	1879
Spouse:	Andrew Dods HANDYSIDE

1.1.4.2.3 Eliza MURRAY
Birth Date:	15 Oct 1846
Birth Place:	Adelaide South Australia
Death Date:	1864

1.1.4.2.4 William MURRAY
Birth Date:	16 May 1848
Birth Place:	McGill / Magill South Australia
Death Date:	1852

1.1.4.2.5 John David MURRAY
Birth Date:	11 Jun 1850
Birth Place:	Ref: Date Found By Barbara Wall
Christen Place:	Above Birth Not Found As Registered Officially In SA Index
Death Date:	1922

1.1.4.2.6 Catherine Helen MURRAY
Birth Date:	3 Jun 1852
Birth Place:	Ref: Date Found By Barbara Wall
Christen Place:	Above Birth Not Found As Registered Officially In SA Index
Death Date:	1933

1.1.4.2.7 George Houston MURRAY
Birth Date:	1854
Birth Place:	Melbourne Victoria Ref 6214
Death Date:	1938

1.1.4.2.8 Edward Stirling MURRAY
Birth Date:	1856
Birth Place:	Melbourne Victoria Ref 11290
Death Date:	1860

1.1.4.2.9 Margaret Brodie MURRAY

Birth Date:	1858
Birth Place:	Melbourne Victoria Ref 10061
Death Date:	1935

1.1.4.2.10 Agnes Andalusia MURRAY

Birth Date:	1863
Birth Place:	Victoria Ref 9392
Death Date:	1863

1.1.4.3 William Richard SPENCE

Birth Date:	1822
Death Date:	1903

1.1.4.4 John Brodie SPENCE Hon.

Birth Date:	15 May 1824
Birth Place:	Scotland
Christen Date:	17 Jun 1824
Christen Place:	Melrose Roxburgh Scotland
Death Date:	7 Dec 1902
Death Place:	Glenelg South Australia
Spouse:	Jessie CUMMING
Birth Date:	28 Mar 1830
Birth Place:	Glasgow LKS Scotland
Death Date:	1910
Spouse Father:	John CUMMING
Marriage Date:	22 Apr 1858
Marriage Place:	Residence Of John Cumming Of Underdale South Australia
Children:	Louisa (Lucy)
	Agnes Helen
	Margaret Ethel (Daisy)

1.1.4.4.1 Louisa (Lucy) SPENCE

Birth Date:	1 Mar 1859
Birth Place:	Adelaide South Australia
Death Date:	1951
Spouse:	James Percy MORICE

Marriage Date: 20 Mar 1886
Marriage Place: Residence Of John Brodie Spence Of Glenelg South Australia

1.1.4.4.2 AGNES HELEN SPENCE

Birth Date: 19 Dec 1863
Birth Place: Glenelg South Australia
Death Date: 1949

1.1.4.4.3 MARGARET ETHEL (DAISY) SPENCE

Birth Date: 26 Aug 1865
Birth Place: Adelaide South Australia
Death Date: 1936

Spouse: George Alexander STEPHEN
Birth Date: 1855
Spouse Father: George Alexander STEPHEN

Marriage Date: 18 Aug 1887
Marriage Place: Unitarian Christian Church Adelaide South Australia

1.1.4.5 CATHERINE HELEN SPENCE

Birth Date: 31 Oct 1825
Death Date: 3 Apr 1910

1.1.4.6 DAVID WAUCHOPE SPENCE

Birth Date: 1827
Death Date: 1890

1.1.4.7 MARY BRODIE SPENCE

Birth Date: 1830
Death Date: 1870

Spouse: William John WREN
Birth Date: 1823
Death Date: 1864

Marriage Date: 1855

Children: Charles William
Margaret Brodie
Eleanor Brodie

1.1.4.7.1 CHARLES WILLIAM WREN
Birth Date:	15 Nov 1856
Birth Place:	North Adelaide South Australia
Death Date:	1934

Spouse:	Eleanor Dora HALL

Marriage Date:	1889

1.1.4.7.2 MARGARET BRODIE WREN
Birth Date:	18 Jun 1858
Birth Place:	North Adelaide South Australia
Death Date:	1858

1.1.4.7.3 ELEANOR BRODIE WREN
Birth Date:	10 Jun 1862
Birth Place:	Stepney South Australia
Death Date:	1948

1.1.4.8 ELIZA BRODIE SPENCE
Birth Date:	1833
Death Date:	1836

1.1.5 MARY BRODIE
Birth Date:	1792
Death Date:	1867

1.1.6 JESSIE BRODIE
Birth Date:	1794
Death Date:	1798

1.1.7 WILLIAM BRODIE
Birth Date:	1798
Death Date:	1842

Spouse:	Jane HOWDEN

Marriage Date:	1837

Children:	Mary Jane

1.1.7.1 MARY JANE BRODIE

1.1.8 JANE BRODIE

Birth Date:	1800
Death Date:	1888
Spouse:	Peter HANDYSIDE
Marriage Date:	1823

1.1.9 JOHN BRODIE

Birth Date:	1802
Death Date:	1849

1. David SPENCE

Spouse:	Mary WAUCHOPE
Children:	William

1.1a William SPENCE*

Spouse:	Janet PARK
Death Date:	1800
Marriage Place:	Marriage One
Children:	John
	David
	Isabella
	Mary
Other Spouses	Katherine SWANSTON

1.1a.1 John SPENCE

Birth Date:	1787
Spouse:	Margaret BELL

1.1a.2 David SPENCE

Birth Date:	1789
Birth Place:	Scotland
Death Date:	29 May 1846
Death Place:	Adelaide South Australia
Burial Place:	West Terrace Cemetery
Spouse:	Helen BRODIE
Birth Date:	1791
Birth Place:	Melrose ROX Scotland
Death Date:	1887
Spouse Father:	John BRODIE (1758-1835)
Spouse Mother:	Nancy (Agnes)
Marriage Date:	1815
Marriage Place:	Scotland

Children:	Agnes
	Jessie
	William Richard
	John Brodie
	Catherine Helen
	David Wauchope
	Mary Brodie
	Eliza Brodie

1.1A.2.1 AGNES SPENCE
Birth Date:	1818
Death Date:	1835

1.1A.2.2 JESSIE SPENCE
Birth Date:	1821
Death Date:	1888
Spouse:	Andrew MURRAY
Birth Date:	1813
Death Date:	1880
Marriage Date:	1841
Children:	Helen
	Mary Anne
	Eliza
	William
	John David
	Catherine Helen
	George Houston
	Edward Stirling
	Margaret Brodie
	Agnes Andalusia

1.1A.2.2.1 HELEN MURRAY
Birth Date:	19 Oct 1842
Birth Place:	Adelaide South Australia
Death Date:	1846

1.1A.2.2.2 Mary Anne MURRAY
Birth Date:	15 Jul 1844
Birth Place:	Adelaide South Australia
Death Date:	1879
Spouse:	Andrew Dods HANDYSIDE

1.1A.2.2.3 Eliza MURRAY
Birth Date:	15 Oct 1846
Birth Place:	Adelaide South Australia
Death Date:	1864

1.1A.2.2.4 William MURRAY
Birth Date:	16 May 1848
Birth Place:	McGill / Magill South Australia
Death Date:	1852

1.1A.2.2.5 John David MURRAY
Birth Date:	11 Jun 1850
Birth Place:	Ref: Date Found By Barbara Wall
Christen Place:	Above Birth Not Found As Registered Officially In SA Index
Death Date:	1922

1.1A.2.2.6 Catherine Helen MURRAY
Birth Date:	3 Jun 1852
Birth Place:	Ref: Date Found By Barbara Wall
Christen Place:	Above Birth Not Found As Registered Officially In SA Index
Death Date:	1933

1.1A.2.2.7 George Houston MURRAY
Birth Date:	1854
Birth Place:	Melbourne Victoria Ref 6214
Death Date:	1938

1.1A.2.2.8 Edward Stirling MURRAY
Birth Date:	1856
Birth Place:	Melbourne Victoria Ref 11290
Death Date:	1860

1.1A.2.2.9 Margaret Brodie MURRAY
Birth Date:	1858
Birth Place:	Melbourne Victoria Ref 10061
Death Date:	1935

1.1A.2.2.10 Agnes Andalusia MURRAY
Birth Date:	1863
Birth Place:	Victoria Ref 9392
Death Date:	1863

1.1A.2.3 William Richard SPENCE
Birth Date:	1822
Death Date:	1903

1.1A.2.4 John Brodie SPENCE Hon.
Birth Date:	15 May 1824
Birth Place:	Scotland
Christen Date:	17 Jun 1824
Christen Place:	Melrose Roxburgh Scotland
Death Date:	7 Dec 1902
Death Place:	Glenelg South Australia
Spouse:	Jessie CUMMING
Birth Date:	28 Mar 1830
Birth Place:	Glasgow LKS Scotland
Death Date:	1910
Spouse Father:	John CUMMING
Marriage Date:	22 Apr 1858
Marriage Place:	Residence Of John Cumming Of Underdale South Australia
Children:	Louisa (Lucy)
	Agnes Helen
	Margaret Ethel (Daisy)

1.1A.2.4.1 LOUISA (LUCY) SPENCE

Birth Date:	1 Mar 1859
Birth Place:	Adelaide South Australia
Death Date:	1951

Spouse:	James Percy MORICE

Marriage Date:	20 Mar 1886
Marriage Place:	Residence Of John Brodie Spence Of Glenelg South Australia

1.1A.2.4.2 AGNES HELEN SPENCE

Birth Date:	19 Dec 1863
Birth Place:	Glenelg South Australia
Death Date:	1949

1.1A.2.4.3 MARGARET ETHEL (DAISY) SPENCE

Birth Date:	26 Aug 1865
Birth Place:	Adelaide South Australia
Death Date:	1936

Spouse:	George Alexander STEPHEN
Birth Date:	1855
Spouse Father:	George Alexander STEPHEN

Marriage Date:	18 Aug 1887
Marriage Place:	Unitarian Christian Church Adelaide South Australia

1.1A.2.5 CATHERINE HELEN SPENCE

Birth Date:	31 Oct 1825
Death Date:	3 Apr 1910

1.1A.2.6 DAVID WAUCHOPE SPENCE

Birth Date:	1827
Death Date:	1890

1.1A.2.7 MARY BRODIE SPENCE

Birth Date:	1830
Death Date:	1870

Spouse:	William John WREN
Birth Date:	1823
Death Date:	1864

Marriage Date: 1855

Children: Charles William
Margaret Brodie
Eleanor Brodie

1.1A.2.7.1 CHARLES WILLIAM WREN
Birth Date:	15 Nov 1856
Birth Place:	North Adelaide South Australia
Death Date:	1934

Spouse: Eleanor Dora HALL

Marriage Date: 1889

1.1A.2.7.2 MARGARET BRODIE WREN
Birth Date:	18 Jun 1858
Birth Place:	North Adelaide South Australia
Death Date:	1858

1.1A.2.7.3 ELEANOR BRODIE WREN
Birth Date:	10 Jun 1862
Birth Place:	Stepney South Australia
Death Date:	1948

1.1A.2.8 ELIZA BRODIE SPENCE
Birth Date:	1833
Death Date:	1836

1.1A.3 ISABELLA SPENCE
Birth Date:	1790
Death Date:	1822

Spouse: John Wesley BARRET

Children: (Daughter)

1.1A.3.1 (DAUGHTER) BARRET
Birth Date:	1822
Death Date:	1822

1.1A.4 MARY SPENCE

Birth Date:	1792
Death Date:	1856

1.1B WILLIAM SPENCE*

(See above)

Spouse:	Katherine SWANSTON
Birth Date:	1757
Marriage Place:	Married Two
Children:	Janet
Other Spouses	Janet PARK

1.1B.1 JANET SPENCE

Birth Date:	1804
Spouse:	Peter REID

Appendix B

Sources of Notes and Additional Information

Biography Index on Cards in the State Library of South Australia

American National Biography, 24 vols., ed. John A. Garraty and Mark C. Carnes (Oxford University Press), Oxford, 1999

Australian Dictionary of Biography, 16 vols., eds Douglas Pike (v. 1–6), Bede Nairn, Geoffrey Serle (v. 7–10), Geoffrey Serle (v. 11), John Ritchie (v. 12–16), (Melbourne University Press), Carlton, 1966–1990

Dictionary of National Biography, eds Leslie Stephen and Sidney Lee, 63 vols. With supplements, (Smith, Elder & Company), London, 1885–1900

Dictionary of New Zealand Biography, 2 vols., eds W.H. Oliver and Claudia Orange, v. 1 (Allen & Unwin and Department of Internal Affairs), Wellington, 1990; vol.2 (Bridget William Books and Department of Internal Affairs), Wellington, 1993

Encyclopaedia Britannica, 29 vols., 11th edition, ed. H. Chisholm, (Cambridge University Press), Cambridge, 1910–1911

Everyman's Encyclopaedia, 12 vols., 4th edition, ed. E.F. Bozman (J.M. Dent & Sons), London, 1958

Oxford Companion to English Literature, ed. Sir Paul Harvey (Oxford at the Clarendon Press) Oxford, 1960

The Penguin Companion to Literature, 4 vols., eds David Daiches, Anthony Thorlby, M. Bradbury, E. Mottram, J. Franco, D.R Dudley and D.M. Lang (Penguin Books), Harmondsworth, 1971

Sir Llewellyn Woodward, *The Age of Reform 1815–1870*, second edition (Oxford at the Clarendon Press), Oxford, 1962

Sir Robert Ensor, *England 1870–1914* (Oxford at the Clarendon Press), Oxford, 1936/1968

Edwin Hodder, *The History of South Australia from its foundation to the year of its Jubilee*, 2 vols., (Sampson Low, Marston & Company), London, 1893

George E. Loyau, *Representative Men of South Australia* (George Howell), Adelaide, 1883

George E. Loyau, *Notable South Australians; or Colonists – Past and Present* (George E. Loyau), Adelaide, 1885

Philip Mennell, *The Dictionary of Australasian Biography*, (Hutchinson), London, 1892

Howard Coxon, John Playford and Robert Reid, *Biographical Register of the South Australian Parliament 1857–1957* (Wakefield Press), Netley, 1985

Wilfrid Prest, Kerrie Round and Carol Fort (eds), *The Wakefield Companion to South Australian History* (Wakefield Press), Kent Town, 2001

Helen Gillman & Stefano Cavedoni, Damien Simonis, Sally Webb, *Italy* (Lonely Planet Publications), Hawthorn, fourth edition, 2000

Italy (Michelin et Cie), Clermont-Ferrand, 1974

Jane Addams, *Twenty Years at Hull House, with Autobiographical Notes*, Illustrated by Norah Hamilton, With an Introduction and Notes by James Hurt (University of Illinois Press), Urbana and Chicago, 1990

Catherine Helen Spence, *Tenacious of the Past: The Recollections of Helen Brodie*, eds Judy King and Graham Tulloch (Centre for Research into New Literatures in English and Libraries Board of South Australia), Adelaide, 1994

Margaret Allen, 'Biographical Background', in Catherine Martin, *An Australian Girl* (ed.), Rosemary Campbell (University of Queensland Press), St. Lucia, 2002

Margaret Barbarlet, *Far From A Low Gutter Girl. The forgotten world of state wards: South Australia 1887–1940* (Oxford University Press), Melbourne, 1983

Lucy Bland, *Banishing the Beast: English Feminism & Sexual Morality 1885–1914* (Penguin Books), London, 1995

Nancy Cott (ed.), *No Small Courage: A History of Women in the United States* (Oxford University Press), New York, 2000

Barbara Goldsmith, *Other Powers: The Age of Suffrage, Spiritualism and the Scandalous Victoria Woodhull* (Harper Perennial), New York, 1999

Patricia Grimshaw, *Women's Suffrage in New Zealand* (Auckland University Press), Wellington, 1972

Pam Hirsch, *Barbara Leigh Smith Bodichon 1827–1891: Feminist, Artist and Rebel* (Pimlico), London, 1999

Raymond V. Holt, *The Unitarian Contribution to Social Progress in England* (The Lindsey Press), London, 1938/1952

Helen Jones, *In Her Own Name: A History of Women in South Australia from 1836* (Wakefield Press), Kent Town, 1994

Ann J. Lane, *To Herland And Beyond: The life and work of Charlotte Perkins Gilman* (Pantheon Books), New York, 1990

Susan Magarey, 'Sex vs Citizenship: Votes for Women in South Australia', *Journal of the Historical Society of South Australia*, no.21, 1993

Susan Magarey, *Unbridling the tongues of women: a biography of Catherine Helen Spence* (Hale & Iremonger), Marrickville, 1985

Susan Magarey, *Passions of the First Wave Feminists* (University of New South Wales Press), Sydney, 2001

Isabel McCorkindale (ed.), *Torchbearers: the WCTU of SA 1886–1948* (Women's Christian Temperance Union), Adelaide, 1949

Jill Roe, *Beyond Belief: Theosophy in Australia 1879–1939* (New South Wales University Press), Kensington, 1986

Elaine Showalter, *A Literature of Their Own: British Novelists from Bronte to Lessing* (Virago Press), London, 1982

Ian Tyrrell, *Woman's World: Woman's Empire: The Woman's Christian Temperance Union in International Perspective, 1880–1930* (University of North Carolina Press), Chapel Hill and London, 1991

Jacqueline Van Voris, *Carrie Chapman Catt: A Public Life* (The Feminist Press at the City University of New York), New York, 1987

Index

Page numbers in italics indicate references to images.

A

A Plea for Pure Democracy, 55–56
A Week in the Future, 10, 159, 268
abbreviations, 217
Aberfoyle Park, 13
Addams, Jane, 108, 161, 220, 337
Adelaide Art Gallery, 46, 77
Adelaide Benevolent and Strangers' Friend Society, 129
Adelaide Democratic Club, 346
Adelaide Morning Chronicle, 40
Adelaide Observer, 48, 149, 219–222, 224, 226, 227, 288 see also *Observer*
Adelaide Register see *Register*
Adelaide Times, 33
Advanced School for Girls, 120, 266
Advertiser, 14, 147, 274, 315, 341
Age, 102, 136, 187, 202, 323, 355
Albury, 193
Alden, Mr, 252–253
Allard, Mrs, 247
Allen, James, 45
America *see* United States of America
American Equal Rights Association, 236
American Proportional Representation League, 155
American Woman Suffrage Association, 236
Ames, Dr Charles Gordon, 151, 223, 233–234, 238
Ames, Julia Frances (Fanny) née Baker, 151, 223, 232, 235, 238, 258–259
 correspondence, 250, 304
An Agnostic's Progress from the Known to the Unknown, 129, 130
An Australian Girl, 115, 222, 226–227, 234, 250
An Autobiography, 2, 8, 11–12, 14, 112, 215–216, 260, 282, 284, 328, 349, 356
Anderson, Elizabeth née Garrett, 161–162, 283–284
Andrews, Dr, 289, 294
Andrews, Elisha Benjamin, 150
Angas, George Fife, 33, 50, 102
Angaston, 33
Anglier, 64
Anstey, Edward Alfred, 197
Anthony, Susan Brownell, 158, 220, 244, 246, 353
Archibald, William Oliver, 318
Argus, 40, 49–50, 52–53, 55, 58, 118, 142, 171, 187, 328, 349, 355–356
Arnold, Matthew, 202
Art Gallery of South Australia, 14, 45
Ash, George, 316
Ashley, Mrs, 223, 236
Ashley, Prof., 151
Atlantic Monthly, 224
Austen, Jane, 60
Austral Examiner, 50
Australasian, 118, 328, 347
Australian Dictionary of Biography, 190
Avery, Rachel Foster, 238–239, 242, 253

B

Backhouse, Alfred Paxton, 190
Baker, Mrs, formerly Annie Herford, née Macnée, 175
Baker, Arthur John, 175
Baker, Miss Ida, 287
Bakewell family, 66
Bakewell, James, 260
Bakewell, Jane née Warren, 48, 82, 260
Bakewell, Mrs J.W., 277

Bakewell, John Warren (Jack), 69, 277
Bakewell, William, 48, 51, 62, 69, 82, 260, 278
Bakewells, the, 66, 260, 277, 285
Balfour, Arthur James, 158, 279, 282
Baltimore, 246, 248, 250
Bank of South Australia, 42, 48
  J.B. Spence, 50, 62
Barnett, Mrs née Henrietta Octavia Rowland, 161, 295
Barnett, Samuel Augustus, 161, 287
Barr Smith Library, 268
Barr Smith, Joanna *see* Smith, Joanna Barr
Barr Smith, Robert *see* Smith, Robert Barr
Barr Smith, Thomas Elder *see* Smith, Thomas Elder Barr
Barrett, Sir James William, 193
Barrington, George, 190
Batchelor, Egerton Lee, 171
Baynton, Barbara née Barbara Janet Ainsleigh Kilpatrick, 189, 343
Beare, Arabella, 43
Beare, Charlotte Hudson, 35
Beare, Eliza (Elizabeth), 43
Beare, Lucy *see* Duval, Lucy (née Beare), 43
Beare, Thomas Hudson, 36, 42–43
Beare, William Loose, 43, 317
Beernaert, Auguste Marie François, 182–183
Bell, Mrs, 261
Bell, Magdelene, 250, 261
Benham, Rosamund, 309–311, 313, 336
Bent, Mr, 262
Bentley, George, 96

Bentzon, Marie-Thérèse (Madame Blanc-Bentzon), 154
Berry, Sir Graham, 136
Besant, Annie, 265
Bevan, Rev. Llewelyn David, 193
Beyer, Mrs, 273
bimetallism, 218
Birkbeck schools, 83–84
Birks, Mrs, 316
Birks, Charles, 316, 322
Birks, Rose née Thomas, 248, 316–318, 320, 322, 324
birthdays, 8, 12, 167, 204, 222, 308, 335–336, 346
  80th, 11
  book, 229
Blackburn, Helen, 161–162, 281
Blackley, Canon, 281
Blackwell, Alice Stone, 236
Blackwell, Dr Elizabeth, 161–162
Blackwell, Henry, 220, 236
Blake, Lillie Devereux, 230
Blankenburg, Rudolph, 249
Blaze de Bury, Baroness Marie Pauline Rose, 162
Blind School, 178
Blyth, Sir Arthur, 101
Blyth, Mrs Howard, 264, 265
Blyth, Neville, 101, 121
Board of Colonization Commissioners, 34
Board of Education, 33, 101
Boarding Out Society (Committee), 99, 101, 103, 317
Bodichon, Barbara Leigh née Smith, 81
Boer War, 179, 180, 328
'Boldrewood, Rolf', 47
book reviews and reviewing, 52–53, 58, 91–92, 111, 118, 131–132, 137, 262, 341, 354
Booth, Mrs Chas, 282

Booth, General William, 107–108
Bosphorus, 54
Boston, 151–153, 222–225, 230, 233–234, 238–239, 251, 258, 280
Boucaut, Sir James Penn, 42, 54
Bowditch, William Lamprey, 187
Bowyear, George John Shirreff, 129
Boys' Reformatory, 103, 105
Brackenridge, Miss, 334
Braddon, Sir Edward Nicholas, 167, 196
Bradlaugh, Charles, 265, 282
Brannlich, Mrs, 256–257
Bray, Caroline [Cara] Hennell, 159, 279
Bray, Charles, 279
Breen, Maggie, 201
Brewster, Sir David, 24
Brient, L.J., 317, 323
Bright, John, 73, 157, 264
Brisbane Courier, 116
British Association for the Advancement of Science, 85, 273
British Linen Company, 27
Brodie, Alexander, 55, 69, 268
  migration, 55
Brodie, James, 69–70, 95, 262, 266, 276
Brodie, John, 26–27
Brodie, Margaret, 27, 69, 71–72
Brodie, Margaret Fernie, 39
Brodie, Mary, 26–27, 70–72, 79
Brodie, William, 310
Broken Hill, 337–338, 346
Brontë, Charlotte later Nicholls, 52
Brooker, T.H., 320
Brothe, Fred, 321
Brown Hill (Brownhill) Creek, 40, 42, 45

Brown, Dr George, 144
Brown, Prof. Jethro, 341
Brown, John, 33
Browne, Thomas Alexander, 47
Browning, Elizabeth Barrett, 65, 72, 97, 147–148, 159
Browning, Robert, 65, 67, 72, 97, 147–148, 178
Bruce, Theodore, 185
Buckley, Dr, 255–256
Bulletin, 112, 189
Bulow, Miss, 290–291, 293, 297
   letters to, 307
Bunyan, John, 129–130
Burdett-Coutts, Angela, 281
Bürkli, Karl, 162, 298, 301
   letters to, 302
Burnet, James, 72, 95
Burnet, John, 70
Burns, Robert, 77
Burra, 47, 52, 55, 62, 168
Buxton, Sir Thomas Fowell, 170
Buxton, Lady Victoria née Noel, 170

C

Caldwell, Robert, 317, 320
Campbell, Sir John Logan, 31
Campbell, Reginald John, 206
Canada, 151
   effective voting, 155
   preaching, 112
Capen, Samuel B., 237
Carlyle, Thomas, 78, 132
Carnegie, Andrew, 234
Carpenter, Edward, 274
Cash, Mary née Sibree, 159, 278
Castine, Major, 316
Castlemaine, 193
Catherine Helen Spence: A Study and an Appreciation, 44

Catt, Carrie Chapman, 229, 334, 351
Chace, Elizabeth, 224
Chalmers Church, 115, 134
Chamber, John, 293
Chamberlain, Joseph, 86
Chambers, Robert, 42, 157, 269
Chapman, Carrie Lane, 244, 250
Charity Organisation Society, 129, 328
Charleston, David Morley, 170, 184, 318
Chicago, 4, 108, 148–150, 219, 221–222, 226, 333, 337, 342
   Alice Henry, 329
   Anthropological Congress, 232
   Charities and Correction Congress, 222
   Congress of Charities, 13
   Hull House, 108, 161, 220, 238
   Keller, Helen, 179
   Women's Christian Temperance Union, 220
   Women's Congress, 243
   Women's Trade Union League, 329
   World Fair, 124, 148, 218–219
   World's Fair Congresses, 144
Childers, J. Wallbanke, 34
Children's Courts, 104–105, 331, 334 *see also* Juvenile Courts
Children's Hospital, 99
Childs, George William, 150
Christian science, 177
Church of Scotland, 42, 71
Church, Mrs, Norah (Nora), 262–263, 265–267, 289, 321
citizenship, 121, 166, 206, 236
civics, 122

Clapperton, Jane Hume, 159, 268, 278, 279, 336
   letters to, 275
Clara Morison – A Tale of South Australia during the Gold Fever, 12, 48, 51–53, 59, 64, 74, 142
Clare, 55
Clark, Caroline Emily, 13, 64, 80, 85, 98–99, *100*, 102–105, 113, 115–116, 133–134, 151, 223, 267, 288, 317, 320, 324, 329, 334
   letters from, 284, 303
Clark, Caroline Emily née Hill, 62, 80, 83, 223
Clark, Rev. Charles, 117
Clark, Emily, 151
Clark, Francis, 62
Clark, John Howard, 62, 80, 97, 101, 114, 129
   death, 116
Clark, Lucy Howard later Bowyear, 129
Clark, Rosa, 85
Clark, Symonds, 85
Clarke, Marcus Andrew Hislop, 132
Clay, Laura, 244
Clayton, Katie, 264, 268, 276, 279–280
Clayton, Canon Lewis, 157, 264, 276
Clayton, Lydia, 282
Clymer, Mrs, 230
Cobbe, Frances Power, 80
Cobden, Richard, 73
Cockburn, Dr, 317
Cockburn, Sir John Alexander, 198
Cockburn, Sarah Holdway née Brown, 198
Colenso, Bishop John, 68, 81
Colonial Convention, 278
Colonization Commissioners, 66
Colton, John, 223

Colton, Mary née Cutting, 99, 104, 223
Conference of Women Suffragists, 351
Congress of Charities, Correction and Philanthropy (International Congress of Charities, Correction and Philanthropy), 13, 148–149, 218
Connor, Mrs, 257
Constitution Amendment Act, 163
Conway, Moncure Daniel, 86
Cook, A., 323
Cook, Harriet, 322
Cook, Mrs, 283
Cooley, Astor, 233, 237, 242, 254–255, 293, 302
Coombe, Ephraim Henry, 197, 206
Cooper, Mr J.A., 290
Co-operative Clothing Factory, 195, 333
Cooperative Housekeeping Association, 231
copyright, 59, 226
Corbet, Mr and Mrs, 281
Corn Exchange, 26, 62, 95
Cornhill Magazine, 59, 72, 96
Cotton, George Witherage, 76
Cotton, Sir John Blacker, 99
Courtney, Mrs, 283, 285
Courtney, Leonard Henry, 158, 179, 266–267, 279–280, 285, 337
letters to, 264
Coutts, Angela Burdett, 281
Couvreur, Jessie, 227
Coventry, 278–279
Cowan, Edith, 330
Cowan, George, 68, 83, 85–86, 290–293
Crabbie, John, 265–266
Craik, Prof. George Lillie, 56, 67

Cridge, Alfred Denton, 145–146, 148, 219, 221, 237, 247–248, 251–252, 254, 259, 299
articles, 257, 308
book on proportional representation, 155
correspondence, 174, 230, 233, 241–242, 251–253, 255, 259, 267, 271, 274–275, 289, 292–293, 295, 301–302, 317, 323
pamphlets, 229, 232–233, 300
Criminological Society, 175–176
Crofton, Sir Walter, 80
Croly, Jane Cunningham, 118, 231, 254, 256
Cross, Ada née Cambridge, 133, 227

D

Daily Telegraph, 52, 56, 189, 317
Dale, Rev. Robert William Dale, 85
Davenport Hill *see* Hill, Davenport
Davenport, Margaret Fraser née Cleland, 99
Davenport, Sir Samuel, 99
David, Mrs Edgeworth née Caroline Martha Mallett, 190
David, Sir Tannatt William Edgeworth, 190
Davidson, Harriet Miller née Miller, 115, 134
Davidson, Rev. John, 115
Davies, Mrs, 324
Davis, Abraham Hopkins, 35
Davison, Mr and Mrs, 229
Day, Mrs, 272
Day, John Medway, 272
Deas, Frank, 274
de Lissa, Miss, 346

Democratic Women's Association of South Australia, 7
Destitute Asylum, 99, 106, 173–174
Destitute Board, 101, 103, 106, 173, 178, 192, 219, 334
destitute children, 13, 80, 103, 153
USA, 149
diaries, 7, 10–11, 116, 213–216, 257, 271–272, 310, 323–324
Dietrick, Ellen Batelle, 233, 235
Digger, Mr, 245–247
Dilke, Mrs Ashton, 283
Dilke, Sir Charles, 79
Doctor's Family, 57
Dolittle, Mrs, 245, 247
Donnelly, Ignatius, 142, 233, 275
Dorling, Miss, 287
Douglass, Frederick, 221
Dowie, Ménie Muriel, 157, 269, 273
Dowie, Mrs Muir, 157, 268–269, 273
Downer, Sir John, 317, 320, 323
Drexel, Anthony Joseph, 150
Droop, H.R., 280
drought, 95
Duke of York, 35–36, 43, 56
Dumfries, 30
Duncan, Mrs, 265
Duncan, Kossuth William, 198, 346
Durning-Lawrence, Sir Edwin, 160
Dutton, Mary Ann later Taylor, 65
Duval, Francis, 43, 56
Duval, Lewis, 324
Duval, Lucy Alice Rose (later Mrs Henry James Hood), 139
Duval, Lucy Anne née Beare, 43, 56

E

Eadnay, Mrs, 258
East Lothian Bank, 27
Eastman, Crystal, 124–125
Eddy, Miss, 258–259
Edinburgh, 26, 77, 157, 264, 267
education, 13, 114, 200, 203, 348, 351
   Birkbeck Schools, 83–84
   church, 83
   citizenship, 121
   elementary, 122
   free, 119
   higher, 123, 161, 283
   New South Wales, 203
   systems, 113
   theories, 122
   USA, 151, 218
   Victoria, 203
   women, 81, 207, 282
Education Act, 200
Education Board, 114
Education Department, 23, 113, 222
   Board of Advice, 119
effective voting *see* proportional representation
Effective Voting League, 112, 185–186, 196, 197, 206
Egremont, 251, 253
Egremonts, 309
Elder family, 41
Elder, Alexander Lang, 41
Elder, Smith and Co, 62
Elder, Thomas, 48, 114
elections, 168, 267, 337
   effective voting, 170
   federal, 187
   mock, 242
   primary, 231
   proportional representation, 55, 184
   secret ballot, 79
   Senate, 13
   South Australian, 1

Electoral Reform Society of South Australia, 55
electoral systems, 13
   reform, 54
Eliot, Miss, 259
Eliot, Mrs, 255
Eliot, George (Marian or Mary Ann Evans), 81, 88, 90–91, 93, 111, 132, 147, 159, 219, 261, 278–279
   lectures on, 241, 243
   letter from, 91–92
   meeting, 91
Ellis, William, 83–84
English, Scottish, and Australian Bank, 65, 126–127, 142
   J.B. Spence, 134
Evans, MaryAnn (Marian) *see* Eliot, George
Evening Journal, 133
executors, 5

F

Fabians and Fabian Society, 157, 219, 263, 265, 268–269, 338
Farr, Rev. George Henry, 104
Farr, Julia Warren née Ord, 104, 317
Fawcett, Henry, 55, 67
Fawcett, Dame Millicent née Garrett (Mrs Fawcett), 161, 283–285
Fay, Miss, 251
Federal Convention, 8, 167–168, 170, 181
federation, 14, 162, 188–189
   proportional representation, 181
female suffrage, 170, 236
   Alice Henry, 199
   New Zealand, 158
   North America, 218
   South Australia, 12
   USA, 229–231, 236

feminism, 4, 11, 80, 89, 207, 328
   Britain, 342
   USA, 124, 147, 150, 231
Ferrer, Francisco, 84
fiction, 118, 159, 226–227, 268, 273
Fields, Annie Adams, 154
Finlayson, John Harvey, 116
Finniss, Boyle Travers, 34
Fitzjames, 103–104
Fleming, Sir Sandford, 155, 251
Fletcher, Alice, 232–233
Flower, B.O., 280
Flurscheim, Mrs, 299–302
Flurscheim, Michael, 263, 265–267, 281, 299–300, 302
   correspondence with, 267, 271, 296, 301, 303–305
Folkes, Mr, 255
Fortnightly, 58, 72–73
Forward Movement, the, 272
Foster, Richard Witty, 317
Fowlds, Sir George, 184
Fox, Sir Frank Ignatius, 189
Fox, William Johnson, 86
Franklin, 247
Franklin, Miles (Stella), 10, 14, 214, 329, 338–339, 341, 343, *344*, 348–349
Franklyn, Mortimer, 138
Fraser, Sir John Foster, 120
Fraser's Magazine, 80, 110
Free Church of Scotland, 37, 71, 115
Freer, Allan, 76
Frome, Captain Edward Charles, 43
Froude, James Anthony, 78, 179

G

Galloway, Louie, 322
Garran, Andrew, 50, 101–102, 118, 188
   letters, 251

Garran, Mary Isham née Sabine, 101–102, 188, 190
Garran, Robert Randolph, 188
Garran, W.L., 293
Garrison, Mrs, 153, 234–237
Garrison, Charlie, 234
Garrison, Frank, 223–224, 235
Garrison, William Lloyd, 152–153, 218, 222–223, 226, 234, 239
　correspondence, 259, 323
Garrisons, 224, 233, 235, 237
Gates, Adelie, 247
Gathered In, 116, 193, 288–291, 293–294, 297
Gawler, 198
Gawler, Col., 35
George, Mrs, 250, 256, 258
George, Henry, 137–138, 153, 155, 184, 218, 231, 234, 250, 258–259
George, Henry, Mrs, 301
George, Mary, 318
Germany, 163
Gilbert, Thomas, 33
Giles, Clement, 318
Giles, William, 36
Gilfillan, John Alexander, 45–46, 77
Gilfillan, Matilda, née Witt, 45
Gilman, Charlotte Perkins *see* Stetson, Charlotte Perkins (Gilman)
Girls' Literary Society, 142
Glenelg, 31, 33, 315, 320, 322, 334
Glenn, John, 246, 248
Glyde, Lavington, 55
Glynn, Patrick McMahon, 170–171, 181, 185
gold
　Pine Creek, 127
　USA reserve, 218
Goldstein, Vida Jane Mary, 207, 254, 331, 335, 347–349, 351
Goodbar, Miss, 288
Goodby, Katharine, 249

Goode, Charles Henry later Sir, 104, 341
Goodham, Miss, 139
Goolwa, 66
Gossip, Miss, 264–265
Gouger, Robert, 32–34
Gould, Sir Albert John, 188
Gove, W.H., 234, 238
Gover, Mrs, 265
Government Gazette, 33
Graham, Mr, 256
Graham, Mrs, 57, 72, 77–78, 94
Grant, Mrs, 264–266
Gray, Jourdiana, 268
Gregory, Ellen Louisa, 1, 5, 7–8, 11, 142, 183–184, 201, 225, 315, 321, 323–324, 335
　age, 4
　CHS's death, 7
　letters from, 241, 248, 264, 268, 292, 303
　letters to, 241, 264, 275, 302
　migration, 5
Gregory, Lizzie, 297
Grey, Sir George, 31, 41, 280
Griffin, Mrs Tom, 291–293, 296
Grote Street Model School, 113–114
guardianships, 56, 66, 184
Guild of Co-operative Women, 157

H
Hailes, Nathaniel, 35
Haining, Jessie, née Grant, 42
Haining, Rev. Robert, 42, 64
Hale, Edward Everett, 230
Hall, Eleanor Dora *see* Wren, Eleanor Dora
Hall, Sir John, 158, 282, 283
Halliwell, Richard P., 233, 237
Hamley Bridge, 345
Handfasted, 5, 13, 131
Handyside, Mrs, 265
Handyside, Andrew Dods, 253
Handyside, Jessie, 267

Handyside, Nicol, 78
Hankey, Mrs Helen, 287, 290, 294
Hankey, Mrs Jameson, 287
Hanson, Sir Richard Davies, 32–33, 109
Hardy, Alfred, 88
Hardy, Arthur, 88
Hare, Mrs Alfred, 280
Hare, Charles Simeon, 57
Hare, Katie, 79, 85, 157
Hare, Thomas, 54–57, 59, 67, 79, 89, 158, 264, 268, 276–277, 282
　proportional representation, 54, 56, 79
　scheme, 55–56
Hare system, 66, 89, 197–198, 298, 337
Harper, Frances Ellen Watkins, 221
Harper, J. Henry, 227, 252
Harper, James, 252
Harper's, 236, 240, 249, 252–257, 278, 333
Hartford, 239–240
Hartley, Mrs, 266, 321, 324
Hartley, John Anderson, 23, 113–114, 121, 201, 203, 218, 266
Harvard University, 151, 153
Hawker, Rev. Bertram, 203
Hawker, Edward, 316
Hawker, George Charles, 203, 316
Hawkins, Miss, 346
Hennell, Charles, 279
Hennell, Sara S., 159, 279
Henry, Alice, 5, 10, 14, 199, 207, 327–331, *332*, 351, 353–355
　Chicago, 329
　in USA, 354
　letters to, 214, 327, 329, 331–350
　proportional representation, 327
　travels, 328

Henry, Josephine K., 244
Herald, 137, 302, 356
Heysen, Hans, 339
Higginson, Rev. Mr, 111
Hill, A.A., 258
Hill, Arthur, 62
Hill, Edwin, 62, 83
Hill, Ellen, 288
Hill, Florence Davenport, 56, 64, 80, 113, 161, 286–289, 292–293, 296, 334
   letters from, 272, 284
Hill, Frederick, 62, 80, 83, 282
Hill, Howard, 64
Hill, Matthew Davenport, 62, 64, 80, 83
Hill, Rosamond (Rosemund), 64, 80, 113
Hill, Sir Rowland, 34, 40, 54, 56, 62, 64, 80, 83
Hindmarsh, Governor, 35, 43
Hindmarsh, Jane, 43
Holden, William, 133
Holder, Sir Frederick William, 168, 323, 347
Holdfast Bay, 31, 33, 39
Holman, William Arthur, 188
Holmes, Dr Bayard Taylor, 148, 174
Holmes, Lucy, 292
Holmes, Oliver Wendell, 153, 223–224, 237, 302
Homestead League, 76
Hood, Catherine (Katherine or Katie), 139, 183–184, 201, 230, 293
Hood, Charles, 139, 183–184
Hood, George, 139, 183–184
Hood, Henry James, 139
Hood, Rose née Duval, 139, 142, 183–184, 315, 317, 321, 324
   death, 183–184
   letters to, 275
Hood, Thomas, 72, 97, 260
Hope, George, 73
Hospital Commission, 166
Hotham, Sir Charles, 53

House of Representatives, 168, 170–171, 181, 183–184
Howe, James H., 317
Howe, Julia Ward, 154, 252
Howell, George, 137
Howland, Isabel, 244, 246–248
Howland, Oliver Aiken, 155, 242–243
Howland, Sir William Holmes, 155, 243
Hubbard, Mrs, 257
Hübbe, Edith formerly Cook, 266, 303, 322
Hughes, Sir Walter Watson, 62, 114
Hull House, 108, 148, 161, 220, 238, 291
Hultin, Ida, 245
Humphreys, John H., 159
Hunt, Mrs Alfred, 281
Hussey, C.H., 48
Hussey, Mary, 258
Hutchins, Mrs, 271
Hutchison, James, 170

I
immigration
   families, 90
   family, 50
   German Lutherans, 33
   laws, 32
   South Australia, 32, 53
   Wakefield principle, 33
   Western Australia, 32
income tax, 138
Indianapolis, 149, 335
Indians (American), 232–233
Ingelow, Jean, 72
Ingram, Mary, 285
International Conference on Charities and Correction, 149
International Council of Women, 198–199, 283
International Women's Year, 10
Italy, 163, 305–306, 309

J
Jefferis, James, 102
Jefferis, Marian née Turner, 102
Jenkins, John Greeley, 317
Jewett, Sarah Orne, 155
Johnson, Prof Edwin, 286, 295
Johnson, Tom Loftin, 234
Jones, Helen, 2, 4, 10, 214
Journal of Australasia, 52
journalism, 132
Juvenile Courts, 199, 353 *see also* Children's Courts

K
Kangaroo Island, 35–36, 43, 134, 315
Kapunda, 55, 137, 309
Kapunda Herald, 181
Kay, Mrs William, 322
Keating, Senator John Henry, 196
Keller, Helen, 178–179
Kelsey, Roland, 315
Kent, Dr, 244, 246–247
Kindergarten Union of South Australia, 203, 336
Kingsley, Charles, 133, 275
Kingston, Charles Cameron, 168–170, 173, 316, 318
Kingston, George Strickland, 34
Kirby, Rev. J.C., 342
Kirkby, Diane, 14, 327, 330
Kirkpatrick, Andrew Alexander, 184
Knibbs, Sir George Handley, 203
Knight, Charles, 81
Knox, John, 23
Kydmann, Mrs, 280–281

L
Labour Party, 54, 198
Laidlaw, Thomas, 31
land, 76, 138
   crime, 177
   land tenure, 122

land, *cont'd*
  laws, 32
  taxation, 122, 136–137
  Wakefield principle, 33
leaflets, 204, 336 *see also* pamphlets
lectures, 175, 238, 240, 251, 265, 278, 286, 333, 346, 349, 351
  ballots, 242
  Boston, 239
  effective voting, 166
  literary, 97, 147, 243
  mock elections, 162
  USA, 4, 156, 219, 231
    effective voting, 146, 148
Lee, Mary, *164*, 318, 320
Lefevre, Shaw, 286
Legislative Council, 316
  NSW, 31, 351
  South Australia, 30, 33, 48, 163, 170, 184–185, 198
    effective voting, 158
  J.B. Spence, 134
  Tasmania, 197
  Victoria, 136
Levens, Miss, 257
Leverson, Dr, 261
Lewes, George Henry, 58, 91
Liberal Woman Suffrage League, 283
Libraries Board of South Australia, 10, 269
Lichanbriggs, 271
Light Square, 14
Light, Colonel William, 34, 80
Lilley, Emmie, 293
Lindsey, Judge Benjamin Barr, 124, 141, 146
Lister, Mrs Watson, 331
Ljungdahl, Lesley Durrell, 159
Lochenbriggs, 271
Locke, Miss Lilian, 334, 336, 355
Lozier, Jennie M., 230
Lubbock, Sir John, 158, 266, 279–280, 282
  letters to, 264

Ludlow, Mrs, 86
Lugarno, 267, 299–300, 302–304

M

McBride, Mrs, 257
McDermott, Harriet, 65
McDougal, 251, 253
Macfie, M., 289
McGlynn, Dr, 252
McGregor, Miss, 334
Mackay, Catherine Edith Macauley *see* Martin, Catherine Edith Macauley (Katie) née Mackay
Mackellar, Mrs, 266
Mackintosh, Dr, 267, 269
Mackintosh, Sir James, 67
Maclaren, Mr, 266
Maclaren, Mrs, 267–268, 273, 283
McLaren, Alexander, 206
McLaren, Priscilla Bright, 157, 264
McMartin, Mr, 310–311
McMillan, Sir William, 188
McPherson, John Abel, 317–318
Magill Democratic Club, 346
Magill School, 99, 101, 104
Magnus, Mrs, 292
Maguire, Judge James George, 146
Mann, Charles, 34
Marjoribanks, Ishbel Maria, 198
Mark Lane, 26, 62, 95
Marston, Mr, 288
Martin, Annie Montgomerie, 320
Martin, Arthur Patchett, 109

Martin, Catherine Edith Macauley (Katie) née Mackay, 133, 222–223, 226–227, 256, 258, 266, 273, 276, 289, 297, 303–311, 323, 329, 335, 342–343, 345–346, 350, 354
  correspondence with, 229–230, 236, 241, 250, 254, 262, 264, 268, 271–272, 275, 286, 290, 292, 296, 299–300, 320
  publications, 115
Martin, Fred, 115, 222–223, 303–306, 308–316, 329, 338, 342, 346
  death, 350
Martin, James, 292, 297
Martin, Mrs James, 297
Martin, James Edward, 42
Martin, Katie or Kate (Mrs Fred Martin) *see* Martin, Catherine
Martineau, David, 294
Martineau, Harriet, 112
Martineau, James, 112, 294
Marxist Social Democratic Federation, 265
Mason, Miss, 255
Mason, Jennie, 355
Mather, John Baxter, 147
Matras, Mr, 291
Matras, Mrs, 291
Matters, Mrs, 318
Maule, Kate, 265, 272–273, 275, 288
  letters to, 268
Maxwell, Mr, 271
Maxwell, Mrs, 77–78, 265
Maxwell, May, 270, 271, 273
Maxwell, W, 270, 273
Maxwells, 272
Mayo, Dr Helen, 346
Melbourne Review, 82, 91–92, 109–111, 118, 132, 136–137
Mellon, Harriot, 281

Melrose, 19–21, 24–27, 29, 38–39, 41, 69, 74, 76, 78, 139, 269
Melrose, George, 31
Mennell, Philip, 273
Mill, Harriet (Harriet Taylor) née Hardy, 88
Mill, John Stuart, 54, 56, 67, 88–90, 282, 298
   proportional representation, 54, 79
   women's suffrage, 89–90
Miller, Annie, 348
Mills, Dr and Mrs, 177
Milne, Agnes, 195
Milne, Eliza née Disher, 30–31
Milne, Sir William, 30
Mitchell, David Scott, 338
Moncrieff, Mr, 321
Monkswell, Lord, 281
Moonta, 62, 65–66
Moore, George, 160, 281
More, Hannah, 87
Morgan, Mr, 293
Morice, Jim, 339
Morice, Lucy (Louise) Spence, 2, *3*, 4, 7, 203, 225, 315–316, 323, 329, 336, 338–339, 342, 346, 347, 355
   CHS's death, 2, 5
   CHS's diaries, 213–215
Morphett, John, 34
Morris, Dr, 339, 342
Morrison, Mr, 296
Mount Gambier, 95, 115, 207, 342, 345–346
Mr Hogarth's Will, 58–59, 350
Mullen, Charles, 94
Mundy, Alfred Miller, 43
Municipal Bill, 40, 54
Murray, Miss, 266, 269, 356
Murray, Mr, 269
Murray, Mrs, 65
Murray, Mrs (CHS's elder sister, wife of Andrew Murray), 274–275
   letters from, 272
   letters to, 275

Murray, Andrew, 19, 40–41, 46, 48–51, 53–54, 64, 142, 269
Murray, D. & W., 77, 292
Murray, David, 77, 250, 274, 278, 297
Murray, Mrs David, 274
Murray, George, 335
Murray, Helen née Cumming, 77, 265, 266, 274, 276
Murray, Jessie née Spence, 5, 19, 25, 42, 64
   childhood, 26
   death, 142
   marriage, 40
   migration, 31
Murray, John David, 5, 83
Murray, Louisa, 267, 269
Murray, Madge, 335
Murray, Mary Anne, 253
Murray, Nene, 249
Murray, Thomas, 23–24
Murray, William, 77, 262, 267, 274–275
Musson, K, 248–249, 252, 254, 257, 317, 323
   letter to, 268
Mutual Improvement Society, 91
Myers, Frederic William Henry, 116
Myers, Mary, 321
Myles, Louisa, 268, 321
Myponga, 47

N

Nanson, Edward John, 187, 193, 194
Naples, 309–310
National American Women's Suffrage Association, 220
National Council of Women, 180, 198–199, 245, 329, 338, 355
   NSW, 245
   USA, 239
   Victoria, 331
National Society for Women's Suffrage, 161, 281

National Women's Suffrage Convention, 220
National Women's Trade Union League of America, 199
Naville, Ernest, 162, 301, 308
New England Women's Club, 233
New South Wales, 142, 187–189
   destitute children, 102
   effective voting, 328
   Electoral Act, 257
   land, 32
   Legislative Council, 31
   National Council of Women, 245
   politics, 192
   proportional representation, 187
   Womanhood Suffrage League, 317
New York, 147, 154–155, 219–222, 225, 227, 230–231, 236, 240, 249
New Zealand, 166, 184, 208, 335
   destitute children, 102
   Labour Party, 185
   progressive taxation, 162
   proportional representation, 184–185
   votes for women, 283
Newell, James Edward, 145
Newton, Frances, 203
Nichols, Elizabeth Webb, 318, *319*
Ningan, Mr, 292
Ningan, Mrs, 292
Ningans, 293
novel writing, 118

O

Observer, 35, 48, 96, 115–116, 131, 133–134, 219–222, 224, 226–227, 232, 259, 316

O'Halloran, William Littlejohn, 43
Oliphant, Mrs Margaret née Wilson, 36, 37, 57–58, 81–82, 93, 116
  Autobiography, 36, 349
O'Regan, Patrick Joseph, 184
Osborne, Miss, 290

P

Palmer, Colonel G., 66
Palmerston, 126–127
Palmyra, 30–31, 66
pamphlets, 57, 67, 117, 160–161, 175, 203, 229, 234, 240, 294, 296, 298–299, 329, 342, 348
  effective voting, 354
  Hare scheme, 55–56
  homeless men, 339
  proportional representation, 292–293
  Register, 11
  sales, 244, 255
Paris, 75, 85, 162
Park, Helen, 27
Park, Janet, 21, 72, 269
Parker, J.W. and Son, 12, 52
Parkes, Mr and Mrs, 292
Parkes, Hilma Olivia Edla Johanna née Ekenberg, 189
Parr, James Hamilton, 62
Parramatta Home for Women, 192, 328
Paul, John Thomas, 184
Peace Society, 180, 329
Pearson, Prof. Charles Henry, 79, 85, 102, 136–137
Peirce, Mrs (Melusine) Fay, 219–220, 230–231, 240–244, 250–259, 278
  correspondence, 253, 268, 274, 293
Peterborough (Petersburg), 206, 248, 345, 346
Petherick Collection, 160, 278

Petherick, Edward Augustus, 160, 277, 284, 291, 297, 347
Petherick, Mary Agatha previously Skeats née Annear 160, 277–278, 284–291, 294–298, 347
  correspondence, 293, 300, 320
Phillips, Mrs, 283
Phin, Sarah, 19, 25, 27, 29, 41, 47, 49, 74–75
Pilgrim, Mr, 271
Pine Creek, 127
Piper, Arthur William, 166
Pitterdriech, Mrs, 274
Plainfield, 240–242
Plea for Pure Democracy, 56, 67, 79, 89
Pocius, Ieva, 14, 39
Pol Study Club, 251, 253, 258–259
Political Education Leagues, 353
politics, 4, 12, 132, 329
  feminist, 328
  NSW, 192
  USA, 146
Pond, Mr, 288
Port Adelaide, 31, 55, 345–346
Port Augusta, 127
Port Pirie, 198, 355
Port Wakefield, 346
Potter, Beatrice *see* Webb, Beatrice
preaching, 37, 82, 112
  Boston, 151
  Melbourne, 144
  USA, 228
preferential voting, 13
  see also proportional representation
Preferential Voting Bill, Victoria, 194
Preston, Margaret, 13, 14
Price, Thomas, 341
Price, Mrs Tom, 355
Prince Alfred College, 113

progressive taxation, 162
proportional representation (effective voting or single transferable voting), 4, 11, 54, 112, 136, 138, 145, 165, 167–168, 170–172, 178, 184–185, 190, 194, 197–198, 201, 204, 207–208, 224, 233, 241–243, 246, 252–253, 277, 279, 287, 292, 301, 328–329, 335–336, 345, 347, 354, 356 *see also* preferential voting *and* quota representation
  articles, 110
  Belgium, 182
  Britain, 157–159, 179, 264
  campaign for, 1
  Canada, 155
  CHS's priority, 98
  Commonwealth, 181
  federation, 181
  female suffrage, 12
  first, 40
  Gove system, 234
  Hare, Thomas, 54, 56
  Hare system, 89
  Hare-Spence, 13
  Henry, Alice, 327
  lectures, 166, 219, 242
  letter writing, 95
  Mill, J.S., 54
  Municipal Bill, 40
  New Zealand, 184–185
  NSW, 187–189, 328
  pamphlets, 292
  promotion of, 8
  South Australia, 171
  Spence, J.B., 135, 143
  support for, 8
  supporters, 54, 79, 188, 197, 261, 308, 318
  Switzerland, 162, 298
  Sydney, 144
  Tasmania, 167, 187, 196
  USA, 146–148, 150, 220, 222, 231, 337

proportional representation, *cont'd*
   vote counting, 8
   Young, Jeanne, 144
Proportional Representation Bill, 336
Proportional Representation Review, 233, 247–248
Proportional Representation Society, British, 159, 280
Proportional Representation Society of New South Wales, 188
Proud, Cornelius, 167, 201, 317
Proud, Dorothea later Pavy, 167
Proud, Emily née Good, 167
Putnam, Mrs, 234

Q

Queensland, 10
   absolute majority, 245
   destitute children, 102
Queenslander, 102, 116
Quick, Sir John, 188
Quilty, Mr, 348
Quilty, John, 1, 7, 201
Quilty, Kate née Breen, 1, 7, 201
quota representation, 40, 80
   see also proportional representation

R

Ralston, Mrs, 268
Reed, Thomas Sadler, 101
Register (South Australian Gazette and Colonial Register), 31, 34, 39, 48, 51, 55–56, 66, 96, 99, 115, 117–118, 131–134, 137, 144, 202–204, 228, 234, 237, 247, 257, 266, 282, 284, 290, 295–296, 302, 315–316, 321, 324, 333, 335, 337, 348, 350, 356

Register, cont'd
   An Autobiography, 1–2, 4, 10, 13, 15
   articles, 203
   contributions, 115
   editor, 116
   editors, 50, 62, 97, 101–102, 116
   education, 114
   first issue, 31–32, 36
   letters to, 89
   proprietors, 35–36, 62
   second issue, 33
   sonnetts, 202
Reid, Lady, 112
Reid, Sir George Houston, 112, 188, 189, 328
Reid, Hugh, 262
Reid, Janet, 74, 76
Reid, Rev. John, 206
Religious Tract Society, 87
Remsen, Daniel S., 231, 241–243, 251–253, 258
Review, 137
   articles, 110, 136
Ridley, John, 49
rights for women, 12, 88, 99, 184
   J.S. Mill, 54
   USA, 229
Riverton, 346
Robbins, Raymond, 339
Robertson, George, 55, 137, 160, 277
Robertson, George (of Angus and Robertson), 137
Robins, Elizabeth, 342
Rosebery, Lord, 110
Rotherham, Mrs, 278
Rothschild, Sir Nathaniel (Lord Rothschild), 282
Rothwell, Mr, 255–256
Rowland, Henrietta Octavia, later Barnett, 161, 287
Royal Colonial Institute, 289
Royal Commission into the Destitute Act, 103

Russell, Frances E., 280
Russell, Percy, 291, 295
Rutherford, William, 48

S

Saddleworth, 346
Salem, 238
Salter, William Mackintire, 249
Samoa, 144–145
Samuel, Herbert, 105
San Francisco, 4, 144–148
San Francisco Chronicle, 148
Sanger, Mrs Margaret, 221–222, 242, 249, 256–257
   correspondence , 304, 309
Sangster, Mrs, 252, 255
Saturday Review, 59
Schlinders, Sol, 230
Schreiner, Olive, 248–249
Scott, Rose, 1–2, 5, 14, 144, 180, 187, 190–192, 328, 334, 338–339, 343, 348, 351, 352, 353–356
   biography, 330
   correspondence, 327, 329
   letters to, 351–357
Scott, Sir Walter, 20, 25, 39, 42, 65, 116, 180
secret ballot, 79, 147
Senate, the, 183
   preferential voting, 13
Senden, William, 40
sermons, 37, 86, 111–113, 341
Seymour, Sara Winthrop Smith, 245
Shakespeare Society, 219
Sharpe, Mrs, 48
Shaw, Flora L. later Lady Lugard, 285–286
Shea, Ann, 245
Sheppard, Kate Wilson, 283
Sherwood, Mary Martha née Butt, 130
Shrew, Miss, 282
Siena, 163, 222, 296, 302–306, 316

Silver Wattle: South Australian Acrostics, 134
Simpson, A.M., 45
Simpson, Jerry, 245
Simpson, Lavinia née Allen, 45
Single Tax League, 218
single transferable voting *see* proportional representation
Sinnett, Frederick, 52, 56, 67, 127
Sinnett, Sophia, 67, 127
Skeats, Mary Agatha née Annear *see* Petherick, Mary Agatha
Smith, Arthur Bruce, 188
Smith, Elder and Co, 59, 91
  Clara Morison, 51–52
  Tender and True, 53
Smith, Prof. Goldwin, 155
Smith, Prof. Henry, 85
Smith, James, 103, 104, 106
Smith, Joanna Barr née Elder, 114, 115, 130, 132, 268, 346
Smith, Richard Bower, 94
Smith, Robert Barr, 48, 114, 115, 143, 130, 132, 268, 347
Smith, Thomas Elder Barr, 268
Smyth, Owen, 104
Smythe, Robert Sparrow, 117
Society for Promoting Useful Knowledge, 31
Society for Psychical Research, 116
Society for the Promotion of Social Purity, 316
Some Social Aspects of South Australian Life, 117
sonnets, 202
Sorosis, 230–231
South Africa, 179–180
  effective voting, 207–208
South Australian, 40–42, 51

South Australian Association, 33–34, 50, 80
South Australian Bank, 35, 126
  J.B. Spence, 47
South Australian Colonization Commission, 33
South Australian Company, 33–36
South Australian Co-operative Clothing Company, Limited, 195–196
South Australian Gazette and Colonial Register, 34–35
South Australian Gazette and Mining Journal, 35
South Australian Institute, 33, 35, 49, 96
  Library, 33
South Australian Library and Mechanics Institute, 49
South Australian Literary Association (Society), 32–33, 49, 109
South Australian Public Library, 32
South Australian Railways, 55
South Australian Register see Register
South Australiana, 97
South Place Ethical Society, 86
Southern Australian, 34
Sowden, William, 10
Spectator, 131
Spence, Agnes, 19, 25, 26, 47–48
Spence, Clara B., 243, 251
Spence, David (CHS's father), 19, 30, 45
Spence, David Wauchope (CHS's brother), 19, 30, 47, 50, 123, 135–136, 146
Spence, Eliza Brodie, 19

Spence, Helen Brodie, 19–20, 24–25, 27, 39, 41, 47, 54–55, 65–66, 70, 72, 132, 139, *140*
  birth, 282
  death, 3–4, 39, 139, 141–142, 314
  marriage, 22, 27, 38
  migration, 30
Spence, Jessie née Cumming (sister in law), 19, 54, 64–65, 77, 316, 322–323
Spence, Jessie (sister) *see* Murray, Jessie née Spence
Spence, John (CHS's uncle), 27–28, 42
Spence, John Brodie, 7, 19, 51, 77, 98, *135*, 166, 168, 171, 203, 219, 222–223, 225, 295, 315–317, 322–323, 349
  Bank of South Australia, 50, 62
  childhood, 21
  correspondence, 228, 237, 251, 253, 257, 259, 263–264, 266–269, 272, 274, 290, 299, 303, 305
  death, 47, 194
  effective voting, 8, 143
  English, Scottish, and Australian Bank, 65, 75, 127
  executor, 5
  Legislative Council, 134
  marriage, 54
  migration, 30
  Official Assignée and Curator of Intestate Estates, 65
  proportional representation, 55
  retirement, 134
  South Australian Bank, 47, 126
  Unitarianism, 64
Spence, Mary (aunt), 25, 27

389

Spence, Mary Brodie *see* Wren, Mary née Spence
Spence, Dr William, 38
Spence, William Richard, 19, 42, 47, 194
Spencer, Rev. Mrs Anna Garlin, 150, 222, 232, 334
Springfield, 48, 236, 239
Stanley, Lady, 282
Star, 147–148, 245
Starr, Ellen, 108, 161, 220
State aid, 50
State Children in Adelaide: a History of Boarding Out in its Development, 13
State Children in Australia, 99, 105, 329, 346
State Children's Congress, 207
State Children's Council, 99, 103, 106–107, 149, 170, 173, 199, 200, 218
State Children's Department, 13, 107, 139, 147, 237
State Library of South Australia, 14, 32, 48–49, 118, 216
Stephens, Edward, 35
Stephens, John, 35–36, 48, 50, 66
Stephens, Samuel, 34–35, 43
Stephens, Mrs Samuel (Charlotte Hudson Beare), 42–43
Stephens, Sophia, 50
Sterling, Mrs, 259
Stetson, Charlotte Perkins (Gilman), 147, 227, 230, 256, 279
  book, 246
  letters to, 252, 292
  poems, 260
Stevens, Bertram William Mathyson Francis, 190
Stevenson, Miss, 267
Stevenson, George, 34–35, 50
Stevenson, Mrs George, 35

Stevenson, Margaret née Gorton, 35
Stevenson, Robert Louis, 145
Stillman, Miss, 252, 255
Stirling, 104, 272, 274
Stirling, Mr, 53, 56, 66
Stirling, Mrs, 53
Stirling, Archie, Mr and Mrs, 281
Stirling, Dr Edward C, later Sir, 48, 62, 65, 69, 103–104, 284
Stirling, Harriet née Taylor, 48
Stone, Lucy, 220, 236
Stowe, Harriet Beecher, 151, 154, 240
Stowe, Isabella Beecher, 240
Strawbridge, Eliza Stockholm, 134
Strong, Rev. Charles, 143–144
Stuart, John McDouall, 126
Stuart, Sir Thomas Peter Anderson, 190
Suffrage Associations, 351
suffragists, 158, 166, 248
  USA, 220
Sutherland, Alexander, 109
Sutherland, Caroline, 167
Swanston, Katherine, 27, 72
Switzerland, 162–163, 299
Sydney Mail, 47, 131, 253
Sydney Morning Herald, 101–102, 118, 131, 137
Symon, Laura, 321
Symonds, R.G., 34

T

Tasmania, 167, 196
  destitute children, 102
  effective voting, 196, 207–208
  proportional representation, 187
Tate, Frank, 203
Taylor, Miss (J.S. Mill's step daughter), 89
Taylor, Eliza, 48

Taylor, Harriet, *see* Stirling, Harriet née Taylor
Taylor, John, 36, 48, 50, 54, 56, 59, 62, 65–66, 71
  Clara Morison, 51
Taylor, John, 88
Taylor, Mrs John, later Knight, 66
Taylor, Mrs John, later Mrs J.S. Mill, 88
Taylor, Thomas, 336
Telegraph, 56, 58, 248, 257–258, 282, 297, 300, 307, 317, 321, 323, 333
Tender and True, 53, 58–59, 74
Tennyson, Alfred, 72
Terowie, 345
Terry, Ellen, 281
The Author's Daughter, 96, 273
The Laws We Live Under, 121–122, 221, 276
The Lone Hand, 189–190
The Silent Sea, 115, 222, 226, 230, 258, 273
The Social and Intellectual Aspects of Australian Life, 289
The Subjection of Women, 90
Thomas, Mrs, 258, 320
Thomas, Mary, 34
Thomas, Robert, 34, 39, 316
Thomas, William Kyffin, 316
Thompson, J. Day, 177
Thomson, Helen, 10, 13, 131
Thornton Loch, 26–27, 56, 69, 72
Three Bells, 64
Thursday Review, 35
Thurston, Sir John Bates, 145
Tinline, George, 42–43, 48
Tipton, Mr, 247
Tipton, Mrs, 245, 247
Tomkinson, Amy Louisa, 200
Torrens, Colonel Robert, 33, 35
Trübner, Nicholas (Nikolaus), 131

Trueman, Mrs, 259
Truth, 189
Tubman, Harriet, 151, 224–225
Turner, Henry Gyles, 82, 91, 109, 111
Turner, Martha *see* Webster, Martha
Twichell, Mrs, 235
Tyson, Robert, 155

U

Unitarian Christian Church, 13, 42, 45, *63*, 204, 206, 316
   Adelaide, 88
   Boston, 151
   Children's Library, 28
   Melbourne, 82, 109, 111, 144
   ministers, 64, 73, 91
   Sunday Schools, 86
   Sydney, 112
   USA, 218, 222
Unitarianism, 64, 180
United Labor Party, 170, 317
United States of America, 4, 13, 146–147, 158, 161, 218–219, 223, 227, 238, 243, 245, 250, 259–261, 295, 322, 343, 349
   National Council of Women, 239
   preaching, 112
   proportional representation, 337
   women's movement, 118
   women's suffragism, 220
University of Adelaide, 33, 62, 103, 115, 134, 222, 268
University Shakespeare Society, 141
Uphill Work, 57–58, 68–69, 78

V

Vardon, Joseph, 196–197
Vaughan, Crawford, 197, 339, 345–346
Vaughan, Howard, 345
Vaughan, John Howard, 197
venereal disease, 339, 342
Victoria, 7, 54, 127, 194
   destitute children, 102
   education, 119, 122
   female suffrage, 12
   gold, 49, 52–53, 61
   National Council of Women, 331
   Preferential Voting Bill, 193
   women's suffrage, 345, 351
Victorian Review, 118, 138
votes for women, 12, 316
   NSW, 180, 329
   New Zealand, 283
   South Australia, 164
   Sydney, 1

W

Wages Boards, 196
Waite, Peter, 347
Wakefield principle, 33, 35
Wakefield, Daniel, 34
Wakefield, Edward Gibbon, 32, 34
Walker, Senator James Thomas, 142, 144, 188
Walker, Thomas, 142
Wall, Barbara, 4, 10, 119, 210, 216
Wallace, Nene, 348
Wallaroo, 62, 117
Warner, Charles Dudley, 154, 240
Warren, Jane *see* Bakewell, Jane née Warren
Washington, 220, 231, 240, 242, 244–246, 248, 253, 283, 351
Watts, Jane Isabella née Giles, 133–134
Watts, Captain John Cliffe, 43
Way, Katharine Gollan formerly Blue née Gordon, 199
Way, Sir Samuel James, 11, 97, 103, 151, 199

W.C.T.U. *see* Women's Christian Temperance Union
Webb, Beatrice née Potter, 269, 301
Webb, Sydney, 269, 301, 318, 338
Webster, Martha née Turner, 13, 82, 109, 111, 114
Wedgwood, Julia, 67
Weekly Mail, 56
Weekly Observer, 35
Wellington, Duke of, 33
Welsh, Jane Baillie (Jeanie), 77, 132
Wendell, Barrett, 237
Wendell, Mrs Barrett, 237
Western Australia, 47, 208, 314
   land, 32
Westlake, Alice née Hare, 67, 81, 158, 162, 276–277, 279–281, 283–284
Westlake, John, 67, 81, 158, 280–282, 284, 296
   correspondence, 268, 293
White Australia, 335
Whitham, Rev. Charles Lawrence, 91, 111
Whiting, John Beeby, 104, 237
Whitridge, William Whitridge Roberts, 50
Whittier, John Greenleaf, 154
will, 5
Willard, Frances, 220
Williams, Miss, 321, 324
Williams, Alfred, 201
Williams, William Smith, 52–53, 58–59, 90–91
Williamson, Charles & Co., 31, 53, 57
Willunga, 49, 53
Wilson, Edward, 49–50, 53–54, 58, 73
Wilson, Thomas Woodrow, 150, 235, 237

Windeyer, Margaret, 149, 220, 245–247, 250, 253, 255, 281, 283
Wise, Bernhard Ringrose, 187–189, 328
Wollstonecraft, Mary later Godwin, 88–89
Wolsely, Lord, 262
Wolstenholme, Maybanke, 258
Womanhood Suffrage League of New South Wales, 189, 200, 317, 355
Women Suffragists, Conference of, 351
Women's Christian Temperance Union (W.C.T.U.), 195, 220–221, 318–319, 351, 353, 355
  New Zealand, 283
Women's Land Reform League, 167
Women's Liberal League, 189
Women's National Council, 180
Women's Non-party Political Association, 207, 329
Women's Political Association, 254
women's suffrage (woman suffrage), 89, 201, 207, 317, 328, 342
  Britain, 157, 161, 264, 283–284
  civics, 122
  Edinburgh, 267
  Mill, J.S., 89–90
  South Australia, 163, 284, 317
  Sydney, 149
  USA, 152
  Victoria, 345

Women's Suffrage Bill, 163, 316, 320
Women's Suffrage League (W.S.L.), 99, 103, 223, 284, 316, 318
Wooden, 25–26
Woods, Rev. John Crawford, 64, 73, 91, 111–112, 114
Working Women's Trade Union, 195
World Fair, Chicago, 149, 218, 219
World's Fair Committee., 245
Wren, Charles William, 3, 65, 98, 126, 142, 223, 241, 253
  birth, 54
  correspondence, 268, 272, 303, 323
  CHS's death, 5
  marriage, 142
Wren, Eleanor Brodie, 2–3, 6–8, 10, 65, 98, 131, 141–142, 218, 241, 249, 334–335, 339, 345, 356
  CHS's death, 2, 5
  CHS's diaries, 213–214
  correspondence, 230, 250, 271, 303, 324
  Darwin, 126–127
  Handfasted, 5
Wren, Eleanor Dora née Hall, 142
Wren, Mary
  Unitarianism, 64
Wren, Mary née Spence, 19, 41–43, 47, 49, 51, 65, 68, 98
  childhood, 26
  death, 3, 5
  marriage, 42, 54

Wren, William John, 19, 64, 68
  death, 65
  marriage, 42, 54
Wright, Edward, 33
Wright, John, 33
Wyatt, Mrs, 321
Wyles, John, 178

Y

Young, Alfred Howard, 8, 341, 346
  CHS's diaries, 214
  CHS's view of, 214
Young, Charles Burney, 101
Young, Courtney Spence, 214, 341
Young, Freda, 335, 346
Young, Jeanne (Sarah Jane Forster), 7–8, 9, 10–11, 47, 167, 170–171, 178–180, 187–188, 193–194, 206–207, 213–214, 328, 335, 341, 345–346, 351
  background, 7
  book on CHS
  CHS's autobiography, 10–11, 14
  CHS's biography, 8, 14, 44, 213
  CHS's death, 2
  CHS's diaries, 213–215
  effective voting, 8, 144
  Effective Voting League, 112
  pamphlets, 354
Young, Mrs Ella Flagg, 119
Young, Sir F., 288
Young Women's Christian Association, 99, 223, 225, 316

Wakefield Press is an independent publishing and
distribution company based in Adelaide, South Australia.
We love good stories and publish beautiful books.
To see our full range of titles, please visit our website at
www.wakefieldpress.com.au.

Wakefield Press thanks Fox Creek Wines
and Arts South Australia for their support.